Copyright Reconstructed

Information Law Series (INFO)

VOLUME 41

Editor

Prof. P. Bernt Hugenholtz, Institute for Information Law, University of Amsterdam.

Objective & Readership

Publications in the Information Law Series focus on current legal issues of information law and are aimed at scholars, practitioners, and policy makers who are active in the rapidly expanding area of information law and policy.

Introduction & Contents

The advent of the information society has put the field of information law squarely on the map. Information law is the law relating to the production, marketing, distribution, and use of information goods and services. The field of information law therefore cuts across traditional legal boundaries, and encompasses a wide set of legal issues at the crossroads of intellectual property, media law, telecommunications law, freedom of expression, and right to privacy. Recent volumes in the Information Law Series deal with copyright enforcement on the Internet, interoperability among computer programs, harmonization of copyright at the European level, intellectual property and human rights, public broadcasting in Europe, the future of the public domain, conditional access in digital broadcasting, and the 'three-step test' in copyright.

The titles published in this series are listed at the end of this volume.

Copyright Reconstructed

Rethinking Copyright's Economic Rights in a Time of Highly Dynamic Technological and Economic Change

Edited by

P. Bernt Hugenholtz

Wolters Kluwer

Published by:
Kluwer Law International B.V.
PO Box 316
2400 AH Alphen aan den Rijn
The Netherlands
E-mail: international-sales@wolterskluwer.com
Website: lrus.wolterskluwer.com

Sold and distributed in North, Central and South America by:
Wolters Kluwer Legal & Regulatory U.S.
7201 McKinney Circle
Frederick, MD 21704
United States of America
Email: customer.service@wolterskluwer.com

Sold and distributed in all other countries by:
Air Business Subscriptions
Rockwood House
Haywards Heath
West Sussex
RH16 3DH
United Kingdom
Email: international-customerservice@wolterskluwer.com

ISBN 978-90-411-9103-8

e-book: ISBN 978-90-411-9124-3
web-PDF: ISBN 978-90-411-9125-0

Contributors

Stefan Bechtold is Professor of Intellectual Property at ETH Zurich. He is a graduate of the University of Tübingen School of Law and of Stanford Law School. Prof. Bechtold has been a Visiting Professor at New York University and the University of Haifa, a Senior Research Fellow at the Max Planck Institute for Research on Collective Goods, and spent research visits in Amsterdam, Berkeley, Munich, and Singapore. He is a member of the Academic Advisory Board of the German Federal Ministry of Economics and Technology. He is the author of the chapter on the EU Information Directive in *Concise European Copyright Law* (2nd ed. 2016), and has written extensively on the economics of copyright and other rights of intellectual property.

Séverine Dusollier is Professor of Intellectual Property and Head of the Master in Innovation Law in the Law School of Sciences Po, Paris. From 2006–2014, she was Professor of Law at the University of Namur, and Director of the CRIDS (Research Centre in Information, Law and Society). She is a founding member of the European Copyright Society and a member of the Executive Board of ATRIP. Prof. Dusollier is the recipient of a European Research Council (ERC) research grant on commons and inclusivity in property.

P. Bernt Hugenholtz is Professor of Intellectual Property Law at the Institute for Information Law (IViR), University of Amsterdam. He is co-author, with Prof. Thomas Dreier (TU Karlsruhe), of *Concise European Copyright Law* (2nd ed. 2016), and general editor of the Information Law Series, published by Kluwer Law International. He is one of the founders of the Wittem Group that drafted the *European Copyright Code*, and founder of the European Copyright Society. He teaches at the University of Amsterdam, the Munich IP Law Centre, and the University of Bergen (Norway). He is also an adjunct-judge at the Court of Appeals in Arnhem.

Martin Kretschmer is Professor of Intellectual Property Law at the University of Glasgow, and Director of CREATe (the Centre for Copyright and New Business Models in the Creative Economy). Prof. Kretschmer specializes in law and economics of intellectual property, and empirical methods. He is the (co-)author of a series of influential policy studies for the European Parliament, the UK Intellectual Property Office, the UK Cabinet Office, and the UK Strategic Advisory Board for IP Policy. In 2015–2016, Prof. Kretschmer served as President of the European Policy for Intellectual Property Association (EPIP).

Ansgar Ohly holds the Chair of Private Law, Intellectual Property and Competition Law at the Ludwig Maximilian University of Munich. He is also a permanent Visiting Professor at the University of Oxford and a Visiting Senior Member of St Peter's College Oxford. He has published widely on all areas of intellectual property law and the law of unfair competition law, with a special emphasis on European developments and the comparison of civil law and common law systems. He is the co-editor of GRUR, the leading German intellectual property journal, and of the commentary on German copyright law founded by G. Schricker.

Joost Poort is Associate Professor at the Institute for Information Law (IViR), University of Amsterdam. He adds an economic perspective to various multidisciplinary research projects at this institute. He studied Physics and Philosophy at the University of Utrecht (The Netherlands) and University College Cork (Ireland). After his graduation, he started working as an economic researcher. He has produced a large number of studies on welfare effects, market structure and regulation in a variety of markets. Over the years, he has specialized in the economics of copyright, telecommunication, media and culture.

João Pedro Quintais is a Postdoctoral Researcher and Lecturer at the Institute for Information Law (IViR), University of Amsterdam. He is a qualified lawyer in Portugal, has an LLM degree in Intellectual Property and Competition Law from the Munich Intellectual Property Law Center in Germany, and a PhD in Law from the University of Amsterdam. His dissertation, entitled *Copyright in the Age of Online Access: Alternative Compensation Systems in EU Copyright Law*, was published in 2017 in the Kluwer Information Law Series. He is also a permanent contributor to the Kluwer Copyright Blog.

Ole-Andreas Rognstad is full Professor at, and former Director of the Department of Private Law, University of Oslo. He teaches a whole range of subjects, including legal methodology and EU/EEA law and intellectual property law, in particular copyright law. He has chaired, and been a member of, a number of public dispute settlement resolution bodies in Norway and is a member of the European Copyright Society and of the Academia Europea.

Alain Strowel is Professor at the UCLouvain and University Saint-Louis, Brussels, where he teaches Intellectual Property and Media Law. He also teaches in the IP/ICT masters of KULeuven and Munich IP Law Center. Alain is avocat at the Brussels bar since 1988. Alain graduated in law, economics and philosophy (UCLouvain and University of Amsterdam). His book publications include *Of Authors and Origins* (1991), *Droit d'auteur et copyright* (1993), *Peer-to-Peer File Sharing and Secondary Liability in Copyright Law* (2009), *Quand Google défie le droit* (2011) and *Droit des médias et de la communication* (2017).

Summary of Contents

Table of Contents

Preface

This book is the result of a collaborative academic research project ('Reconstructing Rights') that ran from the Autumn of 2014 to the Summer of 2017. The aim of the project was to 'reconstruct' the economic rights protected under EU copyright law, by bringing these rights more in line with economic and technological realities.

The project – designed as a thinking exercise – brought together a small group of leading, forward-looking legal and economic scholars in the field of European copyright law: Stefan Bechtold (ETH Zurich), Séverine Dusollier (Sciences Po, Paris), Ansgar Ohly (LMU Munich), Joost Poort (Institute for Information Law, University of Amsterdam), Ole-Andreas Rognstad (University of Oslo) and Alain Strowel (UC Louvain). The project was directed by Bernt Hugenholtz (Institute for Information Law, University of Amsterdam), in cooperation with Martin Kretschmer (CREATe, University of Glasgow).

Each member of the group was charged with drafting (individually or in co-authorship) an ideal model of economic rights, and presenting and discussing this – as a work in progress – in regular project group meetings. Full drafts of the papers were thereafter presented at a public symposium in Brussels on 26 September 2016. Earlier and later drafts were also presented at the EPIP Conferences in Glasgow (2015) and Bordeaux (2017).

I wish to thank the members of the project group for joining me on this sometimes perilous, 'utopian' adventure, for their constructive cooperation on the project, for the inspiring and insightful debates we have had over the course of these three years, and most of all for the thought-provoking essays and studies that are presented in this book.

We wish to thank Microsoft Europe for generously funding the project, for hosting project meetings, for providing logistical support, and – most importantly – for letting us design, develop and carry out this research project with complete academic independence. Our thanks are also due to Sara Moran for immaculate copy editing.

Bernt Hugenholtz

Chapter 1

Reconstructing Rights: Project Synthesis and Recommendations

P. Bernt Hugenholtz & Martin Kretschmer

1.1 INTRODUCTION

As recent jurisprudence of the European Court of Justice and ongoing discussions in the European Union (EU) legislature illustrate,[1] the existing set of economic rights granted to right holders under EU copyright law – the rights of reproduction, communication to the public and distribution – have become disordered. While the right of reproduction, due to its all-encompassing definition in the Information Society Directive,[2] already covers every imaginable – direct or indirect, temporary or permanent, partial or integral – act of (digital) copying, the right of communication to the public is being extended well beyond its originally intended scope and purpose, to include acts of hyperlinking, facilitating file sharing and possibly even large-scale content aggregation.[3] Recent CJEU decisions have also stretched

1. *See* e.g., European Commission, Proposal for a Directive of the European Parliament and of the Council on Copyright in the Digital Single Market, Brussels, 14 September 2016, COM(2016) 593 final. The proposed Directive confronts several scope-related issues, such as text and data mining (Art. 3) and large-scale content aggregation (Art. 13).
2. Directive 2001/29/EC of 22 May 2001 on the harmonisation of certain aspects of copyright and related rights in the information society, OJ No. L 167/10, 22 June 2001 (Information Society Directive), Art. 2.
3. CJEU 13 February 2014, Case C-466/12 (*Svensson and Others*); CJEU 8 September 2016, Case C-160/15 (*GS Media*); CJEU 26 April 2017, Case C-527/15 (*Stichting Brein,*

the right of distribution to include acts of online dissemination of software, thus extending the exhaustion rule to digital resale of software licences[4]. By contrast, the European Court has very narrowly construed the right of communication to the public in cases of distribution of broadcast television programme-carrying signals to signal redistributors.[5]

As a consequence, the scope of copyright protection in the EU has become increasingly difficult to predict, at the expense of legal certainty, and EU copyright law's delicate structure of rights and exceptions is becoming gradually unbalanced. Another concern is that in the digital environment the rights of communication to the public and of reproduction increasingly overlap, requiring providers of digital content services to negotiate multiple permissions from concurrent right holders for acts that – seen from an economic perspective – amount to single acts of usage (e.g., content streaming).

While the economic rights protected under copyright are historically patterned on nineteenth and twentieth century modes of exploitation of copyright works, such as theatrical performance, printing and broadcasting, due to the proliferation of digital media technologies in recent decades these media-specific rights have given way to a structure of more abstractly worded, general exclusive rights. As a result, the natural link with economic exploitation has been lost, causing a growing disconnect between the scope of protection and the economic and technological realities of the twenty-first century. This has in some cases led to overprotection or, occasionally, underprotection of copyright works, and is therefore likely to act as a disincentive for investment in innovative content and information services.

At the international level the core economic rights are harmonized only to a limited extent. The main international treaties (Berne Convention, TRIPs Agreement, WIPO Copyright Treaty)[6] leave contracting states considerable freedom to implement and interpret the economic rights as they see fit. Consequently, definitions and interpretations of these rights differ markedly between, for example, the EU and the United States.[7] This is particularly vexing in a networked world where acts of usage of copyright works almost inevitably occur on a global or regional scale rather than on a purely national territorial basis.

'Filmspeler'); CJEU 14 June 2017, Case C-610/15 (*Stichting Brein, 'The Pirate Bay'*). *See also* Proposal for a Directive of the European Parliament and of the Council on Copyright in the Digital Single Market (note 1), Art. 13.

4. CJEU 3 July 2012, Case C-128/11 (*UsedSoft*); CJEU 12 October 2016, Case C-166/15 (*Ranks and Vasiļevičs*).
5. CJEU 19 November 2015, Case C-325/14 (*SBS Belgium*).
6. The 1886 Berne Convention for the Protection of Literary and Artistic Works, the 1994 Agreement on Trade-Related Aspects of Intellectual Property Rights, and the 1996 World Intellectual Property Organization Copyright Treaty.
7. Paul Goldstein & P. Bernt Hugenholtz, *International Copyright. Principles, Law, and Practice*, 3rd ed., New York: Oxford University Press 2012, pp. 306 ff.

This book is the result of a collaborative research project ('Reconstructing Rights') that normatively examined the core economic rights protected under EU copyright law, with the aim of realigning these rights with economic and technological realities.[8] While the collaborators in the project, as the following chapters reveal, propose diverse models to 'reconstruct' copyright's structure of exclusive rights, all authors start from the common assumption that in an ideal copyright system the scope of copyright's economic rights should more adequately reflect the justifications of copyright protection – economic or otherwise.

The project that produced this book was fashioned in the form of a three-year long interdisciplinary dialogue between some of Europe's leading copyright scholars and copyright economists. While the project's aim was to rethink European copyright law with an eye towards future reform, it was primarily a theoretical, 'utopian' exercise. Its results therefore are not a recipe for EU copyright amendment in the short term.

This book is structured as follows. Following a historical chapter (by Quintais & Poort) that illustrates how a structure of media-specific economic rights has developed in international copyright law as copyright's catalogue of rights followed new markets enabled by new media technologies, a number of alternative models for 'reconstructing rights' are presented in the form of essays. While some of the models concur in their approach or outcome, not all are mutually compatible, nor are they meant to be. Nevertheless, as will be pointed out in the final part of this introductory chapter, the models do occupy significant common ground.

1.2 METHODOLOGY

In copyright doctrine, 'economic rights' are understood as exclusive rights that contrast with 'moral' or personality-based rights that persist even after the transfer of the exclusive rights (such as the right of the author to be named and to object to certain modifications).[9] In addition, remuneration rights (i.e., rights to benefit from the exploitation of a copyright work) are sometimes attached to economic rights, for example, if there is a compulsory licensing scheme for the broadcasting right.[10] A further complication is

8. Reconstructing Rights. Rethinking Copyright's Economic Rights in a Time of Highly Dynamic Technological and Economic Change, *see* project description at https://www.ivir.nl/nl/projects/reconstructing-rights-rethinking-copyrights-economic-rights-in-a-time-of-highly-dynamic-technological-and-economic-change/ (accessed 14 December 2017).
9. Berne Convention, Art. 6*bis*(1).
10. Berne Convention, Art. 11*bis*(2). The European Union has established several remuneration rights, including the public lending right (Directive 2006/115/EC, Art. 6), and the resale right (Directive 2001/84/EC, Art. 1(1)).

introduced by limitations and exceptions to the economic rights that limit the control right holders can exercise over their works.[11]

All these aspects of copyright law will have market effects and can, in principle, be subjected to economic analysis. So, the core regulatory question for the best design of copyright law relative to its policy aims appears to be a behavioural question. Which activities in the market should be restricted, and which should be possible without obtaining the right holders' permission? However, the interplay of exclusive rights, moral rights, remuneration rights, and limitations and exceptions has become extraordinarily complex and, as history shows, intractable.

The premise of this project was that we must return to a more intuitive starting point. If the core economic rights are seen as a stack of exclusions (defining the ability of the copyright owner to say 'No'), what might a coherent formulation of these rights look like? In order to make progress on this question, we decided to engage in a sustained interdisciplinary dialogue that went beyond the orthodox 'law and economics' assumption that the allocation of resources simply requires precision in defining copyright as a property right (so that it can be transacted in the most efficient way). Welfare economics allows a more subtle discussion that extends from conditions for production and use of creative works to their communicative function.

As a focus for the project, we selected five examples of potentially copyright relevant acts that lie at the borders of exclusive rights: (a) digital resale, (b) private copying, (c) hyperlinking and embedding, (d) cable retransmission, and (e) text and data mining. Should these acts fall within the scope of exclusive rights and, if so, under what conditions? There are rapidly evolving precedents from the European Court of Justice which seems to understand copyright relevant use as *economically exploiting copyright subject matter with respect to a (new) public*. Our discussions with economists over the past three years were designed to challenge legal scholars to explore the reasons behind where to draw the line on these borderline cases, and link these back to fundamental principles about the function of copyright law.

Initially, each author offered a new normative model that might govern the scope of exclusive rights. Perhaps unsurprisingly, several contributions took inspiration from branches of law where economic reasoning had already been absorbed into doctrine, such as unfair competition law, trademark law and antitrust (competition) law. More radical proposals offered new groundings from principles of public communication rather than the economic conditions of creative production. In half-yearly workshops with invited guests, authors presented drafts and were challenged to extract economic reasoning from legal doctrine, and vice versa.

11. These vary greatly by jurisdiction, and are circumscribed by the so-called three-step-test (Berne Convention, Art. 9; TRIPs Agreement, Art. 13; Information Society Directive, Art. 5(5)).

The resulting proposals for reconstructing economic rights that are presented in this volume, and are summarized in the next section of this chapter, can be labelled as follows:

- *'Regulatory toolbox'* (Bechtold): shape rights by an empirically testable link between scope of protection and intended purpose.
- *Copyright as a right to prevent unfair uses* (Ohly): reconstruct copyright as a three-tiered system of rights and exceptions (per se infringements, acts that cause negative market effects, and acts that are unfair).
- *Copyright as a right to reasonable exploitation* (Rognstad and Poort): replace the current multi-layered copyright structure by a single comprehensive exploitation right restricting acts that conflict with the economic interests of the right holder.
- *Copyright as a right to control public circulation of works* (Dusollier): copyright should allow the creator control over uses of her work in the public sphere.
- *Copyright as a right to prevent use of work 'as a work'* (Strowel): non-communicative uses are not actionable.
- *Remuneration rights for non-commercial consumptive uses online* (Hugenholtz and Quintais): where exclusive rights are unenforceable, convert economic rights into compensation schemes.

In the final part of this book (Chapter 9) Joost Poort examines what the proper scope of the economic rights should be from a perspective of welfare economics, with a special focus on acts that cause market failure. This economic study, making synthetic recommendations on the borderline cases, serves as important background material for the normative chapters, and is therefore regularly referenced throughout this book.

1.3 COMPARING THE MODELS

Following Chapter 2's 'history of value gaps', which shows that over time new rights were introduced and expanded as new media technologies facilitated novel modes of exploitation, Chapters 3 to 8 present a variety of models for reconstructing copyright's economic rights.

To begin with, Stefan Bechtold 'deconstructs' copyright by comparing copyright's system of predefined economic rights to the more open and malleable structure of antitrust (competition) law. As Bechtold explains, this flexible structure allows competition authorities and courts to apply ad hoc economic analysis on a case-by-case basis. Might a similar 'effects-based' approach be applied in copyright, moving away from the paradigm of ex ante defined property rights? As Bechtold points out, such a 'deconstruction' of copyright would require courts to assess the effects on the market and society at large in the process of awarding or denying copyright protection in each individual case. Are courts equipped for this task? And would it be possible to design a 'more economic' structure of copyright without completely abandoning the legal certainty that comes with predefined rights?

In Chapter 4, Ansgar Ohly draws inspiration from bodies of law somewhat closer to copyright, in particular unfair competition law and trademark law. In his *Fairness-Based Approach to Economic Rights,* Ohly diagnoses copyright's main shortcoming as an overly formalistic structure that does not take economic reality into account. Unlike fairness-based intellectual property rights, such as trademark and unfair competition law, copyright lacks 'market-sensitivity'. Ohly's 'therapy' is to inject a measure of fairness into the European copyright system, somewhat similar to the fair use doctrine that allows US courts to consider (*inter alia*) market impact in copyright infringement cases. Ohly proposes to implement his 'fairness-based approach' as a three-tiered system of rights and exceptions: (1) a 'black list' of well-defined, hard-core cases of infringement, subject only to specific exceptions; (2) a broader list of exceptions subject to a market-effect test; and (3) a general clause of unfair use.

In Chapter 5, Ole-Andreas Rognstad and Joost Poort join forces in an attempt to concretize the 'right to reasonable exploitation' that Rognstad first developed in an earlier publication.[12] This all-encompassing right would systemically simplify copyright by replacing the current six-stage structure of economic rights (rights, limitations, secondary liability rules, safe harbours, protection of technical protection measures and corresponding exceptions) by a single, comprehensive right. But how to give normative content to 'reasonable exploitation'? The authors propose to concretize this norm by operationalizing the right of exploitation as a right to control the use of the work to the extent necessary to secure current or future exploitation opportunities for the right holder. The 'reasonableness' of the exploitation is determined primarily on the basis of a broad conception of social welfare, 'filtered through' the guiding principle of efficiency. Ultimately, other guiding principles, such as freedom of expression and information, may further mitigate the scope of the right.

In Chapter 6, Séverine Dusollier moves further away from a purely economic, market-oriented approach. Like other authors she starts by observing that the economic rights 'have become estranged from exploitation', but she then goes on to point out that 'exploitation' is not a purely economic notion. According to Dusollier, the main function of copyright is to promote and regulate *the circulation of works in the public sphere*; this 'communicative function' of copyright should therefore be restored. Reasoning from this Habermasian conception of copyright, Dusollier posits the economic right as a right to control relevant means of communicating a

12. O.-A. Rognstad, 'Restructuring the Economic Rights in Copyright – Some Reflections on an "Alternative Model"', Journal of the Copyright Society of the U.S.A 62(4), 503–544.

work, including: (1) marketing a work for permanent use; (2) providing a service or an experience of the work; and (3) exploiting a derivative work.

In Chapter 7, Alain Strowel attempts to reconcile copyright's increasingly prominent economic functions with doctrinal 'fundamentals'. Strowel proposes to delimit the reproduction right by introducing an infringement requirement that would limit its scope to uses of the work *as a work* – thus ruling out, for example, copies made in the context of text and data mining. As for the right of communication to the public, Strowel proposes applying economic analysis when considering whether a use is a communication to the public, by adding a double market test.

The final model, presented by Hugenholtz and Quintais in Chapter 8, differs from the others in that the authors propose to partially replace an economic right by a right to remuneration. The premise underlying this model is that copyright enforcement against non-commercial, consumptive online uses has negative overall welfare effects. Not only is enforcement largely ineffective, and enforcement costs disproportionate, but it is also harmful to the open internet by forcing intermediaries to block access to infringing content. In light of empirical research showing that consumers are willing to pay for unencumbered access, the authors propose a statutory licence permitting non-commercial online uses of music, video, images and text, subject to a right to fair remuneration for creators, which would be payable by the internet access providers to designated collecting societies.

1.4 COMMON GROUND AND CONCLUSIONS

While the various legal models for reconstructing the economic rights presented in this book are diverse, and not designed to concur or even to be mutually compatible, there is substantial common ground between them. In this final part of the introductory chapter, the main common features are identified. Thereafter, the implications of the proposed legal models for the 'borderline cases' examined in Poort's economic analysis (Chapter 9) are briefly evaluated. Finally, a few general conclusions from the entire research project are drawn.

1.4.1 Definition of Rights Too Formalistic

Not surprisingly, all authors accept the general premise of this project, i.e., that the main economic rights currently protected under EU copyright law are crafted too formalistically, and require (more) normative anchoring. This is the case, clearly, for the reproduction right in its present, largely technical, definition. But it may also be true for the right of communication to the public, which due to its very abstract wording is similarly disconnected from any impact on the market. As a consequence, the reproduction right is generally overprotective, whereas the communication right may be either overreaching or underprotecting.

1.4.2 'Economic Effects'; Combine Rules with Standards

Another idea common to many of the models presented is to move away from formalist exploitation rights towards a 'rule-of-reason' guided by economic effects in the market. Here, copyright might learn from antitrust (competition) law, unfair competition law and trademark law. As several authors observe, there are some indications that the copyright jurisprudence of the European Court of Justice is already moving in this direction. Similar to present trademark law, a copyright law thus reconstructed might combine clearly defined, per se infringement rules that apply to clear-cut cases of negative market impact with more flexible 'fairness' or 'reasonableness' standards that would apply to harder cases.

1.4.3 Functionalist Approach

All authors agree that copyright's catalogue of exclusive economic rights should be reconstructed in light of copyright's (multiple) functions or rationales. This functionalist approach can be based on utilitarian premises that underpin economic thinking about the efficient allocation of scarce resources, but might also take account of copyright's other societal functions, such as facilitating speech in the public sphere, or promoting fairness. Reconnecting rights to function would also immediately solve the copyright problem of text and data mining. By limiting the scope of the reproduction right *to uses of the work as a work*, performing data analysis on copyright works would not give rise to infringement.

1.4.4 Right to 'Reasonable', 'Fair' Exploitation

Regardless of copyright's functions or rationales, there is also some consensus that the scope of exclusion defined by the so-called economic rights ideally be crafted as, or derived from, a general right to 'reasonable' or 'fair' exploitation that would more directly connect copyright protection to market-relevant acts of exploitation. This approach would have the added advantage of making an extensive list of copyright limitations and exceptions largely redundant. In some cases, efficiency and fairness might justify replacing an exclusive right by a right to remuneration for creators and other right holders where enforcement is disproportionate or inefficient.

Will it make a difference which of the proposed reconstructions of economic rights may be adopted by future policymakers or courts? The relationship between doctrine and market effects is difficult to evaluate. Higher courts are often said to reason back from the desired outcome. Within this research project, we therefore encouraged the authors to commit to what they believe would be the behavioural consequences of their revisionary normative models. The following summary attempts to illustrate what these outcomes might be.

1.4.4.1 Digital Resale

Under Ohly's fairness-based approach, negative market effects of permitting digital resale should be balanced against user interests and free movement interests. Poort and Rognstad suggest that resale without multiplication is unproblematic and that contracts which override resale should be subject to general rules of consumer protection and fair business. Dusollier sees successive sales of artistic works as a way of transmitting creative value to the public that should be subject to a *droit de suite*.

1.4.4.2 Private Copying

According to Poort and Rognstad, most private copies can be priced into the purchase and create no market failure. Under Dusollier's right to control public circulation of works, reading, viewing, receiving and enjoying a work are not exploitation activities. On the other hand, social networks institute a public sphere that need to be licensed. Hugenholtz and Quintais define online activities carried out by individuals for personal enjoyment as non-commercial uses that should be subject to compensation. For Ohly, private copying normally has negative effects and should be prohibited.

1.4.4.3 Hyperlinking and Embedding

Under Poort's welfare analysis, linking to legal content is presumed to be copyright irrelevant. However, there should be an opt-out for embedding, and a notice-and-takedown process or levy for links to illegal content. Ohly argues that no negative market effect can be presumed but it may be established where there is substitution or a commercial benefit is derived from embedded content. For Dusollier, links to copyright works that are already in the public sphere should be permitted.

1.4.4.4 Cable Retransmission

Under Dusollier's right to control public circulation of works, retransmission constitutes exploitation. Ohly too assumes that retransmission resulting in profit is unfair without compensation. Under Poort's welfare analysis, right holders do already exert control over exploitation opportunities if the original transmission took place without access control and within the original reception area.

1.4.4.5 Text and Data Mining

For Strowel, copying for the purpose of providing information is not 'use as a copyright work', and should be outside the scope of exclusive rights. Poort and Rognstad argue that the value users derive from text and data mining can largely be priced into access contracts. There is no market failure. Dusollier argues that text and data mining does not result in the public circulation of the processed works and that the act is therefore outside of the scope of her proposed exclusive right.

In conclusion, there is considerable consensus among the proposals for reconstructing economic rights that the current scope of copyright easily leads to perverse outcomes, with aspects of over- or underprotection that cannot easily be reconciled with any underlying rationale for copyright protection. For example, text and data mining would not be treated as a copyright relevant act under any of the models under discussion. But for most borderline cases, assessment of effects appears to be conditional. Compared to antitrust (competition law), functionalist theories of copyright law may need to assess long-term dynamic effects, for example on future creation. This is difficult to draft in legislation and for courts to operationalize, as the current wave of uneven and unpredictable jurisprudence of the European Court of Justice perhaps already illustrates.

In sum, reconstructing copyright is not for the impatient or the faint-hearted; there remains much work to be done.

Chapter 2

A Brief History of Value Gaps: Pre-Internet Copyright Protection and Exploitation Models

João Pedro Quintais & Joost Poort*

2.1 INTRODUCTION

A premise of this book and its underlying research project is that the historical evolution of copyright has led to a growing disconnect between the legal definitions of economic rights and the business and technological realities they regulate. Whereas such legal definitions were in the nineteenth and twentieth centuries patterned on different modes of commercial exploitation of copyright works, they have in the twenty-first century lost that connection, leading to an erosion of copyright's normative content and focus. The result of this mismatch is a deficient design of the scope of economic rights, with likely negative consequences on incentives to invest 'in innovative content and information services'.[1]

The present chapter explores this premise from a historical perspective by examining how the increase in the scope of copyright protection tracked the progress of business models and technology. The chapter describes the

* We are grateful to Bernt Hugenholtz for comments and suggestions on earlier drafts, and to Anne Bruna and Jasmin Hohmann for valuable research assistance. Parts of this chapter are based on and develop the research in J.P. Quintais, *Copyright in the Age of Online Access: Alternative Compensation Systems in EU Law*, Kluwer Law International (2017).

1. *See* the introductory chapter by P.B. Hugenholtz and M. Kretschmer in this volume.

evolution of economic rights recognized in international copyright law in the pre-internet era, against the background of related developments in the commercial exploitation of works and technological development. The focus lies on rights relating to communication technology and the corresponding exploitation models. To this end, it analyses four case studies: public performance (section 2.2), radio and TV broadcasting (section 2.3), cable retransmission (section 2.4), and commercial rental (section 2.5). In each case, the history of protection under international and EU copyright law is described, starting from the Berne Convention and its revisions, and leading on to the TRIPS Agreement, the WCT (where relevant), and the EU copyright directives prior to the InfoSoc Directive.[2] Alongside this, the development of relevant technology and exploitation models are described.

All case studies focus on activities and technologies relating to communication and dissemination of works, rather than reproduction.[3] The first reason for this focus is that reproduction rights emerged much earlier in history than communication rights. Indeed, although the birth of copyright law is often associated with the Statute of Anne adopted in England in 1710,[4] long before that copying restrictions were enforced by 'Guild regulations and royal printing privileges,' some of which stemmed from even earlier practices in the territories of Venice and Rome.[5] The second and more

2. *See*: Berne Convention for the Protection of Literary and Artistic Works, of 9 September 1886 (last revised at Paris on 24 July 1971, and amended on 28 September 1979) [Berne Convention or BC]; Agreement on Trade-Related Aspects of Intellectual Property Rights, 15 April 1994, Marrakesh Agreement Establishing the World Trade Organization, Annex 1C, The Legal Texts: The Results of The Uruguay Round Of Multilateral Trade Negotiations 320 (1999), 1869 U.N.T.S. 299, 33 I.L.M. 1197 (1994) [TRIPS]; WIPO Copyright Treaty, adopted in Geneva on 20 December 1996 [WCT]; and Directive 2001/29/EC of 22 May 2001 on the harmonisation of certain aspects of copyright and related rights in the information society, OJ L 167/10, 22.06.2001 [InfoSoc Directive]. This chapter focuses solely on 'copyright', understood as authors' rights. It therefore excludes so-called related or neighbouring rights.
3. Legally, all cases except commercial rental are currently associated with what in EU Law falls under the umbrella of the right of communication to the public. *See* Art. 3 InfoSoc Directive, Art. 8 Council Directive 92/100/EEC, of 19 November 1992 on rental right and lending right and on certain rights related to copyright in the field of intellectual property, 1992 O.J. (L 346/61) as republished and amended by Directive 2006/115/EC of the European Parliament and of the Council of 12 December 2006 (codified version), 2006 O.J. (L 376/28) [Rental and Lending Directive], and Art. 4 Council Directive 93/83/EEC of 27 September 1993 on the coordination of certain rules concerning copyright and rights related to copyright applicable to satellite broadcasting and cable retransmission, OJ L 248/15, 6.10.1993 [SatCab Directive].
4. An Act for the Encouragement of Learning, by Vesting the Copies of Printed Books in the Authors or Purchasers of Such Copies, During the Times therein mentioned, 1710, 8 Anne, c.19 [Statute of Anne].
5. Cf. L. Bentley, 'Introduction to Part I; The History of Copyright'; R. Deazley, 'What's New About the Statute of Anne? *Or* Six Observations in Search of an Act'; and W. Grosheide, 'Transition from Guild Regulations to Modern Copyright Law – a View from the Low Countries', in: *Global Copyright: Three Hundred Years since the Statute of Anne,*

important reason is that, despite the perpetual presence of unauthorized copying, from the sheet music pirates of the eighteenth and nineteenth century[6] to the internet 'pirates' of today, the right of reproduction (a 'copy-right') appears to have been less controversial than various rights relating to communication or making works available to the public.[7]

After examining the case studies, section 2.6 critically discusses their common patterns. The evolution of rights could be summarized in a critical fashion by observing that each time a new exploitation model or technology enabled entrepreneurs to generate money using copyright-protected works, new rights were created to reap some of these benefits. This development is consistent with the premise outlined above, as the expansion of economic rights appears to closely track the evolution of economic and technological realities. This is not to say that the development was a direct and necessary result of the copyright infringing nature of the activities of these entrepreneurs. Think for instance of a theatre company staging a play purchased in print from the authorized publisher, or an orchestra performing a symphony from legally obtained sheet music. Rather, it stems from the assertion by rights holders of an entitlement to the value created in connection with 'their works', and the materialization of that assertion into law. Fast-forward to the twenty-first century, and this reveals a stunning resemblance to the 'value gap' debate in current EU copyright law and the initiative to create new exclusive rights for publishers of press publications.[8] Thus, from this perspective, we can read the historical evolution of copyright as a tale of value gaps.

This chapter explores this analogy, examining whether past arguments for copyright protection and the design of legal entitlements presented a clearer connection to the technological development in modes of exploitation. This link, it is argued, has been eroded in contemporary copyright law

---

from 1709 to Cyberspace, L. Bently, U. Suthersanen & P. Torremans (eds), Edward Elgar (2010), pp. 7–13, 26–53, and 79–102. *See also* F. Kawohl and M. Kretschmer, 'Abstraction and Registration: Conceptual Innovations and Supply Effects in Prussian and British Copyright (1820-50)', *Intellectual Property Quarterly*, 2003-2, pp. 209–228; and M. Rose, *Authors and Owners: The Invention of Copyright*, Harvard University Press (1993), pp. 9–24.

6. *See* R. Towse, 'Economics of Music Publishing: Copyright and the Market', *Journal of Cultural Economics*, 2016, pp. 1–18.
7. A notable exception is the perennial controversy surrounding the application of the reproduction right to private copying activities. For a discussion of legal and economic aspects of private copying, *see*: J. Poort and J.P. Quintais, 'The Levy Runs Dry: A Legal and Economic Analysis of EU Private Copying Levies', *Journal of Intellectual Property, Information Technology and Electronic Commerce Law* (*JIPITEC*) 4(3), pp. 205–224. For a discussion of the historical background of private copying, *see* P.B. Hugenholtz, 'The Story of the Tape Recorder and the History of Copyright Levies', in: *Copyright and the Challenge of the New*, B. Sherman & L. Wiseman (eds), Kluwer Law International (2012), pp. 179–196.
8. *See* Proposal for a Directive of the European Parliament and of the Council on copyright in the Digital Single Market, COM(2016) 593 final, Arts 11–13.

and policy, in part due to the increasingly abstract and generic mode in which economic rights are formulated. This erosion in turn raises the crucial question of how to justify the expansion in scope of economic rights to appropriate (some of) the downstream value.

2.2 PUBLIC PERFORMANCE

The earliest copyright laws, such as the Statute of Anne (1710), regulated the printing, reprinting, and sale of books. Only later were other types of work added, such as sheet music and theatre plays.[9] In modern-day language, one can say that in the early days copyright was almost entirely *exhausted* upon sale: no restrictions existed regarding the public performance of these works, their translation, or adaptation through musical arrangements. Only reprinting a legally obtained copy was forbidden. This began to change from the end of the eighteenth century onwards, starting with France.

2.2.1 The Emergence of a Public Performance Right in France

The legal recognition of a public performance right is intertwined with the birth of collective rights management in France, which dates back prior to the *Ancien Régime*. The origins of collective management are often traced back to the *Bureau de legislation dramatique*, a venture designed by playwrights to defend their interests against the actor-controlled *Comédie Française*, which held a theatre monopoly in Paris in the eighteenth century.[10] The *Bureau* was created at a famous dinner on 3 July 1777, by the popular playwright Beaumarchais (born Pierre Augustin-Caron) and twenty-two colleagues disgruntled with the remuneration received from theatres for the performance of their works.[11] Thanks to the popularity and lobbying of

9. Kawohl and Kretschmer 2003, p. 219.
10. S. Nérisson, 'Collective Management of Copyright in France', in: *Collective Management of Copyright and Related Rights*, D. Gervais (ed.), Kluwer Law International (2016), p. 176; *See also* N. Piaskowski, 'Collective Management of Copyright in France', in: *Collective Management of Copyright and Related Rights*, D. Gervais (ed.), Kluwer Law International (2010), p. 171, SACD, *Two centuries of experience*, https://www.sacd.fr/en/two-centuries-experience (accessed 26 September 2017) [SACD Two Centuries of experience]; and J.C. Ginsburg, 'Tale of Two Copyrights: Literary Property in Revolutionary France and America', *Tulane Law Review* 64, 1989–1990, pp. 991, 996–997: 'the Crown also regulated rights of public performance of dramatic works by vesting in the *Comédie Française* the exclusive right to perform such works'. Other than the *Comédie Française*, the *Comédie-Italienne* and the *Opera* also enjoyed privileged status until 1789. *Id.* p. 998; and S. Maslan, *Revolutionary Acts: Theatre, Democracy, and the French Revolution*, The Johns Hopkins UP (2005), p. 14.
11. *See*: A.C. Renouard, Traité *des Droits d'Auteurs dans la Littérature, les Sciences et les Beaux Arts*, Paris: Chez Jules Renouard et Cie (1838), pp. 212–225; F. Hardison Londré

Beaumarchais and his contemporaries, the *Bureau* obtained royal support and a 'concession from the *Théâtre Français* for playwrights to be remunerated not only by the honour to be performed, but also with royalties'.[12] At the time, the main concern of the *Bureau* was theatrical works, as music was deemed a 'minor art', and music publishers viewed as 'shopkeepers'.[13]

In 1789, the French Revolution brought the abolition of privileges. As a result, the interests of musical authors had to wait a couple of years to return to the political agenda.[14] This occurred in January 1791 in the form of a decree from the National Assembly. As Ginsburg notes, the main motivation for the decree was 'to break the *Comédie Française*'s monopoly on the works of Corneille, Moliere, and Racine'; hence, 'the decree's recognition of authors' rights principally was a means to terminate that monopoly'.[15] Nonetheless, the decree recognized an exclusive performing right (*droit de représentation*) for dramatic and musical works lasting for five years after the author's death.[16] The law stated that 'the performance of a theatre play requires the express and written consent of its playwright'.[17] The penalty for unauthorized performance was 'confiscation of the entire income of the spectacle'.[18] Later that year, a new decree specifically recognized 'public performing rights including concerts, thereby giving rise to what today we consider the rights of authors and composers'.[19]

The 1791 laws, by releasing the theatres from governmental control or censorship, are said to have directly contributed to the rise in the number of theatres. In Paris, Kennedy reports an increase from nineteen to thirty-five

and M. Berthold, *The History of World Theater: From the English Restoration to the Present*, A&C Black (1999), pp. 173 et seq.; and Piaskowski 2010, p. 171.

12. Nérisson 2016, p. 176. The relevant articles of the *arrêt* (9 December 1780) in question are reproduced in Renouard 1838, pp. 220–221.
13. SACEM (Society of Actors, Composers and Publishers of Music), Historical Background, '1777', https://societe.sacem.fr/en/history (accessed 26 September 2017) [SACEM Historical Background].
14. *Ibid.*, '4 August 1789'.
15. Ginsburg 1990, p. 1005.
16. S. Ricketson, *The Berne Convention for the Protection of Literary and Artistic Works: 1886–1986*, Kluwer (1987), p. 5. *See also* F. Rideau, *Nineteenth Century Controversies Relating to the Protection of Artistic Property in France*, OpenBook Publishers (2010), p. 242.
17. 'Décret relative aux spectacles' (dated 13–19 January 1791) [Loi des 13/19 janvier 1791 relative aux spectacles (complétée par un decret des 19 juillet/6 août 1791)]. Cf. A. Bertand, *Le Droit d'Auteur et les Droits Voisins*, Masson (1991), pp. 26–27.
18. S. Depreeuw, *The Variable Scope of the Exclusive Economic Rights in Copyright*, Kluwer Law International (2014), p. 249.
19. SACEM Historical Background, 'July–August 1791'. *See also* Bertand 1991, pp. 26–27. For the analysis of a subsequent 1792 decree that further regulated dramatists' public performance rights in France (including subjecting them to formalities) and the first full-fledged French copyright law (Law of 19–24 July 1793), *see* Ginsburg 1990, pp. 1006–1014.

within one year.[20] This growth is confirmed by a short reference in Charles-Augustin Renouard's *Traité des Droits d'Auteurs* (of 1838), which mentions the existence of thirty-eight theatres in Paris in 1791. [21] Susan Maslan's work provides additional information. She notes that 'with the end of legal privileges the construction of new theaters was unleashed': 'At least one thousand new plays were written and performed, approximately fifty new theaters opened, and there were roughly twenty-five theatrical performances every day in Paris during the revolutionary decade.'[22] Note, however, that Maslan links this heyday for theatres in Paris to the abolition of the existing legal privileges, not to the recognition of performing rights for playwrights.

On the basis of the 1791 decrees, Framery founded the *Societé des Auteurs* with the objective of managing and enforcing the newly created performing right, as well as collecting royalties from theatres across the country. The organization obtained authorization from authors for the exercise of this right against theatres, in what is viewed as 'the origin of the collective management of copyright'.[23] In 1829, the *Societé* merged with a competing agency to form the Society of Dramatic Authors and Composers (SACD), 'the first and oldest CMO in France'.[24]

One of the most colourful episodes in the history of collective management and public performance took place in 1847, more than half a decade after the recognition of some types of performance rights in France. At the concert-café *Les Ambassadeurs* on the Champs-Elysées, author (playwright, lyricist, and librettist) Ernest Bourget famously refused to pay a bill because the café did not remunerate him for the public performance of his compositions. This led to a lawsuit. The ensuing judgment awarded damages to Bourget and prohibited the café from playing his works.[25]

This litigation demonstrates the dynamic nature of the concept of 'public performance', which evolved from its initial application in concert halls or theatres to cover concert-cafés as well. Although it is difficult to determine the revenue generated from the 'business model' of concert-cafés in France at the time, it was clearly a popular phenomenon during the *belle époque*. It could be argued that they became even more popular than theatres for enjoying performances. The *Encyclopedia of Contemporary French Culture* notes that these establishments became popular in France in the 1860s and that 'by 1890 there were some 200 in Paris alone'. They are

20. E. Kennedy, M.L. Netter, J.P. McGregor and M.V. Olsen, *Theatre, Opera, and Audiences in Revolutionary Paris*, Greenwood P (1996), pp. 45, 89.
21. Renouard 1838, p. 212.
22. Maslan 2005, pp. 14–15.
23. Nérisson 2016, pp. 176–177.
24. *Ibid.*, p. 177. On the transition from the collection agency *Agence Framery* to the SACD, and the role played by Beaumarchais in the same, *see* Piaskowski 2010, p. 171.
25. SACEM Historical Background, '1847'.

historically important establishments due to the fact that they were frequented by the public to listen to music 'rather than joining in the singing of popular songs'.[26] This is anecdotally illustrated in the works by Édouard Manet depicting scenes in concert-cafés, while Edgar Degas even made a famous painting of the aforementioned concert-cafés – *Les Ambassadeurs*. Herbert writes: 'Many indoor cafés-concert had rather small stages, but new ones were built in the 1860s and 1870s with huge stages, rather like music halls. Outdoor cafés-concerts used covered pavilions fronting on fenced-off areas where the clients sat. Both indoor and outdoor types charged extra for the entertainment, either by elevating the prices of their drinks, or by levying an entry fee or seat charge.'[27] This makes clear how these establishments monetized the value generated by the performances and – in present-day language – a value gap was created, which the public performance right ought to fill.

The following years saw a proliferation of similar lawsuits, all favourable to Bourget and his colleagues. These established a line of case law supporting authors' claims to exclusive rights for the performance of their works.[28] In 1850, the union started to collect royalties from café owners for public performances of musical pieces.[29] This laid the foundation for the incorporation, on 31 January 1851, of the *Société des Auteurs Compositeurs et Éditeurs de Musique* (SACEM), with the primary aim of enforcing the performing rights of authors against concert-cafés.[30] SACEM is to this day one of the biggest and most important collective rights management organizations (CMOs) in Europe.

Of course, while France was taking the lead in this area, several other national copyright laws recognized public performance rights under different models.[31] At an international level, the first instances of recognition of such rights are found in nineteenth century bilateral treaties, which granted the right for musical, dramatic, and dramatico-musical works, subject to the

26. I. Pickup, 'Café-Concert', in A. Hughes & K. Reader (eds), *Encyclopedia of Contemporary French Culture*, Routledge (1998), p. 86.
27. R.L. Herbert, *Impressionism*. Yale University Press (1988), p. 76.
28. SACEM Historical Background, '28 April 1849', referring in particular to the decision of the Court of Justice of Paris of 28 April 1849.
29. Piaskowski 2010, p. 172, noting that at this time the union operated under the name *Agence Centrale pour la Perception des droit des Auteurs et Compositeurs de Musique*.
30. *See*: SACEM Historical Background, '31 January 1851'; Piaskowski 2010, p. 172; and Nérisson 2016, p. 177, noting that SACEM is an interesting CMO insofar as it represents both authors and publishers.
31. Ricketson 1987, pp. 12, 14, and 426, making reference to the UK, Netherlands, Finland, and Switzerland. For a study on the origins of performing rights in Britain, *See* I. Alexander, *The Birth of the Performing Right in Britain*, OpenBook Publishers (2010), pp. 321–346. For examples in the 1837 Prussian Copyright Act and 1886 Belgian Copyright Act, *see* Depreeuw 2014, p. 249.

principle of national treatment and other conditions.[32] Dissatisfaction with this bilateral approach led to the initial steps towards a first multilateral treaty. These steps included different international meetings and congresses on the topic of literary and artistic works, taking place in Brussels (1858), Antwerp (1861 and 1877), and under the auspices of the Universal Exhibition of 1878 in Paris.[33]

In 1878, following these congresses, the meeting of the International Literary Congress in Paris, under the presidency of Victor Hugo, led to the foundation of the International Literary Association. This was extended and renamed in 1884 as the *International Literary and Artistic Association* (ALAI). Among the resolutions passed at the founding meeting was that:[34]

> All literary, scientific and artistic works will be treated, in all countries other than their country of origin, according to the same laws as those applicable to works of national origin. The same system will apply to the performance of dramatic and musical works.

The ALAI played a key role in the drawing up and establishment of the Berne Convention, signed on 9 September 1886.[35] Through the principles of national treatment and reciprocity, the Berne Convention 'allowed foreign authors to benefit from rights currently in force in countries where their works were performed'.[36]

2.2.2 Public Performance Right in International Law

The Berne Convention has been revised multiple times since 1886. The version currently in force suffered its last major revision in Paris in 1971 (with subsequent minor amendments in 1979). The convention establishes minimum standards. These include rights to be protected, subject to certain reservations and to exceptions or limitations. Among the minimum rights is the exclusive right in Article 11 to authorize the *public performance of dramatic, dramatico-musical, and musical works*, which is the main focus of this section.[37]

---

32. S. von Lewinski, *International Copyright Law and Policy*, Oxford University Press (2008), p. 17; *See also* Ricketson 1987, pp. 29, 32.
33. von Lewinski 2008, pp. 23–32.
34. Association Littéraire et Artistique Internationale – Son Histoire, Ses Travaux (1878–1889), Bibliothèque Chaconac (1889), pp. 112–113.
35. *See* SACD Two Centuries of experience, '1878'; von Lewinski 2008, pp. 26–32; Ricketson 1987, pp. 46–55.
36. SACD Two Centuries of experience, '1886'.
37. We focus here on the right of public performance proper, as distinguished from the other rights that relate to making the work perceptible (by sound or vision) in the presence of a public. These include the right of public recitation for authors of literary works (Art. 11*ter* BC) and the right of public performance of cinematographic adaptations and cinematographic works (Arts 14 and 14*bis* BC).

2.2.2.1 Evolution of Protection Between 1886 and 1971

The initial version of this public performance right was found in Article 9 of the Berne Convention (1886). It granted national treatment to citizens of other Union countries in relation to the public presentation (*représentation publique*) of dramatic or dramatico-musical works and translations thereof, whether or not they are published.[38] The provision also applied national treatment to the public performance of (published or unpublished) musical works.

For musical works, however, this was conditional on the author attaching a notice of reservation on the title page of the sheet music. This requirement resulted in many composers of musical works losing their performance rights due to a classic *principal-agent problem*: many publishers neglected to meet the requirement as they benefited from the sale of sheet music and not from the performance rights.[39] Hence, by leaving the reservation notice off, publishers hoped to increase the number of public performances of works, leading to more copies sold. Naturally, this strained their relationship with composers, who complained of 'discriminations against their interests'.[40]

The issue was debated at the 1896 Paris Conference. In the interest of the authors and composers, the French Government tried to remove the requirement of prior notice, only to meet opposition from the German and British delegations, who argued that 'public opinion in their countries would find it difficult to adjust to a situation where they would be prevented from performing musical works which contained no notice of reservation',[41] for example, 'in social clubs, by students or military music bands'.[42] The outcome was to maintain the status quo, but to issue a declaration stating that national laws should fix the boundaries for the next conference to 'adopt the principle that published musical works should be protected against unauthorized execution, without a need for a prior reservation in this respect by the author'.[43]

In the 1908 Berlin Act, the requirement for advanced reservation of rights was abolished. This Act made it impossible for national laws to curtail recognition of the rights of public performance (musical works) and presentation (dramatic and dramatico-musical works) through the application

38. *See* Ricketson 1987, p. 425.
39. This problem, also referred to as the 'agency problem' or 'agency dilemma', refers to a situation in which an agent (in this case the publisher) acts on behalf of a principal (the composer) while having interests that are not fully aligned with those of the principal. *See*, e.g., S.A. Ross, 'The Economic Theory of Agency: The Principal's Problem', *The American Economic Review*, 63(2), 1973, pp. 134–139.
40. Ricketson 1987, p. 426.
41. *Ibid.*, p. 426.
42. Depreeuw 2014, p. 249.
43. Ricketson 1987, p. 427.

of national treatment in combination with a notice of reservation requirement.[44]

Although the 1908 Act did not grant a general public performance right, it recognized more specific performance rights in two fields. First, Article 13(1) granted a new minimum right of public performance of musical works by means of *mechanical reproduction instruments*.[45] Clearly, this introduction of a mechanical performance right in international law was a response to technological and market developments. Player pianos (pianolas) playing 'recorded' music rolls had been developed in the last quarter of the nineteenth century to challenge the hegemony of live performances in concert halls and concert-cafés up to that point.[46] Around the same time, Thomas Edison had invented the phonograph (in 1877) and Emile Berliner the gramophone (1887). By 1898, Berliner's company had produced over 11,000 gramophone players and more than 400,000 records.[47] And by 1914, six years after the Berlin Act, more than 27 million records had been printed. In 1919, record production had reached 107 million.[48] By that time, this technological development had already given rise to domestic court decisions in Belgium and France, which qualified the playing of recorded phonograms by means of a phonograph (a 'graphophone') and the public listening to a disc as a public performance (*exécution*).[49]

Second, Article 14 granted a public representation right for 'cinematographic adaptations and reproductions of literary, artistic and scientific works'.[50] Again, this was a response to rapid technological development. The Lumière brothers held the first (private) screening of motion pictures in Paris in March 1895, and the first commercial public screening charging admission fees was in Berlin later that same year.[51] The advance of cinema had made it clear by then that this 'was another means by which works could be reproduced and performed'. Thus, the recognition of such rights was seen as the 'natural corollary of the rights of mechanical and cinematographic

44. *Ibid.*, p. 427.
45. Article 13, first paragraph, of the 1908 Berlin Act of the BC states: '*Les auteurs d'oeuvres musicales ont le droit exclusive d'autoriser: … l'exécution publique de Mêmes oeuvres au moyen de ces instruments [intruments servant à les reproduire mécaniquement].*' On the historical evolution of this provision in tandem with that of the mechanical reproduction right, *see* Depreeuw 2014, pp. 253–254.
46. Towse 2016.
47. P. Gronow and I. Saunio, *International History of the Recording Industry*, Cassell, (1999), p. 9.
48. J.R. Ogden, D.T. Ogden and K. Long. 'Music Marketing: A History and Landscape', *Journal of Retailing and Consumer Services* 18(2), 2011, pp. 120–125.
49. *See* Depreeuw 2014, pp. 252–253, and the early case law cited therein.
50. Ricketson 1987, p. 428. Art. 14 of the 1908 Berlin Act makes reference to 'représentation publique'. *Id.*, p. 95.
51. Wikipedia, *Auguste and Louis Lumière,* Other early cinematographers, https://en.wikipedia.org/wiki/Auguste_and_Louis_Lumi%C3%A8re (accessed 26 September 2017).

reproduction'; following a French proposal, they were 'adopted with little discussion once the decision to protect the latter rights had been agreed'. This proposal aligns with a French Court decision of the same year, which considered the screening of the opera Faust in two cinemas in Paris to be a public representation.[52] As granted, the right covered the public projection of fixated cinematographic works, whether accompanied by sound or not (i.e., a silent film).[53]

The 1928 Rome Act was relatively inconsequential as regards the public performance right. There was debate on the topics of mechanical reproduction and performance rights, but the delegations could not agree on changes. Many Union countries had reservations about a general right. This was due to concerns about the practice of collective management of the public performance of musical works during the interwar period. Existing CMOs had developed monopolies (or quasi-monopolies) in the field, raising public interest concerns as to artificially high price setting for public performance licences. These concerns led some countries to propose legislation to control the activities of CMOs. Such countries felt, even in 1928, that a general public performance right would restrict their ability to regulate CMOs.[54]

The 1948 Brussels Act brought substantive changes in this area by introducing a general public performance right in Article 11.[55] From this point onwards, reservations to the right on the basis of national treatment were barred. The right was proposed in the preparatory works by the Belgian government and the International Office, on the basis of several different arguments. First, the need for unambiguous recognition of a general right on a par with the existing public performance rights (for translations, mechanical reproduction of musical works, and cinematographic adaptations). Second, the argument that such a general right would not hinder the control of CMOs via competition law. Third, the fact that Union countries would continue to be allowed minor reservations and exceptions for certain types of public performance.[56]

The original proposal mentioned an exclusive right for 'the public transmission of representations and performances of their works by telephone or any other analogous means'. According to Ricketson, telephone should be read here as the 'théâtrophone' or 'theatre phone', a popular invention at the time.[57] Invented as early as 1881, this was 'a telephonic distribution system available in portions of Europe that allowed the subscribers to listen to opera and theatre performances over the telephone lines':[58]

---

52. Depreeuw 2014, pp. 254–255, and references cited therein.
53. *Ibid.*, p. 256.
54. Ricketson 1987, 428–429.
55. von Lewinski 2008, p. 76. This was also the Act that granted a general reproduction right.
56. Ricketson 1987, p. 429.
57. *Ibid.*, p. 430.
58. Wikipedia, *Théâtrophone*, https://en.wikipedia.org/wiki/Th%C3%A9%C3%A2trophone (accessed 26 September 2017).

music streaming *avant la lettre*. Remarkably, in 1899 a Belgian court had already qualified transmission over the telephone of a performance of Verdi's Rigoletto to the visitors to an electricity fair against the payment of a fee as an act covered by the domestic right of public performance.[59]

Coming back to the Brussels conference fifty years later, opponents to the proposal contended that a general right was unnecessary and undesirable.[60] The discussion led to a redrafting of the provision into a more general right (deleting the reference to the 'theatre phone') and making a clear demarcation from the rights of broadcasting (Article 11*bis*) and mechanical reproduction (Article 13), by stating that their application was 'reserved'.[61] The final version of Article 11(1) adopted in Brussels grants authors of dramatic, dramatico-musical, and musical works an exclusive right to authorize: '(i) the public presentation and public performance of their works, and (ii) the public distribution by any means of the presentation and performance of their works'.[62]

Important was the fact that delegates recognized that the general right was subject to the minor exceptions or reservations doctrine and, furthermore, each state retained the power to impose competition law controls in their territories.[63] In addition to the general public performance right, the Brussels Act also introduced two important changes. First, in Article 11*ter*, it granted an exclusive right for authors to authorize the public recitation of their literary works. Second, it amended Article 14 on cinematographic works, changing the formulation of the right to cover public presentation *and performance*.

59. *See* Depreeuw 2014, pp. 300–311, and references cited therein.
60. Ricketson 1987, p. 430. Opponents considered national treatment sufficient and were concerned a general right would lead to a reduction in protection, namely if certain restrictive conditions from national law were adopted in the text of the convention. In addition, it was feared that a general right would limit the space available for national restrictions and 'anti-monopoly controls'.
61. Article 11(1)(i), second sentence, BC. *See* Guide to the Copyright and Related Rights Treaties, Administered by WIPO, and Glossary of Copyright and Related Rights Terms, WIPO Publication 891(E), Geneva (2003) [WIPO Guide 2003], p. 68.
62. Article 11(1) BC of the Brussels Act (1948). *See* Ricketson 1987, pp. 430–431, describing the reference to 'public distribution' as 'an unfortunate translation of the original French word transmission'; the most accurate translation being 'transmission or communication'. This mistake was corrected in the Stockholm revision, which replaced the term 'distribution' with 'communication' in the official English text of the Convention.
63. *Ibid.*, pp. 421, 431. On this point it is noteworthy that the UK made a declaration – jointly with other countries – to reserve 'its freedom to promulgate legislation where necessary in the public interest to oppose or remedy the abuse of this right by copyright owners within the UK'. Cf. *ibid.*, p. 111. On the Agreed Statement on minor reservations included in the General Report of the Brussels revision conference, *see* WIPO Guide 2003, p. 70, citing *Documents de la Conférence réunie a Bruxelles du 5 au 26 Juin 1948* (Berne: Bureau de l'Union Internationale pour la Protection Des Œuvres Littéraires et Artistiques, 1951) [Records BC Brussels 1948].

The change brought about by the Stockholm Act in 1967 was the extension of the scope of the general right of public performance by the addition, in Article 11(1)(i), of the expression 'including such public performance by any means or process'. This *general-purpose* wording took the scope of the right beyond direct presentation by natural persons, to include performances through the use of any equipment – including the 'public rendition of *recorded* performances or by other technical means'[64] – making it future-proof with respect to new technologies and exploitation models for public performance. At the same time, from a societal perspective, it introduced the risk that certain activities would come to fall under the right without clear normative justification. The change brought within the scope of Article 11, acts previously covered by Article 13 on public performance of musical works by means of mechanical reproduction instruments. The latter article was therefore 'completely transformed'.[65]

The same addition was made to Article 11*ter*, regarding public recitation of works. The provision was further extended in scope to include the communication to the public of the recitation of works. A paragraph (2) was also added to grant authors of literary works the same rights in respect of translations thereof.

2.2.2.2 Current Level of Protection

The current version of Article 11 of the Berne Convention contains a right of public performance[66] for three types of work: *dramatic*, *dramatico-musical*, and *musical* works. The scope of the public performance right covers the performance of such works by a natural person to a public that is present or 'at a place open to the public, without the need for any transmission'.[67] The exclusive right to authorize the public performance of cinematographic adaptations and works is laid down in Articles 14 and 14*bis*.[68]

The natural person in question is a human actor or performer, e.g., a musician in a concert, an opera singer, or a theatre actor in a play. As in the Stockholm Act (1967), the performance can be by 'any means or process', such as 'by means of sound recordings, tapes and other devices in which

64. Depreeuw 2014, pp. 247–248.
65. WIPO Guide 2003, p. 68.
66. In this version, and since the Stockholm Act, the English term performance corresponds to the French terms '*représentation et exécution*'. Cf. Ricketson 1987, p. 425. Note that Art. 11(1)(ii) contains a *distinct* exclusive right of communication to the public of the protected performances. Furthermore, the right of public performance is distinct from that of public recitation in Art. 11*ter*, which applies to 'performing' a literary work in the sense of reading it out loud or reciting it. *Id.*, p. 433.
67. von Lewinski 2008, p. 147.
68. WIPO Guide 2003, p. 68. Art. 14(1) also encompasses communication to the public of works 'of the works thus adapted or reproduced'. Note that pursuant to Art. 14*bis*, the owner of copyright in a cinematographic work shall enjoy a similar right to the author.

these works may be embodied'.[69] This extended the scope of the right beyond human performances to mechanical performances.

A key aspect of the right is that a performance is made to a 'public' that is 'present at the *location* of the (human or mechanical) performance, at the *time* it takes place'.[70] On the qualification of 'public', the text and preparatory works of the Convention provide little guidance beyond the exclusion of 'private' communications.[71] Thus, it is for national laws to precisely demarcate public from private in such a way as to not 'prejudice the author's right to exploit his work by means of public performance'.[72] According to the WIPO guide to this Convention, the dominant view is that an act of communication is made to the 'public' when it goes beyond the communicator's 'circle of family and its close social acquaintances'.[73] Furthermore, the actual presence of the public is not required. It suffices that 'the performance is made in a place open to the public' and that the public has the opportunity to attend it.[74]

Note that what is protected is the performance to the public as an act of *exploitation*, not the reception or enjoyment of the work (or of the performance of the work) by audience members.[75] Finally, the Berne public performance rights are subject to the application of 'minor reservations' by Union members. This covers *de minimis* performances that do not have a commercial character, nor are they carried out for profit-making purposes.[76]

2.3 RADIO AND TV BROADCASTING

Broadcasting is the transmission of sounds and/or images for reception by a dispersed audience using electromagnetic radiation or waves, without the

69. Ricketson 1987, p. 431. The expression therefore includes, as illustrated by von Lewinski, 'devices from which the works can be made audible or visible at a place open to the public or in its presence, such as the playing of musical works in a discotheque, bar, or at a choreographic performance in a theatre, or the showing of an audiovisual recording of a theatre play, opera, or concert to the public at an educational establishment'. Cf. von Lewinski 2008, p. 148.
70. Depreeuw 2014, p. 258 (emphasis original).
71. On the basis of the pecuniary nature of the exclusive right, Ricketson argues that the 'public' should include 'those who are willing to pay for the benefit of hearing or seeing the work performed', thereby excluding from the concept 'only performances in the immediate family circle'. Cf. Ricketson 1987, pp. 432–433.
72. Ricketson 1987, p. 433.
73. WIPO Guide 2003, p. 68.
74. *Ibid.*, p. 69. For a detailed treatment of the concept of 'public' in the BC, *see* Depreeuw 2014, pp. 257–259, 329–341.
75. Depreeuw 2014, pp. 258–259.
76. WIPO Guide 2003, pp. 70–73. *See also* Depreeuw 2014, p. 258.

assistance of 'artificial means of guidance or support', like wire or cable.[77] Where such artificial means are used, the transmission in question can be called a 'cable retransmission' – a topic examined below in section 2.4.

2.3.1 The Early Days of Radio and TV

Discussion on the technology dates as far back as the 1880s, and the first experiences with radio-communications systems, by Marconi and Tesla, from 1896 and 1897.[78] In the early 1890s, the German scientist Heinrich Hertz discovered electromagnetic or 'Hertzian' waves, initially used to 'communicate the telegraphs dots and dashes'; around that period, the first reports surfaced of use of radio signals by the United States (US) Navy.[79]

As early as 1905–1906 it is possible to identify the amateur pioneers of broadcasting in the US, who operated rudimentary radio stations, talked with each other, and listened to 'radio signals from ships at sea'.[80] These experimental amateur activities significantly preceded the first commercial radio transmissions in 1919–1920, distributed through radio waves from transmitters to receiving devices with antennae.[81] The early days of radio broadcasting in the US were characterized by the co-existence of different models, from amateur radio clubs, to radio stations of universities, churches, hotels, newspapers, the US military, and a few commercial stations. Radio was mostly local, partly due to limitations in the range of transmissions, and the content transmitted was irregular.[82] Between 1912 and 1922, the combination of 'massive amateur and commercial exploitation' with war production led to a boom in radio innovation in the US.[83] By 1924, more than a thousand broadcast stations existed and over 2 million broadcast-ready radio sets had been sold.[84] By the end of 1934, over 65% of households in

77. *See* Ricketson 1987, p. 435. When such artificial means are used, the transmission in question can be called a 'cable retransmission'.
78. *See* G. Austin, 'Radio: Early Battles over the Public Performance Right', in: *Copyright and the Challenge of the New*, B. Sherman & L. Wiseman (eds), Kluwer Law International (2012), pp. 117–118, noting that both men held patents on the technology in the US and UK.
79. Austin 2012; T. Wu, *The Master Switch: The Rise and Fall of Information Empires,* Alfred A Knopf (2011), p. 34.
80. Wu 2011, pp. 34 et seq., noting that, in their contemporary dictionaries, 'broadcast' was a seeding technique meaning '[c]ast or dispersed in all directions, as seed from the hand in sowing, widely diffused'.
81. *See*, generally, Austin 2012; Ithiel de Sola Pool, *Technologies of Freedom*, Harvard University Press (2009); Wu 2011.
82. *Ibid.*
83. Y. Benkler, 'Open Wireless vs. Licensed Spectrum: Evidence from Market Adoption', *Harvard Journal of Law & Technology*, 26(1), 2012, pp. 69–163.
84. Pool 2009; Wu 2011. On the development of the US radio industry and its regulation in this period, *see* Austin 2012; Benkler 2012; and Wu 2011.

the US had at least one radio receiver.[85] Interestingly, by 1923, 47% of radio stations with known ownership in the US were owned by radio manufacturers, who apparently saw radio stations primarily as a medium to promote the sales of receivers. 'Commercial establishments like department stores, art dealers, or jewelry and music stores' owned another 20%, the rest being educational or amateur stations.[86]

Across the Atlantic, the development of broadcasting suffered an interruption during the First World War (1914–1918). There is evidence that the first broadcast programmes on a fixed schedule were made in the Netherlands in late 1919, by an early Dutch radio pioneer, Mr Hanso Schotanus à Steringa Idzerda.[87] Between July 1922 and July 1923, the Daily Mail in the United Kingdom (UK) covered the costs of two weekly broadcasts in the Netherlands. A little later, in 1924, broadcasts were resumed by a Dutch manufacturer of transmission equipment, the 'Nederlandse Seintoestellenfabriek' who later allowed the 'Hilversumsche Draadlooze Omroep' to make use of its transmission equipment.[88] Thus, the early days of Dutch radio were partly sponsored by manufacturers who hoped to open this new market, just like in the US.

Meanwhile, in 1922, a UK consortium of radio manufacturers formed the BBC, which came into existence as a public 'crown' corporation in 1927, one year before the Rome Act of the Berne Convention.[89] In Germany, the first radio stations went on air in Berlin in 1923.[90] In most of Western Europe, radio broadcasting quickly turned into a state monopoly, 'defined and structured by regulation', which lasted until the 1980s.[91] By the 1930s, radio challenged the influence of film and had become the 'dominant form of entertainment'.[92]

In 1928, the first experimental demonstrations of electronic televisions (by Farnsworth and Baird) took place, as well as the introduction of the first mechanical televisions on the market (by General Electric). This period also

---

85. H. Leblebici, G. Salancik, A. Copay and T. King, 'Institutional Change and the Transformation of Interorganizational Fields: An Organizational History of the U.S. Radio Broadcasting Industry', *Administrative Science Quarterly,* 36(3), September 1991, pp. 333–363.
86. *Ibid.*
87. W.B.H.J. van de Donk et al., *Media Policy for the Digital Age*, WRR, Amsterdam University Press (2005), p. 29.
88. A.A.M. Enserinck (1933). *De Nederlandse radio-wetgeving geschiedkundig ontwikkeld.* N. Samson N.V., Alphen aan den Rijn, p. 69.
89. Lord Windlesham (1980). *Broadcasting in a Free Society*, Blackwell, pp. 18–23; Wu 2011.
90. Wikipedia, *History of Broadcasting*, https://en.wikipedia.org/wiki/History_of_broadcasting#Germany (accessed 26 September 2017).
91. B. O'Neill and H. Shaw, 'Radio Broadcasting in Europe: The Search for a Common Digital Future', in O'Neill, B., M. Ala-Fossi, et al., (eds), *Digital Radio in Europe: Technologies, Industries and Cultures*, Bristol, Intellect Books (2010), pp. 27–42.
92. Austin 2012; Wu 2011.

marks the beginning of television broadcasts in the US. In Europe, following the first experimental broadcasts in 1929, the BBC started its regular television broadcasting in 1936; one year earlier, in 1935, television broadcasts had started in Nazi Germany. However, this development was put on hold due to the Second World War,[93] and in many countries in Europe no television service was developed until the 1960s.[94] During the first decades of its existence, television broadcasting in most European countries was operated by the state, a notable exception being Luxemburg.[95] The major breakthrough for television in terms of household penetration came with the introduction of the colour TV. In the US, the percentage of households with a colour TV increased from 5% in 1965 to over 50% seven years later, a diffusion speed similar to that of the internet two decades later and exceeding that of the Personal Computer and the Video Cassette Recorder (VCR). A similarly rapid growth was recorded in for instance France, after a 5% penetration rate was reached eight years later.[96] By 2015, 96% of EU households had access to a television, making television broadcasting a multi-billion euro business in the EU alone.[97]

European commercial broadcasting by satellite began with ASTRA in 1989.[98] By 1991, approximately 2.5 million households in Western Europe had direct satellite reception, mostly in the UK and Germany.[99] In terms of coverage, satellite could be received by 56 million households (35% of total households) in twenty-two European countries in 1995.[100] By 2015, 24% of EU households were receiving satellite television. In Western European countries, the penetration of satellite is even higher, at around 29% of TV households, totalling 50 million households, 26 million of whom have free-to-air and 24 million pay satellite.[101]

The major technology shift produced by broadcasting, when compared with telegraph technology, was an evolution from one-to-one to one-to-many communication of messages to multiple devices. When compared to distribution of public performances 'by any means' as discussed in the previous

93. *See* Wu 2011.
94. J. Bignell and A. Fickers, 'Introduction. Comparative European Perspectives on Television History', in: *A European Television History*, J. Bignell and A. Fickers (eds), Wiley-Blackwell (2008), p. 5.
95. M.J. Rusher, in: *World Broadcasting: A Comparative View*, Alan Wells (ed.), Ablex Publishing Corporation (1996), p. 30.
96. OECD 2004, *OECD Information Technology Outlook 2004*, Paris, pp. 142–144.
97. European Commission (2016), *E-Communications and the Digital Single Market. Special Eurobarometer 438*.
98. R. Collins, *Satellite Television in Western Europe*, John Libbey (1990).
99. Rusher 1996, p. 32.
100. R. Collins, *Satellite Television in Western Europe*. John Libbey (1990).
101. Broadband TV News, *Digital TV Western Europe Forecasts report* (2016). The countries studied in this report are Austria, Belgium, Denmark, Finland, France, Germany, Iceland, Ireland, Italy, Luxembourg, Malta, the Netherlands, Norway, Portugal, Spain, Sweden, Switzerland, and the UK.

section, there is a similar distinction: broadcasting, as a medium of mass communication, allowed all within reach of the broadcast to 'see or hear the same program at the same time' without requiring 'that the public is assembled in one location'.[102] Radio, in its early days, became 'the technological vehicle that allowed synchronized communication to a new audience'.[103]

Broadcasting also had a profound effect on copyright, mainly because protected works constituted a significant portion of the content transmitted.[104] The programming of radio broadcasting, for example, primarily consisted of phonograph musical recordings.[105] Broadcast music became part of social interactions and firms' business practices, a tool to promote musical works and artists, the technology itself, and other types of content (e.g., newspapers, films).[106] Advertising grew into the standard business model for radio, proving in time 'almost a license to print money' and, together with sponsorship, 'gave radio stations a sustainable financial basis'.[107] Even for government-run television channels in Europe, advertising became an important source of revenue in most countries, alongside licence fees levied upon the purchase or ownership of television sets.[108] A powerful illustration of the economic significance of broadcasting and advertising revenues through broadcasting is the fact that by 1983 advertising revenues from radio and television had outgrown box office receipts from cinemas in most Western European countries.[109]

The question facing copyright policymakers in the early days of broadcasting was how to balance 'the traditional view of authors' rights with these new modes of communication: are new formulations of rights required, or do old formulations still hold good, necessitating only a flexible interpretation to apply to these changed conditions?'[110] Just as in the previous case of public performance, the issue was not that radio stations had somehow acquired the recordings they played illegally. Rather, the call for the extension of existing rights or the creation of new rights stemmed from the recorded music industry's view that airplay would hurt record sales.[111]

102. Depreeuw, 2014, pp. 268–269.
103. Austin 2012.
104. *Ibid.*, pp. 436–437.
105. *Ibid.*, p. 121.
106. *Ibid.*, pp. 122–123.
107. Wu 2011.
108. J. Tydeman and E.J. Kelm, *New Media in Europe. Satellites, Cable, VCR and Videotex* (1986), McGraw-Hill, pp. 54–55.
109. *Ibid.*, pp. 54–55, 79. In real terms, box office revenues had stagnated in most Western European countries between 1970 and 1982.
110. Ricketson 1987, pp. 436–437.
111. Leblebici et al. 1991, pp. 333–363.

In the US, court battles in the 1920s 'established that radio broadcasting implicated public performance rights of copyright owners'.[112] Ginsburg speculates that this was due to economic reasons and fears that unlicensed and free broadcasting would undercut rights holders' revenues.[113]

The move allowed US performing rights organizations representing owners of copyright in musical works (ASCAP, BMI, and SESAC) to access the operation of radio broadcasters, setting the stage for a blanket voluntary collective licensing system under which the organization provides access to its repertoire against a percentage of the radio station's revenues. That system survives to this day. It is noteworthy that the system initially applied to commercial establishments such as hotels, restaurants, and bars. As technology evolved, the licences were extended first to radio broadcasters, and later to 'television broadcasters, movie and television show producers and webcasters'.[114]

In Europe, the potential for exploitation of works through broadcasting became apparent only after the First World War, namely through the transmission of musical compositions and plays to individual receivers in people's homes, a 'far wider audience than possible at one specific location'.[115] For the most part, domestic legislators grappled with the new reality by interpreting existing law to protect authors against unauthorized exploitation of works through the new technology.[116]

2.3.2 Protection under International Law

2.3.2.1 Radio and Television

In a 1925 resolution, the ALAI urged that 'radio electric transmission' of literary and artistic works be treated as a public performance.[117] This was in the middle of the period of consolidation of broadcasting, but almost a decade before the advent of FM radio transmission.[118] The ALAI resolution

112. Austin 2012, pp. 123–128.
113. J. Ginsburg, 'Toward Supranational Copyright Law? The WTO Panel Decision and the "Three-Step Test" for Copyright Exceptions', *Revue Internationale du Droit d'Auteur (RIDA)* (2001), pp. 1620–1621.
114. G. Lunney, 'Copyright Collectives and Collecting Societies: The United States Experience', in: *Collective Management of Copyright and Related Rights*, D. Gervais (ed.), Kluwer Law International (2016), D. Gervais ed. (2016), pp. 319–348 (cit. p. 323, discussing ASCAP). *See also* Austin 2012, pp. 127–128.
115. Ricketson 1987, pp. 434–435.
116. Depreeuw, 2014, p. 267 (& n. 65); Ricketson 1987, p. 437.
117. *Actes de la Conférence réunie a Rome du 7 Mai au 2 Juin 1928* (Berne: Bureau de l'Union Internationale pour la Protection Des Œuvres Littéraires et Artistiques, 1929) [Records BC Rome 1928], p. 59, referring to the 1925 ALAI conference.
118. On the development of FM radio transmission as from 1934, *see* Wu 2011.

eventually led to the discussion of a broadcasting right in the 1928 Rome revision conference of the Berne Convention.[119] The programme proposal initially referred to a right of communication to the public by 'telegraphy', 'telephony', or 'other analogous means serving to transmit the sounds or images'.[120] The reference to 'artistic works' and 'images' seems to indicate the 'possibilities posed by the imminent advent of television'.[121] However, television was still in its infancy, explaining why specific discussions regarding television broadcasting are found only in the preparatory works of the 1948 Brussels Act of the Berne Convention.

The wording finally adopted in the Rome conference of 1928, in Article 11*bis*, referred to an exclusive right for authors to authorize the communication to the public of their works 'by radio-diffusion'.[122] The provision was described as a reaction to the 'new discovery of broadcasting', an innovative medium for dissemination of works that introduced 'a dramatically different vehicle of thought'.[123] Its regulation, through the 'application of the principle of the exclusive privilege to radio broadcasting ... whatever may be the conditions governing the exercise of the privilege that national legislation adopts', was classified as a 'victory for copyright of considerable importance'.[124]

The article was balanced by the introduction – in paragraph (2) – of the possibility to subject the right to compulsory licensing. This was justified by a combination of public interest associated with the educational and informative role of broadcasting – as 'in many countries this function was carried out by, or under the close supervision of, governmental or public authorities' – with the specific group interest of broadcasters.[125] In particular, broadcasting organizations were concerned that CMOs representing the broadcasting rights of authors would abuse their monopoly positions on national markets in negotiations with commercial users.[126] In sum, the purpose of the provision 'was to enable the contracting states to balance the

119. Note that the term 'broadcasting' was only adopted in the 1971 Stockholm Act of the BC as the English translation of the French '*radiodiffusion*'. Until then, both English and French texts used 'radiodiffusion'. This terminology choice, however, does not imply the exclusion of broadcasting of visual content from the scope of the provision. *See* Depreeuw 2014, pp. 268–270; and Records BC Rome 1928, p. 76.
120. Records BC Rome 1928, p. 76.
121. Ricketson 1987, p. 437.
122. *See* Depreeuw, p. 269, noting the different definitions of the term advanced in the reports of the 1928 Rome Conference and concluding that, although no definition was provided, the notion 'was quite clear in the then technical and socio-economic context'.
123. Records BC Rome 1928, p. 255 (General Report).
124. *Ibid.* (statement by Mr Caselli, Rapporteur-General to the 1928 Rome revision conference).
125. Ricketson & Ginsburg 2006, p. 819.
126. Ricketson & Ginsburg, 2006, p. 819 (& n. 283), citing the comments of the national delegations (of Australia, New Zealand, Scandinavia, and the Netherlands) in the records of the 1928 Rome revision conference.

author's exclusive rights with other policy considerations in other domains (e.g., education and culture)'.[127] When all is said and done, this article was considered one of the most important achievements of the conference.[128]

After the war, in 1948, the Brussels Act amended the Berne Convention regulation of broadcasting in an attempt to capture the developments of radio broadcasting and the relatively new invention of television.[129] The Brussels Act extended the scope of the exclusive right in Article 11*bis*(1) by introducing new items: point *(ii)* on communication to the public by wire or by rebroadcasting by a different organization, and point *(iii)* on communication by loudspeaker. From this moment onwards, the provision also covered acts of rebroadcasting, such as cable retransmission (*see* section 2.4 below). These new means of exploitation were therefore included in the scope of the author's exclusive right.

The Brussels conference also incorporated a corresponding scope extension in paragraph (2) through some minor drafting changes and, more substantially, replacing 'right' with 'rights', thus covering all the new entitlements in paragraph (1), including cable retransmission.[130] This simple solution hides the 'impassionate debate' behind the adoption of paragraphs (2) and (3), which saw the opposing tendencies that manifested in 1928 resurface with vigour.[131] The conference did not yield a definition of broadcasting. The likely reason was the existence of a general international understanding of the term as an act of communication to the public.[132] The

---

127. *Ibid.*, p. 297.
128. Records BC Rome 1928, p. 248 (General Report). The other main achievement was the recognition of the protection of moral rights in Art. 6*bis* BC. For further detail on the historical background of Art. 11*bis*(2), *see* Quintais, 2017, pp. 61–70.
129. In a communication before the ALAI Congress in 1958 on copyright and television, a former head of the copyright division at UNESCO argued for the need for an analogy between the legal regimes for radio broadcasting and television. *See* M.F. Hepp, 'Droit d'Auteur et Télévision', in: ALAI 1955–1958, *Compte Rendu du 47ème Congrès d'Amsterdam (3-8 septembre 1956) et des Journées 'Art et Droit d'Auteur' de Knokke-le-Zoute (14-17 mai 1958)*', pp. 190–192. For a discussion on the interpretation of Art. 11*bis* and its application to television after the Brussels Acts, *see* G. Straschnov, 'Television and the Berne Convention', *Revue Internationale du Droit d'Auteur* (*RIDA*) 9 – 10, 1955, pp. 40–59.
130. *See* Proposal for a Council Directive on the coordination of certain rules concerning copyright and neighbouring rights applicable to satellite broadcasting and cable retransmission, COM(91) 276 final – SYN 358, 11 September 1991 [Explanatory Memorandum SatCab Directive], p. 16.
131. Records BC Brussels 1948, pp. 263–264 (General Report).
132. *See* M.H. Pilcher, *Copyright Problems of Satellite and Cable Television in Europe*, Martinus Nijhoff (1987), p. 22, and Ricketson 1987, p. 440. This understanding was embodied in the radio regulations of the International Telecommunications Union, which in that same year defined broadcasting as a 'radiocommunications service of transmissions to be received directly by the general public'.

consensus as to the meaning of the term is also apparent from the preparatory documents of the Brussels Act.[133]

The 1967 Stockholm revision introduced an important clarification in terminology by adopting the term 'broadcasting' as the English translation of the French '*radiodiffusion*'. Until then, both English and French texts used '*radiodiffusion*'.[134] The impact of broadcasting was magnified by the advent of satellites (and later cable), which expanded its scope 'enormously', making possible 'the diffusion of programmes from one continent to another, and even to most of the world at one time'. The result was an erosion of the relevance of national boundaries in the realm of communications technology, and 'profound effects' on fields like 'popular education and entertainment, the conduct of international trade and business, diplomacy and defense'.[135]

This more versatile use of wireless technologies, as well as technical solutions for rebroadcasting and communication by wire, complicated the task of copyright. In particular, the introduction of separate technical steps in the process of disseminating the signals to the public (e.g., intermediary transmissions between providers before reaching the public) meant that copyright law struggled to qualify these technical acts.[136]

The current scope of Article 11*bis*(1) grants authors different exclusive rights to authorize the broadcasting of their work:

- Communication to the public by broadcast or by means of wireless diffusion.
- Communication to the public by wire or by rebroadcasting.
- 'Public communication' of broadcasts by loudspeaker or any other analogous instrument.[137]

---

133. Records BC Brussels 1948, p. 265.
134. *See* Depreeuw 2014, pp. 268–270; Ricketson 1987, pp. 438–439. Note that in Stockholm there was an unsuccessful proposal to exclude certain uses of cinematographic works from the scope of the compulsory licence. However, the licence remained unchanged as it 'provided an acceptable compromise between opposing interests'. Actes de la Conférence de Stockholm de le propriété intellectuelle: 11 juin–14 juillet 1967: Records of the intellectual property conference of Stockholm: 11 June to 14 July, 2 vols (Geneva: OMPI/WIPO, 1971) [Records BC Stockholm 1967], pp. 1168, 1181–1182.
135. Ricketson 1987, pp. 436–437. *See also* Austin 2012.
136. Depreeuw 2014, pp. 264–265, 273, 280–282.
137. We are using 'public communication' here to mean something different from 'communication to the public'. Following Ricketson and Ginsburg, the first term refers to secondary communication to a public place, rather than communication to a remote audience (the primary act). *See* S. Ricketson and J. Ginsburg, *International Copyright and Neighbouring Rights: The Berne Convention and Beyond* (Vol. I) (2nd ed.), Oxford University Press (2006), pp. 750–754 (*Comparative Table of Performance and Communication Rights*, 12.63).

2.3.2.2 Satellite

At this stage, it is important to note that the Berne Convention does not deal expressly with satellite broadcasting. The communicative capacities of satellites were recognized early on, after the launch of the first satellites in 1957 by the USSR (Sputnik 1) and in 1958 by the US (Explorer I). Their use for telecommunications proved to be an affordable and reliable alternative means of long-distance transmission of information, especially when compared to conventional broadcasting. Such use was 'particularly revolutionary in the field of television transmission', where it brought about 'a dramatic increase in the number of potential viewing audiences'.[138] In 1965, the first commercial communications satellite INTELSAT I[139] entered geostationary orbit, triggering the spectacular growth in the adoption of this type of satellite.[140] In 1981, the European spacecraft launcher Ariane launched its first satellites, soon to be followed by dozens more.[141]

Despite not expressly mentioning communication by satellite, Article 11*bis*(1) Berne Convention applies to most acts of satellite broadcasting, as well as to acts of retransmission via wire or cable (on which *see* section 2.4 below).[142] In particular, this provision covers transmission of copyright-protected content by satellite where the signals are received directly by members of the public through the use of the necessary equipment (e.g., a satellite dish).

More controversial was the case of *intermediate* satellite transmission, where the 'content is transmitted between distributors by means of satellite signals that cannot be captured by means normally at the disposal of the general public' but that eventually reach that public over cable networks through the intervention of a cable distributor that picks up the transmission and distributes the signal to its subscribers.[143] These transmissions between point-to-point and distribution satellites, as opposed to direct-broadcasting satellites, were not aimed at reception by the public (through satellite dishes), but were rather intended 'to assist programmers and broadcasting organizations to distribute their signals'.[144] Depending on its legal qualification, the

138. Pilcher, p. 8.
139. Nicknamed 'Early Bird' after the proverb 'the early bird catches the worm'.
140. Pilcher, pp. 9–10. *See also*, International Telecommunication Union, *Overview of ITU's History*, http://search.itu.int/history/HistoryDigitalCollectionDocLibrary/12.28.71.en.pdf (accessed 26 September 2017).
141. Tydeman and Kelm, p. 86.
142. Explanatory Memorandum SatCab Directive, pp. 9–13, describing the application of Art. 11*bis* BC to different acts of satellite broadcasting. *See also* Depreeuw 2014, p. 389, explaining the development of the international understanding of the scope of Art. 11*bis* to the acceptance 'that satellite transmissions that the public could receive directly were also *broadcasts*'.
143. Depreeuw 2014, p. 318.
144. Pilcher 1987, p. 26. *See also* E. Ulmer, 'Protection of Authors in Relation to the Transmission via Satellite of Broadcast Programmes', *RIDA* 93 – 07, 1977, pp. 4–41.

'injection' or uplink of the work into the satellite by the broadcaster would be free from copyright (because it did not reach a 'public') or a restricted act of broadcasting. The issue was hotly debated, but no unanimous consensus on the qualification of intermediate satellite transmissions as acts of broadcasting emerged, leaving the issue to be determined by national laws and courts.[145]

Outside the Berne Convention, no international *copyright* instrument dealt with satellite broadcasting in the decades following the Stockholm Act, notwithstanding some attempts to do so in the context of UNESCO, WIPO, and the ILO.[146] In fact, only the broad exclusive right of communication to the public for authors in Article 8 WCT deals with this reality at an international level. [147] This right, which applies without prejudice to the different rights of communication in the Berne Convention,[148] covers any communication to the public of works by wire or wireless means, thereby applying to all types of broadcasting of works, including by satellite.

In the EU, despite there having been discussions on copyright aspects of satellite broadcasting since at least the 1970s, the issue was only settled in the 1993 SatCab Directive, following the CJEU decision in *Coditel I* (1980), the Green Paper on Television without Frontiers (1894), and the White Paper setting out the Commission's intention to create a 'Single European Broadcasting Area' (1985), a Commission Notification, and a Discussion Paper.[149] The directive recognizes, *inter alia*, an exclusive right for the

145. For a description of the relevant discussions, *see*: Ulmer 1977; H. Cohen Jehoram, 'Legal Issues of Satellite Television in Europe', *RIDA* 122 – 10, 1984; Pilcher 1987, pp. 26–38; and Depreeuw 2014, pp. 318–329.
146. *See* Pilcher 1987, pp. 6–7, making reference to different initiatives. Note that the Brussels Convention of 1974 is not a copyright convention *stricto sensu* and deals primarily with the problem of unauthorized interception of signals. *Id.*, pp. 27–30.
147. Performers and phonogram producers are granted more limited exclusive rights of making available in Arts 10 and 14 WPPT, as well as a right to remuneration for broadcasting and communication to the public in Art. 15 WPPT.
148. Articles 11(1)(ii), 11*bis*(1)(i) and (ii), 11*ter*(1)(ii), 14(1)(ii), and 14*bis*(1) BC.
149. *See*, CJEU Case 62/79, *SA Compagnie générale pour la diffusion de la télévision, and others v. Ciné-Vog Films and others*, 19.03.1980 [*Coditel I*]; European Commission, 'Television without Frontiers', Green Paper, COM (84) def, Brussels, 14.06.1984 [Green Paper 'Television Without Frontiers']. European Commission, 'Completing the Internal Market, White Paper from the Commission to the European Council' (Milan, 28–29 June), COM (1985) 310 final, June 1985; Communication of the Commission to the Council and Parliament on Audiovisual Policy of 21 February 1990, COM (1990) 0078 final; European Commission, *Broadcasting and copyright in the internal market. Discussion paper*, III/F/5263/90-EN, Brussels, November 1990, p. 2. For earlier discussions, *see* A. Lokrantz-Bernitz, 'Telecommunications with Satellites and Copyright', *RIDA* 68 – 04, 1971; R. Plaisant, 'Intellectual Property and Communications by Satellites', *RIDA* 70 – 10, 1971 (citing studies by BIRPI/WIPO and UNESCO on the topic); ALAI, *Compte Rendu des Journées D'Études tenues à l'Hôtel de Massa à Paris (Société des Gens de Lettres) du 3 au 8 juillet 1972*, Paris (1974), pp. 152–171, containing the communications of J.V. Ungern-Sternberg ('*La transmission*

author to authorize the communication to the public by satellite of copyright works.[150]

The right applies to all types of satellite transmissions (whether from direct broadcasting or point-to-point satellites), whether the signal is received directly, or after decoding by an intermediary.[151] The right applies only where the signals are introduced into an uninterrupted chain of communication leading to the satellite and down towards the earth, under the control and responsibility of the broadcasting organization, for reception by the public.[152] An important feature is that this is a 'Community-wide right' protected only in the Member State of origin of the satellite transmission, i.e., in the country where 'uplink of the programme-carrying signal occurs' rather than the countries in the reception area.[153] This right has been for the most part superseded by Article 3 InfoSoc Directive, which provides for a general right of communication to the public, including acts of satellite broadcasting.[154]

2.4 CABLE RETRANSMISSION

This section addresses cable retransmission, meaning the secondary communication, by cable networks to subscribers, of an initial transmission of originally broadcast or otherwise transmitted programmes. It does not discuss the initial transmission of 'cable-originated' programmes, also known as 'cable-casting'.[155]

---

d'émissions de radiodiffusion par satellites et le droit d'auteur'), and R. Castelain ('*Les satellites*'). *See also* Pilcher 1987, pp. 18–50.

150. Article 2 SatCab Directive. Art. 1(1) and 1(2) define the act and place of the communication to the public by satellite. Note that the directive clarifies in Art. 4 that the concept of 'broadcasting by wireless means' under Arts 8 and 10 Rental Right Directive also encompasses 'communication to the public by satellite'. *See also* Common Statement by the Council and Commission at the internal market Council meeting of 18 June 1992. The Rental and Lending Rights Directive contains specific exclusive and remuneration rights regarding acts of broadcasting and communication to the public for related rights holders.
151. Articles 1(1) and (2)(c) and recital 6 SatCab Directive.
152. Article 1(2)(a) SatCab Directive. On the interpretation of these conditions, *see* Depreeuw 2014, pp. 370–381.
153. Hugenholtz 2009, p. 9, notes that 'Art. 1(2)(b) does not rule out that licence fees and other contractual conditions take into account the size of the footprint (i.e., the number of countries reached) of the satellite broadcast.' In this respect, *see* recital 17, which encourages parties to 'take account of all aspects of the broadcast, such as the actual audience, the potential audience and the language version'.
154. Hugenholtz 2009, p. 10; P.B. Hugenholtz, in Dreier/Hugenholtz, *Concise Copyright*, 'Satellite and Cable Directive' (2016), p. 322.
155. For a distinction between these two different types of service, *see* Pilcher, pp. 56–58.

2.4.1 The Rise of Cable Retransmission

Just as for broadcasting, retransmission of radio signals preceded that of television. In the early twentieth century, radio retransmission over telephone lines served two distinct purposes. First, and primarily in the US, point-to-point telephone line connections were used to increase coverage of radio stations. Rather than using more powerful transmitters, less powerful radio stations were connected using telephone lines to create national coverage. Second, and primarily in Europe, radio lines were used as early as the 1920s in a point-to-multipoint setting to deliver radio signals to subscribers without the need to obtain a radio receiver.[156]

Retransmission gained economic significance in the 1950s, when subscription-based cable retransmission of commercial television channels, known as Community Antenna Television (CATV), was introduced in the US, to provide reception in areas where there was no or poor reception of the broadcast signal. Initially, commercial entrepreneurs built antennae to capture existing broadcast signals from neighbouring communities. The Federal Communications Commission did not require a licence for such retransmission, as long as no new services were included and the entrepreneurs were allowed to charge a fee to subscribers.[157] Cable television proved popular, and from 1959 onwards it was no longer limited to providing access to locally available television stations: its *raison d'être* started shifting towards providing access to remote channels. As a consequence, the industry tripled between 1959 and 1965.[158]

In Europe, cable networks developed more slowly than in the US. Master Antenna Television (MATV), aimed at improving the reception for apartment complexes or blocks of houses in cities (and at getting rid of individual rooftop antennae), emerged simultaneously with more extensive CATV networks operated by public entities. Either way, improving reception of national broadcast channels and in some cases receiving foreign channels, were the main purposes of cable networks. In many European countries the public telephony incumbents initially had a monopoly on the construction and operation of cable systems. The growth of (commercial) cable in the US rekindled the interest in cable networks in Europe. Still, by 1985, the European cable industry was claimed to be where the US industry had been ten years earlier, i.e., only on the brink of commercialization. In that year, there were about 12.3 million cable households in Western Europe. The

---

156. T.H. White, *United States Early Radio History*, http://earlyradiohistory.us/index.html (accessed 26 September 2017).
157. Tydeman and Kelm, p. 131.
158. N. Schaumann, 'Copyright Protection in the Cable Television Industry: Satellite Retransmission and the Passive Carrier Exemption', *Fordham Law Review* 51(4), 1983, pp. 637–665.

countries with the largest percentage of cable subscribers were Belgium (80%), The Netherlands (70%), and Switzerland (40%).[159]

During the 1980s and 1990s, cable networks in Europe expanded rapidly, spurred by the development of satellite and commercial television, and followed by privatization and consolidation of local networks throughout much of Europe, which turned cable television into a multi-billion euro industry in Europe alone. By 2014, the average coverage (homes passed) of cable in the EU-28 was 54%. Excluding Italy and Greece where there is no coverage, this percentage was 63%, while in some countries, such as Belgium and the Netherlands, it is more than 95%.[160] About 29% of EU households with a television subscribed to a cable TV network (20% digital, 9% analogue) in 2015.[161] This made it the second largest TV infrastructure in Europe, after digital terrestrial television (DTT). Including TV reception of telephone networks, wired television accounts for 41% of EU households.

2.4.2 Protection under International Law

The history of the legal protection of cable retransmission acts in the Berne Convention is intertwined with that of broadcasting, described above in section 2.3. As noted, wireless broadcasting (then: *radiodiffusion*) came under the Convention with the Rome Act of 1928. At that time, there was already discussion on the possible protection of retransmission and other secondary use of radio broadcasts. Yet, despite a proposal to that effect by the French Delegation, this did not come to pass.[162]

The issue was debated in national laws and courts. In the Netherlands, for instance, the 1930 *Radiocentrale* judgment of the Supreme Court ruled that a system allowing the passing of signals from a commercial broadcast, through a radio distribution system owned by a third party, to paying members of the public did not involve the rights of performance or reproduction. The decision turned on the fact that the broadcast signal was already available to the public in that geographic reception zone for the average consumer, and that the radio distribution system merely facilitated and simplified its reception.[163] However, this judgment was overturned eight

159. Tydeman and Kelm, pp. 131 138

160. Arthur D. Little, *Cable Operator's Contribution to the European Digital landscape*, http://www.cable-europe.eu/wp-content/uploads/2010/09/ADL-full-report.pdf (accessed 26 September 2017).

161. European Commission (2016), *E-Communications and the Digital Single Market. Special Eurobarometer 438*, p. 23.

162. M. de Cock Buning, 'Cable Retransmission and Other Secondary Use', in: *A Century of Dutch Copyright Law: Auteurswet 1912–2012*, DeLex (2012), p. 261.

163. Supreme Court of the Netherlands, 3 April 1930, *NJ* 1931, p. 53 (*Radiocentrale*). Cf. De Cock Buning 2012, pp. 271–272; and Depreeuw 2014, pp. 306–307.

years later in *Caféradio*.[164] In this later case, the Supreme Court considered the use in a café of 'service equipment with which radio signals could be received and made perceptible through speakers' to be a restricted act of communication to the public, more precisely a secondary and simultaneous *openbaarmaking*.[165]

Turning back to the Berne Convention, the matter was considered in greater detail in Brussels (1948) when discussing proposed amendments to Article 11*bis*, aimed at accounting for different methods and techniques for exploitation of works in broadcasting and communication to the public.[166] The inclusion of retransmission and other secondary use of radio broadcasts was proposed by the *Bureau de l'Union* and the Belgian Government. Retransmission acts were necessary to respond to certain technical limitations of territorial broadcasting at that time, largely concerning the reach and quality of the signal.[167]

The proposal was for a new paragraph 2, which mentioned an exclusive right to authorize '*toute nouvelle communication publique, soit par fil, soit sans fil, de l'oeuvre radiodiffusée*'.[168] The idea was therefore to distinguish primary communications (the original transmission) from subsequent secondary use, such as retransmission by cable. The latter use would require the author's consent if it reached a new circle of listeners as compared to the primary transmission.[169]

During the discussions it became clear that the criterion of 'new audience' – which can also be perceived to underlie the Dutch Supreme Court's decision in *Radiocentrale* – was of difficult application. It was noted that, regardless of whether a new audience was reached, the broadcasting organization authorized to carry out the primary transmission should not require a separate authorization for the secondary transmission.[170] In this light, and facing opposition from other delegations, the Belgian delegation suggested replacing the word '*nouvelle*' with the sentence '*lorsque cette communication est effectuée par un autre organisme que celui d'origine*', i.e., replacing the criterion of 'new audience' or 'new public' with that of 'new organization' (i.e., 'a body other than the original one'). This more functional requirement was considered 'easier to apply in practice because the identity of the retransmitting organisation can usually be readily

164. Supreme Court of the Netherlands, 6 May 1938, *NJ* 1938, 635 (*Caféradio*).
165. De Cock Buning 2012, p. 272.
166. Guide to the Berne Convention for the Protection of Literary and Artistic Works, WIPO Geneva (1978) [WIPO Guide 1978], p. 66.
167. Depreeuw 2014, pp. 278, 280.
168. Records BC Brussels, 1948, p. 270.
169. De Cock Buning 2012, p. 264.
170. *Ibid.*, pp. 263–264, describing the discussions of the amendment to Art. 11*bis* in 1948, and in particular the positions expressed by the Delegations of Monaco, the Netherlands, and Luxembourg.

ascertained'.[171] Although this makes practical sense, it is questionable whether the organizational structure of the industry should determine whether a retransmission requires authorization, especially due to the risk that such a requirement may incentivize vertical integration to avoid payment of retransmission fees.

The current wording of the provision was thus settled, having remained unchanged in the Stockholm (1967) and Paris (1971) revision conferences, with the exception of linguistic changes 'to provide a more suitable translation in the newly authentic English text'.[172] Article 11*bis*(1)(ii) grants authors an exclusive right for secondary acts of communication by wire of the broadcast of the work, when made by an organization other than the original one. This means that the author has the right to authorize the cable retransmission of his works. As noted in section 2.3 above, the acts of cable retransmission covered by this provision are subject to the possibility of compulsory licensing under Article 11*bis*(2) Berne Convention.

Although the Berne Convention text appears to clearly cover secondary acts of cable retransmission, it is noteworthy that the 1970s and 1980s witnessed serious debates as to the legal qualification of certain activities under this right. In particular, national legislators and courts struggled with the technological overlap between broadcasting and cable retransmission, and whether the retransmission right should apply solely to a 'new public'. The latter theory also went by many other names, sometimes referred to as arguments for each theory: 'double payment', 'direct reception zone', 'license area', or 'service area' (*see* section 2.3 above).[173]

However, and despite certain deviations, a mid-1980s study on, *inter alia*, the national legislation and higher court decisions in key European jurisdictions shows a trend towards the autonomous recognition of a cable retransmission right and the rejection of the 'new public' approach.[174] This trend coincided with the growing importance of cable networks for the reception of television in European households, and the commercialization of cable networks, described above. To apply the anachronism once more, it can be argued that a substantial and widening value gap had emerged, which the recognition of the retransmission right aimed to bridge.

For the sake of completeness, it is noted that cable retransmission is covered by the general right in Article 8 WCT, which refers to the respective provision in Article 11*bis*(ii) Berne Convention, discussed in section 2.3

171. P.B. Hugenholtz and S.C. van Velze, 'Communication to a New Public? Three Reasons Why EU Copyright Law Can Do Without a "New Public"', *International Review of Intellectual Property and Competition Law (IIC)* 47(7), 2016, p. 808.
172. WIPO Guide 1978, p. 66.
173. H. Cohen Jehoram, 'General Report: Cable Television, Media and Copyright Law Aspects', in ALAI Symposium 1982 on 'Cable Television: Media and Copyright Law Aspects' (Paris, 1983), pp. 217–233. *See also* Pilcher 1987, pp. 66–76.
174. Pilcher 1987, pp. 76–96, noting that countries were more divided on the introduction of systems of non-voluntary licence. *See also* Cohen Jehoram 1983, pp. 225–231.

above. Interestingly, the Basic Proposal for the WCT made no reference to Article 11*bis*(ii), leading to speculation that the WCT covered only primary acts of communication (e.g., broadcasting), but not secondary cable retransmission. Still, the provision did however apply to communication 'by wire or wireless means', leaving the status of cable retransmission unclear.[175] This apparent shortcoming was corrected in the final version by adding the safeguard reference to the Berne provision. As a result, the broad exclusive right of communication to the public in Article 8 WCT is without prejudice to the continued applicability of the Berne right of cable retransmission.

2.4.3 Protection under EU Law

In EU law, the SatCab Directive makes a legal distinction between satellite broadcasting and cable retransmission, the latter regulated by Articles 8–12. Like satellite broadcasting, the recognition of copyright protection in the EU for cable retransmission can be traced back to the *Coditel I* judgment (1980) and the Green Paper on 'Television without Frontiers' (1984).[176]

In *Coditel I*, the Court refused to recognize the application of the exhaustion doctrine to acts of cable retransmission.[177] At stake was the unauthorized retransmission in Belgium of a film broadcast in Germany with the authorization of the rights holder. The Court recognized the territorial exclusivity of the film producer's right, which prevailed over the freedom to provide services across borders (Article 56 TFEU; ex Article 59 EC Treaty). To arrive at this decision, the Court relied on the fact that, at the time, television broadcasting services in the Member States were 'traditionally organized on the basis of national monopolies'.[178] Article 8 SatCab Directive can be viewed as the legislative confirmation of this ruling. [179]

The 1984 Green Paper pointed out national differences regarding the scope of national rights of retransmission, reserved to the author under Article 11*bis*(1)(ii) Berne Convention. This right, and the existing national differences, posed a conflict with the freedom to provide services, at least regarding the possibility that rights holders could prevent unauthorized cable

175. Records of the Diplomatic Conference on Certain Copyright and Neighboring Rights Questions 1996 (vols I and II), WIPO Publication 348 (WIPO: Geneva 1999) [Records WIPO Treaties], p. 12 (Art. 10 Basic Proposal for the 1996 Diplomatic Conference).
176. Cf. Pilcher 1987, pp. 52–56, referring also to a number of studies in the context of WIPO, UNESCO, and the Council of Europe.
177. M. van Eechoud, P.B. Hugenholtz, S. van Gompel, L. Guibault & N. Helberger, *Harmonizing European Copyright Law. The Challenges of Better Lawmaking*. Kluwer Law International (2009), p. 312.
178. Van Eechoud et al. 2009, p. 312. Cf. *Coditel I*, paras 15–17.
179. Hugenholtz 2016, p. 327.

retransmissions in territories other than that of an initial authorized transmission.[180]

To deal with potential obstacles to the free flow of broadcasts, the Commission considered dealing with cable retransmission through a system of statutory licensing.[181] However, by the time of the 1990 Discussion Paper, this possibility was off the table. This was largely due to existing contractual arrangements under the framework of collective rights management schemes in different Member States, such as Belgium, the Netherlands, and Germany – the most significant countries in Europe for cable retransmission.[182] The success of these arrangements led the Commission to suggest a mandatory collective management scheme for the cable retransmission right.[183]

The directive does not mandate an exclusive right for cable retransmission per se, but merely requires these acts to be restricted under copyright.[184] However, as Depreeuw notes, several elements in the directive confirm the exclusive nature of the retransmission right, and exclude the possibility of subjecting it to statutory licensing.[185]

The right applies only to simultaneous, unaltered, and unabridged retransmissions by cable of television or radio programmes for reception by the public originating in another Member State, following an initial transmission over the air or (unlike the Berne Convention) by wire.[186] The scope of the right aligns with economic reality, as in the 1980s this was already the most important 'form of border-crossing television programmes'.[187] Furthermore, the right by definition requires a primary transmission and the use of the specific technology of cable as the means for the secondary transmission.[188] Unlike Berne, no requirement of a 'new organization' applies.

The reason why the directive focuses on cross-border cable retransmission of broadcasts is related to competence. There was no established case for harmonization of purely national retransmissions, since these did not affect the main objective of creating a single European audiovisual area. The directive also leaves to national law the issue of retransmissions of programmes originating from outside the EU.[189]

---

180. Green Paper on the Establishment of the Common Market for Broadcasting, especially by Satellite and Cable, 'Television Without Frontiers', COM (84) 300 final/annex, Communication from the Commission to the Council, 1984 [Green Paper 1984], p. 304.
181. *Ibid.*
182. EC Discussion Paper 1990, p. 27.
183. *Ibid.*, pp. 80–82; Explanatory Memorandum SatCab Directive, pp. 4–5, 8, 24–25.
184. Depreeuw 2014, p. 393.
185. *Ibid.*, p. 402, referring to recital 27 and the wording of Art. 8 SatCab Directive, which mentions individual or collective contractual agreements.
186. Articles 1(3) and 8 SatCab Directive.
187. Pilcher 1987, p. 96.
188. On the requirements of initial transmission and retransmission by cable, *see* Depreeuw 2014, pp. 393–400.
189. *See* Explanatory Memorandum SatCab Directive, p. 23; and Hugenholtz 2016, p. 320.

The exercise of the right is subject to a special regime of mandatory collective management in Articles 9–12 SatCab Directive, from which only broadcasting organizations are exempt. Still, despite this special regime, the right remains exclusive.[190] In essence, the proposed scheme determines the conditions of exercise of the right. This solution, consistent with Article 11*bis*(2) Berne Convention, enhances the bargaining position of authors, who retain the (collective) right to prohibit the exploitation of their works.[191]

The main rationale behind this option was not so much the protection of authors' interests but the facilitation of 'the practicable exploitation of programmes'.[192] The objective was to put in place a system that ensured cable operators could acquire cable retransmission rights in a timely manner and in their entirety.[193] Mandatory collective management would shield cable operators from refusals to licence by individual rights holders not represented by CMOs, in relation to their rights in retransmitted programmes (the so-called outsider problem).[194] Such refusals would have the effect of creating '"black-outs" in programmes retransmitted by cable operators'.[195] The system would likewise provide that rights holders interested in cable retransmission 'would not be prevented from exploiting their rights'.[196]

Finally, it should be noted that the cable retransmission right was at a later date substantively harmonized (for authors) by Article 3(1) InfoSoc Directive as an integral part of that provision's broad right of communication to the public.

In sum, the recognition of a cable retransmission right in EU law, in line with the protection granted in the Berne Convention, was the result of a need to articulate the protection of rights holders with the fundamental freedom to provide services. The exclusive right prevailed as an exception to that freedom, but its exercise is restricted by a special regime of mandatory collective management, justified by the need to enable the exploitation of rights across the EU. Like with the Berne Convention's rejection of the 'new public' criterion in favour of that of a 'new organization', practical considerations related to the application of the right and its commercial exploitation shaped the choices for its legal design.

---

190. Hugenholtz 2006, p. 280. Art. 10 SatCab Directive contains the exemption for broadcasting organizations.
191. Depreeuw, 2014, pp. 403–404.
192. *Ibid.*, p. 406.
193. Explanatory Memorandum SatCab Directive, p. 32.
194. Depreeuw, 2014, pp. 402–403; and J. Rosén, 'The Satellite and Cable Directive', in: *EU Copyright Law. A Commentary, Cheltenham,* I. Stamatoudi & P. Torremans (eds), Edward Elgar (2014), pp. 234–235. *See also* Explanatory Memorandum SatCab Directive, pp. 20, 24, 32.
195. Hugenholtz 2016, p. 309.
196. Explanatory Memorandum SatCab Directive, p. 32.

2.5 COMMERCIAL RENTAL

From a legal perspective, rental can be defined as 'the transfer of the possession of a *copy* of a work or an object of *related rights* for a limited period of time, and for direct or indirect economic or commercial advantage'.[197] Some national laws include the concept under the general right of distribution, as an exception to or deviation from the exhaustion of the distribution right resulting from first sale or transfer of ownership of a physical copy. Other laws grant a specific right of rental alongside the right of distribution.[198]

2.5.1 The Rise and Fall of Commercial Video and DVD Rental

Commercial rental of print books (outside the school book segment) never gathered steam for several reasons. For one thing, there is competition from public libraries lending books for free or against highly subsidized prices for social reasons. Second, the timeframe within which commercial rental of a specific title would be attractive is relatively short, as readers will want to keep rental books for a number of weeks at least, unlike video rentals. Rentals would be most attractive over such a period of high demand, but it would take a large number of copies during a brief window to actually make money. Lastly, delivery and return of print books involve significant costs and books are prone to damage and stains.[199] These arguments apply far less to commercial rental of, in particular, audiovisual material, which can explain why commercial rental of copyright works only became a business model of significance after the mass introduction of the video cassette recorder (VCR).

VCRs were introduced in the late 1970s, and in Europe there were initially three competing formats: VHS developed by JVC, Beta developed by Sony, and V-2000 developed by Philips and Grundig.[200] VHS eventually became the most widely adopted standard; despite its alleged technical superiority, V-2000 lost the race because of its relatively late market introduction and the unavailability of porn for this format.[201] Until 1979, total sales of VCRs in Western Europe were only 340,000, but sales more than doubled in each of the ensuing three years. By the end of 1984, VCRs' penetration had exceeded 20% of households in the UK, Western Germany,

197. WIPO Guide 2003, p. 307.
198. *Ibid.*, p. 307.
199. J. Poort, I. Akker, N. van Eijk, B. van der Sloot & P. Rutten (2012), *Digitally Binding. Examining the Feasibility of Charging a Fixed Price for e-books*. SEO-report 2012-18, p. 72.
200. Tydeman and Kelm, p. 160.
201. M. Naaijkens, *Video 2000 vs VHS*, http://www.briljantemislukkingen.nl/nl/2012/02/03/video-2000-vs-vhs/ (accessed 26 September 2017).

the Netherlands, Ireland, and Norway.[202] It continued to grow rapidly in the following years and, according to estimates from the OECD for a selection of countries, diffusion from 20% to 50% penetration only took between three and six years. This diffusion rate is inferior to that of the PC and is largely comparable to that of the colour TV.[203]

The two main reasons for people to buy a VCR were time-shifting programmes broadcast at inconvenient times and – particularly in countries with limited local programming or poor reception – to rent or buy pre-recorded cassettes. In Europe, halfway through the 1980s, 80% of pre-recorded tapes were commercially rented rather than bought and rental outlets had sprung up across Europe.[204] Tape rental boomed throughout the 1990s. From the development of the DVD standard in 1995 onwards, VHS rental gradually lost terrain to this digital video disc of superior technical quality. Including sales, the home video industry (DVD plus video-cassette) was the largest source of revenue for the film industry in the US in 1999, when it accounted for 55% of industry revenues. About half of this came from rental, the other half from sales.[205] In the Netherlands, turnover from VHS and DVD rentals was roughly equal to that from cinema and art-house theatre admissions during the first few years of the century.

Around 2005, however, the rental market started to decline very rapidly. This can be linked to the emergence of digital rental (video on demand), streaming video subscriptions, and unauthorized file sharing. To illustrate this: between 1998 and 2004, there were between 1,000 and 1,150 DVD/ video rental shops in the Netherlands. In the following years, this number declined by more than 10% each year, and there were only 470 such shops left by the end of 2008.[206] By February 2015, this number had dropped to 176,[207] and by 2017 there seem to be only a few left.[208]

2.5.2 Protection under EU Law

In international law, despite discussions in the context of WIPO in the 1980s, a right of rental is only granted in TRIPS (1994) and in the WIPO Treaties

202. Tydeman and Kelm, p. 159.
203. OECD 2004, *OECD Information Technology Outlook 2004*, Paris, pp. 143–144.
204. Tydeman and Kelm, p. 165.
205. Video Software Dealers Association (VSDA), *Annual Report on the Home Video Market* (2000).
206. CBS, *Aantal videotheken gehalveerd in tien jaar tijd*, https://www.cbs.nl/nl-nl/nieuws/2008/47/aantal-videotheken-gehalveerd-in-tien-jaar-tijd (accessed 26 September 2017).
207. RTL, *Wanneer verdwijnt de laatste videotheek*, https://www.rtlnieuws.nl/economie/home/wanneer-verdwijnt-laatste-videotheek (accessed 26 September 2017).
208. For example *see*: M. van den Tempel, *Longread, Last Action Heroes: de laatste videotheken van Nederland*, http://revu.nl/uit-ons-archief/longread-last-action-heroes-de-laatste-videotheken-van-nederland/ (accessed 26 September 2017); J. Chorus, *De laatste videotheek*, https://www.nrc.nl/nieuws/2016/08/28/de-laatste-videotheek-4036790-a1518381 (accessed 26 September 2017).

(1996). In EU law, the right is found in the Computer Programs Directive (1991, codified 2009) and in the Rental and Lending Rights Directive (1992, codified 2006).[209] Because the European directives preceded the international provisions, they are addressed here first.

Having said that, legal discussions on copyright and video-cassettes largely predate the boom in the market for VCRs and cassette tapes, and can be traced back as early as the 1960s. For example, based on a Report by Professor Torben Lund, an ALAI Resolution of 1961 advocates the participation of authors in the revenues from the rental of books and records.[210]

About a decade later, it is possible to find discussions on the topic in the 1972 ALAI conference, which contains a couple of reports and communications on the legal aspects of the use of works on video-cassettes. However, the legal questions that arose relate mainly to the rights of reproduction (namely private use) and '*représentation*' of video-cassettes, despite some prescient references to the possibility of rental.[211]

In a 1983 study on rental of videograms and related market phenomena, Karnell discusses the commercial practices emerging at the beginning of the decade, including the practice by videoclubs to enable both the hire (rental) and 'swapping' (exchange) of videograms. At this time, the growing relevance of these practices for the general public meant that the retail sale of videograms was already but a 'marginal part of the market'.[212] A key element in the discussions at the time was the uncertain application of the exhaustion principle to the right(s) of distribution and rental in different national laws, seen as one of the main 'evils … haunting the videogram (and phonogram) market'.[213]

The Computer Programs Directive was the first copyright instrument to be adopted in the EU following the publication of the White Paper on completing the Single Market by 1992. The directive was adopted in 1991 and repealed, replaced, and codified in 2009. Prior to its adoption, in 1989,

209. Directive 2009/24/EC of the European Parliament and of the Council of 23 April 2009 on the legal protection of computer programs (Codified version). This instrument repeals Directive 91/250/EEC, as amended [Computer Programs Directive]. For the international discussions in the 1980s, *see* Karnell 1983, p. 79; and T. Desurmont, 'The Author's Right to Control the Destination of Copies Reproducing His Work', *RIDA* 134 – 10, 1987, p. 8.

210. *See* ALAI Congress 1961 (Florence), 11–16 September, pp. 161–162, Resolutions et Voeu, 'Pret et Location des Livres et des Disques'.

211. ALAI 1974, pp. 95–139, containing the Reports and Communications of D. Gaudel ('*Videogrammes et droits d'auteurs': Droit Français et Convention de Berne*); M. Fabiani ('*les Aspects Juridiques de L'Utilisation par Video-Cassete dóeuvres protegees*'); and G. Karnell ('*Les Problèmes des Video-Cassettes Envisagées du Point de Vue Scandinave*'). The latter authors make express mention of renting as a problem 'relating to the ulterior use of copies of works'. *Id.*, pp. 131–133.

212. G. Karnell, 'Rental and Related Market Phenomena Concerning Videograms and the Right of Distribution', *RIDA* 115 – 01, 1983, p. 83.

213. G. Karnell 1983, pp. 93 et seq. (cit. p. 95).

available figures showed that the cost of piracy of computer programs in seven countries of the Community alone amounted to USD 4.5 billion. The directive was therefore aimed at stemming 'this enormous illicit trade in computer programs'.[214]

The directive has its roots in the 1985 White Paper on the Completion of the Internal market and the 1988 Green Paper on Copyright and the Challenge of Technology.[215] The rationale for the grant of a rental right is explained in the 1989 proposal for a directive.[216] Contrary to analogue private copies of music and video content, which were of inferior quality to originals, it was possible to make a large number of perfect digital copies of software from a single copy. This increased the risk that an unregulated rental market would potentially substitute for the sale of copies by rights holders.[217]

Among the restricted acts identified in the directive, Article 4(1)(c) grants an exclusive right 'to do or to authorise … any form of distribution to the public, including the rental, of the original computer program or of copies thereof'. Article 4(2) clarifies that the right of distribution of a copy of a program is subject to exhaustion after the 'first sale in the Community of a copy of a program by the rightholder or with his consent', but that such exhaustion does not apply to 'the right to control further rental of the program or a copy thereof'. The right is granted to authors, legal persons (where allowed by national law[218]), or employers (by virtue of a legal presumption[219]).

The year after the adoption of the Computer Programs Directive, the EU adopted the Rental and Lending Rights Directive, which contained a more general approach to the rental right. The directive was preceded by two significant developments in 1988: the landmark CJEU (then ECJ) judgment in *Warner v. Christiansen* (17 May), and the aforementioned Green Paper on Copyright and the Challenge of Technology (7 June).[220]

214. European Commission, Press Release, *The Twelve Decide To Protect Computer Programs: Piracy Costs More Than Four Billion Dollars A Year*, 15.05.1991, http://europa.eu/rapid/press-release_IP-91-420_en.htm (accessed 26 September 2017).
215. European Commission, 'Completing the Internal Market', White Paper, COM (85) 310 final, Brussels, 14.06.1985 [White Paper 1985], and European Commission, 'Copyright and the Challenge of Technology', Green Paper, COM (88) 172 final, Brussels, 07.06.1988 [Green Paper 1988]. For a historical account of the development of copyright protection for software, *see* T. Dreier, 'The International Development of Copyright Protection for Computer Programs', in *A Handbook of European Software Law*, Lehman and Tapper (eds), Oxford (1993), pp. 216–238.
216. Proposal for a Council Directive on the legal protection of computer programs, COM (1988) 816.
217. *Ibid. See also* Walter & von Lewinski, p. 140.
218. *See* Art. 2(1) *in fine* Computer Programs Directive.
219. *See* Art. 2(3) Computer Programs Directive.
220. CJEU, Case C-158/86 *Warner Brothers Inc. and Metronome Video ApS v Erik Viuff Christiansen* [*Warner v. Christiansen*].

By way of background, it is noted that in 1988 there were substantial differences in national laws regarding the rental right for sound recordings. In a first group of countries, the right was exhausted on first sale (Italy, Netherlands). In a second group there was no exhaustion (Denmark, Spain, and Portugal). In a third group, no clear right of rental existed, although a similar effect could sometimes be achieved through contract or conditional exercise of the reproduction right. For the most part the right belonged to the author, only rarely to producers, and never to performers.[221] The situation was similar for rental of video recordings, with the significant difference that film producers were considered authors pursuant to Article 2(1) Berne Convention.[222]

The first major development in 1988 was the *Warner v. Christiansen* judgment, which laid bare the community dimension of rental rights. The case concerned the interpretation of Articles 30 and 36 of the EEC Treaty (current Articles 34 and 36 TFEU) and the compatibility of the freedom to provide services with national copyright legislation. By that time, Danish copyright law already contained a lending right, giving authors the right to authorize or prohibit the hiring-out of video-cassettes. This right was to apply even when the same cassettes were put into circulation with his consent in another Member State whose legislation allows authors to control the initial sale but not the subsequent hiring-out.[223]

In this case, a video-cassette was purchased in the UK and then imported to Denmark by the manager of a video shop in Copenhagen, for the purpose of hiring it out to his clients. The rental right recognized under Danish law had not been cleared by the video shop owner, who was relying on its exhaustion. However, Danish law applied without distinction to video-cassettes produced in situ or imported from another Member State, merely distinguishing the type of transaction in question, i.e., whether it was a sale or a rental. The Court took this into consideration to conclude that the national law did not operate an arbitrary discrimination in trade between Member States, rejecting exhaustion of the rental right.[224]

The Court pointed out the emergence of a specific market for hiring-out of video-cassettes, distinct from their sale.[225] It further noted that granting

221. Green Paper 1988, pp. 157–159. Note that the exceptional cases where the right also belonged to producers were Portugal and France.
222. Green Paper 1988, p. 159.
223. *Warner v. Christiansen*, paras 1–9.
224. *Ibid.*, paras 12, 18.
225. *Ibid.*, para. 14: 'The existence of that market was made possible by various factors such as the improvement of manufacturing methods for video-cassettes which increased their strength and life in use, the growing awareness amongst viewers that they watch only occasionally the video-cassettes which they have bought and, lastly, their relatively high purchase price. The market for the hiring-out of video-cassettes reaches a wider public than the market for their sale and, at present, offers great potential as a source of revenue for makers of films.'

right holders control only over sales would be insufficient to secure 'for them a satisfactory share of the rental market'. This explained why some national laws (such as in Denmark) already contained a specific rental right. For the Court, this made such a right 'clearly justified on grounds of the protection of industrial and commercial property pursuant to Article 36 of the Treaty'.[226] In this light, it stated that the lawful putting into circulation of a video-cassette in a Member State that does not specifically protect hiring-out of the same, will not prevent the rights holder from benefitting from this type of protection in another Member State where such a right is granted.[227]

In the end, the legislation at issue was considered compatible with the freedom to provide services, meaning that rights holders could rely on it to exercise their exclusive right of rental, even if a video-cassette was lawfully acquired in another Member State.[228] In essence, like with the cable retransmission right in *Coditel*, the Court established that the doctrine of exhaustion did not apply to the rental right.

Similar to what was observed in the cases discussed in the preceding sections, the motivation to create rental rights in EU Law was primarily the fact that the rental market generated revenues that rights holders felt entitled to, and could not be captured by the reproduction right: a new value gap was born. In the Green Paper on Copyright and the Challenge of Technology, the Commission set out its rationale for introducing a general rental right in EU law. The paper analyses rental in the context of distribution of sound and video recordings.[229] It states that commercial exploitation of rental is profitable where the recording media is less susceptible to damage. This was for example the case for tape cassettes and (laser-read) Compact Discs (CDs). For sound and video recordings, different factors were considered to have a negative effect on the income of rights holders. First, the development of the audio tape recorder allowed high quality and low-cost home copying by hirers. Second, the increasing number of VCR rental outlets in and outside of Europe was diverting legitimate business from licensing distributors. Third, those outlets often rented out pirated copies. For VCR in particular, rental had become the predominant distribution method, due to the high price of purchasing a cassette and the degradation in quality resulting from repeated playing.[230] It is worth pointing out that some of these factors are remarkably similar to the arguments advanced at national and EU level to justify the adoption and continuing extension of private copying levies.[231]

Against this background, the Commission was of the view that commercial rental would be of increasing importance as a means of

226. *Warner v. Christiansen*, para. 16.
227. *Ibid.*, para. 18.
228. *Ibid.*, para. 19.
229. Green Paper 1988, pp. 155–166.
230. *Ibid.*, pp. 155–157.
231. *See*, e.g., Poort and Quintais.

distribution. It argued that uncontrolled rental posed a risk of economic damage to rights holders, who would likely respond by raising sales prices, therefore also prejudicing the position of consumers intending to purchase recordings.[232]

After a narrower initial proposal, comments and suggestions on Chapter 4 of the Green Paper (1 December 1988), and hearings held by the Commission in 1989, the proposal for a directive was finalized in December 1990 and published on 24 January 1991.[233] The proposal defined rental as an exclusive right and extended its scope to include all categories of rights holders and subject matter.[234] The exclusive nature of the right was justified on the need to prohibit rental to preserve the sales in certain sectors (e.g., newly released CDs) and to provide rights holders with a stronger bargaining position in licensing negotiations.[235]

Following some amendments proposed by the European Parliament, and a few additional steps in the legislative proposal, the directive was finally adopted on 19 November 1992.[236] It requires Member States to provide exclusive rental rights for originals and copies of works and related subject matter.[237] 'Rental' is defined as the 'making available for use, for a limited period of time and for direct or indirect economic or commercial advantage'.[238] It is distinguished from 'lending', which refers to the same type of use but 'not for direct or indirect economic or commercial advantage, when it is made through establishments which are accessible to the public'.[239] Rental rights are not subject to exhaustion.[240]

The exclusive right belongs to authors (for the original and copies of his work), performers (for fixations of their performances), phonogram producers (for their phonograms), and producers of the first fixation of a film (for the original and copies of their films).[241] There is a presumption of transfer

232. Green Paper 1988, pp. 161–165. *See also* Reinbothe & von Lewinski 1993, p. 5.
233. For a historical account, *see* Reinbothe & von Lewinski 1993, pp. 5–6; Green Paper 1988, pp. 161–165; and Follow-up Green Paper – Working Programme of the Commission in the Field of Copyright and Neighbouring Rights, COM (90) 584 final, 17.01.1991 [Follow-up Green Paper 1991].
234. Follow-up Green Paper 1991, p. 15; Reinbothe & von Lewinski 1993, pp. 6–7.
235. Reinbothe & von Lewinski 1993, pp. 10–12, and 16–19 (on the reception of the proposal by the affected stakeholders).
236. For the relevant documents, *see* Procedure 1990/0319/SYN, COM (1990) 586: Proposal for a Council Directive on Rental Right, Lending Right, and on Certain Rights Related to Copyright, http://eur-lex.europa.eu/procedure/EN/1990_319 (accessed 26 September 2017).
237. Article 1(1) Rental and Lending Rights Directive.
238. Article 2(1)(a) Rental and Lending Rights Directive.
239. Article 2(1)(b) Rental and Lending Rights Directive.
240. Article 1(2) Rental and Lending Rights Directive, referring to 'any sale or other act of distribution of originals and copies of copyright works and other subject matter'.
241. Article 3(1) Rental and Lending Rights Directive.

of rental rights of performers in favour of producers in the context of film production contracts, a presumption which might be extended to authors.[242]

In addition, if an author or performer transfers or assigns their right concerning a phonogram or an original or copy of a film to a phonogram or film producer, that author or performer retains an unwaivable right to equitable remuneration.[243] This right can be subject to mandatory collective management by a CMO, who will claim and collect the remuneration from parties to be identified by law, typically producers and rental shops.[244] As regards subject matter, although the right applies to all works, its main focus of protection is video and sound recordings, as these generated the highest economic investments.[245] Only excluded are buildings or works of applied art.[246] Furthermore, the directive is without prejudice to Article 4(c) of the Computer Programs Directive, discussed above. As a final remark, it is noted that subsequent judgments of the CJEU, and the InfoSoc Directive, confirm that the exhaustion of the distribution right does not apply to the rental right.[247]

2.5.3 Protection under International Law

The TRIPS Agreement contains two provisions on rental rights: Articles 11 and 14(4). It is the first international agreement to recognize such a right, and is therefore considered to be 'Berne-plus' in this respect. The background to these provisions can be found in the 1990 *Anell* (23 July) and *Brussels* (3 December) drafts of the agreement.[248]

The discussions on the *Anell Draft* clarify that national delegations could not agree on the recognition of a general distribution right. Rather, agreement was only possible on a subset thereof – a rental right – as applied to two categories of works: computer programs and cinematographic works.[249] The right to control commercial rental of computer programs in

242. *See* Arts 3(3)–(5) Rental and Lending Rights Directive.
243. Article 5(1)–(2) Rental and Lending Rights Directive.
244. Article 5(3)–(4) Rental and Lending Rights Directive.
245. Recital 5 Rental and Lending Rights Directive.
246. Article 3(2) Rental and Lending Rights Directive.
247. *See* CJEU, Case C-61/97 *Laserdisken*; and CJEU, Case C-200/96 *Metronome Musik v. Music Point Hokamp. See also* recital 28 and Art. 4 InfoSoc Directive.
248. GATT, Negotiating Group on Trade-Related Aspects of Intellectual Property Rights, including Trade in Counterfeit Goods, Anell Draft (MTN.GNG/NG11/W/76), 23 July 1990; Trade Negotiations Committee, Draft Final Act Embodying the Results of the Uruguay Round of Multilateral Trade Negotiations, (MTN.TNC/W/35/Rev.l), 3 December 1990.
249. UNCTAD–ICTSD, *Resource Book on TRIPS and Development*, Cambridge: CUP (2005), p. 173.

particular 'was considered a priority by many negotiators', as such rental activities had led to widespread copying by users.[250]

By the time of the *Brussels Draft,* no proposals for a general distribution right were advanced.[251] This draft subjected the obligation to grant the rental right to a material impairment test vis-à-vis the reproduction right. That is to say, Members only had to grant the right if the rental of works led to their 'unauthorized' copying. Such term was later replaced by 'widespread' copying, thereby shifting the core of the material impairment test from the *illegal nature* of copying activities to their *economic impact.* [252] Here, as with the debate at the EU level, the justification of the rental right as a means to preserve the economic core of the reproduction right – a 'legal firewall' of sorts – comes to the surface, as do echoes of the economic concerns with private copying activities.

According to Gervais, one of the aims of the impairment test was to ensure the imposition of the rental right 'on as many countries as possible, while leaving in particular the United States out'. Such a right had failed to make it into legislation in the US, despite lobbying from the film industry. It was therefore politically difficult to pass it at this stage. Thus, forcing the US to accept it 'could have endangered ratification of the Round as a whole'.[253]

In the US, section 106(3) of the Copyright Act gives copyright owners the exclusive right 'to distribute copies or phonorecords of the copyrighted work to the public by sale or other transfer of ownership, or by rental, lease, or lending'. This right is subject to a general limit, known as the first sale doctrine (the US equivalent of the European exhaustion doctrine), codified in section 109. That provision allows the owner of a particular copy or phonorecord that was lawfully made, or any person authorized by such owner, to sell or otherwise dispose of the possession of that copy or phonorecord without the owner's prior consent. However, section 109 excludes from its scope the rental, lease, or lending of sound recordings and computer programs, prohibiting such subsequent uses without the express permission of the copyright owner.[254]

Despite the aforementioned lobbying efforts, the US movie and video rental industry never benefited from this exclusion. As an alternative, that industry developed – with great commercial success – 'a pricing structure for new-release videos that is designed to compensate for the rental market',

250. D. Gervais, *The TRIPS Agreement: Drafting History and Analysis*, 1st ed., Sweet & Maxwell (1998), p. 84.
251. Note that this draft 'still contained a bracketed reference to a remuneration right as an alternative to the right to prohibit or authorize the commercial rental of copyrighted works'. Cf. UNCTAD–ICTSD 2005, p. 174.
252. UNCTAD–ICTSD 2005, p. 174.
253. D. Gervais, *The TRIPS Agreement: Drafting History and Analysis*, 3rd ed., Sweet & Maxwell (2008), p. 231.
254. J.E. Cohen, L.P. Loren, R.L. Okediji, and M.A. O'Rourke, *Copyright in A Global Information Economy.* 3rd ed., Wolters Kluwer (2010), pp. 351–352.

coupled with technological protection measures to limit follow-on copying of rental videos.[255] By the time the TRIPS Agreement was being negotiated, the prevailing view in the US favoured this approach and opposed restricting the commercial rental of films. It was this context that led to the current version of Article 11 TRIPS.[256]

The final version of the provision grants authors and their successors an exclusive right regarding the 'commercial rental to the public' of originals or copies of their copyright works. The provision sets a minimum standard: it is applicable 'at least' in respect of computer programs and cinematographic works, but members can extend the right to other subject matter.[257] The right has further qualifications. First, protection of cinematographic works is subject to an impairment test. There is only an obligation to grant the right if the rental of such works has led to their widespread copying and this is materially impairing the exclusive right of reproduction conferred in that Member country. Second, regarding computer programs, the obligation to grant protection is only imposed where the program itself is not the essential object of the rental.[258]

Article 14(4) TRIPS applies the provisions of Article 11 in respect of computer programs *mutatis mutandis* to phonogram producers and any 'other right holders in phonograms' under a Member's law. Other rights holders likely include the authors of the underlying musical composition and lyrics, as well as performers. The *mutatis mutandis* application means that there is no obligation to grant protection to rentals where the phonogram itself is not the essential object of the rental.[259]

The provision is limited by a 'grandfathering clause'. The clause allows the survival of existing equitable remuneration systems for rental of phonograms, provided that on the relevant date (15 April 1994) 'the commercial rental of phonograms is not giving rise to the material impairment of the exclusive rights of reproduction of right holders'.[260]

The WIPO Treaties recognize exclusive rental rights for authors, performers, and phonogram producers.[261] A general rental right in the WCT was initially advanced by Article 9(1) of the Basic Proposal I for the 1996 Diplomatic Conference.[262] Article 9(2) of the proposal allowed the exclusion of specific types of works from the general right, but prohibited such exclusion from applying to computer programs, collections of data or other

255. *Ibid.* p. 352.
256. *Ibid.* pp. 351–352.
257. Dreier and Hugenholtz, in: *Concise Copyright* (2016), 'TRIPS', Art. 11, note 1, p. 228.
258. This aspect is a novelty in relation to the Brussels Draft. Cf. UNCTAD–ICTSD 2005, p. 174.
259. Dreier and Hugenholtz, in: *Concise Copyright* (2016), 'TRIPS', Art. 14, note 5, p. 235.
260. Article 14(4) TRIPS. *See also* P. Kamina, in: Cottier/Véron (eds), *Concise IP Law*, 'TRIPS Agreement' (2015), Art. 14, note 5.
261. Article 7 WCT and Arts 9 and 13 WPPT.
262. Records WIPO Treaties, p. 10.

material in machine-readable form, and musical works embodied in phonograms.[263]

Despite the initial approach favouring a general right, it was ultimately agreed not to go beyond the TRIPS level of harmonization. The final version of the WIPO Treaties was adopted on 20 December 1996, and they were implemented in the EU on 16 March 2000.[264] The WCT grants a general distribution right in Article 6 and specific rental right in Article 7. The latter provision grants authors of: (i) computer programs, (ii) cinematographic works, and (iii) works embodied in phonograms, an exclusive right to authorize the 'commercial rental to the public of the originals or copies of their works'.[265]

The right comes with restrictions similar to TRIPS. For computer programs, it does not apply if the program itself is not the essential object of the rental. For cinematographic works, recognition of the right is only possible if such commercial rental has led to widespread copying of such works, materially impairing the exclusive right of reproduction.

The WCT deviates from Article 14(4) TRIPS in relation to phonograms. First, the WCT recognizes a rental right for authors of works embodied in phonograms, in terms to be defined by national law.[266] Second, it grandfathers 'pre-existing national practices dealing with record rentals' – namely systems of equitable remuneration of authors for the rental of copies of their works embodied in phonograms – by subjecting them to an identical impairment test to that applied to audiovisual works.[267]

2.6 PATTERNS AND CONCLUSIONS

This chapter described the evolution of economic rights recognized in international copyright law in the pre-internet era, against the backdrop of

263. *Ibid.*
264. Council Decision of 16 March 2000 on the approval, on behalf of the European Community, of the WIPO Copyright Treaty and the WIPO Performances and Phonograms Treaty, OJ L 089, 11/04/2000 pp. 6–7.
265. According to the Agreed Statements on Arts 6 and 7, the expressions 'copies' and 'original and copies', being subject to the right of rental under this provision 'refer exclusively to fixed copies that can be put into circulation as tangible objects'.
266. UNCTAD–ICTSD 2005, p. 176, noting that Art. 14(4) TRIPS recognizes such a rental right for 'producers of phonograms and any other right holders in phonograms as determined by domestic law'. The Agreed Statements on Art. 7 clarify that 'the obligation under Article 7(1) does not require a Contracting Party to provide an exclusive right of commercial rental to authors who, under that Contracting Party's law, are not granted rights in respect of phonograms. It is understood that this obligation is consistent with Article 14(4) of the TRIPS Agreement.'
267. Article 7(3) WCT. Regarding performers and phonogram producers, Arts 9 and 13 WPPT are similar to their TRIPS counterparts, differing solely on the beneficiary rights holders. *See* UNCTAD–ICTSD 2005, p. 176.

related developments in the commercial exploitation of works and technological development. It did so by analysing four case studies that relate to communication and dissemination of works: public performance, radio and TV broadcasting, cable retransmission, and commercial rental. In each case, the history of protection under international and EU copyright law is described. Alongside this, the development of relevant technology and exploitation models was outlined.

The first reason to focus on the communication and dissemination of works in the selected case studies, rather than on reproduction, is that reproduction rights emerged much earlier in history than communication rights. The second, and more important, reason is that the right of reproduction appears to have been less controversial than various rights relating to communication or making works available to the public.

The discussion of the evolution of the *public performance right* reveals that it started in France in 1777 on the basis of a claim by playwrights for remuneration for the public performance of their plays. This was a time when theatres were important in social and cultural life in France. The rise in the number of theatres in Paris, and the production and performance of many new plays around the end of the eighteenth century, however, is linked to the abolition of the existing legal privileges and government control over theatres in 1791, not to the recognition of performing rights for playwrights.

Extension of the public performance right to musical works occurred in 1847, around the time café-concerts became the epicentre of social life in Paris. It was clear that these establishments monetized the value generated by the performances by charging entry fees and raising the price of their drinks. The performance right transferred some of that value to the authors.

Between then and 1971, the scope of the right was gradually expanded in response to technological and commercial developments, such as the introduction of pianolas and gramophone records, cinema, and the theatrophone. A public performance right was also recognized in the Berne Convention, albeit through the mechanism of national treatment. By 1971, a general exclusive public performance right had been introduced in the Berne Convention (in the 1948 Act), taking the scope of the right beyond direct presentation by natural persons to include performances through the use of *any* equipment. Meanwhile, the protected subject matter was broadened to include musical and dramatico-musical and (in a separate provision) cinematographic reproductions and adaptations of works. The general formulation of a performance right in relation to any equipment made it future-proof with respect to new technologies and exploitation models for public performance. At the same time, however, it introduced the risk that certain activities would come to fall under the right without clear normative justification.

Radio broadcasting emerged in the interbellum of the twentieth century. By the 1930s, radio challenged the influence of film and had become the dominant form of entertainment. In the early days, radio manufacturers were an important sponsor of radio broadcasts, hoping to sell more radio sets and transmitters. However, in most of Western Europe, radio broadcasting quickly turned into a state monopoly which lasted until the 1980s. Although the first *television broadcasts* started halfway through the 1930s, due to the Second World War no television service was developed in most European countries until the 1950s. Like radio, in those days television broadcasting was commonly operated by the state. The major breakthrough for television in terms of household penetration came with the introduction of the colour TV in the late 1960s.

Since protected works, such as phonograph recordings, constituted a significant portion of the content transmitted, there was a clear link between broadcasting and copyright. Music radio broadcasts became part of social interactions as well as a tool to promote musical works and artists, the technology itself, and other types of content. Advertising grew into the standard business model for radio, together with sponsorship. Even for government-run television channels in Europe, advertising became an important source of revenue.

In the early days of broadcasting, the question of how to balance this new means of communication with the rights of authors arose. The call for extending existing rights or creating new ones stems from the view of the recorded music industry that airplay would hurt record sales while radio, and later television stations, were generating considerable amounts of money through advertising and sponsorship.

As with broadcasting, radio preceded television in the field of *cable retransmission*. In the early twentieth century, radio retransmission over telephone lines was used to increase coverage of radio stations via point-to-point connections. In Europe, radio lines were also used as early as the 1920s in a point-to-multipoint setting to deliver radio signals to subscribers without the need to obtain a radio receiver: an early case of music streaming.

In economic terms, retransmission did not become significant until the introduction of subscription-based cable retransmission of commercial television in the US. In Europe, cable networks developed more slowly than in the US, and improving reception of national broadcast channels and in some cases receiving foreign channels were the main purpose of these networks. From the 1980s onwards, cable networks in Europe expanded rapidly, followed by privatization and consolidation of local networks throughout much of Europe. This turned cable television into a multi-billion euro industry.

The history of the legal protection of cable retransmission is intertwined with that of broadcasting. Initially, the idea was to distinguish the original broadcast from subsequent secondary use, such as cable retransmission, which would require authorization from rights holders if it reached a new audience as compared to the primary transmission. However, from the mid-1980s onwards, there has been a trend in judicial interpretation towards the autonomous recognition of a cable retransmission right and the rejection of the 'new public' approach, consistent with the text of the Berne Convention since its Brussels Act of 1948 (which adopted a 'new organization' criterion instead). This trend coincided with the growing importance of cable networks for the reception of television in European households and the commercialization of cable networks.

Finally, *commercial rental* gained economic significance with the diffusion of the VCR in the 1980s, followed by the DVD player in the late 1990s. For about two decades, rental outlets for physical carriers of audiovisual works boomed and provided a revenue stream comparable to that of cinemas. At the beginning of this century, however, this industry collapsed as quickly as it had grown, due to the emergence of digital rental, streaming video subscriptions, and unauthorized file sharing.

Halfway through this golden age of commercial rental, a separate rental right was created in EU Law in 1991, which was not subject to exempting exhaustion. This was meant to harmonize diverging national laws, which oscillated between those that had no such right and those where such a right was recognized, but exhausted at first sale. Justification for the creation of a separate rental right was found in the possibility of making good quality home copies from rented tapes, the emergence of a booming rental industry, and the renting out of pirated copies by some rental shops. It is noteworthy that some of these justifications mirror those advanced in the private copying levies debate. For the introduction of a rental right in TRIPS, concerns with widespread home copying and its potential harmful effects on the exploitation of the reproduction right of copyright owners appeared to be more pivotal.

What general patterns can be discerned throughout these cases and what lessons can be learnt or conclusions drawn? A first overarching observation is that the scope of rights has expanded gradually over time. Since the early days of the Statute of Anne, the protected acts in national laws and international treaties have stretched to include all kinds of public performance, wired and wireless transmission or retransmission, and rental. Furthermore, rights have been recognized in international treaties as substantive minima, beyond the mere protection pursuant to reciprocity or national treatment mechanisms.

The focus of this chapter (and indeed this book) is on the evolution of the scope of economic rights in relation to the development of business models and technology. Through that lens, it can be observed in each of the case studies that whenever a new exploitation model or technology enabled entrepreneurs to generate money using copyright-protected works, new rights were tailored to reap some of these benefits. This is what happened to theatres and café-concerts staging plays and musical performances, radio and television stations broadcasting music and audiovisual works, cable networks retransmitting free-to-air television broadcasts, and rental shops renting out cassette tapes and DVDs. This development is consistent with the premise underlying the project that led to this book, as the expansion of economic rights appears to track the evolution of economic and technological realities.

The call for the creation of additional rights stems from the assertion by rights holders of an entitlement to the value created in connection with 'their works' by those performers, radio and television stations, cable networks, and rental shops, and the materialization of that assertion into law. In the cases discussed here, the expansion of rights takes place with the emergence and adoption by the public of new technologies and exploitation models: new technological means for works to reach an audience and new ways for entrepreneurs to create value with a work are generally followed (or occasionally anticipated) by new exclusive or remuneration rights. Each time a new exploitation model or technology enabled entrepreneurs to generate money using copyright-protected works, new rights were created to reap some of these benefits. Often, this is supported by the claim that the new model is undermining existing revenue streams, such as with radio broadcasting and rental harming record and video sales.

Fast-forward to the twenty-first century, and this resembles the 'value gap' debate in current EU copyright law and the initiative to create new exclusive rights for publishers of press publications.[268] Thus, from this perspective, we can read the historical evolution of copyright as a tale of value gaps, and the creation of new rights to bridge these gaps. History suggests that if a business user generates value by developing a new product or service where protected works play a role, this will trigger debates about creating new rights – or extending existing rights – to cover that product or service.

A difference in this value gap analogy is that past claims for extension of protection and the corresponding evolution in the legal definition of rights presented a clear and incremental link to novel technology-influenced modes of exploitation. This link is not always visible in contemporary copyright policy debate, as a consequence of the increasingly abstract and generic formulation of economic rights. While such formulation may have served the purpose of making copyright law technologically neutral and future-proof, it likewise enhances the risk of overprotection – 'false positives' – and may undermine copyright's normative content and focus. These observations raise a related but fundamental question of how to justify or explain the proliferation of rights to capture (some of) the downstream value.

From a utilitarian or normative economic perspective, the above is unsatisfactory. As argued by Poort in his chapter of this volume, downstream value can, to a large extent, be appropriated through the initial sale or access

268. *See* Proposal for a Directive on copyright in the Digital Single Market 2016, Arts 11–13.

agreement as long as these new business models acquire the content they work with legally.[269] If that is accepted, then one must turn to a 'natural rights' perspective for a more compelling background to understand the historical evolution of rights.[270]

269. For a more extensive discussion of the utilitarian justification of copyright, *see* J. Poort in this volume.
270. This perspective is epitomized by the Lockean labour-desert (fairness) theory. Under such theory, one could argue that the author is entitled, as reward for his intellectual labour, to rents from the future exploitation (by whichever method) of his work. Following this logic, a broad application of the fairness theory for copyright could be used to justify the continual creation of new copyright entitlements whenever new technology or business models emerge in connection with the use of protected works. On the application of the fairness theory to copyright, *see* e.g., W. Fisher, 'Theories of Intellectual Property', in: *New Essays in the Legal and Political Theory of Property*, S.R. Munzer (ed.), Cambridge University Press (2001), pp. 168–200; and D.J. Gervais, 'Human Rights and the Philosophical Foundation of Intellectual Property', in: *Research Handbook on Human Rights and Intellectual Property*, C. Geiger (ed.), Edward Elgar (2015), pp. 89–97, pp. 89–90.

Chapter 3
Deconstructing Copyright

Stefan Bechtold*

3.1 INTRODUCTION

When the United States (US) Congress enacted the Sherman Act in 1890, it created a regulatory system whose power unfolded only in the following decades. The Act prohibited 'every contract, combination or conspiracy in restraint of trade', as well as every monopolization 'or attempt to monopolize … any part of the trade or commerce among the several States, or with foreign nations'.[1] US Congress did not merely prohibit such activities. It also criminalized them, thereby providing a particularly powerful tool against anticompetitive behaviour by corporate executives.

What the Sherman Act did not provide, however, was clear guidance to courts on how they should assess firm conduct. When it came to determining whether a contract actually restrains trade or whether conduct monopolizes trade, it was up to the courts to decide whether and how to analyse the economic effects of firm conduct. In *Standard Oil Co. v. United States*,[2] the US Supreme Court introduced a rule of reason standard into antitrust

* The author would like to thank Rainer Bechtold, Séverine Dusollier, Bernt Hugenholtz, Matthias Leistner, Bertin Martins, Ansgar Ohly, Alexander Peukert, Joost Poort, and Ole-Andreas Rognstad.

1. 15 U.S.C. §§ 1, 2.
2. 221 U.S. 1 (1911).

analysis.[3] This standard allows courts to analyse the competitive effects of firm conduct and to determine whether a restraint of trade is reasonable or not. At the same time, the court classified certain conduct as anticompetitive by its very nature and character. For such classes of anticompetitive conduct, courts would not have to engage in a rule of reason analysis, as such conduct was assumed to be unreasonable, and there was no way to rebut the assumption.

In its early days, US antitrust law was dominated by per se rules: classes of firm conduct were assumed to be unreasonable and courts did not challenge this assumption. Increasingly, however, courts realized that they needed more flexibility in adjudicating antitrust cases. In addition, significant improvements in the understanding of the economics of antitrust policy, industrial organization, and game theory had a deep impact on antitrust law. Most conspicuously, starting in the 1970s, prominent members of the Chicago School – such as Robert Bork and Richard Posner – challenged many decisions by the Supreme Court which had held various types of firm conduct as per se illegal. They pointed out that in many cases, the firm behaviour actually had pro-competitive effects or that its potentially negative effects were negligible at least.

As a response to such critics, courts increasingly relied on the rule of reason standard and began to investigate the economic effects of restrictive firm conduct on a case-by-case basis. Over time, the Supreme Court overturned various old antitrust decisions, abandoned the per se illegality of certain restrictive firm conduct and increasingly adopted a rule of reason analysis.[4] As a result, US antitrust enforcement has gradually moved from per se rules to rule of reason standards over the last few decades.

While per se rules have the advantage of being clear and easy to interpret, they become problematic if they are applied to cases where it is ambiguous whether the restrictive firm conduct is actually unreasonable. As the Chicago School challenges led to a more nuanced understanding of the interaction between firm conduct and market forces, it was a logical step to subject antitrust doctrine to more flexible legal standards. However, such transition came at a cost. Determinations under a rule of reason standard are inherently complex, consume a significant amount of time and effort, may lead to indeterminate results, and raise numerous questions about the rule of law and burdens of proof. As a result, neither a system of antitrust that is built

---

3. This story has often been told. *See*, e.g., William E. Kovacic & Carl Shapiro, Antitrust Policy: A Century of Economic and Legal Thinking, J. Econ. Pers. 14 (2000), 43.
4. *See*, e.g., *Continental Television v. GTE Sylvania*, 433 U.S. 36 (1977) (holding that franchise business practices must be analysed under the rule of reason standard); *State Oil c. v. Khan*, 522 U.S. 3 (1997) (holding that vertical price-fixing should be evaluated under the rule of reason standard); *Leegin Creative Leather Products, Inc. v. PSKS, Inc.*, 551. U.S. 877 (2007) (overruling *Dr Miles*, a decision by the Supreme Court from 1911, and holding that vertical price restraints should be judged under the rule of reason standard).

fully upon per se rules, nor one that relies fully on rules of reason seems feasible or convincing.

In order to escape the dichotomy between strict per se rules and a full-blown rule of reason assessment, courts and antitrust agencies in the US have also relied on a method that lies in between both extremes. Under a 'quick look' analysis, the agency or court determines whether 'an observer with even a rudimentary understanding of economics could conclude that the arrangements in question have an anticompetitive effect on customers and markets'.[5] If this is not the case, a full-blown rule of reason analysis is necessary. Otherwise, no such inquiry is warranted as the conduct is presumed unlawful. It is then up to the defendant to explain how his conduct might produce economic benefits.[6]

The central theme of US antitrust law over the last century has been to situate this area of law between a per se rule, a rule of reason standard, and approaches that lie between both extremes, such as a 'quick look' analysis. This calibration has been motivated by an epic battle on how to ensure that antitrust law achieves its intended economic goals while still being administrable and predictable.

The calibration between per se rules and rule of reason standards is neither restricted to particular jurisdictions, nor to particular areas of law. Just as the Chicago School revolutionized US antitrust law at the time, some decades later the 'more economic approach' brought European antitrust law in line with (post-Chicago) economics.[7] In the 1990s, it became apparent that European antitrust law had fallen out of sync with the transformation that economics had brought to US antitrust law over the last few decades: concurrent antitrust investigations on both sides of the Atlantic showed significant differences in how antitrust agencies applied antitrust laws, and academics point to important conceptual differences.[8] In 2002, the General Court annulled three merger-control decisions by the European Commission because of serious errors of assessment, including disregard of contemporary economic theory.[9] This shock prompted the European Commission to overhaul European antitrust law in fundamental ways. A 'more economic

5. *California Dental Association v. Federal Trade Commission*, 119 S. Ct. 1604, 1606 (1999).
6. On the detailed allocation of burdens of proof under this standard, *see* Alan J. Meese, In Praise of All or Nothing Dichotomous Categories: Why Antitrust Law Should Reject the Quick Look, 104 Georgetown L.J. 835, 858–859 (2016).
7. *See* Heike Schweitzer & Kiran Patel, EU Competition Law in Historical Context, in: Patel & Schweitzer (eds), The Historical Foundation of EU Competition Law, Oxford 2013, pp. 207, 208.
8. For a detailed account, *see* Anne Witt, *The More Economic Approach to EU Antitrust Law*, Oxford 2016, pp. 11 et seq. (referring to the antitrust investigations into the proposed Boeing/McDonnel Douglas merger, the proposed General Electric and Honeywell merger, and the investigations into Microsoft's conduct concerning Windows and web browsers).
9. Court of First Instance, *Airtours v. Commission of the European Communities*, case T-342/99, 6 June 2002, ELCI:EU:T:2002:146; *Schneider Electric v. Commission of the*

approach' was applied to Articles 101 and 102 of the Treaty on the Functioning of the European Union (TFEU) as well as to European Union (EU) merger control, thereby bringing European antitrust law more in line with concurrent economic theory and methodology.[10] By reducing the importance of per se prohibitions and increasing the significance of rule of reason assessments, the more economic approach has had a deep impact on European competition law.[11]

US securities law provides another example:[12] in order to recover damages in a securities fraud class action, investors must prove that they relied on the seller's misrepresentation. In a decision from 1988, the US Supreme Court had held that investors could satisfy this reliance requirement based on the 'fraud-on-the-market theory' without actually proving that they had relied on the seller's misrepresentation.[13] In 2014, the Supreme Court considered overruling this cornerstone of modern private securities litigation in the US. This was prompted by the significant progress that economic analysis of financial markets has made over the last few decades. In particular, the analysis has demonstrated how behavioural effects can undermine the efficient market hypothesis, thereby also undermining the 'fraud-on-the-market theory'. While the Court ultimately declined to overrule the 'fraud-on-the-market theory',[14] this is another area of the law where advances in economic research have encouraged changes from strict rules to open-ended standards.

As this short review indicates, various areas of business law have been fundamentally affected by advances in economic theory and empirical research over the last few decades. They have responded to the resulting scientific challenge in very different ways. On a conceptual level, the influence of economics has been to encourage legal scholars, courts, and enforcement agencies to reconnect the scope of the law with its underlying economic purpose, to synchronize legal and economic concepts, and to take a less broad-brush approach to designing legal systems. On a somewhat

---

European Communities, case T-310/01, 22 October 2002, ECLI:EU:T:2002:254; *Tetra Laval v. Commission of the European Communities*, case T-5/02, 25 October 2002, ECLI:EU:T:2002:264.

10. *Witt*, *supra* n. 8, pp. 34–35, 40–74.
11. Schweitzer & Patel, *supra* n. 7, pp. 207, 220: 'The "more economic approach" is arguably the most fundamental challenge to EU competition law as it evolved between 1958 and the late 1980s.'
12. For another example of a move to an effects-based approach, *see* Armin Steinbach, Effect-based Analysis in the Court's Jurisprudence on the Euro Crisis, forthcoming 2017 in the European Law Review.
13. Under the efficient market hypothesis, an asset's market price reflects all material public information. Under the 'fraud-on-the-market theory', all investors are presumed to have relied on the integrity of the market price. If an investor can show that a security was traded in an efficient market, they are also presumed to have relied on the seller's misrepresentation. *See Basic Inc. v. Levinson*, 485 U.S. 224 (1988).
14. *Halliburton Co. v. Erica P. John Fund, Inc.*, 134 S. Ct. 2398 (2014).

amusing note, economists have shown lawyers that one should be careful with unwarranted generalizations and broad per se rules, because it all depends on the (economic) circumstances.

As this chapter intends to show, we are currently experiencing similar developments in European copyright law, albeit we are at a different stage from antitrust or securities law.[15] While the history of copyright law is traditionally told as a story of an area of the law that responds to technological changes,[16] this chapter demonstrates that its history could also be told as a story of how an area of the law responds to changes in markets and advances in economic research.

For a long time, the economics of copyright consisted of a rather simple public goods argument. As information is non-exclusive in consumption and non-rivalrous in use, it has the characteristics of a public good, similar to lighthouses or military defence.[17] Under a rational choice model, no individual has an incentive to produce public goods, resulting in a market failure: while there is a demand for such goods, nobody wants to produce them. The government must take action in order to overcome this market failure. In the case of copyright, the government has chosen to provide a property right to creators so that they can recoup their investments in the production of works. This, effectively, turns information into an exclusive good, thereby solving the original market failure.[18]

Today, research on the economics of copyright has moved far beyond this foundation. On the one hand, scholars have challenged whether creators actually need incentives provided by the law in order to be creative.[19] Important examples include open source software,[20] fashion design,[21]

15. *See also* Christina Bohannan & Erik Hovenkamp, IP and Antitrust: Reformation and Harm, 51 B.C. L. Rev. 905 (2010) (arguing on p. 913 that current US intellectual property law closely resembles antitrust policy in the 1960s).
16. *See*, e.g., Tim Wu, Copyright's Communications Policy, 103 Mich. L. Rev. 278 (2005); Stefan Bechtold, Der Schutz des Anbieters von Information: Urheberrecht und Gewerblicher Rechtsschutz im Internet, ZUM 1997, 427, 446–448.
17. Ronald H. Coase, The Lighthouse in Economics, J. L. & Econ. 17 (1974), 375.
18. William Landes & Richard Posner, An Economic Analysis of Copyright Law, 18 J. Legal Stud. 325 (1989), William Landes & Richard Posner, *The Economic Structure of Intellectual Property Law*, Cambridge 2003, pp. 37 et seq. This analysis applied to patents and copyright, not to trademark protection.
19. *See also* Rochelle C. Dreyfuss, Does IP Need IP? Accommodating Intellectual Production Outside the Intellectual Property Paradigm, 31 Cardozo L. Rev. 1437 (2010), Diane L. Zimmerman, Copyrights as Incentives: Did We Just Imagine That? Theor. Inq. L. 12 (2011), 29.
20. Josh Lerner & Josh Tirole, Some Simple Economics of Open Source, J. Ind. Econ. 50 (2002), 197; Yochai Benkler, Coase's Penguin, or, Linux and the Nature of the Firm, 112 Yale L.J. 369 (2002).
21. Kal Raustiala & Christopher Sprigman, The Piracy Paradox: Innovation and Intellectual Property in Fashion Design, 92 Va. L. Rev. 1687 (2006), Kal Raustiala & Christopher Sprigman, The Piracy Paradox Revisited, 61 Stan. L. Rev. 1201 (2009).

cooking recipes,[22] TV show formats,[23] and art in general.[24] More importantly for our purposes, significant methodological advancements in empirical methodology[25] have had a deep impact on empirical legal scholarship.[26] It is methodologically increasingly feasible, if the right data and institutional setup exist, to identify causal relationships between particular aspects of intellectual property laws and creative behaviour. There is a nascent scholarship from both law and economics applying state-of-the art experimental and quasi-experimental methods on issues of copyright law and policy.[27] While there are still too many blind spots on the economic map of copyright law, our empirical knowledge of the effects of copyright law has increased considerably over the last two decades.

Given the substantial and methodological advances in our understanding of the economics of copyright, one may wonder whether copyright law will follow a pattern similar to antitrust and securities law. In fact, empirical insights about the effects of copyright protection have become part of the general scholarly discourse in copyright law. As many contributions in this

22. Emmanuelle Fauchart & Eric von Hippel, Norms-Based Intellectual Property Systems: The Case of French Chefs, Organization Sci. 19 (2008), 187; Christopher Buccafusco, On the Legal Consequences of Sauces: Should Thomas Keller's Recipes be Per Se Copyrightable?, 24 Cardozo Arts & Ent. L.J. 1121 (2007).
23. Stefan Bechtold, The Fashion of TV Show Formats, 2013 Mich. St. L. Rev. 451.
24. Martin Kretschmer & Philip Hardwick, Authors' Earnings from Copyright and Non-Copyright Sources: A Survey of 25,000 British and German Writers, 2007, available at https://microsites.bournemouth.ac.uk/cippm/files/2007/07/ACLS-Full-report.pdf (accessed 2 October 2017); Martin Kretschmer et al., Copyright Contracts and Earnings of Visual Creators: A Survey of 5,800 British Designers, Fine Artists, Illustrators and Photographers, 2011, available at http://ssrn.com/abstract=1780206 (accessed 2 October 2017); Peter DiCola, Money from Music: Survey Evidence on Musicians' Revenue and Lessons About Copyright Incentives, 55 Arizona L. Rev. 301 (2013); Jessica Silbey, The Eureka Myth: Creators, Innovators, and Everyday Intellectual Property, Stanford 2015.
25. Joshua D. Angrist & Jörn-Steffen Pischke, The Credibility Revolution in Empirical Economics: How Better Research Design Is Taking the Con out of Econometrics, J. Econ. Persp. 24(2) (2010), 3.
26. Daniel Ho & Donald Rubin, Credible Causal Inference for Empirical Legal Studies, Ann. Rev. Law & Soc. Sci. 7 (2011), 17.
27. *See*, e.g., Kai-Lung Hui & I.P.L. Png, On the Supply of Creative Work: Evidence from the Movies, Am. Econ. Rev. 92 (2002), 217; Megan MacGarvie & Petra Moser, Copyright and the Profitability of Authorship: Evidence from Payments to Writers in the Romantic Period, in: Goldfarb et al. (eds), Economic Analysis of the Digital Economy, Chicago 2015, p. 357; Xing Li et al., Dead Poets' Property: How Does Copyright Influence Price?, 2014, available at http://ssrn.com/abstract=2170447 (accessed 2 October 2017); Christopher Buccafusco & Christopher Sprigman, Valuing Intellectual Property: An Experiment, 96 Cornell L. Rev. 1 (2010); Christopher Buccafusco & Christopher Sprigman, The Creativity Effect, 78 U. Chi. L. Rev. 31 (2011); Stefan Bechtold, Christopher Buccafusco & Christopher Sprigman, Innovation Heuristics: Experiments on Sequential Creativity in Intellectual Property, 91 Ind. L.J. 1251 (2016); Stefan Bechtold & Christoph Engel, The Valuation of Moral Rights: A Field Experiment, 2017, available at https://ssrn.com/abstract=2941499 (accessed 12 December 2017).

volume demonstrate, European scholars worry about an increasing disconnect between the formalistic exploitation rights granted by copyright law and the underlying economic purpose copyright law is supposed to achieve. This is also reflected in increasing attempts by courts to limit the scope and effects of exploitation rights to their intended purpose.

This chapter conjectures as to where a transition from a copyright system that is based primarily on formalistic exploitation rights to a system that includes flexible rule of reason analyses will take us, where the pitfalls for such a transition lie, and how far one should push the transition. The goal of this chapter is threefold. First, the paper identifies signs in case law and scholarship that the design of exploitation rights in copyright law is out of sync with copyright's underlying purpose (*see infra* section 3.2). Second, the article analyses what actions copyright law could take to resynchronize the effects of the law with its economic purpose (*see infra* section 3.3). Third, the article identifies general challenges and dangers that could arise along the way (*see infra* section 3.4). Finally, the article closes with a call for the introduction of modestly flexible property rights and identifies conceptual problems that must be resolved before such a system can be implemented (*see infra* section 3.5).

3.2 SIGNS OF THE TIME

The Court of Justice of the EU has become an active and important shaper of European copyright law in recent years.[28] The court has not only harmonized areas of European copyright law that had not been harmonized by EU Directives;[29] it has also limited exploitation rights in order to link their scope to their underlying purpose. A prominent example is the right of communication to the public in Article 3 of the Information Society Directive.[30] The court has stated in recent case law that in order for a broadcast to be a 'communication to the public', the work needs to be transmitted to a 'new' public, i.e., a public which was not taken into account by the authors when they authorized the use of the work for communication

28. *See* Matthias Leistner, Europe's Copyright Law Decade: Recent Case Law of the European Court of Justice and Policy Perspectives, Common Market L. Rev. 51 (2014), 559; Matthias Leistner, Copyright at the Interface between EU Law and National Law: Definition of 'Work' and 'Right of Communication to the Public', J. Intell. Prop. L. & Practice (10) 2015, 626.
29. Most prominently, starting with the *Infopaq* decision, the Court of Justice has harmonized originality standards across various categories of work, *see Infopaq International A/S v. Danske Dagblades Forening*, 16 July 2009, case C-5/08, E.C.R. [2009] I-06569.
30. Directive 2001/29/EC of the European Parliament and of the Council of 22 May 2001 on the Harmonisation of Certain Aspects of Copyright and Related Rights in the Information Society, O.J. L 167, 22 June 2001, p. 10.

to the original public.[31] By introducing the requirement of a new public, the court intends to ensure that right holders receive appropriate remuneration 'which takes account of all aspects of the broadcast, such as its actual audience and its potential audience'.[32] Thereby, the court determines the scope of the exploitation right by its underlying economic purpose.[33]

Likewise, the court held in its *Allposters* decision that the unauthorized transfer to a canvas of a painting which is printed on a poster violates the copyright owner's right of distribution, even if the right owner has authorized the distribution of the original poster. The court stressed that the alteration of the medium on which the painting is printed means that the copyright owner's distribution right is not exhausted. The court noted that if the owner's distribution right was exhausted, the transfer of the painting would deprive them of an 'appropriate reward for the commercial exploitation of their work'.[34] This is another example where the court determines the scope of an exploitation right by its underlying economic purpose, i.e., to provide a financial reward to the painter. More generally, in its analyses of exploitation rights, the court seems increasingly willing to move away from arguments that conceptualize exploitation rights as mere static legal monopolies. Rather, the court analyses the economic effects that an unauthorized use has on the copyright owner in order to determine the scope of his exploitation rights.[35]

Until now, the Court of Justice of the EU has only explored very cautiously how to link the scope of exploitation rights to their economic purpose. It is not surprising that European copyright scholars have accepted the challenge more directly. As part of this volume, Séverine Dusollier has proposed replacing the current system of differentiated exploitation rights with a broad right of exploitation that is related to the function of copyright.[36]

---

31. *Sociedad General de Autores y Editores de España (SGAE) v. Rafael Hoteles*, 7 December 2006, case C-306/05, ECR [2005] I-11519, at paras 40, 42; *Football Association Premier League and Others v. QC Leisure and Others*, 4 October 2011, case C-403/08, ECR [2011] I-9083, at para. 197; *Airfield v. Gelgische Vereniging van Auteurs, Componisten en Uitgevers (Sabam)*, 13 October 2011, joint cases C-431/09 and C-432/09, ECR [2011] I-9363, at para. 72; *ITV Broadcasting and Others v. TVCatchup*, 7 March 2013, case C-607/11, EU:C:2013:147, at para. 32; *OSA v. Léčebné lázně Mariánské Lázně*, 27 February 2014, case C-351/12, ECLI_EU_C_2014:110, at para. 31; *Nils Svensson and Others v. Retriever Sverige*, 13 February 2014, case C-466/12, EU:C:2014:76, at para. 24.
32. *Airfield v. Belgische Vereniging van Auteurs, Componisten en Uitgevers (Sabam)*, 13 October 2011, joint cases C-431/09 and C-432/09, ECR [2011] I-9363, at para. 73.
33. For a critical reflection, *see* P. Bernt Hugenholtz & Sam C. van Velze, Communication to a New Public? Three Reasons Why EU Copyright Law Can Do Without a 'New Public', International Review of Innovation and Competition Law (47) 2016, 797.
34. *Art & Allposters International v. Stichting Pictoright*, 22 January 2015, case C-419/13, EU:C:2015:27, at para. 48.
35. Matthias Leistner, Europe's Copyright Law Decade, *supra* n. 28, at 570, 572–573; Alain Strowel (in this volume).
36. Séverine Dusollier (in this volume).

Ansgar Ohly has explored whether copyright could be remodelled after unfair competition law, thereby prohibiting a core set of infringing activities, while leaving more ambiguous activities to a system of flexible property rights, a market-effect clause, and a general clause of unfair use.[37] Ole-Andreas Rognstad and Joost Poort have proposed focusing copyright law on a single exclusive right to reasonable exploitation, thereby simplifying copyright law's structure radically.[38] In addition, Sari Depreeuw has explored how the act of exploitation could be used to clarify the scope of the rights of reproduction and communication to the public.[39] While these proposals differ in detail, they are all united in their desire to link the scope of exploitation rights back to the purpose of copyright protection.

Copyright scholarship in the US has been even more explicit in resynchronizing the design of property rights with their intended economic purpose. Thomas Cotter has argued that, when applying the fair use doctrine, courts should focus on whether the unauthorized use creates cognizable harm to the copyright owner's exploitation interests.[40] Sara Stadler has proposed reconceptualizing the distribution right on unfair competition grounds.[41] Christina Bohannan has argued that copyright law requires a theory of harm in order to limit copyright protection and enable creative reuse.[42] Together with Herbert Hovenkamp, she has also suggested the concept of 'IP injury', which would restrict intellectual property remedies to situations in which the intellectual property owner has suffered harm that is sufficiently linked to the purpose of intellectual property law.[43] Shyam Balganesh has explored how the foreseeability of consequences that are far removed from the author's actions influence his *ex ante* incentives and how this should, indirectly, affect the scope of copyright protection.[44] Brett Frischmann and Mark Lemley have suggested limiting the scope of exploitation rights to what is necessary to recoup the author's investment costs.[45] Thomas Nachbar has investigated how the distinction between rules and standards can be used to think about

37. Ansgar Ohly (in this volume).
38. Ole-Andreas Rognstad, Restructuring the Economic Rights in Copyright – Some Reflections on an 'Alternative Model', 62 J. Copyright Soc'y U.S.A. 503 (2015); Ole-Andreas Rognstad & Joost Poort (in this volume).
39. Sari Depreeuw, *The Variable Scope of the Exclusive Economic Rights in Copyright*, Alphen aan den Rijn 2014, pp. 514–538.
40. Thomas Cotter, Transformative Use and Cognizable Harm, 12 Vand. J. Ent. & Tech. L. 701 (2010).
41. Sara Stadler, Copyright as Trade Regulation, 155 U. Penn. L. Rev. 899 (2007).
42. Christina Bohannan, Copyright Harm, Foreseeability, and Fair Use, 85 Wash. U. L. Rev. 969 (2007); Christina Bohannan, Copyright Infringement and Harmless Speech, 61 Hastings L.J. 1083 (2009).
43. Bohannan & Hovenkamp, *supra* n. 15.
44. Shyam Balganesh, Foreeability and Copyright Incentives, 122 Harv. L. Rev. 1569 (2009).
45. Brett Frischmann & Mark Lemley, Spillovers, 107 Colum. L. Rev. 257 (2007).

the timing of policy decisions in the copyright system.[46] Moreover, Christopher Sprigman has analysed how the rule of reason doctrine stemming from antitrust law could be used to reduce the growing disconnect between copyright's utilitarian rationale and copyright law itself.[47] While US copyright law is in practice far from implementing such far-reaching proposals, US copyright theory has developed a growing array of overlapping proposals to reconnect the scope of copyright protection with its economic purpose.

3.3 DECONSTRUCTING COPYRIGHT

This is not the place to unveil an exhaustive critique of the current copyright system. Suffice it to say that current copyright law seems to struggle with adapting to changing technological environments; balancing the interests of creators, intermediaries, users and the public at large; ensuring proper revenue streams for creators and intermediaries; resisting overly strong influence from lobbyism groups; and retaining sufficient acceptance by the general public. There are signs that some of these problems are, to some extent, related to the inflexible design of current European copyright law. By relying on a static, rather formalistic definition of exploitation rights, European copyright law forces courts to engage in doctrinal assessments that are unrelated to any of the policy rationales underlying copyright protection. The various scholarly initiatives portrayed in the preceding section of this chapter intend to reduce the reliance of copyright law on formalistic conceptions of static property rights and increase the flexibility with which courts can decide copyright cases. While much of the discussion focuses on the use of copyright works on the Internet, the scholarly debate has a broader agenda: It scrutinizes whether the copyright system needs to be rethought and redesigned, irrespective of the technology that is used to disseminate copyright works.

This section does not intend to propose yet another system of more flexible exploitation rights. Rather, it presents the regulatory toolbox which is available to courts and policymakers who intend to provide a better link between the scope of copyright protection and its intended purpose. The tools will be presented roughly in order of how revolutionary they may be, compared to the current state of copyright doctrine.

---

46. Thomas Nachbar, Rules and Standards in Copyright, 52 Hous. L. Rev. 583 (2014).
47. Christopher Sprigman, Copyright and the Rule of Reason, 7 J. Telecomm. & High Tech. L. 317 (2009).

3.3.1 Copyright Limitations

If courts want to resynchronize copyright law with its intended purpose, the easiest (although not necessarily the best) way is probably to rely on flexible copyright limitations. In the European context, the three-step test of Article 5(5) of the Information Society Directive[48] could play such a role. Various scholars have suggested using the test as a tool to interpret copyright limitations in a more flexible manner.[49] Others have explored whether European countries should switch to a system of fair use, as in the US.[50] Under the US fair use doctrine, one factor to determine whether a use is fair – and, therefore, does not require the authorization of the copyright owner – is the effect the use has upon the market for the copyright work (17 U.S.C. § 107(4)). However, both the three-step test and the fair use doctrine have their shortcomings. The Court of Justice of the EU has only rarely relied expressly on the three-step test as laid down in the Information Society Directive.[51] Moreover, while the fair use doctrine takes the effect of the use on the market into account, this effect is only one among four factors the court has to consider. Furthermore, what constitutes a harmful effect in the context of the fair use defence is not well defined. Finally, and most importantly for our purposes, the fair use doctrine provides an affirmative defence only. The burden of proof is on the defendant: he has to demonstrate that his use creates no harm.[52]

3.3.2 Scope of Exploitation Rights

If courts want to go one step further in reconciling copyright protection with its underlying economic purpose, they can link protection and purpose when determining the scope of exploitation rights. The Court of Justice of the EU in its *UsedSoft v. Oracle* decision, for example, had to decide whether the unauthorized sale of used software licences violates the distribution right of

48. *See supra* n. 24.
49. Kamiel Koelman, Fixing the Three-step Test, E.I.P.R. 2008, 407; Martin Senftleben, L'application du triple test: vers un système de fair use européen? Propriétés Intellectuelles 2007, 453; Christopher Geiger, Flexibilising Copyright: Remedies to the Privatisation of Information by Copyright Law, IIC 2008, 178; Christopher Geiger et al., Declaration: A Balanced Interpretation of the 'Three-Step Test' in Copyright Law, JIPITEC (1) 2010.
50. *See* Antony Dnes, Should the UK Move to a Fair-Use Copyright Exception? IIC 2013, 418.
51. *See Public Relations Consultants Association v. Newspaper Licensing Agency and Others*, case C-360/13, 5 June 2014, EU:C:2014:1195.
52. Bohannan & Hovenkamp, *supra* n. 15, at 973–974; Bohannan, Copyright Harm, Foreseeability, and Fair Use, *supra* n. 42; Sprigman, *supra* n. 47, at 328.

Article 4 of the Computer Programs Directive.[53] In affirming that the distribution right can become exhausted if a software program has been downloaded over the Internet, the court noted that '[t]he on-line transmission method is the functional equivalent of the supply of a material medium'.[54] The court released itself from a formalistic interpretation of the term 'distribution'. Such an interpretation may have only included the physical transmission of an object and would thereby have excluded the exhaustion principle from being applicable in the *UsedSoft* case. Rather, the court adopted a functional approach by investigating the purpose of the provision in question. It could not observe a functional difference between the offline and online transmission of a computer program and, therefore, applied the exhaustion principle to online transmissions as well.[55]

Proposals to link the scope of exploitation rights to their underlying purpose come in other flavours as well. Some proposals intend to limit the scope of protection to what the author could foresee and reasonably expect at the time of creating his work. Shyam Balganesh, for example, starts with the premise that copyright law intends to provide incentives to creators at the time of creation. When the author decides whether and what to create, any legal consequences that are – temporally or causally – far removed from his decision will not have a significant impact on his decision. Therefore, Balganesh proposes limiting the scope of exploitation rights *ex post* according to a 'foreseeability test', i.e., to situations where an unauthorized use was reasonably foreseeable *ex ante* – because this is the time at which copyright's incentive is intended to operate.[56]

Other proposals link the scope of copyright protection directly to the harm an unauthorized use inflicts upon the author. If there is cognizable harm, a copyright infringement has occurred; if there is none, copyright law has not been violated. Christina Bohannan, for example, adopts an *ex ante* perspective. She is interested in the harm an unauthorized use of a work causes, as such harm would probably have a material effect on the author's

---

53. Directive 2009/24/EC of the European Parliament and of the Council of 23 April 2009 on the Legal Protection of Computer Programs, O.J. L 111, 5 May 2009, p. 16.
54. Court of Justice of the European Union, *UsedSoft v. Oracle International*, case C-128/11, 3 July 2012, EU:C:2012:407, para. 61.
55. This is not to say that the court has ruled that the exhaustion principle always applies to online transmissions. In fact, the court has only ruled with regard to the distribution right provided in Art. 4 of the Computer Programs Directive, not with regard to the distribution right provided in Art. 4 of the Information Society Directive. Both the *UsedSoft* and the *Allposters* decisions as well as Recital 29 of the Information Society Directive raise doubts as to whether the Court would treat online transmissions under the Information Society Directive in a similar way to online transmissions under the Computer Programs Directive; *see* Stefan Bechtold in: Thomas Dreier & P. Bernt Hugenholtz (eds.), *Concise European Copyright Law*, 2nd edition, Alphen aan den Rijn 2016, commentary on Art. 4 Information Society Directive, p. 450.
56. Balganesh, *supra* n. 44.

decision to create or distribute a work. Only if such harm can be shown, have the owner's exploitation rights been violated.[57]

3.3.3 Effects-Based Analysis

Linking the scope of copyright protection to the harm an unauthorized use creates is already a significant step away from the current copyright system. Even more radical approaches rely on a case-by-case analysis of the welfare effects of an authorized use of a copyright work. One of the most sweeping versions of such an approach has been tried out by the European Commission. In its *Microsoft* decision from 2004, the Commission had to analyse whether Microsoft was required to provide protocol information and specifications about its file, printer, and user directory service ('Active Directory') to firms who compete on the market for workgroup server operating systems. If competitors had access to such information, the argument goes, they could modify their operating systems in order to provide interoperable directory services in a systems environment dominated by Microsoft, thereby reducing Microsoft's dominance.[58]

The Court of Justice of the EU developed a set of requirements in its *Magill*[59] and *Bronner*[60] decisions under which the refusal of dominant firms to supply intellectual property rights to competitors can violate Article 102 of the TFEU.[61] In its own decision, the Commission noted that there was no persuasiveness in an approach that relied on an exhaustive checklist of exceptional circumstances under which a refusal to supply intellectual property rights violated Article 102.[62] Rather, the Commission stressed that it must analyse the entirety of the circumstances of Microsoft's behaviour and base its decision on the results of such a comprehensive examination.[63]

This is not surprising. In fact, every good antitrust authority should do so. Rather, the way in which the Commission conducted its investigation

57. Bohannan, *supra* n. 42; Bohannan & Hovenkamp, *supra* n. 15; *see also* Cotter, *supra* n. 40.
58. Commission of the European Communities, Commission Decision of 24.03.2004 relating to a Proceeding under Art. 82 of the EC Treaty (Case COMP/C-3/37.792 Microsoft), C(2004)900 final, available at http://ec.europa.eu/competition/antitrust/cases/dec_docs/37792/37792_4177_1.pdf (accessed 2 October 2017).
59. Court of Justice of the European Union, *Radio Telefis Eireann and others v. Commission of the European Communities*, joint cases C-241/91 and C-242/91, 6 April 1995, E.C.R. [1995] I-743.
60. Court of Justice of the European Union, *Oscar Bronner v. Mediaprint Zeitungs- und Zeitschriftenverlag and Others*, case C-7/97, 26 November 1998, E.C.R. [1998] I-7791.
61. The Court of Justice published its *IMS Health* decision only four weeks after the Commission's *Microsoft* decision.
62. Commission of the European Commission, *Microsoft* decision, *see supra* n. 58, at p. 149, Rec. 555.
63. *Id.* at p. 150, Rec. 558.

may come as a surprise. Instead of putting Microsoft's alleged intellectual property rights at the centre of its analysis, the Commission merely noted, in passing, that Microsoft had claimed copyright, trade secret, and patent protection on some of its protocol information.[64] It also noted that the mere fact that Microsoft may own intellectual property rights to some of the information does not justify a refusal to license it to competitors.[65] The Commission then conducted a detailed comparison between the welfare effects if Microsoft were allowed to keep the protocol information secret and the effects if Microsoft were required to disclose it to competitors. Thereby, the Commission intended to determine whether the need to provide Microsoft with incentives to innovate outweighed any detrimental effects on competitors and consumers.[66] The Commission investigated the effects a refusal to license has on technical development and consumer welfare.[67] It concluded that, 'on balance, the possible negative impact of an order to supply on Microsoft's incentives to innovate is outweighed by its positive impact on the level of innovation of the whole industry (including Microsoft)'.[68]

For our purposes, the analysis of the decision by the European Commission is illuminating in how it dealt with intellectual property rights. The Commission acknowledged that Microsoft's protocol information may be protected by intellectual property rights. However, in a decision that extended over 300 pages, the Commission never actually determined whether the protocol information was protected by intellectual property laws or not.[69] Instead, the Commission engaged in a direct welfare analysis regarding what implications an order to supply protocol information to competitors would have on *ex ante* incentive effects and *ex post* competitive effects. Whether the Commission was correct in its welfare analysis, is not the subject of this chapter.[70] What is interesting is that the Commission decided to move away from intellectual property rights and focus instead on welfare effects directly.[71] This seems the most extreme way to realign

64. *Id.* at p. 55, Rec. 249, and at p. 147, n. 658.
65. *Id.* at p. 191, Rec. 712.
66. *Id.*
67. *Id.* at pp. 186 et seq.
68. *Id.* at p. 208, Rec. 783.
69. *See id.* at p. 147, Rec. 546: ' … it cannot be excluded that ordering Microsoft to disclose such specifications … restricts the exercise of Microsoft's intellectual property rights'.
70. *See*, e.g., François Lévêque, Innovation, Leveraging and Essential Facilities: Interoperability Licensing in the EU Microsoft Case, World Comp. 28 (2005), 71; Simonetta Vezzoso, The Incentive Balance Test in the EU Microsoft Case: A Pro-Innovation 'Economics-Based' Approach, Eur. Comp. L. Rev. 2006, 382.
71. In the later decision of the Court of First Instance, the court analysed Microsoft's behaviour primarily under the standards of *Magill* and *IMS Health*, a decision by the Court of Justice which had been published after the Microsoft decision by the Commission, *see* Court of First Instance, *Microsoft v. Commission of the European Communities*, case T-201/04, 17 September 2007, E.C.R. [2007] II-3619, at Rec. 336 et

copyright with its underlying economic purpose: property rights are dissolved in an *ex post* case-by-case analysis by an administrative agency.

3.4 RECONSTRUCTING COPYRIGHT

As the introduction has indicated and the preceding two sections have attempted to demonstrate, copyright law and scholarship are on a road towards increasingly flexible property right allocations, an increased tailoring of exploitation rights to particular cases, and a growing dependency on the factual circumstances of individual cases. At first sight, such trends seem convincing: Who could object to a legal system that is better designed to achieve its intended purpose and leads to fewer unintended consequences for unaffected third parties? In addition, these trends are fashionable. Evaluating the effectiveness of an area of the law according to economic criteria is *en vogue* in an era of evidence-based policymaking and regulatory impact assessments.

Nevertheless, the trend towards more a more flexible copyright law generates many novel questions. In particular, it is not clear how far we should follow this trend. Should we end up with a copyright system in which courts use the *ex ante* incentive effects of court decisions as a guiding principle in delineating exploitation rights? Should we apply the European Commission's refusal-to-license analysis in the Microsoft decision to other cases as well? In the following section, various stumbling blocks will be presented that may inhibit overly extensive attempts to move copyright from a property-based to an evidence-based system of individual allocations of bargaining power.

3.4.1 Rights Versus Effects

The main purpose of the reform proposals described in this chapter is to realign copyright protection with its underlying economic purpose, i.e., to incentivize the production of new creative works.[72] The closer the link between copyright protection and its underlying purpose becomes, however, the more fine-grained and nuanced the protection tends to become. By moving an area of the law from rules to standards, the area may become more

seq. The Court also noted that it was not possible for the Commission to evaluate Microsoft's claims concerning various intellectual property rights as the relevant specifications were not available for scrutiny, *see id.* at Rec. 285.

72. On competing purposes of copyright protection, *see infra* section 3.4.4.

malleable and adaptive to individual circumstances. However, this comes at the cost of reduced predictability and legal certainty.[73]

In addition to this general trade-off between rules and standards, another dimension of the rules versus standards debate becomes important in copyright law. Copyright rules are typically determined by parliament before an author creates a work. It is relatively easy to determine the incentive effects of such rules, as they exist at the time the author decides whether to create a work or not. Copyright standards, however, are implemented by courts typically once a work has been used without authorization. As the courts attempt to determine what effect their decisions would have on authors from an *ex ante* perspective, another level of complexity and uncertainty is introduced.[74] If courts were always well equipped to determine the *ex ante* effects of their decisions, implementing a rule-based copyright system could be an attractive option. Unfortunately, courts may not have the necessary information or educational background to make the determinations required. They run the risk of false positive and false negative errors. Therefore, in individual cases, courts may cut back exploitation rights too much or too little.

In addition to this time dimension, copyright law adds a trading dimension to the rules versus standards debate. This debate plays an important role in areas of law such as antitrust or torts. As opposed to antitrust or torts, entitlements must not only be enforceable in copyright law, they must also be tradable. If a property right becomes too murky because it relies extensively on standards, transaction costs for trading the right may become prohibitively high. It is not only the copyright owner, but also his potential licensees who have to understand the scope of the property right.[75] Tradability and predictability put a natural limit on attempts to move copyright protection fully to a standards-based system.

3.4.2 Litigation Versus Regulation

Christina Bohannan and Herbert Hovenkamp compare the influence special interest groups have had on antitrust and intellectual property policy in the US in their proposal to introduce the concept of 'IP harm' into intellectual property law. They submit that intellectual property statutes have been affected more by lobbyism than antitrust statutes. They trace this difference back to the less robust nature of economic models of innovation compared to

73. On the general debate between rules and standards, *see* Isaac Ehrlich & Richard Posner, An Economic Analysis of Legal Rulemaking, 3 J. Legal Stud. 257 (1974); Louis Kaplow, Rules versus Standards: An Economic Analysis, 42 Duke L.J. 557 (1992).
74. On this point, *see* Nachbar, *supra* n. 46.
75. For a different perspective, *see* Dan L. Burk, Muddy Rules for Cyberspace, 21 Cardozo L. Rev. 121 (1999).

economic models of competition.[76] '[W]hen an area of enterprise is not well-understood, lawmakers are more vulnerable to special interests', they argue.[77] As courts are more insulated from the influence of special interest groups, they hope that a shift towards standards in copyright law would make this area of law less prone to lobbyism.[78]

While this is a plausible effect, an important difference between antitrust and copyright law remains. Antitrust laws are typically enforced by antitrust authorities. They are equipped with special means to gather evidence and to hire specialized personnel; they have assembled large amounts of tacit knowledge and deal with antitrust cases all the time. The same is not true for courts dealing with copyright cases. A court which is charged with determining the detailed welfare effects of a judicial intervention in copyright law may arrive easily at its practical limits. The shift from rules to standards in copyright law should not be misunderstood as a shift from a system of litigation between private parties to a system of regulation between an administrative agency and private companies.[79]

3.4.3 Intuition Versus Knowledge

The move towards a system of more flexible exploitation rights leads to novel data requirements. At some point, courts, scholars, and policymakers will need data on the effects that particular copyright doctrines have on markets. For a long time, many areas of copyright law have been based on assumptions, political views, and prior decisions rather than exact knowledge of causal relationships.[80] Empirical data is gradually becoming available which may provide novel insights for copyright policy. A system of flexible exploitation rights will have to integrate such insights. One example may illustrate this point: a large-scale empirical study by Lesley Chiou and Catherine Tucker has analysed how Internet users use information aggregators such as Google News. They show that Internet users do not use Google News as a full substitute for news websites which are indexed by Google News. Instead, Google News seems to enable users to better investigate additional, related content comprehensively. According to the data analysed

76. Bohannan & Hovenkamp, *supra* n. 15, at 923–926.
77. *Ibid.*, at 926.
78. *Ibid.*, at 923–926, 979–980 (noting that the influence of special interests depends on the robustness of the economic models under which policymakers work).
79. On this debate, *see Verizon Communication v. Law Office of Curtis v. Trinko*, 540 U.S. 398 (2004).
80. On a related, provocative note, *see* Mark Lemley, Faith-Based Intellectual Property, 62 UCLA L. Rev. 1328 (2015).

by Chiou and Tucker, this not only benefits users, but also benefits news websites indirectly.[81]

Such empirical insights can be informative when designing property rights for news websites. If the analysis by Chiou and Tucker is correct, it is not obvious that news aggregators create harm for right owners. The point here is not to analyse whether copyright law should provide protection to news websites against Google News. The point is to show that data will become increasingly available which may demonstrate unexpected welfare effects of copyright doctrines, thereby challenging traditional assumptions. A system of flexible exploitation rights will have to develop methods to absorb such information.

While copyright law should attempt to integrate available empirical knowledge into its doctrines, one should also note that empirical knowledge about copyright law is most likely unevenly distributed. While we may have a good understanding of the real effects of some copyright doctrines, our understanding of other doctrines may be much more blurred. The data necessary to analyse copyright doctrines is often unavailable, or the available empirical methods have methodological shortcomings. The uneven distribution of empirical knowledge on the effects of copyright doctrines puts another limit on the introduction of a flexible system of property rights.

3.4.4 Efficiency Versus Other Goals

Finally, and most importantly, all proposals that attempt to link copyright protection to its underlying purpose have to define what the purpose of copyright protection actually is. This may sound easier than it is. While this chapter starts from the premise that the goal of copyright protection is to incentivize creative production, many other potential goals of copyright protection exist. The protection of personality interests of authors may be the most important alternative goal in the European context.[82] Compared to antitrust law, copyright scholars and courts seem to agree much less on the ultimate goal of copyright protection. A system of flexible exploitation rights can only be effective, however, if the underlying purpose of copyright and the link to the exploitation rights are well defined.[83] This is not to say that copyright should necessarily only care about incentives and welfare maximization. As centuries of experience with this area of the law demonstrate,

81. Lesley Chiou & Catherine Tucker, Content Aggregation by Platforms. The Case of the News Media, 2015, available at http://ssrn.com/abstract=1864203 (accessed 2 October 2017).
82. *See* Bechtold & Engel, *supra* n. 27.
83. For a similar discussion in antitrust law, *see Roger Blair & Daniel Sokol*, The Rule of Reason and the Goals of Antitrust: An Economic Approach, 78 Antitrust L.J. 471 (2012).

this cannot and should not be the case.[84] But even if there was wide consensus that the primary goal of copyright law is to incentivize the creation of new works, the proposed increase in the flexibility of copyright law would leave courts with ample opportunities to take account of other values such as free speech, access, or the protection of property interests.

3.5 OUTLOOK

As the preceding section has shown, there are multiple stumbling blocks on the way to introducing more flexibility into copyright's exploitation rights. An effects-based approach towards copyright runs the risk of dissolving property rights; turning courts into regulators; requiring data that is not available; and suppressing values that are not compliant with the economic justification of copyright law. Nevertheless, courts and scholars who aim to add more flexibility to the copyright system seem to be on the right track. In this concluding section, the paper will first discuss how a reformed copyright system may look. It will then identify conceptual problems that must be resolved before such a system can be implemented.

3.5.1 Flexible Property Rights

Various proposals to make copyright law more flexible have been introduced on both sides of the Atlantic over the last few years. While the details of the proposals differ, some similarities are apparent. First, many proposals intend to link the scope of copyright protection to its underlying purpose by either introducing a concept of harm into copyright doctrine[85] or by directly investigating the *ex ante* effects of an unauthorized use on the incentives to create.[86]

Many proposals operationalize this link by introducing different categories of unauthorized use into copyright doctrine. In Europe, Ansgar Ohly has proposed prohibiting clear cases of copyright infringement per se without the need to demonstrate any harm, while subjecting less clear cases to more flexible provisions and general clauses of unfair behaviour.[87] Ole-Andreas Rognstad and Joost Poort have proposed a catalogue approach, under which the legislator would list typical, but not all conceivable conduct that infringes

---

84. *See*, however, for a strong defence of a utilitarian vision of copyright law, Lemley, *supra* n. 80.
85. *See*, e.g., Bohannan & Hovenkamp, *supra* n. 15, at 976, 985; Bohannan, Copyright Harm, Foreseeability, and Fair Use, *supra* n. 42; Sprigman, *supra* n. 47, at 320.
86. *See*, e.g., Balganesh, *supra* n. 44.
87. Ohly (in this volume).

copyright law.[88] In the US, Christopher Sprigman has proposed subjecting consumptive uses to a per se rule, while subjecting transformative uses to a rule of reason standard.[89]

The general idea behind these proposals is to distinguish between instances where copyright provisions have clear and undisputed effects on markets (such as the unauthorized offering of a work to the public for permanent download) and areas with ambiguous effects (such as transformative uses). For areas of copyright law with clear effects, strict rules seem appropriate. For other areas, variations of standards would provide courts with the necessary flexibility to develop an appropriate body of case law.

3.5.2 Will Reform Help?

While expanding flexibility in copyright along these lines seems a laudable goal, some questions remain: will such reform actually produce a better copyright system in practice? To what extent does the success of copyright law really depend on the internal structure of its doctrines? Why are courts not able to achieve the goals they deem appropriate under the current system of copyright law?

Indeed, one may doubt whether a reformed copyright law will necessarily lead to a better copyright system. A system with more flexible property rights could introduce a substantial amount of uncertainty, at least in an extensive transition period. It could also lead to substantial divergence in case law between courts from different Member States of the EU and beyond. Furthermore, current copyright law may seem more static to outside observers than it actually is to courts. All this could suggest that moving to a copyright system with more flexible exploitation rights may not be worth the effort or may start copyright law on a journey with an uncertain outcome.

In order to make the reform a success, proposals should not analyse only the substantive aspects such as when to rely on rules versus standards in copyright law. Rather, they should also investigate how the proposal could be implemented on a procedural level. Most importantly, reform proposals could rely on a staggered system of burdens and standards of proof. In many copyright systems, the copyright owner has to prove infringement, while the unauthorized user has to prove that the benefits from a limitation to copyright infringement. When moving to a copyright system that takes the underlying purpose into account, the allocation of the burdens of proof could be different.

---

88. Rognstad & Poort (in this volume). They also point to the abstract analysis of the advantages of such catalogues by Gideon Parchomovsky & Alex Stein, Catalogs, 115 Colum. L. Rev. 165 (2015).
89. Sprigman, *supra* n. 47, at 334–340.

In cases of close or verbatim unauthorized copying of a work, Christina Bohannan and Christopher Sprigman have proposed providing a rebuttable presumption of harm. In cases of more remote unauthorized use of a work, they argue that the copyright owner, not the unauthorized user, should provide proof that the unauthorized use actually harmed the owner.[90] This would not only limit the scope of copyright protection to the harm created by the unauthorized use, but, by requiring copyright owners to provide proof of actual harm, this would also produce helpful public information about the effects of transformative unauthorized use on authors.[91]

The combination of a system of flexible exploitation rights with a staggering of burdens of proof is promising on various dimensions. First, a staggered system of burdens of proof could also deal with cases in which the unauthorized use does not harm, but actually benefits the author.[92] In such cases, copyright law could allocate the burden of proof to the unauthorized user. In order to escape liability, the user would have to prove that his use benefited the author and that the author could not have materialized the benefit without him.[93] Second, the combination of flexible exploitation rights and staggered burdens of proof could enable fine-grained solutions for borderline cases. In the case of digital resales, for example, a copyright system could subject such resales to a per se prohibition; or to a rule of reason analysis in which it is presumed that such resale harms the copyright owner, although the reseller may prove otherwise; or to a rule of reason analysis in which it is presumed that such resale does not harm the copyright owner generally, although the resale will be an infringement if the author is able to prove harm that materially impacted the copyright owner's *ex ante* incentives to innovate. The third alternative may be the most appropriate solution to the problem of digital resale. Similarly, hyperlinking and private copying cases could be subject to a rule of reason analysis with a rebuttable presumption that they do not harm copyright owners. Conversely, retransmission cases could fall under a rule of reason analysis with a rebuttable presumption that they harm copyright owners. Linking a system of flexible exploitation rights with staggered burdens of proof greatly expands the regulatory toolbox available to courts and policymakers. In fact, the Court of Justice of the EU has already experimented with such an approach. In the *GS Media* case, the court held that providing a hyperlink to an unauthorized reproduction of a work that its copyright owner has not yet published may violate the right of communication to the public. Most interestingly for our

90. Bohannan, Copyright Harm, Foreseeability, and Fair Use, *supra* n. 42, at 1019–1020, 1028; Sprigman, *supra* n. 47, at 323.
91. Sprigman, *supra* n. 47, at 324.
92. For the study by Chiou and Tucker on Google News, *see supra* text accompanying n. 81; *see also* Bohannan, Copyright Harm, Foreseeability, and Fair Use, *supra* n. 42, at 1028–1030 (noting how the publication of Dan Brown's *The Da Vinci Code* increased demand for the earlier book *The Holy Blood and the Holy Grail*).
93. This system remotely resembles the efficiency defence in antitrust law.

purposes, the court held that, if the hyperlink is posted for profit, a rebuttable presumption exists according to which the provider of the hyperlink had full knowledge that he may be linking to an unauthorized, unpublished version of the work. This is not the place to analyse the doctrinal and systematic merits of the decision.[94] This is just to note that, even under the current copyright system, courts are experimenting with procedural approaches concerning the scope of copyright protection.

As this discussion shows, a reform of copyright law with more flexible exploitation rights will only be successful if it also addresses who bears the burden of proof in rule of reason cases. Such reform should also take into account that, in reality, it may be difficult for an alleged infringer to prove that his conduct does not cause harm to the copyright owner if the copyright statute assumes otherwise; or, vice versa, for a copyright owner to prove that the conduct of an alleged infringer actually harms the copyright owner, despite an assumption to the opposite in copyright law. Experience from antitrust law shows that the procedural design of the burden of proof can have a decisive impact in many cases.[95]

In addition to this procedural aspect, a system of flexible exploitation rights has to ensure that flourishing licensing markets can develop on top of the exploitation rights. For more flexible exploitation rights that are granted under a rule of reason regime, one has to ensure that these entitlements are not so vague that it becomes impossible to write contracts based on them. In particular, it may be difficult for contracting parties to assess the value of flexible exploitation rights as their value will only be determined *ex post* by a court. It is, therefore, very important that courts develop a steady body of case law on exploitation rights under a rule of reason regime, in order to increase the predictability and assessability of such rights.

A copyright reform along the lines described in this chapter will not be easy to design and implement, nor will it solve all the problems with the current copyright system. This chapter has used the development of antitrust as an indication of how copyright doctrine may evolve. However, the example of antitrust also shows that clear-cut answers to difficult problems at the intersection of law and economics are rare. Despite all the influence that economics has had on the evolution of European competition law, the rights-based approach still plays an important role in decisions by antitrust

94. Birgit Clark & Sabrina Tozzi, 'Communication to the Public' under EU Copyright Law: An Increasingly Delphic Concept or Intentional Fragmentation? E.I.P.R. (2016), 715; Michael Grünberger, Zugangsregeln bei Verlinkungen auf rechtswidrig zugänglich gemachte Werke ZUM 2016, 905.
95. Damien Geradin, Merger Control Policy: How to Give Meaningful Consideration to Efficiency Claims? Common Market L. Rev. (2003), 1367; Alan Fisher & Robert Landes, Efficiency Considerations in Merger Enforcement, 71 Cal. L. Rev. 1582 (1983); Stefan Bechtold, Die Kontrolle von Sekundärmärkten: eine juristische und ökonomische Untersuchung im Kartell- und Immaterialgüterrecht, Baden-Baden 2007, pp. 61–65.

enforcement agencies and courts.[96] One should neither expect nor hope that the copyright system of the future will be entirely or even primarily based on a rule of reason.

Introducing some flexibility into copyright's exploitation rights may not be sufficient to change the course of modern copyright law. However, a clever combination of per se rules and rule of reason standards with staggered burdens of proof and institutional safeguards to secure vibrant licensing markets may do the trick. Copyright law will become less of a personality right and more akin to unfair competition and antitrust law. It will become more dependent on economic research and less dependent on doctrinal arguments. It will lead to the increased availability of data on the economic effects of copyright protection. It may become more harmonized across countries. It may require copyright scholars to develop an integrated view of copyright law and comparable methods of protection (Digital Rights Management, contracts, and database protection), as these methods may be effective substitutes for copyright protection.[97] At the same time, copyright law may suffer from some uncertainty during periods of transition. It may gain predictability in some areas, while losing predictability in others. Most importantly, copyright law will hopefully become more effective in achieving its central economic goal: to incentivize.

96. Schweitzer & Patel, *supra* n. 7, at 222–223.
97. Stefan Bechtold, Digital Rights Management in the United States and Europe, 52 Am. J. Comp. L. 323 (2004); Stefan Bechtold, *Vom Urheber- zum Informationsrecht: Implikationen des Digital Rights Management*, München 2002.

Chapter 4

A Fairness-Based Approach to Economic Rights

Ansgar Ohly

4.1 INTRODUCTION: PURPOSE AS JUSTIFICATION AND LIMITATION

Intellectual property rights interfere with markets. They artificially restrict the use of intangible subject-matter. But they are not ends in themselves. They serve purposes which both justify and delimit them. This is particularly evident in US law, where the nexus between right and purpose is famously expressed in the Copyright Clause,[1] which empowers Congress to pass legislation 'to promote the Progress of Science and useful Arts, by securing for limited Times to Authors and Inventors the exclusive Right to their respective Writings and Discoveries'. Once it is acknowledged that a right is both justified and limited by its purpose, the rules determining the content and scope of the rights are open to challenge. They can be tested against economic and social reality, in particular by means of economic analysis.

Industrial property law has by and large been responsive to this challenge. *Patent law* went through a crisis in the second half of the nineteenth century. At that time the justification for patent law was doubted, and the Netherlands even went so far as to abolish patent protection

1. Article 1 s. 8 US Constitution.

altogether.[2] This forced the proponents of the patent system to come up with convincing justifications.[3] While patents are now well-established in the modern canon of rights, they have always been subject to important restrictions:[4] their term is restricted to twenty years, they cannot be infringed by private acts and they can be subject to compulsory licences, for which both patent law and competition law can provide the basis. *Trade marks* have traditionally not been regarded as intellectual property rights at all, but rather as tools preventing unfair competition.[5] While the modern development has been characterized by an expansion of trade mark law and emancipation from its unfair competition law roots,[6] trade marks have never developed into full monopoly rights. They remain restricted by their function, as the Court of Justice of the European Union (CJEU) never ceases to stress.[7] *Unfair competition* law is almost by definition market-sensitive. Under the EU Unfair Commercial Practices Directive (UCPD),[8] misleading or aggressive practices are in principle[9] only regarded as unfair when they affect the consumers' economic behaviour. While the UCPD protects consumers and is hence not closely related to intellectual property law, other areas of unfair competition law protect trade values. Between these doctrines and classical intellectual property rights there exists what could be referred to as a 'continuum of propertization'. In modern legislation there is a trend towards 'legal hybrids',[10] which combine certain elements of property with infringement provisions depending on flexible notions of fairness or misappropriation. Trade secrets are an example in point: they can be assigned and licensed, but the secret information is not made the object of a full exclusive

2. The economic effects of this step are still the subject of academic controversy, *see* on the one hand J.P. Smits, *The Determinants of Productivity Growth in Dutch Manufacturing, 1815-1913*, 4 Eur. Rev. Econ. Hist. 223–246 (2000), on the other hand P. Moser, *How Do Patent Laws Influence Innovation? Evidence from 19th-Century World Fairs*, 95 Am. Econ. Rev. 1214–1236 (2005).
3. F. Machlup & E. Penrose, *The Patent Controversy in the Nineteenth Century*, 10 J. Econ. Hist. 1–29 (1950).
4. This is not to say that the present patent system does not have its shortcomings, *see* A.B. Jaffe & J. Lerner, *Innovation and Its Discontents: How Our Broken Patent System Is Endangering Innovation and Progress, and What to Do About It* (Princeton: Princeton University Press, 2004).
5. *See* n. 47–49.
6. *See* 4.2.3.1 *infra.*
7. *See* 4.2.3.2 *infra.*
8. Directive 2005/29/EC of the European Parliament and of the Council of 11 May 2005 concerning unfair business-to-consumer commercial practices in the internal market and amending Council Directive 84/450/EEC, Directives 97/7/EC, 98/27/EC and 2002/65/EC of the European Parliament and of the Council and Regulation (EC) No. 2006/2004 of the European Parliament and of the Council OJ L 149/22.
9. The cases proscribed in the 'black list' are the exception: *see* 4.2.2.2 *infra.*
10. J.H. Reichman, *Legal Hybrids Between the Patent and Copyright Paradigms*, 94 Colum. L. Rev. 2432 (1994).

right. The EU Trade Secrets Directive[11] in particular aims at reconciling effective protection with proportionality and with the freedoms of trade and expression.

Copyright law, however, has partly become detached from commercial reality. It follows the classical property paradigm: the owner is allocated broad exclusive rights which are subject to certain exceptions. In US law the fair use test,[12] whose elements include economic factors, reconnects copyright protection with market reality. EU copyright law, however, has not only been influenced by the utilitarian approach which prevails in common law jurisdictions, but also by the natural rights tradition of continental European legal systems.[13] According to this approach copyright is not an economic right but a cultural right, which is mainly designed to serve the author's commercial and ideal interests. The economic rights which stem from copyright law mirror the economic reality of the analogue world. Unlike in trade mark law, there is no distinct infringement test.[14] Anyone who performs one of the acts covered by the exclusive rights will commit a prima facie infringement. And unlike in US law, there is no market-sensitive fair use exception which would counterbalance the broad prima facie allocation of rights.

This chapter will look at some of the more market-oriented approaches which exist in other areas of intellectual property and competition law, notably the concept of fairness in unfair competition and trade mark law (section 4.2). The approach of copyright law, in contrast, will be shown to be predominantly formalist (section 4.3). Drawing inspiration from trade mark and unfair competition law, this chapter will propose a fairness-based approach which adds a market effects criterion to the infringement test and which can be cast into a three-level model (section 4.4).

Traditionally-minded copyright lawyers might resent this approach. As *Alois Troller* once noted, some copyright specialists even tend to feel offended when common features between their realm of high culture and the mundane world of industrial property and competition law are pointed out.[15] But it will be argued here that copyright law and theory could benefit from a more function-oriented analysis. A more market-sensitive approach can

11. Directive (EU) 2016/943 of the European Parliament and of the Council on the protection of undisclosed know-how and business information (trade secrets) against their unlawful acquisition, use and disclosure, OJ No. L 157/1.
12. On which *see* 4.4.3.1 *infra*.
13. *See* 4.4.2.2 *infra*.
14. Although courts sometimes distinguish between scope and infringing acts, *see infra* at 4.3.1.
15. A. Troller, *Immaterialgüterrecht* (3rd ed., Basel: Helbing & Lichtenhahn, 1983), 102: 'Heute sind sogar die einzelnen Gebiete des Immaterialgüterrechts so weit auseinandergeraten, daß … der Spezialist des Urheberrechts die Erhabenheit seines Gebietes durch die behauptete Verwandtschaft mit dem gewerblichen Rechtsschutz angegriffen sieht …'.

help to overcome the often-bemoaned crisis of copyright law in the digital age.

4.2 MARKET-SENSITIVE APPROACHES IN UNFAIR COMPETITION AND TRADE MARK LAW

4.2.1 Unfair Competition, Intellectual Property and Legal Hybrids

The term 'intellectual property' suggests a bipolar structure which consists of property rights such as patents and copyright on the one hand and tort law, including unfair competition law, on the other. The existence of property rights depends on certain conditions of protection, they have a well-defined scope and they are subject to certain exceptions. Unfair competition law, on the other hand, seems to be tort law which regulates market behaviour without creating exclusive rights.

This analysis, however, is inaccurate both empirically and normatively. As, in particular, *Jerome H. Reichman* has pointed out, there is a trend in modern legislation towards what he refers to as 'legal hybrids'.[16] While he mainly challenges the bipolar structure of patent and copyright law and discusses hybrids between both paradigms, he also focuses on regimes which combine proprietary elements with more flexible misappropriation approaches. These regimes mediate between formal intellectual property law and free competition[17] by making protection dependent on flexible factors such as unfair misappropriation. *Reichman* analyses several examples, notably trade secret protection, technology protection in unfair competition law and database protection. On the basis of this analysis he recommends a new, flexible liability regime which protects applied know-how.

While *Reichman* pursues a research objective which differs from the one discussed here, the notion of 'legal hybrids' is not only accurate as a description of the present system, but it also indicates a way of making intellectual property more flexible. Several unfair competition law doctrines protect trade values against misappropriation. The common law tort of passing off provides owners of goodwill with remedies against damage caused by misleading consumers about the trade source of goods.[18] Misappropriation doctrines in French, Dutch or German unfair competition law can be relied on in order to protect the investment in product image or quality

16. Reichman, *supra* n. 10, at 2432.
17. *Ibid.* at 2438.
18. *See* R. Arnold, *English Unfair Competition Law*, IIC 63, 73–75 (2013); C. Wadlow, *The Law of Passing-Off: Unfair Competition by Misrepresentation* (5th ed., London: Sweet & Maxwell, 2016), paras 1-15-1-17.

against misappropriation.[19] Systematically these doctrines are part of unfair competition law, but they partly overlap with trade mark law. The law of trade secrets is a half-way house between unfair competition law and intellectual property law. The EU directive[20] distinguishes trade secrets from intellectual property[21] and only prohibits the unfair acquisition, use or disclosure of confidential information.[22] At the same time the remedies provided by the directive are closely modelled on the IP Enforcement Directive[23] as, indeed, Article 39 of the Agreement on Trade-Related Aspects of Intellectual Property Rights (TRIPS) requires. A lot of ink has been spilt over the question of whether trade secrets are property and whether they should be.[24] But this question is partly irrelevant and partly misguided. It is irrelevant because modern trade secrets law creates a legal hybrid[25] which combines elements of intellectual property and of competition law. And it is misguided because it suggests that the level of protection would depend on this classification.

Some of the rights which are considered as intellectual property also contain elements of unfair competition law. This is most obvious in trade mark law. But some of the neighbouring rights protected under EU law also protect competitive interests. In the law of databases, the sui generis right is only afforded to databases which are the result of substantial investment and it is only infringed by the transfer of a 'substantial part' or by 'the repeated and systematic extraction and/or re-utilization of insubstantial parts of the contents of the database implying acts which conflict with a normal exploitation of that database or which unreasonably prejudice the legitimate

---

19. For an overview *see* A. Kamperman Sanders, *Unfair Competition Law* (Oxford: Clarendon Press, 1995), 24–77, 121, 153; A. Ohly, *The Freedom of Imitation and its Limits – A European Perspective*, IIC 506, 515–524 (2010), and the country reports in F. Henning-Bodewig (ed.), *International Handbook on Unfair Competition* (Munich: Beck, 2013).
20. *See supra* n. 11.
21. Recital 39: 'This Directive should not affect the application of any other relevant law in other areas, including intellectual property rights and the law of contract'.
22. Articles 3–5.
23. Directive 2004/48/EC on the enforcement of intellectual property rights, OJ No. L 195/16, 2 June 2004.
24. There is a controversial debate about whether trade secret protection can be regarded as a form of intellectual property, *see* on the one hand, M. Lemley, *The Surprising Virtues of Treating Trade Secrets as IP Rights*, 61 Stan. L. Rev. 311 (2008); M. Bronckers & N. McNelis, *Is the EU Obliged to Improve the Protection of Trade Secrets? An Inquiry into TRIPS, the European Convention on Human Rights and the EU Charter of Fundamental Rights*, EIPR 673, 677 et seq. (2012); A. Ohly, *Harmonising the Protection of Trade Secrets: Challenges and Perspectives*, in: J. de Werra (ed.), *La protection des secrets d' affaires / The Protection of Trade Secrets* (Zurich: Schulthess, 2013), 25, 33–35; on the other hand G. Ghidini & V. Falce, in: R.C. Dreyfuss & K.J. Strandburg, *The Law and Theory of Trade Secrecy, A Handbook of Contemporary Research* (Cheltenham: Edward Elgar, 2011), 141 et seq.
25. Reichman, *supra* n. 10, at 2519–2556.

interests of the maker of the database'.[26] Other neighbouring rights are cast in the form of exclusive rights, although in terms of history and policy they are rooted in competition law.

Reto Hilty has recently suggested a three-tier structure consisting of unfair competition law, medium types of protection and full intellectual property rights.[27] But the examples given above defy such a clear classification. Rather, there is a continuum of protection which ranges from mere conduct-based rules such as the prohibition of unfair business-to-consumer practices in the UCPD, over the conduct-based protection of trade values by torts like passing off in English law or parasitic competition in French law, over 'semi-proprietary' regimes like the law of trade secrets and competition-based neighbouring rights, to rights which fully correspond to the classical property paradigm. This idea of a continuum is also more attractive in terms of legal policy than any binary approach distinguishing between 'property' and 'non-property', as it avoids legislation being confronted with the difficult choice between granting property rights and lesser forms of protection. Rather than criticizing property-based approaches, the way forward seems to be a flexibilization within intellectual property law, which is already underway in several areas. This is particularly true for copyright policy: this chapter will not suggest the abolition of copyright as an intellectual property right, but rather the introduction of flexibility borrowed from some of the 'legal hybrids'.

4.2.2 Unfair Competition Law

4.2.2.1 Unfair Competition and Copyright

At first sight, unfair competition law and copyright law seem to have little in common. Unfair competition law regulates trade practices, it sets the 'rules of the game' rather than creating property rights. Hence it is not surprising that unfair competition law does not adhere to the 'property logic' of scope and exceptions. In practice, however, unfair competition law has always supplemented intellectual property protection. While imitating a product is lawful outside the ambit of intellectual property, the marketing of a lookalike product may well fall foul of the harmonized provisions on misleading

26. Article 7(1), (5) Directive 96/9/EC of the European Parliament and of the Council of 11 March 1996 on the legal protection of databases, OJ No. L 77/20, 27 March 1996 (Database Directive).
27. R. Hilty, *Paper Given on the Occasion of the 50th Anniversary of the Max Planck Institute*, 13 May 2016.

practices or unfair comparative advertising.[28] Confidential information can be protected both by intellectual property and under the law of trade secrets. Several, if not all EU Member States have doctrines under which the misappropriation of trade values may be regarded as unfair.[29] Some of these doctrines have been relied on by the courts in order to protect investments related to copyright law before they became protected by neighbouring rights.[30]

In particular, two aspects deserve attention. First, the methodology of unfair competition law consists of an interesting mix of per se rules, of rules proscribing certain types of unfair conduct and of general clauses (2.2.2). Secondly, unfair competition law is market-sensitive, but the need for speedy injunctions often prevents a full market analysis. It is interesting to see how unfair competition law deals with this issue (2.2.3).

4.2.2.2 Methodology

Since its origins, unfair competition law had to answer to two challenges. First, the notion of 'fairness' is vague and elusive. As a nineteenth century English court famously put it: 'To draw a line between fair and unfair competition, between what is reasonable and unreasonable, passes the power of the courts.'[31] Secondly, markets are dynamic. As *Josef Kohler* noted, unfair competition is 'a Proteus which takes on a thousand different shapes in order to avoid statutory proscriptions'.[32] Hence the law must be flexible enough to react to new trade practices and to changed circumstances.

In early unfair competition law systems case law developed by the courts provided the solution. While initially cases were decided on their

---

28. *See* in particular, Art. 4 lit. f, g of Directive 2006/114/EC of the European Parliament and of the Council of 12 December 2006 concerning misleading and comparative advertising, OJ No. L 376/21, 27 December 2006 and CJEU, case C-487/07, *L'Oréal v. Bellure*, ECLI:EU:C:2009:378.
29. § 4 No. 3 of the Unfair Competition Act (Germany), Art. 11 Unfair Competition Act (Spain), on the French doctrine of parasitic competition *see* P. Le Tourneau, *Le Parasitisme* (Paris: Litec, 1998); A. Lucas, H.-J. Lucas & A. Lucas-Schloetter, *Traité de la propriété littéraire et artistique*, para. 21 (4th ed., Paris: LexisNexis, 2012); on Dutch law *see* D. v. Engelen, *The Misappropriation Doctrine in the Netherlands*, (1991) IIC 11.
30. The German Supreme Court, for example, granted protection to broadcasters and to organizers of concerts and other events at which works are performed on the basis of unfair competition law before the respective neighbouring rights were provided by §§ 81, 87 Copyright Act 1965, *see* BGH GRUR 1962, 470, 474–476 – *AKI*; BGH GRUR 1963, 575 – *Vortragsabend [Recitation Soiree]*.
31. *Mogul Steamship v. McGregor, Gow & Co.*, 23 QBD 598, 625–626 (1889) per Fry L.J.
32. J. Kohler, *Recht des Markenschutzes* (Würzburg: Staehl, 1884), 60: 'die Unredlichkeit ist ein Proteus, der sich in tausend Formen flüchtet und gerade die gesetzlich verpönten Gestalten vermeidet, um in unzähligen Verkleidungen dem loyalen Verkehr die Früchte seiner redlichen Bemühungen abzujagen: ein Proteus, welcher daher nur mit einem ebenso gestaltenreichen Rechtsprincip, nicht durch das Spezialmittel eines einzelnen formalen Rechtsinstituts wirksam bekämpft werden kann'.

individual merits only, gradually clusters of cases emerged which were increasingly governed by judge-made rules. The categories of unfair competition developed by the French courts under section 1382 *Code civil* and the *Fallgruppen* of the former section 1 of the German Act against Unfair Competition of 1909 are examples in point.[33] In modern legislation these judge-made doctrines have increasingly been replaced by non-exhaustive statutory catalogues of unfair practices, which are supplemented by a general clause. Article 10*bis* of the Paris Convention provides an early example of this legislative technique. More elaborate catalogues of unfair practices were introduced in the 1980s and 1990s, for example in Switzerland and Spain. German law followed in 2004, when the former judge-made categories were codified.

Thus the modern answer to the double challenge outlined above consists of a combination of specific examples and general catch-all provisions. Meanwhile the prime example is provided by the UCPD. First, a 'black list' proscribes thirty-one rather well-defined practices as unfair. In these cases there is no need to show any particular impact on consumer behaviour or on markets. These practices are irrebuttably presumed to have an impact on the consumer's decision-making process. Secondly, provisions of a medium level of abstraction prohibit the most typical forms of unfair trading: misleading practices, violations of duties of information and aggressive practices. These provisions have a defined scope, but they allow the courts to take account of all circumstances of the case. They do not prohibit the respective practices per se, but they are subject to an impact test: the practice must be likely to cause a consumer to take a transactional decision that he would not have taken otherwise. Thirdly, a general clause prohibits unfair commercial practices in general. The term 'unfair' is not defined, but Article 5(2) UCPD provides two guidelines: the practice must be contrary to the requirements of professional diligence; and it must have a negative impact on the consumer's economic behaviour. Since the UCPD pre-empts both more liberal and stricter national laws, several Member States had to replace former per se prohibitions by market effect rules. For example, Belgian,[34] Austrian[35] and German[36] bans on combined offers were held to be inconsistent with the UCPD. As a consequence, German law now only

33. *See* A. Ohly, *Richterrecht und Generalklausel im Recht des unlauteren Wettbewerbs* (Köln, Berlin, Bonn, München: Carl Heymanns, 1997), 253–310, 315–326.

34. CJEU, cases C-261/07, C-299/07, *VTB-VAB v. Total Belgium and Galatea v. Sanoma*, ECLI:EU:C:2009:244.

35. CJEU, case C-540/08, *Mediaprint v. 'Österreich'-Zeitungsverlag*, ECLI:EU:C:2010:660.

36. CJEU, case C-304/08, *Zentrale zur Bekämpfung des unlauteren Wettbewerbs v. Plus Warenhandelsgesellschaft*, ECLI:EU:C:2010:12.

objects to combined offers when they are misleading or when they have any other negative impact on the consumer's economic behaviour.[37]

The strength of this approach is that it combines certainty in clear cases with flexibility to deal with unforeseen situations. It also requires an economic effect and only waives this requirement in well-defined clear cases. But the model also has its drawbacks. The 'black list' has been criticized for compiling partly irrelevant, partly ill-defined cases. The 'consumer effects' test is often bypassed because the courts tend to assume a negative impact once a misleading or aggressive practice has been established. The general provision of 'unfair practices' is notoriously difficult to apply. Commentators have found it difficult to agree on cases beyond misleading and aggressive practices. While these objections show the difficulties involved in formulating a convincing 'black list' and in applying any market effects tests, they do not undermine the three-step approach as such. It remains a promising model for other areas of market-related regulation.

4.2.2.3 How to Apply Market Effects Tests?

Most provisions of unfair competition law prohibit a trade practice only when it has an effect on consumers or markets. As explained above, the UCPD only proscribes the 'black listed' practices per se. In all other cases trade practices are only unfair if they affect the economic behaviour of consumers. According to section 3a of the German Act against Unfair Competition of 2015, the breach of a statutory duty is only unfair if it is likely to affect the interests of consumers, competitors or other market participants. The common law tort of passing off has three elements, all of which are market-sensitive: there must be goodwill, a misrepresentation and damage. Some authors who think that unfair competition law should allow courts to fill gaps in the intellectual property system often make such additional protection dependent on proof of a market failure.[38] This criterion has been adopted by some courts.[39]

In this respect there is an obvious parallel between unfair competition law and antitrust law, which also looks at the effects that competitive acts have on markets. There is, however, an important procedural difference. Competition authorities have the factual possibility and the legal power to

37. *See* BGH GRUR 2011, 532 – *Millionen-Chance II [Million Chance II]*. In 2015, the former ban on linking the sale of goods with lotteries or prize competitions (§ 4 No. 6 Unfair Competition Act 2004) was abolished altogether.
38. A. Peukert, *Güterzuordnung als Rechtsprinzip* (Tübingen: Mohr Siebeck, 2008), 812–813; A. Ohly, *Hartplatzhelden.de oder: Wohin mit dem unmittelbaren Leistungsschutz?*, GRUR 2010, 487, 492–493.
39. BGH GRUR 2016, 729, para. 28 – *Pippi-Langstrumpf-Kostüm II [Pippi Longstocking Costume II]*.

investigate market circumstances.[40] As a result, their decisions usually provide extensive facts about the particular market situation. The downside is that competition proceedings can take a very long time. In unfair competition law, however, lengthy proceedings are unacceptable. Often unfair practices must be enjoined immediately. A misleading advertisement, for example, will not usually be available for a very long time. Consumers, competitors and other market participants can only be protected effectively if speedy injunctive relief is available. In countries where administrative authorities enforce unfair competition law, these authorities must have the power to stop unfair practices immediately. In systems which mainly rely on civil law enforcement, claimants often seek interlocutory relief. In such cases a rich investigation of market structures and effects would simply take too much time.

In practice it is probably fair to say that unfair competition courts rely on simple heuristics rather than on sophisticated market analyses. The EU unfair competition law directives are based on a model of rational consumer behaviour, although an analysis informed by behavioural economics shows that consumers are biased in several respects.[41] When applying national provisions implementing the UCPD, courts tend to assume an effect on the consumer's economic behaviour without further investigation.[42] Even protection against misappropriation is sometimes granted without any evidence of a market failure; sometimes unfair competition courts are driven by a strong urge to prevent imitation and neglect the limits of intellectual property law.[43] On the other hand there are examples of misappropriation cases in which the courts at least examine the legal framework and discuss whether it already provides for sufficient protection. The German Federal Supreme Court, for example, was invited by a regional football association to enjoin the operation of a website which allowed football fans to upload video clips

40. On assessing market effects in competition law, *see* the contribution by S. Bechtold to this volume.

41. *See* M. Leistner, *Behavioural Economics und Lauterkeitsrecht, Versuch einer Annäherung*, ZGE/IPJ 3–58 (2009).

42. Article 7 UCPD prohibits the omission of material information, provided the omission is likely to influence the consumers' transactional decisions. However, in BGH GRUR 2013, 1169, para. 19 – *Brandneu von der IFA [Brand New from the IFA]* the German Supreme Court held that the omission of material information necessarily has an impact on the consumers' decision process. Meanwhile, the BGH seems to have abolished this approach and seems to assess the influence on consumers on a case-by-case basis, *see* BGH GRUR 2016, 1076, para. 55 – *LGA-tested*.

43. *See* W. Gordon, *On Owning Information: Intellectual Property and the Restitutionary Impulse*, 18 Va. L. Rev. 149, 150–163; D. Visser, *Intellectual Property and Unfair Competition Law*, in: A. Ohly (ed.), *Common Principles of European Intellectual Property Law* (Tübingen: Mohr Siebeck, 2012), 246, 248–254; M. Leistner, in: O. Teplitzky, N. Peifer, M. Leistner (eds), *UWG, Großkommentar* vol. 2 § 4 No. 9 para. 170 (2nd ed., Berlin: De Gruyter, 2013); A. Ohly, in: A. Ohly & O. Sosnitza (eds), *UWG, Kommentar*, § 4 paras 3/13, 3/61, 3/62 (7th ed., Munich: Beck, 2016).

showing short scenes of amateur matches. The Court decided in favour of the defendants: first, property law already provided sufficient protection, secondly the freedom of expression militated against an injunction.[44] This is a normative legal rather than an empirical economic analysis, but it does show that the Court took the market effects of a prohibition into account.

4.2.3 Trade Mark Law

4.2.3.1 Emancipation and Extension

Trade marks have only rather recently been admitted to the intellectual property club. While signs have been protected since ancient times, they were not regarded as the object of property for most of their history. Rather, it was seen as the role of public and criminal law to guarantee the good and well-established rules of trading.[45] The origins of civil law protection lie in causes of action against deceit or fraud.[46] But even in the nineteenth century, when intellectual property received its modern shape, trade mark protection was widely seen as a part of unfair competition law. In the UK, the regime of registered trade marks branched off from the common law action for passing off;[47] in Germany, until the 1970s, trade mark law was seen as a part of unfair competition law. The leading commentaries such as *Rudolf Callmann's*[48] or that founded by *Adolf Baumbach* and continued by *Wolfgang Hefermehl* combined both fields of law in one volume.[49] Hence, historically, copyright and trade marks do not seem to have much in common, as trade mark law does not protect creators or creations, but market transparency.

In the past decades, however, trade marks have increasingly become accepted as intellectual property rights. As *Andreas Sattler* has shown in his historical analysis, the modern development of trade mark law has been one of emancipation and extension.[50] Trade marks have become independent

44. BGH GRUR 2011, 436, paras 19–32 – *Hartplatzhelden.de*.
45. D. Klippel, in; F.L. Ekey, A. Bender, G. Fuchs-Wissemann, *Markenrecht* vol. 1, E 1, paras 2–4 (3rd ed., Heidelberg: C.F. Müller, 2014).
46. For English law *see* Wadlow, *supra* n. 18, at paras 1-37-1-42; for Roman and German law *see* Kohler, *supra* n. 32, at 38–41.
47. Wadlow, *supra* n. 18, at paras 1-51-1-52.
48. R. Callmann, *Der unlautere Wettbewerb* (Mannheim: Bensheimer, 1932). The same applies to the commentary founded by Callmann after his emigration to the US: R. Callmann, *The Law of Unfair Competition and Trade-Marks* (2nd ed., Chicago: Callaghan, 1950).
49. From the first edition: A. Baumbach, *Kommentar zum Wettbewerbsrecht* (Berlin: Otto Liebermann, 1929), until the 11th ed.: A. Baumbach & W. Hefermehl, *Wettbewerbs- und Warenzeichenrecht* (11th ed., Munich: Beck, 1974).
50. A. Sattler, *Emanzipation und Expansion des Markenrechts. Die Entstehungsgeschichte des Markengesetzes von 1995* (Tübingen: Mohr Siebeck, 2015), 457–478 et passim; *see*

objects of intellectual property. They can be freely transferred and separated from the goodwill of their initial owner. International agreements and regional laws treat trade marks as intellectual property rights, subject to the same standards of enforcement that apply to copyright and patent law. According to Article 10(1) of the EU Trade Mark Directive 2015 (TMD),[51] 'the registration of a trade mark shall confer on the proprietor exclusive rights therein'. At the same time, trade mark law has expanded beyond the protection against confusion. Under Article 16(3) TRIPS, Member States are under an obligation to protect well-known marks against dilution by tarnishment and by blurring. EU law goes further by allowing the owner of a well-known mark to prevent misappropriation without having to show damage. On its face, Article 10(1)(a) TMD comes close to a communication monopoly over a sign by prohibiting the use of an identical sign for identical products per se, thereby granting 'absolute' protection.

4.2.3.2 The Importance of Trade Mark Functions

But despite this apparent extension and despite intensive lobbying by trade mark owners, trade mark law has not lost sight of its inherent limits. One tool which has been used by courts in many jurisdictions was the requirement of 'trade mark use', according to which not every use of a sign counts as infringing.[52] The sign must be used in a trade mark sense, i.e., the average consumer must understand it as an indicator of commercial origin. This would not be the case when the sign is used as a mere ornament or as a mere description.[53] However, the doctrine of trade mark use has been criticized by authors who consider it too formalistic and who advocate a broader perspective which focuses on the context of the use.[54] The case law of the CJEU seemed unstable for a while, but meanwhile the theory of trade mark functions has replaced the 'trade mark use' test. Rather than requiring use 'as a mark', the Court enquires whether the defendant uses the sign in the course of trade for his or her own goods or services and whether the use is likely to

also A. Sattler, *Dilution of Well-Known Trademarks – an Analysis of Its Foundations in Germany and the European Union*, (2011) ZGE/IPJ 304–328.

51. Directive 2008/95/EC of the European Parliament and of the Council of 22 October 2008 to approximate the laws of the Member States relating to trade marks (codified version), OJ No. L 299/25, 8 November 2008 (replacing Council Directive 89/104/EEC of 21 December 1988 to approximate the laws of the Member States relating to trade marks, OJ No. L 40/1, 11 February 1989, as amended).
52. For German law *see* S. Eichhammer, *Die markenmäßige Benutzung* (Tübingen: Mohr Siebeck, 2008), for English law *see* *R. v. Johnstone*, UKHL 28, paras 74–75 (2003).
53. A. Strowel draws on this criterion and suggests a 'use of the work as a work' test as a factor limiting copyright infringement in his contribution to this volume.
54. G.B. Dinwoodie & M.D. Janis, *Confusion Over Use: Contextualism in Trademark Law*, 92 Iowa L. Rev. 1597, 1622–1662 (2007); A. Kur, *Confusion Over Use? – Die Benutzung 'als Marke' im Lichte der EuGH-Rechtsprechung*, GRUR Int. 2008, 1, 11–12.

affect the protected functions of the mark.[55] According to the Court, these functions go beyond the function of indicating commercial origin, they also encompass the quality, advertising, investment and communication functions.[56] The function analysis plays a different role in each of the three categories of infringement.

In cases of double identity (Article 10(2)(a) TMD), the likelihood of a negative impact on one of the functions has effectively become an additional condition of infringement. A line of cases in point are the keyword advertising cases.[57] The CJEU has held that the use of another trader's mark as a keyword by a competitor only interferes with the origin function of a trade mark when the advertisement 'does not enable an average internet user, or enables that user only with difficulty, to ascertain whether the goods or services referred to therein originate from the proprietor of the trade mark or an undertaking economically connected to it'.[58] The investment function is affected when the use 'substantially interferes with the proprietor's use of its trade mark to acquire or preserve a reputation capable of attracting consumers and retaining their loyalty'.[59] This approach has met with significant criticism from authors who have pointed out that it results in legal uncertainty and that it overstretches the limits of Article 10(1)(a).[60] In the discussions preceding the recent trade mark law reform, the Commission recommended restricting double-identity infringement to cases in which the origin function is affected,[61] but this proposal has not been adopted. While this criticism has not lost its force, it must be acknowledged that the CJEU has been able to achieve balanced results on the basis of the function theory. In the *Interflora* case, the Court stressed the potential of keyword advertising

---

55. CJEU, case C-487/07, *L'Oréal v. Bellure*, ECLI:EU:C:2009:378, paras 58–65; cases C-236/08 – C-238/08, *Google France v. Louis Vuitton* et al., ECLI:EU:C:2010:159, paras 75–98.
56. CJEU, case C-487/07, *L'Oréal v. Bellure*, ECLI:EU:C:2009:378, para. 58.
57. CJEU, cases C-236/08 – C-238/08, *Google France v. Louis Vuitton* et al., ECLI:EU:C:2010:159; case C-558/08, *Portakabin v. Primakabin*, ECLI:EU:C:2010:416; case C-323/09, *Interflora v. Marks & Spencer*, ECLI:EU:C:2011:604.
58. CJEU, case C-487/07, *L'Oréal v. Bellure*, ECLI:EU:C:2009:378, para. 84.
59. CJEU, case C-323/09, *Interflora v. Marks & Spencer*, ECLI:EU:C:2011:604, para. 62.
60. M. Senftleben, *Function Theory and International Exhaustion: Why It Is Wise to Confine the Double Identity Rule in EU Trade Mark Law to Cases Affecting the Origin Function*, EIPR 518, 518–521 (2014); A. Ohly, *Keyword Advertising or Why the ECJ's Functional Approach to Trade Mark Infringement Does Not Function*, IIC 897 (2010); A. Ohly, *Die Markenverletzung bei Doppelidentität nach L'Oréal: eine Kritik*, in: W. Erdmann et al. (eds), *Festschrift für Michael Loschelder zum 65. Geburtstag* (Köln: Otto Schmidt, 2010), 265–278, but *see* the reply by A. Kur, *Trade Marks Function, Don't They? CJEU Jurisprudence and Unfair Competition Principles*, IIC 434, 442–447 (2014).
61. Articles 10(2)(a) TMD and 9(2)(a) Council Regulation (EC) No. 207/2009 of 26 February 2009 on the Community trade mark, OJ L 78/1 (CTMR), of the Commission proposals published on 27 March 2013, COM(2013) 162 final (amendments to the CTMR) and COM(2013) 161 final.

to contribute to consumer information and to allow a fair comparison between products.[62]

Causing a likelihood of confusion (Article 10(1)(b) TMD) remains by far the most important category of infringement. There is a strong economic justification for preventing confusion, which does not need to be rehearsed here.[63] The likelihood of confusion is assessed from the perspective of an average consumer. Legal systems differ as to how close this assessment should be to market reality. The traditional European test has tended to be rather abstract: confusion is judged on the basis of three general criteria: similarity between the registered mark and the sign used by the infringer, similarity of products and distinctiveness of the mark.[64] In this respect there used to be a difference between trade mark confusion and misleading practices in unfair competition law, the determination of which always requires an analysis of all circumstances of the case. In the US, the infringement test always seemed to be more fact-sensitive. But the recent case law of the CJEU also shows a tendency to take more account of the specific circumstances of the case. This is particularly evident in cases concerning keyword advertising, in which the CJEU has applied one and the same test to determine whether the origin function has been affected and to assess the likelihood of confusion.[65] It has directed the national courts to enquire whether the particular advertisement causes consumers to assume a business relation between the owner of the mark and the user.

In the third category of infringement the effects-oriented approach is even more evident. Well-known marks are protected against dilution and misappropriation, but the likelihood of these effects must be shown by the claimant, and the court must take all circumstances of the case into account. A finding of damage to the distinctiveness of the mark, for example, requires 'evidence of a change in the economic behaviour of the average consumer'.[66] The test applied by the CJEU to cases of misappropriation of reputation, however, has been less specific. The Court enquires whether the defendant, by using the mark, is riding on 'the coat-tails of the mark with a reputation in order to benefit from the power of attraction, the reputation and the

62. CJEU, case C-323/09, *Interflora v. Marks & Spencer*, ECLI:EU:C:2011:604, paras 57–58, 64.
63. On the economic analysis of trade mark law *see* W.M. Landes & R.A. Posner, *The Economic Structure of Intellectual Property Law* (Cambridge (Mass.) and London: Belknap Press, 2003), 166–209; N.S. Economides, *The Economics of Trademarks*, 78 TMR 523 (1988); G.B. Ramello, *What's in a Sign, Trademark Law and Economic Theory*, in: M. McAleer & L. Oxley (eds), *Economic and Legal Issues in Intellectual Property* (Malden (Mass): Blackwell, 2007), 65.
64. CJEU, case C-39/97, *Canon v. MGM*, ECLI:EU:C:1998:442, paras 15–19.
65. CJEU, case C-278/08, *BergSpechte v. trekking.at Reisen*, ECLI:EU:C:2010:163, paras 38–40.
66. CJEU, case C-252/07, *Intel v. CPM United Kingdom*, ECLI:EU:C:2008:655, para. 77.

prestige of that mark and to exploit, without paying any financial compensation, the marketing effort expended by the proprietor of the mark in order to create and maintain the mark's image'.[67] This rather emotive formula, which is strongly reminiscent of the French doctrine of '*parasitisme*', has been criticized both judicially[68] and in the academic literature, precisely because it allows courts to disregard the market realities and to assume misappropriation in cases in which a no-name manufacturer makes a reference to luxury products. Once dilution or misappropriation is established, the courts still need to enquire whether such use is unfair and without due cause. These flexible notions allow for a balancing of interest, although the courts do not always take this possibility seriously.

4.3 FORMALISM AS THE PROBLEM OF DIGITAL COPYRIGHT LAW

4.3.1 Formalism and Economic Reality

As regards market-sensitivity, copyright law compares unfavourably with trade mark and unfair competition law. Copyright is infringed when: (a) the subject-matter in issue is protected as a work or as the object of a neighbouring right, (b) the infringing act falls within the scope of copyright and constitutes an infringing act and (c) no defences are made out. The subject-matter of copyright and neighbouring rights (a) is defined in very broad terms. The originality threshold may contribute to the balance between protection and the public domain, but it is very low or, in the case of some neighbouring rights, non-existent. Copyright scope (b1) [69] presents a problem when only parts of the work are used or when the work is adapted.[70] Here, courts have some flexibility, but the criteria for determining whether an

67. CJEU, case C-487/07, *L'Oréal v. Bellure*, ECLI:EU:C:2009:378, para. 49.
68. *L'Oréal v. Bellure*, [2010] EWCA Civ 535, paras 17–20 per Jacob L.J.
69. M.A. Lemley & M.P. McKenna, *Scope*, 57 Wm. & Mary L. Rev. 2197 (2015–2016) have recently argued in favour of taking the determination of scope, not only in patent law, more seriously.
70. The distinction between scope and infringing acts is often not drawn as openly in copyright law as it is in patent law. The adaptation right, in particular, conflates both. Art. 12 of the Berne Convention classifies the adaptation right as an independent economic right, although the extent to which copyright law provides protection against the use of a work in an altered form is essentially an issue of scope, *see*, for German law, BGH GRUR 2014, 258, paras 32–48 – *Pippi-Langstrumpf-Kostüm I [Pippi Longstocking Costume I]*, headnote translated in [2014] IIC 467, and M. Loschelder, *Vervielfältigung oder Bearbeitung? – Zum Verhältnis des § 16 UrhG zu § 23 UrhG*, GRUR 2011, 1078, 1082–1083. English courts tend to ask whether the defendant has reproduced a substantial part of the work (s. 16 (3)(a) Copyright, Designs and Patents Act 1988) rather than applying the adaptation right, *see Designers Guild Ltd. v. Russell Williams (Textiles) Ltd.*

adaptation is still a use of the work or whether the use of a part is substantial are predominantly non-economic. There is no independent definition of infringement. Rather, any act which falls within the broadly defined economic rights constitutes a prima facie infringement (b2). In US law, the fair use defence gives some flexibility for fine-tuning and allows the consideration of economic effects (c). In EU law, however, there is an exhaustive list of more or less well-defined defences.[71]

In particular, the economic rights, which are the focus of this chapter, are defined in abstract terms as categories of acts which only the owner is allowed to perform or to authorize. Whenever a person carries out any of the acts allocated to the owner without being able to invoke a statutory exception, he or she infringes. This approach is formalist. It does not consider the economic consequences of individual acts, but judges them on the basis of a formal classification.

It must be admitted that a list of per se prohibitions is not necessarily inappropriate. As seen above, even unfair competition law, despite being highly market-sensitive, provides for a black list. But per se rules are only acceptable when economic experience permits a presumption to the effect that the proscribed acts have a negative impact on markets or in any other way interfere with the function of the right.

This is borne out by a comparison with patent law, which, like copyright, applies property logic by defining the scope of the right and infringing acts, and by providing for a list of exceptions. But nevertheless the conditions of patent infringement mirror the economic reality. First, private acts are exempted from infringement. Secondly, the infringing acts correspond to commercial reality. When Article 25 of the Agreement on a Unified Patent Court (UPC Agreement) confers on the patent owner the exclusive right of 'making, offering, placing on the market or using a product which is the subject-matter of the patent, or importing or storing the product for those purposes', it reflects the usual ways of marketing technical products. Certainly the modern patent system is not beyond criticism.[72] Critics argue that the patentability threshold may be too low, that the patent system should not have been extended to new subject-matter such as genes or computer software, that some exceptions are too narrow, that compulsory licences should be granted more frequently or that courts in Continental Europe should not grant injunctions as a matter of course. But rarely, if ever, are the 'economic rights' stemming from a patent criticized as inappropriate.

[2001] FSR 11, paras 23–30; *Baigent v. Random House Group Ltd.*, [2006] EWCA Civ 247, paras 67–94. Again, the substantiality test determines the scope of copyright.

71. Although economic considerations sometimes play a role when courts interpret these provisions, especially when they are interpreted in the light of the three-step test.

72. *See supra* n. 4.

In copyright law, however, the system of economic rights mirrors the economic reality of the late nineteenth and early twentieth century. This system has been imposed on digital communication in a maximalist way. This is particularly evident with respect to the reproduction right. Other economic rights allow a more nuanced application, but courts still have the tendency to interpret them *in dubio pro auctore*.

4.3.2 Reproduction

Historically, the reproduction right was the earliest economic right. Copyright emerged at a time when printing technology was widely available and when reprints became a problem. The Statute of Anne of 1710 was the legislative answer to a dispute between the London Stationers and other, non-privileged printers.[73] In Germany, the debate preceding the first copyright acts is known as *die Nachdruckdebatte*, which translates into 'the reprinting debate'.[74] While it has been pointed out that even then it was the unauthorized distribution rather than the reprint which affected the authors' and initial printers' markets, printing was an act which produced a marketable product.[75] As the experience of patent law shows, it seems fair and reasonable to extend intellectual property protection to steps which directly precede the marketing. Users, on the other hand, did not print, and private copying by hand did not harm the right owners' markets. Even after the advent of photocopying technology the reproduction right made economic sense. Private copying now became a challenge, but as long as photocopiers were distinct machines levy systems provided satisfactory answers.

In the digital context, however, the economic and social significance of reproduction has changed dramatically, as has been pointed out by many copyright scholars[76] and, indeed, by most members of our research group.[77]

73. *See* B. Sherman & L. Bently, *The Making of Modern Intellectual Property Law* (Cambridge: CUP, 1999), 11–15.
74. *See* M. Vogel, in: U. Loewenheim, M. Leistner & A. Ohly (eds), *Urheberrecht, Kommentar*, (5th ed., Munich: Beck, forthcoming), Einleitung, paras 117–123; D. Klippel, *Ueber die Unzulässigkeit des Büchernachdrucks nach dem natürlichen Zwangsrecht. Der Diskurs über den Büchernachdruck im Jahre 1784*, in: T.J. Chiusi (ed.), *Das Recht und seine historischen Grundlagen: Festschrift für Elmar Wadle zum 70. Geburtstag* (Berlin: Duncker & Humblot, 2008), 477–498.
75. As has been pointed out by many authors. *See*, for example, the contribution by S. Dusollier to this volume, and D. Gervais, *Towards a New Core International Copyright Norm: The Reverse Three-Step Test*, 9 Marq. Intell. Prop. L. Rev. 1, 10 (2005).
76. *See*, for example, A.F. Christie, *A Proposal for Simplifying United Kingdom Copyright Law*, EIPR 1 (2001); S. Depreeuw, *The Variable Scope of the Exclusive Economic Rights in Copyright* (Alphen aan den Rijn: Wolters Kluwer, 2014); J. Litman, *Revising Copyright Law for the Information Age*, 75 Oregon L. Rev. 19 (1996).
77. *See* the contributions by S. Dusollier and A. Strowel to this volume. O. A. Rognstad, in his contribution, notes that the artificial isolation of reproduction leads to unnecessary

It is impossible to enjoy works in digital form without reproducing them at least temporarily.[78] Reproductions may create a marketable commodity, but unlike in the case of commercial printing it is impossible to presume that a reproduction is usually followed by an act of marketing. Indeed, as the case of inline linking shows, internet actors can use works for commercial purposes without having reproduced them first. Nevertheless legislation not only extended the reproduction right to the digital sphere, it did so in a maximalist way. Despite suggestions to the contrary,[79] EU legislation allocated the right to make or authorize permanent, but also transient reproductions to the right owners. The users' interest in free browsing is accommodated by the mandatory exception provided by Article 5(1) InfoSoc Directive,[80] but this exception is fraught with open and unclear terms which have given rise to considerable litigation.[81]

4.3.3 Communication to the Public

The right of communication to the public is better suited to capturing the use of works in the digital context. The terms 'communication' and 'public' are both rather general and allow the courts a certain leeway. Nevertheless, Article 3 of the InfoSoc Directive does not refer to the economic effects of the act of communication. On the contrary, Recital 23 stresses that the right should be understood in a broad sense and that it should cover any transmission or retransmission.

---

complexity when dealing with online exploitation: *Restructuring the Economic Rights in Copyright: Some Reflections on an 'Alternative Model'*, 62 J. Copyright Soc'y U.S.A. 503, 525, 535 (2014–2015).

78. R. Sucker, *Der digitale Werkgenuss im Urheberrecht* (Tübingen: Mohr Siebeck, 2014), 177–193 et passim.
79. *See* P.B. Hugenholtz et al., *The Recasting of Copyright & Related Rights for the Knowledge Economy*, 2006, 47–48 (with further references), available at http://ec.europa.eu/internal_market/copyright/docs/studies/etd2005imd195recast_report_2006.pdf (accessed 12 December 2017).
80. Directive 2001/29/EC of 22 May 2001 on the harmonisation of certain aspects of copyright and related rights in the information society, OJ No. L 167/10, 22 June 2001.
81. *See* CJEU, case C-360/13, *Public Relations Consultants Association v. Newspaper Licensing Agency*, ECLI:EU:C:2014:1195; the issue of whether reproductions made in the course of watching a video stream amount to an infringement when the streaming is carried out without the consent of the right owner was left open by the CJEU in case C-314/12, *UPC Telekabel v. Constantin Film*, ECLI:EU:C:2014:192, and is still moot, *see* for example, AG Potsdam ZUM-RD 2014, 587; M. Stieper, *Rezeptiver Werkgenuss als rechtmäßige Nutzung – Urheberrechtliche Bewertung des Streaming vor dem Hintergrund des EuGH-Urteils in Sachen FAPL/Murphy*, MMR 2012, 12–17.

The CJEU's case law on Article 3 has been the object of widespread analysis,[82] not least in our research group.[83] Three remarks may therefore suffice.

First, the Court has used the abstract and general language of the directive as a starting-point for the development of its own case law. Early cases such as *SGAE v. Rafael*[84] were very much decided on their own merits. But gradually a two-step test has emerged, which was restated in cases like *Svensson*[85] and *OSA*[86] and which has since then been repeated on several occasions. The Court enquires whether there is: (1) an act of communication and whether it is (2) to the public. The term 'act of communication' is defined in very broad terms as every kind of deliberately making available, the Court even regards hyperlinking as a form of communication. The Court has been invited both by academic authors[87] and by AG Wathelet[88] to give up this approach. But the CJEU is highly unlikely to admit a mistake: it has meanwhile confirmed that linking is in itself an act of communication.[89] The test of whether a communication is made 'to the public' has two prongs. The first element is quantitative: the public consists of a 'fairly large' and indeterminate group of persons. The second element, which could also be seen as an independent third condition of 'communication to the public', is that the communication must either use a new kind of technology or reach a 'new public', i.e., a public which is different from the one the copyright owner initially had in mind. Methodologically, this development from individual judgments to a more rule-based approach, which becomes increasingly refined, bears strong resemblance to the unfair competition law methodology outlined above.

Secondly, the CJEU's judgments on communication to the public differ in their degree of formalism. Sometimes the two-step test outlined above has

---

82. *See* the overviews given by M. Grünberger, *Bedarf es einer Harmonisierung der Verwertungsrechte und Schranken?*, ZUM 2015, 273; M. Leistner, *Urheberrecht an der Schnittstelle zwischen Unionsrecht und nationalem Recht*, GRUR 2014, 1145, 1149–1153; A. Lucas-Schloetter, *Das Recht der öffentlichen Wiedergabe in der Rechtsprechung des Europäischen Gerichtshofs*, ZGE/IPJ 5 (2013) 84–102; J. v. Ungern-Sternberg, *Urheberechtliche Verwertungsrechte im Lichte des Unionsrechts*, GRUR 2012, 1198.
83. Strowel, *supra* n. 53, at 8 et seq.
84. CJEU, case C-306/05, *SGAE v. Rafael Hoteles*, ECLI:EU:C:2006:764.
85. CJEU, case C-466/12, *Svensson v. Retriever Sverige*, ECLI:EU:C:2014:76, paras 16–24.
86. CJEU, case C-351/12, *OSA v. Léčebné lázně*, ECLI:EU:C:2014:110, paras 25–31.
87. European Copyright Society, *The Reference to the CJEU in case C-466/12 Svensson*, available at https://ssrn.com/abstract=2220326 (accessed 12 December 2017); E. Arezzo, *Hyperlinks and Making Available Right in the European Union – What Future for the Internet After Svensson?*, IIC 524, 539 (2014).
88. Opinion in CJEU, case C-160/15, *GS Media v. Sanoma Media, Playboy Enterprises and Dekker*, ECLI:EU:C:2016:221, para. 54.
89. CJEU, case C-160/15, *GS Media v. Sanoma Media, Playboy Enterprises and Dekker*, ECLI:EU:C:2016:644, para. 50.

been applied in a rather technical way[90] without regard to the underlying economic interests. In *Svensson*,[91] the Court did not overtly address the copyright owner's interest in being protected against links to pirate websites or the public interest in the freedom of communication online. It applied its methodology and concluded very briefly that there was no 'new public' when the target website had already been accessible to the general public. In *BestWater*, the German Supreme Court had given reasons in its reference as to why it thought that framing differed from mere surface linking: whereas a hyperlink is a reference to another website, framing may allow the operator of a website to fully enjoy the economic benefits of using the work. For the user, it may be a perfect technical substitute for hosting the file on his own site. The CJEU disregarded these arguments, considered the cases of linking and framing to be 'identical' in the sense of Article 99 of the CJEU's Rules of Procedure and hence decided *BestWater* by reasoned order with a mere reference to the reasons given in *Svensson*.[92] The recent *GS Media* judgment,[93] however, is different. It concerned a hyperlink to a website where a work had been made available without the author's consent. The *Svensson* test seemed to point to an all-or-nothing solution: [94] either there is always a 'new public' in this situation because the owner had never given his consent[95] or there is no 'new public' when the website had been freely available before.[96] The Court, however, does not apply the *Svensson* test in a formalistic way. It addresses the tension between a high level of copyright protection and the right to freedom of expression and it notes that it may be difficult for persons placing a link to find out whether the work on the target website was made available with the right owner's consent. The Court goes on to use its case law as a tool-box and attaches weight to two criteria which are not mentioned in the directive and which were irrelevant under more traditional approaches to 'communication to the public'. It enquires whether

---

90. M. Grünberger refers to this as a 'more technogical approach': *supra* n. 82, at 276.
91. CJEU, case C-466/12, *Svensson v. Retriever Sverige*, ECLI:EU:C:2014:76, paras 16–24.
92. Hence the order is only available in German and French: CJEU, case C-348/13, *BestWater v. Mebes and Potsch*, ECLI:EU:C:2014:2315.
93. CJEU, case C-160/15, *GS Media v. Sanoma Media, Playboy Enterprises and Dekker*, ECLI:EU:C:2016:644.
94. But *see* A. Kur, *Completely Exhausted or Just Relaxed? Some Thoughts on the CJEU's 'New Exhaustion Principle' in Internet Linking Cases*, in: G. Karnell et al., *Liber Amicorum Jan Rosén* (Visby: eddy.de, 2016), 443.
95. This is how the *Svensson* and *BestWater* judgments were interpreted by the German Federal Supreme Court in its follow-up decision to *BestWater:* BGH GRUR 2016, 171, para. 34 – *Die Realität II [The Reality II]*; *see* the criticism by G. Spindler, *Das Ende der Links: Framing und Hyperlinks auf rechtswidrige Inhalte als eigenständige Veröffentlichung?*, GRUR 2016, 157, 159–160. This understanding is also in line with the ALAI Report and Opinion on the making available and communication to the public in the internet environment – focus on linking techniques on the Internet of 16 September 2013, pp. 7–8, available at http://www.alai.org/assets/files/resolutions/making-available-right-report-opinion.pdf (accessed 12 December 2017).
96. This is how Grünberger, *supra* n. 82, at 280–282 interpreted the judgment.

the use was or was not for profit, and restricts a potentially overbroad liability by a requirement of actual or constructive knowledge.[97] This flexible approach, which has been confirmed in the *Filmspeler*[98] and *Pirate Bay*[99] judgments, almost turns Article 3 InfoSoc Directive into a 'fair use' provision.

Thirdly, some of the criteria the CJEU applies under Article 3 InfoSoc Directive are based on economic considerations, especially when the Court asks whether the use is made for profit[100] or whether the defendant is using the work in the course of offering an autonomous service.[101] Since the Court, due to the cryptic style of its judgments, never elaborates on the economic basis of its criteria, it is hard to say whether they are rooted in economic analysis or whether they only reflect the intuition of judges who, for better or worse, have not been socialized in the copyright law world. The conclusions reached by the Court are not always plausible.[102] But the reasoning in cases concerning communication to the public clearly shows a tendency away from formalism to an approach which is more open to economic reasoning.

4.3.4 The Liability of Intermediaries

One of the most pressing challenges posed to copyright law in the internet context is the liability of intermediaries. EU law imposes an obligation on states to provide for injunctions against intermediaries, but it leaves the details to the Member States, which still apply very different models, ranging from rather detailed court orders in the UK to the German concept of '*Störerhaftung*' (interferers' liability). Looking in more detail, EU law regulates exceptions from liability for internet service providers, but Articles 12–15 of the E-Commerce Directive[103] only apply to conduct which is

97. CJEU, case C-160/15, *GS Media v. Sanoma Media, Playboy Enterprises and Dekker*, ECLI:EU:C:2016:644, paras 45–53.
98. CJEU, case C-527/15, *Stichting Brein v. Wullems*, ECLI:EU:C:2017:300.
99. CJEU, case C-610/15, *Stichting Brein v. Ziggo BV and XS4All Internet BV*, ECLI: EU:C:2017:456.
100. CJEU, case C-160/15, *GS Media v. Sanoma Media, Playboy Enterprises and Dekker*, ECLI:EU:C:2016:644, para. 51; case C-527/15, *Stichting Brein v. Wullems*, ECLI: EU:C:2017:300, paras 34, 51; case C-610/15, *Stichting Brein v. Ziggo BV and XS4All Internet BV*, ECLI:EU:C:2017:456, paras 29, 46.
101. Joined CJEU cases C-431/09 and C-432/09, *Airfield and Canaal Digital*, ECLI: EU:C:2011:648, para. 80.
102. *See* for example, the more or less open contradiction between CJEU case C-135/10, *SCF v. Del Corso* and case C-117/15, *Reha Training v. GEMA*.
103. Directive 2000/31/EC of the European Parliament and of the Council of 8 June 2000 on certain legal aspects of information society services, in particular electronic commerce, in the Internal Market (Directive on electronic commerce), OJ No. L 178/1, 17 July 2000.

merely technical, automatic and passive. Thus at the moment the harmonization achieved 'applies in an evasive, negative fashion, dictating only when Member States "cannot" impose liability for intermediary activities, not when they can'.[104] What is more, the present regime does not cater for service providers who play an active role and who derive a significant economic benefit from hosting works.

Drawing the line between primary infringement and the liability of intermediaries can be a difficult task. In some trade mark cases, the CJEU has attempted a distinction. A search engine operator who operates a keyword advertising system does not use trade marks which are registered as keywords in its own commercial communication.[105] Hence it can only be liable as an intermediary. The same is true for the operator of an online marketplace.[106] In copyright cases, however, this line gets blurred, as two examples show. First, platforms like YouTube may be seen as intermediaries, because they only allow users to upload video clips.[107] On the other hand YouTube provides an independent service which is, at least partly, a substitute for commercial services like Spotify.[108] Indeed, the CJEU has held the operators of the platform 'The Pirate Bay' to be liable for primary infringement, despite the fact that they do not host any infringing files themselves.[109] Secondly, a person who places a link seems to be a typical intermediary. But in its hyperlink cases, the CJEU has not discussed the distinction between immediate users and intermediaries. Indeed, in its recent judgment in *GS Media*,[110] the Court draws some of the distinctions that have previously been made by national courts in the framework of intermediary liability.

National case law has in part been sensitive to the different economic roles of intermediaries. In German law the scope of the duties of care imposed on intermediaries vary depending on several criteria including the

---

104. C. Angelopoulos, *Beyond the Safe Harbours: Harmonising Substantive Intermediary Liability for Copyright Infringement in Europe*, (2013) IPQ 253.
105. Joined CJEU cases C-236/08 – C-238/08, *Google France v. Louis Vuitton* et al., ECLI:EU:C:2010:159, paras 55–58.
106. CJEU, case C-324/09, *L'Oréal v. eBay*, ECLI:EU:C:2011:474, para. 102.
107. But *see* the opinion of AG Szpunar in case C-610/15, *Stichting Brein v. Ziggo BV*, ECLI:EU:C:2017:99, paras 44–54 in which the AG considers a BitTorrent tracking site like The Pirate Bay as a primary infringer, provided the operators have knowledge of the infringement.
108. On the distinction between primary and secondary liability *see* the Sirinelli report, *Rapport de la mission sur la révision de la directive 2001/29/CE sur l'harmonisation de certains aspects du droit d'auteur et des droits voisins dans la société de l'information*, available at http://www.ladocumentationfrancaise.fr/rapports-publics/154000036/index.shtml (accessed 12 December 2017); and M. Leistner, *Reformbedarf im materiellen Urheberrecht: Online-Plattformen und Aggregatoren*, ZUM 2016, 580, 590.
109. CJEU, case C-610/15, *Stichting Brein v. Ziggo BV and XS4All Internet BV*, ECLI:EU:C:2017:456, paras 36–38.
110. *Supra* n. 97.

profit the intermediary derives from its activity and the degree to which the risk of infringement is increased.[111] In this sense, the German criteria of secondary liability are at least more market-sensitive than those of primary liability. But while courts in several EU jurisdictions have found effective ways of preventing intermediaries from enabling infringement, they have not been able to translate the economic role of modern intermediaries into the law.

4.4 TOWARDS A FAIRNESS-BASED MODEL

4.4.1 Fairness as Market-Sensitivity

In unfair competition law, parts of trade mark law and the law of trade secrets, the standard of fairness plays a central role. At first sight, this standard may seem extremely vague. It also seems to have moral undertones and to draw on the idiosyncratic notions of what individual judges consider as fair or unfair. For this reason the concept of unfair competition has been criticized by common law judges.[112] Indeed it is easy to find judgments which, without any economic foundation, consider market practices as unfair, just because they are unusual or because they take advantage of another trader's efforts. In recent decades, however, the standard of fairness has been refined, both by statutory lists of examples and by courts on a case-by-case basis. In the case law of the CJEU there has been cross-fertilization between trade mark law and the directives on unfair commercial practices and on comparative advertising which, notably, *Annette Kur* regards as the nucleus of a European standard of fair competition.[113] In particular, there are signs in both trade mark and unfair competition law that the courts take more account of the market effects of unfair practices. While Article 39(2) TRIPS puts an obligation on the Member States to prohibit any use of trade secrets which is 'contrary to honest commercial practices'

111. *See* the overviews by Angelopoulos, *supra* n. 104, at 264–270; M. Leistner, *Structural Aspects of Secondary (Provider) Liability in Europe*, JIPLP 75–90 (2014).

112. *See* the Australian case *Moorgate Tobacco Co. Ltd. v. Philip Morris Ltd.*, 3 I.P.R. 545 (1984) per Deane J.: 'The rejection of a general action for "unfair competition" involves no more than a recognition of the fact that the existence of such an action is inconsistent with the established limits of the traditional and statutory causes of action which are available to a trader in respect of damage caused or threatened by a competitor. ... Neither legal principle nor social utility requires or warrants the obliteration of that boundary by the importation of a cause of action whose main characteristic is the scope it allows, under high-sounding generalizations, for judicial indulgence of idiosyncratic notions of what is fair in the market place.'

113. A. Kur, *Europäische Harmonisierung des Lauterkeitsrechts – Verbraucherschutz und danach?*, presentation given on the occasion of the 70th birthday of Karl-Heinz Fezer, 18 April 2016 (forthcoming).

without defining this broad notion in greater detail, the draft EU directive fleshes out this standard by giving examples of unfair behaviour. Thus 'fairness' in unfair competition and trade mark law is a broad and flexible concept which allows the balancing of interests. In modern law it does not draw on extra-legal concepts of morality, but rather on economic concepts, and also on general legal principles and fundamental rights.

But the notion of fairness obviously also forms a part of the concepts of 'fair use' and 'fair dealing' in US and UK copyright law, respectively. Again, 'fairness' in this sense has little to do with morality. In US law, the fair use standard has been concretized by a non-exclusive list of four factors.[114] At least the first and fourth of these factors openly draw on economic criteria. 'Fair use' can be the mirror image of copyright justifications, especially in cases in which 'fair use' prevents a reverse market failure.[115] But again, the fair use and fair dealing clauses allow the courts to take more general principles like the importance of the freedom of expression into account. Thus, despite the different systematic nature of 'unfairness', which gives rise to a cause of action in unfair competition law, and 'fair use', which is a defence in US copyright law, both concepts have striking parallels.

The following approach draws two inspirations from unfair competition and trade mark law. The first is of a substantive nature: it will be argued that copyright law should become more market-sensitive and that, to a varying degree, the infringement test itself should contain a clause which allows the courts to consider the market effects of use. The second is methodological. Copyright law should distinguish between clear cases of uses which amount to infringements per se unless a defence is made out, and cases in which the first allocation of a right already depends on a balancing exercise.

This dual approach could either be referred to as a 'market effects approach' or as a 'fairness based approach'. One can object to the concept of 'fairness' in this context, because it may seem high-sounding, but extremely vague. To paraphrase a wry observation made by Jacob L.J.: we are all against unfairness, just as we are all in favour of mother and apple pie.[116]

114. 17 USC § 107 provides that in determining whether a use is fair 'the factors to be considered shall include –

(1) the purpose and character of the use, including whether such use is of a commercial nature or is for non-profit educational purposes;
(2) the nature of the copyrighted work;
(3) the amount and substantiality of the portion used in relation to the copyrighted work as a whole; and
(4) the effect of the use upon the potential market for or value of the copyrighted work'.

115. W.J. Gordon, *Fair Use as Market Failure: A Structural and Economic Analysis of the Betamax Case and its Predecessors*, 82 Colum. L. Rev. 1600, 1657 et passim (1982).

116. The original dictum is: 'We are all against misappropriation, just as we are all in favour of mother and apple pie', *L'Oréal v. Bellure* [2007] EWCA Civ. 968, para. 160.

Also, it carries with it several connotations which may even differ between unfair competition and copyright law. Nevertheless, for several reasons I think 'fairness' is an appropriate basis for the following approach. First, as seen above, the concept of 'fairness' can accommodate market effects both in unfair competition and in copyright law. But, secondly, it is not restricted to market effects. Factors which are not strictly related to the incentive theory of intellectual property can also play a role. Thirdly, methodologically modern concepts of fairness represent a mixture of flexibility, because fairness is an open concept, and foreseeability due to catalogues of examples and lists of criteria to be taken into account.

4.4.2 PURPOSE AS A LIMITING FACTOR

4.4.2.1 The Importance of Market Effects

Our analysis of unfair competition and trade mark law has shown that liability in both areas of law depends on adverse effects on markets or on the interests of other traders. The three categories of infringement in EU trade mark law are a prime example: double-identity infringement is only actionable when trade mark functions are adversely affected. The likelihood of confusion is to be determined from the point of view of an average consumer, and it can be presumed to interfere with market transparency. Causing damage or taking advantage of the distinctiveness or reputation of a well-known mark is only considered an infringement if it is unfair and without due cause. We have also seen that there is no comparable effects-based test in European copyright law, even though courts sometimes draw on economic considerations openly or tacitly when determining scope, when analysing economic rights or when interpreting defences.[117]

But there seems to be growing uneasiness with copyright formalism on both sides of the Atlantic. In the US, there is widespread awareness of the purpose-bound nature of copyright law, not least because the constitutional Copyright Clause binds legislative power to the purpose of 'promoting science and useful arts'. Hence the US Supreme Court has held that uses which 'have no demonstrable effect upon the potential market for, or the value of, the copyrighted work need not be prohibited in order to protect the author's incentive to create'.[118] While neither the Supreme Court nor the lower courts have consistently required harm in a strict sense, there is a considerable body of literature on what amounts to a 'cognizable harm' in

117. *See* 4.3.1, 4.3.3 *supra.*
118. *Sony v. Universal Studios*, 464 U.S. 417, 456 (1984).

copyright law and on where in the infringement test it should be assessed.[119] Several authors connect harm to the incentive function of copyright and conclude that copyright should only prohibit acts which, if permitted and if the author had expected them to be permitted, would have discouraged him or her from creating.[120]

In Europe, the CJEU has stressed that restrictions of fundamental freedoms or competition are only justified for the purpose of safeguarding the 'specific subject-matter' of copyright:

> It is clear from settled case law that the specific subject-matter of the intellectual property is intended in particular to ensure for the right holders concerned protection of the right to exploit commercially the marketing or the making available of the protected subject-matter, by the grant of licences in return for payment of remuneration ... However, the specific subject-matter of the intellectual property does not guarantee the right holders concerned the opportunity to demand the highest possible remuneration. Consistently with its specific subject-matter, they are ensured – as recital 10 in the preamble to the Copyright Directive and recital 5 in the preamble to the Related Rights Directive envisage – only appropriate remuneration for each use of the protected subject-matter.[121]

As seen above,[122] when applying the right of communication to the public, the Court also draws on economic criteria at times, although not consistently. Interpretations such as the one in the *GS Media* case would stand on much firmer ground if the provisions constituting the economic rights required some sort of market effect as a condition of infringement. Market effects criteria have also been proposed by European copyright scholars.

---

119. *See* C. Bohannan, *Copyright Harm, Foreseeability, and Fair Use*, 85 Wash. U. L. Rev. 969 (2007); C. Bohannan & H. Hovenkamp, *IP and Antitrust: Reformation and Harm*, 51 B.C. L. Rev. 905 (2010); T.F. Cotter, *Transformative Use and Cognizable Harm*, 12 Vand. J. Ent. & Tech. L. 701 (2009–2010); S.K. Stadler, *Copyright as Trade Regulation*, 155 U. Pa. L. Rev. 899 (2006–2007); S. Balganesh, *Foreseeability and Copyright Incentives*, 122 Harv. L. Rev. 1569 (2009); *see also* the review by S. Bechtold, *supra* n. 40.
120. *See* in particular, Balganesh, *ibid.* An interesting test question is whether the Sonny Bono Copyright Term Extension Act was consistent with the Copyright Clause. The Supreme Court, by majority, upheld the copyright extension, *see Eldred v. Ashcroft*, 537 US 186 (2003).
121. Joined CJEU cases C-403/08 and C-429/08, *Football Association Premier League v. QC Leisure and Karen Murphy v. Media Protection Service*, ECLI:EU:C:2011:631, paras 107–108.
122. *See* 4.3.3 *supra*.

4.4.2.2 The Limiting Factor: 'Cognizable Harm' or Also 'Unjust Enrichment'?

But there is one considerable difficulty here: there is no agreement about what the proper function of copyright is.

A host of literature has been written about the justification of copyright.[123] The main distinction seems to be between deontological approaches which assume the author's natural entitlement to the fruits of his labour or to the emanations of his personality, and consequentialist approaches, which are mainly economics-based. More recently, communitarian, democratic or communication-based theories have been added to the list. Even authors inspired by economy differ as to whether the proper function of copyright is only to encourage authors to create and media companies to invest or whether copyright should, more generally, create an atmosphere in which authors can live from their creations and afford to dedicate time to writing, painting or composing.[124] The InfoSoc Directive suggests the latter: copyright is a way to ensure 'that European cultural creativity and production receive the necessary resources and of safeguarding the independence and dignity of artistic creators and performers'.[125] This begs the question of whether an effects-based criterion should only consider the harm which a particular use is causing to the right owner's market position or whether it should also take the unjust enrichment made by the user into account.

Consider the following example. In 1974 the band Lynyrd Skynyrd released its hit song 'Sweet Home Alabama,' which consists of a chorus and verses, a guitar solo and a piano outro. Several bands have covered the entire song since then. In his 2008 hit 'All Summer Long,' Kid Rock sampled the guitar solo and the piano outro. Although both are clearly recognizable, the song is an independent creation, it became a number one hit in many countries and it may well have increased the popularity of 'Sweet Home Alabama.' Would Kid Rock have needed a licence (which he probably had)? And how about a band which samples just four notes of the guitar solo, loops it and creates a piece of music which nobody relates to 'Sweet Home Alabama'?

---

123. On copyright justifications in common law and civil law jurisdictions *see* A. Strowel, *Droit d'auteur et copyright, Divergences et convergences* (Brussels, Paris: Bruylant & LGDJ, 1993); C.G. Stallberg, *Urheberrecht und moralische Rechtfertigung* (Berlin: Duncker & Humblot, 2006); W. Fisher, *Theories of Intellectual Property*, in: S.R. Münzer (ed.), *New Essays in the Legal and Political Theory of Property* (Cambridge: CUP, 2005), 168 et seq.

124. For broader consequentialist approaches *see* J.E. Cohen, *Copyright as Property in the Post-Industrial Economy: A Research Agenda*, (2011) Wisconsin Law Review, 141–165 (2011); O. Bracha & T. Syed, *Beyond Efficiency: Consequence-Sensitive Theories of Copyright*, 29 Berkeley Tech. L.J. 229–316 (2014).

125. Recital 11.

The lowest common denominator seems to be that copyright should bite when someone else uses the work in a way which substitutes the original work. In our example, copyright should prevent anyone from uploading 'Sweet Home Alabama' on the internet and making it available for free. Nobody would buy the song anymore; the market would collapse. The same is probably true for full cover versions, which some fans may even prefer to the original song. There is less agreement about Kid Rock's sample. The guitar solo and the piano outro are probably original enough to qualify as works by themselves. Under both the *Infopaq* test proposed by the CJEU[126] and the common law[127] substantiality test[128] a reproduction of these solos would probably fall within the scope of copyright, although they might be regarded as fair use or quotation. Economists who insist on a strict incentive function will probably take issue with this view and might even go so far as to refer to this rule as a 'jealousy tax':[129] the market for the original song is not adversely affected, and if the composers had been told in 1974 that the law would tolerate samples of this kind, their incentive to create would not have been lessened. But if you take the view that copyright law should also protect authors against 'unjust enrichment' – uses which derive a significant economic benefit from the original work – you will be likely to agree with present copyright law and consider this adaptation as at least prima facie covered by copyright. The last variant, digital sampling of minuscule parts not qualifying for copyright protection, has been the subject of court decisions in at least in the US and Germany. Both the Sixth Circuit Court of Appeals[130] and the German Federal Supreme Court[131] regarded digital sampling of this kind as an infringement of the neighbouring right in the sound recording. The German judgment was recently reversed by the Federal Constitutional Court, because the Supreme Court had not given due weight

126. According to CJEU case C-5/08, *Infopaq International A/S v. Danske Dagblades Forening*, ECLI:EU:C:2009:465, para. 48, a reproduction of an extract amounts to a 'reproduction in part' within the meaning of Art. 2 of the InfoSoc Directive, 'if that extract contains an element of the work which, as such, expresses the author's own intellectual creation'.
127. On the impact of the CJEU approach on UK law *see* L. Bently & B. Sherman, *Intellectual Property Law* (4th ed., Oxford: Oxford University Press, 2014) 205–206.
128. *See* the Australian case of *Larrikin Music Publishing Pty. Ltd. v EMI Songs Australia Pty. Ltd.* [2010] FCA 29, paras 218–229: a rock band had reproduced two bars from the refrain of the iconic Australian song 'Kookaburra Sits in the Old Gum Tree'. The Federal Court held that the refrain was a 'hook', i.e., the part of the song which everyone remembers, and that two of the four bars of the 'hook' were a substantial part.
129. *See* the contribution by J. Poort to this volume.
130. *Bridgeport Music v. Dimension Films*, 410 F.3d 792 (6th Cir., 2005). But *see VMK Salsoul, LLC v. Madonna Louise Ciccone*, 824 F.3d 871 (9th Cir., 2016), recognizing a *de minimis* threshold.
131. BGH GRUR 2009, 403 – *Metall auf Metall I.*

to the constitutionally protected freedom of art.[132] Again, copyright lawyers may differ as to which solution is the right one. Under a strict incentive-based approach there is no justification for allowing an action based on the sound recording right, because, again, the sound recording company's market remains entirely unaffected. If, however, every use which benefits from the original recording requires the right holder's authorization, the Sixth Circuit is right in saying: 'Get a licence or do not sample'.[133] But in the German discussion at least many authors steer a middle course. While not rejecting an unjust enrichment approach per se, they support the Federal Constitutional Court's view: first there is a case for a *de minimis* threshold even with respect to neighbouring rights, secondly the law should also take into account that the taking of a minuscule part should be set off against the creative effort which went into the new song.[134]

This is not the place for a critical analysis of all copyright justifications, for following up the debate between consequentialist and 'faith-based' approaches in the US[135] or for reviewing all the different types of incentive approaches. Ultimately the decision in favour of a particular theory of justification may well be a matter of personal conviction, not only of logic. In my view, which is certainly contestable, there are three arguments against a strict incentive-based approach which does not allow for remedies against 'unjust enrichment'. First, it does not take sufficient account of artistic creativity. Often authors do not need an incentive for a particular creation, but they need time and leisure. Even on a consequentialist view it may thus be insufficient to only protect copyright owners against acts which have a negative impact on their markets, but there may be a case for allowing authors to benefit from their creativity. Secondly, and this may well be a credo rather than scientific analysis, copyright differs from patent law in that it is not an exclusively economic right. Personality-based aspects cannot entirely be left out of the equation. The more a work is the emanation of the author's personality, the more he or she should be given a remedy not only against harm but also against unjust enrichment. Thirdly, while excessive copyright protection should be curbed, it is politically unrealistic to reduce copyright to a harm-based approach.

---

132. BVerfG GRUR 2016, 690 – *Metall auf Metall III*. Meanwhile, the German Supreme Court has referred the case to the CJEU, *see* BGH GRUR 2017, 895 – *Metall auf Metall III*.
133. *Bridgeport Music v. Dimension Films*, 410 F.3d 792, 801 (6th Cir., 2005); but *see also VMG Salsoul, LLC v. Ciccone*, 824 F.3 d 871 (9th Cir. 2016).
134. *See* M. Leistner, *Die 'Metall auf Metall'-Entscheidung des BVerfG*, GRUR 2016, 772, 774–777; R. Podszun, *Postmoderne Kreativität im Konflikt mit dem Urheberrechtsgesetz und die Annäherung an 'fair use' Besprechung zu BVerfG ZUM 2016, 626 – Sampling*, ZUM 2016, 606, 609–611; A. Ohly, *Urheberrecht in der digitalen Welt, Gutachten F zum 70. Deutschen Juristentag* (Munich: Beck, 2014), F 41.
135. *See* R.P. Merges, *Justifying Intellectual Property* (Cambridge (Mass.): Harvard University Press, 2011), and the sharp criticism by M.A. Lemley, *Faith-Based Intellectual Property*, 62 UCLA L. Rev. 1328–1346 (2015).

But it does not follow that every possible use of the work should be actionable. Again, trade mark law offers an interesting example. Causing confusion with another trade mark is prohibited per se, subject to certain exceptions. But taking advantage of another trader's well-known mark is only actionable when it is unfair and when it takes place without due cause. In other words the onus of proof for justification is different. In the clear case of a likelihood of confusion, it is on the alleged infringer. But protection against 'reaping without sowing' is subject to a balancing exercise. This model could inform copyright legislation. Uses which are clearly harmful should be proscribed per se, whereas cases in which the economic harm is doubtful or which only constitute 'unjust enrichment' should be subject to a more flexible standard, which allows, first, setting the negative economic consequences for the copyright owner off against pro-competitive effects, and, secondly, allocating greater weight to countervailing interests when the economic case for protecting the right owner is not overwhelming.

4.4.3 Methodology: A Three-Layer Model of Economic Rights

4.4.3.1 Fair Use or Multi-Level Flexibility?

If we are prepared to accept that the test of copyright infringement should be market-sensitive and that it should not only look at harm, but also at the user's unjust profits, there are two ways of implementing this approach.

One way is the current US approach, which consists of a low originality threshold and a broad definition of economic rights, coupled with a market-sensitive fair use clause. This approach combines clarity at the step of initial entitlement with flexibility at the step of defences. There are sound arguments for initially defining the scope of intellectual property rights broadly and for then balancing the competing interests at the stage of copyright exceptions.[136] While it is true that the fair use clause avoids some of the shortcomings of the European system, the initial prima facie entitlement is overly broad because US law, very much like EU law, has extended the classical economic rights from the analogue world to the digital environment. Once the broad prima facie entitlement has been established, the onus of proof for showing fair use is on the defendant. The prima facie allocation of rights may also give rise to the circular argument that the copyright owner is prima facie entitled to a licence for acts of reproduction, distribution, communication to the public and adaptation and that hence every unlicensed use has a negative impact on the owner's market.

---

136. *See* A. Rahmatian, *Originality in UK Copyright Law: The Old 'Skill and Labour' Doctrine Under Pressure*, IIC 4, 28 (2013); for trade mark law *see* G.B. Dinwoodie & M.D. Janis, *supra* n. 54, at 1662.

The second option seems preferable: the option of multi-level flexibility, which allows taking economic effects into account at all stages. First, there may be economic reasons for excluding certain subject-matter from copyright or for requiring a higher originality threshold for certain kinds of works, although this thought cannot be developed here. Our focus is on economic rights. As the example of trade mark and unfair competition law shows, there are advantages to an effects-based infringement test over a broad allocation of economic rights. Many uses in the digital context are ambivalent. The economic effect is unclear. Take the case of linking and framing: it would go too far to consider every type of linking as a communication to the public which prima facie requires the right owner's consent, but it also seems inappropriate to allow framing per se, as certain kinds of framing can create substitutes for the right owner's products or services. It is understandable that the CJEU attempts to distinguish between kinds of linking which constitute acts of communication to the public and others which do not. But the law would be clearer if this distinction could be based on a clear statutory market effects test.

There are two objections against this approach. The first is that it may lead to legal uncertainty and that the courts may not be able to assess the economic effects of a particular use with sufficient precision. Indeed, the economic function of copyright not only depends on the correct calibration of rights and exceptions, but also on the possibility to contract. Rights should be defined clearly enough to write licences and to allow for the collective administration of copyright.[137] But it is submitted that the system proposed here provides a sufficiently clear basis for contracting. Uses which must clearly be allocated to the right owner are to be defined even more clearly than they are today.[138] Licences can also cover cases in which infringement depends on an assessment of market effects. Again, trade mark licensing is not jeopardized by the fact that the protection of well-known marks is flexible. Whether the courts can assess economic effects is another matter. The CJEU seems to assume that they can: the guidelines given in cases such as *GS Media* make it mandatory for national courts to consider economic criteria. Initially there may be difficult cases in which more evidence is necessary than under the present system. But over time, a system of precedents will develop which clarify some basic questions.

Secondly, one might object that a 'double fair use standard' would be tautological, because the same market effects test would have to be applied twice. Again, trade mark law helps to explain why this is not the case. Causing a likelihood of confusion is a core case of trade mark infringement. It is prima facie prohibited, but there are possible defences. If my name happens to be identical with a trade mark, I am allowed to use it, even for similar goods or services, but I must take all necessary precautions to avoid

137. As S. Bechtold rightly points out in his chapter, *supra* n. 40.
138. *See infra* at 4.4.3.2.

undue confusion. But taking advantage of a well-known mark is only prohibited if it is unfair and without due cause. In this context, the trade mark exceptions lose their independent significance, but they can be the basis of a 'due cause'. Similar considerations apply under the model proposed here. First, there are also cases of clear infringement, which can only be justified by a defence. In these cases there will be an interrelation between market effects and justification: the stronger the market effects, the higher the threshold of justification. Secondly, the provisions on prima facie infringement proposed here are not suited as a basis for levy schemes. Collecting societies need clear rules. Levies could not be collected on an ad hoc basis. What is more, liability rules in present copyright acts usually concern uses of economic relevance, in which there is a case for compensating the right owner. So under the model proposed here, there is a prima facie entitlement. Thirdly, it is true there may be cases in which the courts need to carry out a balancing exercise at the level of prima facie infringement. Nevertheless, there is a distinction between prima facie infringement and defences in this regard. The effects clause at the step of assessing infringement should be restricted to market effects. Hence courts can set off the negative effects on the right owner's market against positive competitive effects. Balancing economic effects against countervailing rights and interests, such as freedom of expression, of research or of art, should rather be carried out when applying defences. It should be added that, according to the idea of multi-level flexibility, exceptions should also become more flexible than they are in present EU law. I have argued elsewhere,[139] that a combination of the present, detailed exceptions with a catch-all fair use clause might combine the best of the two worlds on both sides of the Atlantic.

4.4.3.2 A Three-Layer Model

Both trade mark law and unfair competition law combine provisions which prohibit core infringements with more open-ended provisions, which apply in the penumbra of protection. This is particularly evident with regard to the three-step approach adopted by the UCPD which prohibits: (1) thirty-one 'black-listed' cases per se without the need to show a negative impact on consumers' behaviour, (2) misleading and aggressive practices by well-defined but nevertheless flexible provisions and (3) unfair behaviour in unforeseen cases by means of a general clause.

The three-layer model which is suggested here is inspired by this methodology. In copyright law it should also be possible to identify clear cases of infringement and to define them in a way which is easily understandable not only by lawyers but also by potential infringers. The

139. Ohly, *supra* n. 134, at F 63–66; *see also* A. Förster, *Fair Use* (Tübingen: Mohr Siebeck, 2008), 221–222. A similar approach is taken by the Wittem Code, Art. 5.5 and note 48.

present economic rights could be retained as provisions of a medium level of abstraction, but they should be combined with a market effects clause. At the highest level of generality there should be a general clause protecting copyright owners against all unfair use of their works.

Level 1: A 'Black List' of Core Infringements

First, there should be a list of well-defined acts which clearly interfere with the specific subject-matter of copyright law. They represent the core area of copyright protection about which lawyers and economists agree. They should be defined as clearly as possible. If the detailed definitions leave gaps, they can be filled on the basis of the more general provisions at steps two or three. All acts in this category should be likely to adversely affect the right owner's market. They should be restricted to uses of the entire work in unaltered form. Whenever parts of the work are used or when the work is adapted, there is the need for a more flexible approach. The 'black-listed' cases should target the supply rather than the demand side. While the basic list should be drawn up through legislation, more details could be regulated by means of a statutory instrument.

These infringing acts would still have to be subject to certain exceptions, as even clearly infringing acts may be acceptable under particular circumstances. Even making available a work online in the course of trade can be acceptable for the purpose of quotation, for example. Including this exception in the definition of the right would result in legal uncertainty, because a clear definition of the infringing act would become impossible. The onus of proof is on the claimant to show that the subject-matter is protected and that a 'black-listed' act has occurred. But very much like in present copyright law, the onus of proof with regard to defences is on the defendant.

Obviously the devil is in the details: right owners and internet users will certainly disagree about which cases are 'clear' and 'evident'. It is not the task of this chapter to discuss and classify all possible uses of copyrightable works. Suffice it to give three examples of cases which could be 'black listed': (1) making available a digital copy of the work to the public online for permanent download, (2) distributing a permanent copy of the work, regardless of whether in digital or analogue form, online or offline (3) transmitting a work to the public by means of broadcast or on-demand streaming. In all of these situations there is obvious competition between the right owner and the user. This is the case regardless of whether the offer is made in the course of trade or without a view to obtaining profit. The copy should be under the control of the user. Either the provision itself or an authoritative explanation should clarify that 'offering' does not include linking. The statutory language could be neutral with regard to the technology used whereas a statutory instrument could give detailed examples relating to particular technologies.

Level 2: Economic Rights Combined with a Market Effects Clause

The second level could resemble the present economic rights. They should, however, be reformulated as a list of infringing acts, and infringement should be subject to a market effects clause. Hence the claimant will have to show that the act complained of is likely to have a negative effect on his market position or derives an undue economic benefit from the use of the work. Subject to economic relevance, the prohibited acts could extend to acts done for private purposes. Again, it is impossible to give a full list of 'level 2' cases, which would constitute a prima facie infringement, subject to the market effects clause. Examples would be: (1) reproducing the work in a permanent form or reproducing a work in a non-permanent form if the reproduction has independent economic significance, (2) offering or making available a derivative work or (3) integrating the work into the user's own website by inline linking.

At least some activities carried out by intermediaries will also fall into this category. While it is not the purpose of this chapter to present a full model of secondary liability, a rule on intermediaries could distinguish between access providers and hosts. Mere access providers should only be under a duty to provide assistance in order to prevent access to works made available illegally.[140] For passive hosts, there should be a general notice and takedown obligation. But when a company derives an independent economic benefit from hosting a work without the right owner's consent, it could be liable under the model proposed here.[141]

Level 3: A General Clause on Unfair Use

Finally the model would be completed by a general clause which prohibits any unfair use of the work. It could cover cases not explicitly dealt with at levels 1 or 2. This part of the model is reminiscent of the 'use right model' proposed by *Ole-Andreas Rognstad* and *Joost Poort*[142] although the general right will be much less important under the fairness-based approach, since the lists of uses at the lower levels should be as comprehensive as possible. The provision should cover any use which unfairly causes a negative impact on the right owner's market position or which takes unfair advantage of the work. Possible criteria for unfairness might be the second and third steps of the three-step test:[143] does the use conflict with the normal exploitation of the work and does it unreasonably prejudice the legitimate interests of the right holder?

140. *See* M. Husovec, *Injunctions against Intermediaries in the European Union: Accountable But Not Liable?*, (Cambridge: Cambridge University Press, 2017).

141. A comparable model is proposed by Leistner, *supra* n. 108, at 589–594.

142. *See* the contribution of O.-A. Rognstad & J. Poort to this volume.

143. This 'reverse three-step test' has been proposed by D. Gervais, *supra* n. 75 at 27–30.

4.4.4 Can This Model Help to Determine Difficult Cases?

Does this model stand the test of concrete examples? Can it provide guidelines for dealing with difficult cases such as hyperlinking, digital resale, private copying or retransmission?

The answer is partly disappointing. The fairness-based approach proposed here consists of an abstract substantive and a concrete methodological component. The substantive proposal is that the law should define infringing acts rather than economic rights, and that a market effect should be a condition of prima facie infringement. The methodological proposal is the three-layer model outlined above. Since the substantive criterion is abstract, it provides a starting-point for the assessment of infringement, but it is not a panacea for difficult cases. Right owners and users are likely to disagree about negative economic effects on the owner's market and positive counter effects. The following examples are mere outlines. A full discussion of the economic effects including reviews of cases and literature would require several articles.

Hyperlinking is not a case in which negative market effects can be presumed. Often hyperlinking will be in the right owner's interest, in many cases the public interest in a functioning search engine infrastructure will outweigh the owner's interest in preventing or licensing links. So hyperlinking would not be a 'level 1' case. At level 2, the level of acts which are prima facie prohibited in the case of a negative market effect, a distinction between surface links and inline links should be drawn. Surface links only have adverse effects on the right owner's market if they circumvent access restrictions or if the work on the target website was made available without the consent of the owner. Hence surface linking should be dealt with in the context of the liability of intermediaries. Users placing a surface link should be subject to notice and takedown, but they should not be exposed to further liability. Framing, however, should be one of the uses which are infringing if a negative market effect can be shown. This is the case where the user offers a substitute to the right owner's services or where the user derives a commercial benefit from embedding the work into his website.

News aggregators also compile hyperlinks, but they combine links and snippets in an independent business model. Aggregating hyperlinks could also be a case for 'level 2'. In the case of news aggregators, the market effects clause is likely to militate against liability. First, there is no significant negative effect on newspaper publishers' markets, as there is evidence that internet users are referred to newspaper websites by news aggregators. While it is true that news aggregators benefit from newspaper websites, this effect is offset by a positive effect on competition: news aggregation websites are an important tool for finding information on the internet. Hence they contribute to the internet infrastructure.

The issue of *digital resale* is very complex. The model proposed here has little to add to the discussion of whether exhaustion can still be a model in digital times. I have expressed my scepticism elsewhere:[144] the doctrine of exhaustion is convincing when the work is embodied in a tangible object, but its economic rationale does not hold in the digital world. It is clear that digital resale interferes with the right owner's market, since the resold data are usually fully substitutable against data sold by the right owner. It would be possible to integrate resale into the model proposed by listing it at 'level 2' and by subjecting it to an economic effects test. It would be the task of the courts to determine the negative economic effect on the owner's market and to decide whether this effect is offset by the user's interest and by the general interest in the free movement of data. But this issue should probably be dealt with by specific legislation.

In most EU countries, *private copying* is allowed by a statutory exception, but subjected to a levy system. As explained above, liability rules should be created by statutory exceptions, not by courts interpreting the provisions of prima facie infringement. Hence, on the basis of this model the present system will remain unaffected. Private copying is not a 'level 1' infringement, but it will normally have negative economic effects on the right owner's market. Hence it usually constitutes a 'level 2' infringement, which is prohibited unless justified by an exception. Allowing private copying in exchange for remuneration is a proven and tested system, which should not be given up.

Retransmission is a typical 'level 2' case: the law needs to draw a distinction based on the economic effects of retransmission. The retransmission of signals to flats in an apartment building does not have a significant economic effect. The owners of the apartments would not be prepared to take out individual licences, they would rather install the technical means necessary to receive the signals directly. Also, the recipients do not make an economic profit which goes beyond the reception of the signals. This result is also reached by the CJEU in a recent judgment.[145] The Court, however, does not refer to any economic criteria, but applies the 'new public' test in a rather formal way, which could lead to inadequate results if the retransmission had a broader coverage than the one in the case decided by the CJEU. In the case of hotels, there is some merit in the approach adopted by the CJEU.[146] While the concept of a 'successive public' may be criticized as doctrinally doubtful, it is true that hotel owners can offer rooms equipped with TVs at a higher price. The retransmission may not harm the right owner's market, as they would probably still have an incentive for creation and investment. But the hotel owner derives a profit from the commercial use

144. A. Ohly, *Exhaustion of Rights: A Concept for the Digital World?*, in: D. Beldiman (ed.), *Innovation, Competition, Collaboration* (Cheltenham: Edward Elgar, 2015), 188–198.

145. CJEU, case C-138/16, *AKM v. Zürs.net*, ECLI:EU:C:2017:218. A similar result was reached by the German Federal Supreme Court, albeit on slightly different grounds: 343 occupants of flats in a housing complex were a 'fairly large', but not an 'indeterminate' number, BGH GRUR 2016, 71, para. 63 – *Ramses*.

146. *See* the references *supra* n. 84, 86.

of the work, which is 'unjust' if made without compensation. In short, the model proposed here will often lead to results similar to those reached by the CJEU. But it makes the criteria of a 'new public' and 'new technical means' superfluous as independent criteria. Rather, the Court should assess the economic impact of the individual retransmission. This may require economic evidence in pilot cases. But once the courts have decided on typical situations, future courts can follow these precedents.

4.5 CONCLUSION

The economic rights are in need of reform. The present system has lost touch with economic reality. The CJEU is reacting by interpreting the right of communication to the public in a creative way. Some of its judgments draw on economic criteria and some are more convincing than others, but many of them represent attempts to reform the law judicially. Legislation, however, should claim back the lead, at least partly. The way forward seems to be a more flexible, market-sensitive infringement test. The 'fairness-based approach' presented here draws on experiences from trade mark and unfair competition law. It suggests a three-level model consisting of a black list of acts which are prohibited per se if done without the right owner's consent, a medium level of acts which only trigger an infringement action if a negative effect on the right owner's market or an unjustified profit of the user is shown, and a broad general clause. This model allows legislation to provide guidelines, but it depends on the courts for full realization. Both the experience from unfair competition law and the recent CJEU decisions suggest that courts are up to this task. But they do much better if they can develop the law within a suitable statutory framework: *intra legem* rather than *praeter* or even *contra legem*.

Chapter 5
The Right to Reasonable Exploitation Concretized: An Incentive Based Approach

Ole-Andreas Rognstad & Joost Poort*

5.1 THE RIGHT TO REASONABLE EXPLOITATION REVISITED

In a previous article, an alternative model for defining the economic rights in copyright was sketched out.[1] This alternative model is predicated on the notion that there is a need for a simplified structure of the economic rights which at the same time is apt to meet the technological challenges of the twenty-first century. The model implies that the right holder has an exclusive *right to reasonable exploitation* of the work (or other protected subject matter), the further scope of which should be specified in statutory provisions. The model is intended to serve as a 'one stage assessment' for the

---

* The authors thank the project team of Bernt Hugenholtz, Stefan Bechtold, Séverine Dusollier, Martin Kretschmer, Ansgar Ohly and Alain Strowel, as well as Lionel Bently, Sari Depreeuw, Estelle Derclaye, Daniel Gervais, Jonathan Griffiths, Matthias Leistner, Bertin Martens, Giuseppe Mazziotti, João Pedro Quintais and Martin Senftleben, and the participants in the 'Reconstructing rights' symposium held on 26 September 2016 in Brussels for their valuable comments on earlier drafts of this chapter.

1. O-A. Rognstad, 'Restructuring the Economic Rights in Copyright – Some Reflections on an "Alternative Model"', *Journal of the Copyright Society of the USA* 62 (2015): 503–544.

delineation of the rights, depending on what is to be considered as reasonable exploitation, instead of the current 'six stage assessment': definitions of exclusive rights, limitations to them, secondary liability, safe harbour and protection of technical protection measures (TPMs) with pertaining exceptions. This implies the abandonment of the traditional rights structure based on a positive definition of acts subject to the exclusive rights, such as reproduction, communication to the public and distribution, which in turn are subject to exceptions that need justification. Furthermore, problems that under the current rights structure are handled under secondary liability and special rules on protection of TPMs are integrated in the right to reasonable exploitation. This means that under the alternative model the rights are delineated through the requirement that the exploitation subject to exclusive rights must be reasonable. This formulation implies, in turn, that copyright shall not expand beyond its purpose and that the alternative model will bring it closer to its rationale than what results from the current structuring of the economic rights.

This chapter intends a further elaboration of this model by developing two main issues. First, the concept of 'reasonable exploitation' is analysed and elaborated on (section 5.2). Subsequently, it is operationalized from a consequentialist, welfare economic perspective (section 5.3). Next, a number of case studies illustrate how the concept may be implemented into the model (section 5.4). These case studies are based on welfare economic reasoning and considerations that are not presented in detail here, but in a separate chapter of this volume.[2] Regarding these case studies, it should be borne in mind that in the previous article it was suggested that statutory provisions could provide partly for general guidelines and partly for a catalogue of examples demonstrating the further scope of the concept of reasonable exploitation. The analysis of the further concretization of the right to reasonable exploitation will be predicated on this way of implementing the alternative model. Still, as with the previous article, it is not the intention to provide a full-fledged copyright reform proposal; rather the purpose of this chapter is to elaborate on the further implications of the proposed right to reasonable exploitation. This includes demonstrating how both the approach to and the outcomes of certain problems will differ compared to how the same problems are treated under current copyright systems (section 5.5). It should also be borne in mind that although the model as such will apply equally to copyright and related rights, the analysis – as in the previous article – will be limited to copyright in works.[3]

2. *See* the chapter by J. Poort, elsewhere in this volume. That chapter follows a welfare economic approach without placing it into the context of a right to reasonable exploitation or any other legal structure.
3. Compare Rognstad (2015), 508.

5.2 THE CONCEPT OF 'REASONABLE EXPLOITATION'

5.2.1 BASELINES

The basic idea behind the right to reasonable exploitation is that it is a 'one stage' test which implies that the delineation of the right lies in the definition of what is reasonable rather than in what constitutes an 'exploitation'.[4] The concept of 'exploitation' is to be understood in its widest sense: it is intended to cover all kinds of behaviour and business models that are in the current or future financial interest of the right holder, including those that rely on advertising revenues or reputation building rather than direct monetary transfers. The concept is to be open-ended, intended to cover not only existing but also yet to be developed exploitation models. As a result, the exclusive right to reasonable exploitation can cover any action that may conflict with these interests of the right holder, including actions that under the current system are handled under doctrines of secondary liability (contributory infringement etc.).

Having said that, the idea is that the *delineation* of the exclusive rights does not follow from a classification of what constitutes an act of 'exploitation' but rather from what is considered as a *reasonable* exploitation.[5] This means that it is most pertinent to elaborate on the concept of *reasonable*. As the purpose of the previous article was to outline the model as a different, and alternative, way of structuring the economic rights, the scope of what is 'reasonable' was not discussed beyond stating that the word 'reasonable is highly ambiguous … depending also on different copyright traditions whether utilitarian or more non-consequentialist oriented, including natural rights concepts',[6] and that it 'will be up to the legislator, within the framework of international obligations, including also human right conventions, to further decide on the implications of that concept'.[7] When elaborating on the possible implications of the model, as is the purpose here, it is, however, necessary to take a normative position on the content of the concept of *reasonable* exploitation. At the same time, it is important to underline that the model may be implemented in different ways from what is suggested here, including in the sense that different approaches to the concept of 'reasonable' may be taken.

Here, it will be suggested that, bearing in mind that the model is meant to be universal,[8] the concept of 'reasonable' should to some extent bridge

4. *Ibid.* 511.
5. *Ibid.* 513.
6. *Ibid.*
7. *Ibid.* 515.
8. *Ibid.* 508.

different copyright doctrines leaving room for both utilitarian and non-consequentialist ideas. In the previous article, it was suggested that inspiration for the guiding principles that should be laid down in the legislation and even serve as overarching guidelines for the courts, could be found in the so-called mid-level principles presented by Robert P. Merges in his book 'Justifying Intellectual Property'.[9] These 'mid-level principles' are 'concepts that run through and tie together disparate doctrines and practices, and provide a common policy vocabulary that bridges different foundational viewpoints such as Kantian and utilitarian'.[10] In Merges' view there are four mid-level principles in IP law: *non-removal* (i.e., the public domain), *proportionality*, *efficiency* and *dignity*.[11] Although the basis for, and the function of, these mid-level principles has been subject to discussion and criticism,[12] they are here considered as useful guidelines for mapping out the content of 'reasonable', precisely because they reflect some basic principles that may be founded in various justification grounds for copyright protection. For this purpose, it is considered appropriate to add two other guiding principles: *freedom of expression*[13] and, in a European context, the principle of *market integration*.

The natural starting point for determining the scope of 'reasonable exploitation' would be *efficiency*. It should not be denied that the utilitarian goal of social welfare maximization is a key element in justifying modern copyright rules.[14] If that is accepted, hard-core economists would hold that, in theory, the welfare economic framework could (and should) include other norms (except for distributional concerns) through their welfare effects, including the other guiding principles mentioned above.[15] The ambition of

9. *Ibid.* 516, fn. 31. *See* R.P. Merges, *Justifying Intellectual Property* (Cambridge MA: Harvard University Press, 2011).
10. Merges (2011), 139.
11. *Ibid.*
12. *See* in particular D.H. Blankfein-Tabachnick, 'Intellectual Property Doctrine and Midlevel Principles', *California Law Review* 101 (2013): 1315–1359. For the author's response, *see* R.P. Merges, 'Foundations and Principles Redux: A Reply to Professor Blankfein-Tabachnick', *California Law Review* 101 (2013): 1361–1386.
13. *See* Rognstad (2015), 516, fn. 31.
14. *See* e.g., Recital 2 of the Infosoc Directive (Directive 2001/29/EC of 22 May 2001 on the harmonisation of certain aspects of copyright and related rights in the information society, OJ No. L 167/10, 22 June 2001) emphasizing that '[c]opyright and related rights play an important role [in the context of the existence of an internal market for new goods and services] as they protect and stimulate the development and marketing of new products and services and the creation and exploitation of their creative content'. *See also* Recital 9. In the US, reference is made to Art. I Sec. 8 Clause 8 in the US constitution, which empowers the Congress to 'promote the Progress of Science and useful Arts, by securing for limited Times to Authors … the exclusive Right to their respective Writings'.
15. In recent scholarship, claims have been made that the economic approach to the utilitarian goal is based on maximization of income or GDP as a proxy for wealth, and it is therefore criticized for not being concerned with well-being as such, *see* e.g., E. Derclaye & T. Taylor, 'Happy IP: Replacing the Law and Economics Justification for Intellectual

such economists would be for those principles, or more precisely the effect on them of certain acts or policy measures, to be measured and expressed in monetary terms or abstract 'utility' to allow for a comparison within the unified welfare economic framework. For instance, the value attributed to privacy or freedom of speech and its importance to democracy, are in theory part of the long-term welfare function an economist maximizes.[16]

In practice, however, it will prove complicated enough to assess the static and dynamic market effects of copyright issues and other more direct economic effects such as transaction costs, without integrating these other guiding principles into the same framework. Rather, these other principles can give reason to amend the normative welfare economic stance in cases where they point in different directions. For instance, it could be decided that the economic position based solely on efficiency would lead to over- or under-protection when efficiency is balanced with the norm on freedom of speech.[17] Amending the normative economic stance on the basis of these other principles therefore seems a more pragmatic and much more viable solution than aiming to express all guiding principles in welfare economic terms. There is a fine line between this approach and Merges' statement that '[e]fficiency cannot explain or justify the foundations of IP law, but as an operational principle it can guarantee that this body of law works smoothly'.[18] The method suggested here for determining the concept of reasonable exploitation is to start from the efficiency principle, and to

---

Property Rights with a Well-Being Approach', *European Intellectual Property Review* (*EIPR*) 37 (2015): 197–209. As far as we are concerned, the concept of *wealth* as used in the early Law & Economics literature (such as R.A. Posner, 'Utilitarianism, Economics, and Legal Theory', *The Journal of Legal Studies* 8 (1979): 103–140) is very similar to the concept of *welfare* as used in this chapter and in the seminal paper on the economics of copyright by W.M. Landes & R.A. Posner, 'An Economic Analysis of Copyright Law', *The Journal of Legal Studies* 18 (1989): 325–363. It can in theory encompass anything we value as a society.

16. In comparison, economists C.N. Teulings, A.L. Bovenberg & H.P. van Dalen, *De Calculus van het publieke belang* (Den Haag Kenniscentrum voor Ordeningsvraagstukken, 2003), 10–11 argue that ultimately, there are only two goals for public policymaking: efficiency and distributional issues. Ideally, these should be decided on independently. A few years earlier, the Dutch Scientific Council of Government Policy had identified five separate principles for good governance: democratic legitimation, equality before the law, legal certainty, effectiveness and efficiency. In response, Teulings et al. argue that effectiveness is not fundamentally distinct from efficiency, while they consider the first three principles to be procedural criteria, which are not goals in themselves but means to achieve the public interests of efficiency and an acceptable distribution of welfare.
17. Compare O. Bracha & S. Talha, 'Beyond Efficiency. Consequence Sensitive Theories of Copyright', *Berkeley Technology Law Journal 29* (2014): 229–315.
18. Merges (2011), 153. The basis for the stand being efficiency 'cannot explain large features of the IP landscape (moral rights being one of many examples)', and 'try as we might, law and economic scholars have never established an efficiency based (or utilitarian) justification for the field. There is no lock-solid proof that overall social welfare would decline if IP protection were suddenly removed. True, there are plenty of *indications*,

consider adjusting the outcome in case it conflicts with the other principles above. The approach will be explained further in section 5.2.3.6 below.

Starting from the point of efficiency, it should be borne in mind that there are aspects of current copyright law other than the scope of the economic rights that can be questioned from the angle of efficiency, e.g., the concept of a 'work', the lack of formality requirements and the term of protection. The fact that we are concentrating on the scope of the economic rights does not imply an ignorance of other aspects of copyright law in need of reform. Still, we believe that the scope of the economic rights can be studied separately from, for example, the term of protection, and that the argument that the term of protection of copyright may be too long from the perspective of efficiency, is no legitimate reason to curb the scope of the rights beyond what is reasonable.

5.2.2 Efficiency

When starting with efficiency, it is important to remember that in general, the economic literature on copyright links the rationale for copyright protection to the incentive to create works of literature, science and art, at the cost of creating a temporary monopoly over these works.[19] As will be elaborated below, static welfare losses due to this monopoly are justified by dynamic welfare gains from new creation. Put simply, this exclusive right to certain acts of exploitation enables a right holder to generate revenues and to recoup the investment made to create the work. As for many other economic activities, the costs precede the benefits and will only be incurred if future benefits can be expected.

Of course, this is a simplification as intrinsic motivation is generally accepted to be highly important for understanding the professional activities of creators and performers.[20] In addition, a sense of fairness can be relevant as an incentive: a survey among a large number of Dutch creators and

---

plenty of data to support the notion that IP rights are overall good for the economy. But there is no proof in the form that a scientist, or even a rigorous social scientist, would accept as unequivocal', *Id.* 6.

19. *See* e.g., W.M. Landes & R.A. Posner, 'An Economic Analysis of Copyright Law', *The Journal of Legal Studies* 18 (1989): 325–363; S.M. Besen & L.J. Raskind, 'An Introduction to the Law and Economics of Intellectual Property', *The Journal of Economic Perspectives* 5 (1991): 3–27; R.A. Posner, 'Intellectual Property: The Law and Economics Approach', *Journal of Economic Perspectives* 19 (2005): 57–73; T.J. Miceli & R.P. Adelstein, 'An Economic Model of Fair Use', *Information Economics and Policy* 18 (2006): 359–373; M.J. Sag, 'Beyond Abstraction: The Law and Economics of Copyright Scope and Doctrinal Efficiency', *Tulane Law Review* 81 (2006): 187–250.
20. For example, *see* B.S. Frey, *Not Just for the Money* (Cheltenham: Edward Elgar Publishing, 1997); R. Towse, 'Copyright and Artists: A View From Cultural Economics', *Journal of Economic Surveys* 20 (2006): 567–585. *See also* the studies referred to by S. Bechtold in his chapter in this volume.

performers showed overwhelming support for introducing legislation to entitle them to additional revenues if their work becomes a great success (the so-called bestseller clause), even though such a clause can be detrimental for them from a strictly rational economic perspective, when taking account of the effect it is likely to have on lump-sum advances in initial contracts.[21] Apart from arguments in terms of fairness, this support for a bestseller clause may also be understood from behavioural economic insights, namely loss aversion or prospect theory (overweighting small chances). Nonetheless, wages and other financial incentives have been shown to play an important role for authors and performers, much like for any other profession. Moreover, economic motivations are essential for publishers and other commercial entities in the copyright industries.

In the economic literature, copyright aims to prevent a situation in which anyone could decide to create and sell copies of a work without permission once the costs of its creation are incurred, thereby reducing the revenues for the initial creator. This would reduce the incentives for the creator to invest in the creation and exploitation of works, leading to a loss of welfare in the long run. In economic terms, the rents from creation are not (or are insufficiently) excludable without intervention and this 'public good' market failure related to the creation of a work can justify copyright legislation. Contractual arrangements – *private ordering* – are a potential substitute for copyright protection. In that sense, the clause 'without permission' at the start of this paragraph is crucial: in a world with perfect and enforceable private contracts, no copying without permission will occur and hence no copyright protection is required. The viability of private ordering as a substitute for copyright will depend on the enforceability and transaction costs of private contracts, as well as on the limits to contractual freedom and the enforcement of contracts on behalf of, for instance, competition policy, unfair business practices and privacy protection.

The optimum scope of copyright in the economic literature follows from the optimum long-term effect it has on total welfare, taking account of the dynamic effects of copyright on the creation and quality of works, and on the incentives it provides for their active exploitation. That is, consumer and producer welfare (surplus) are given equal weight and neither right holders nor consumers enjoy a privileged status. In the digital age, the costs of making good quality copies of many kinds of work have decreased sharply relative to the initial costs of creation. This applies not only to the initial creator or right holder but also to others, despite the development of TPMs which aim to prevent unauthorized copying or distribution, which implies that without certain forms of copyright protection others can undermine the exploitation potential for the creator. As a result, and despite the fact that the

21. *See*: J.N.T. Weda, J.P. Poort & I. Akker, 'Makers over speerpunten. Opvattingen van makers en uitvoerend kunstenaars over de speerpuntenbrief Auteursrecht 20©20', *AMI* 2011-5 (2011): 164–170.

costs of creating many types of work have also decreased because of technological progress, the economic need for some form of copyright protection in the digital age may be stronger than ever before: the costs and quality deterioration of copying no longer provide a 'natural protection', but at the same time the enforcement of copyright seems more difficult than ever before.

There are, however, also costs (welfare losses) associated with copyright protection, which need to be taken into account. Landes & Posner mention the costs of administering copyright, which are likely to increase with the number of works created and with the strength of protection. The transaction costs of licensing copyright or obtaining consent for certain acts which may be copyright-relevant are considered to fall within the same broad category of transaction costs of copyright.[22]

A second general type of cost of copyright protection stems from the fact that whenever it allows works to be priced above their marginal costs, this is likely to cause demand to decrease below the level that is optimum from a static perspective. This entails a static loss of welfare through so-called *dead-weight losses*, and in a static framework marginal cost pricing would be preferable to a uniform price above marginal costs. Alternatively, refined price schemes may be used to minimize dead-weight losses.

A third type of cost is related to the former but appears in a dynamic perspective.[23] Works protected by copyright often serve as an input for other works and stronger economic rights will generally limit the possibilities for new creators to access works for inspiration or study, since they will cause works to be supplied at a higher price and prevent a free exchange of copies of earlier works. Moreover, it will limit their ability to utilize works for transformative use as this would likely be an infringement. Relatedly, uncertainty about the scope of copyright and whether or not certain acts will be an infringement will discourage risk-averse agents from making certain uses of works or even developing certain business models, leading to so-called chilling effects. These notions imply that there is an inverted u-shaped relation between the strength of economic rights and creation: beyond the strength of copyright protection that yields the maximum level of creation, a further increase in the strength leads to a *decrease* in the number of works created.

---

22. Landes & Posner (1989), 326. Posner (2005) adds that these costs also increase over time, as identifying a copyright holder to license from usually becomes more difficult over time: the copyright holder may well be the heir of the initial creator, or a company obtaining the rights after the bankruptcy of a first company which the initial creator transferred her economic rights to, etc. These increasing costs over time limit the optimal duration (term) of copyright. Although copyright term could also be studied from a perspective of reasonable exploitation and economic welfare, it falls outside the current chapter and should be studied independently from the scope of copyright, *see* the closing remarks in s. 5.2.1 above.
23. For example *see* Landes & Posner (1989), 332.

As a result of these three types of cost, the level of copyright protection that maximizes *efficiency* (economic welfare) lies *not* where creative output is highest, but somewhere on the left-hand slope of this inverted u-shaped curve.[24] The reasons for this are the increasing costs of administering copyright, and the dead-weight losses of stronger protection via the higher prices it entails. The further implications of this for the implementation of the right to reasonable exploitation are discussed in section 5.3 and the subsequent case studies.

5.2.3 Other Guiding Principles and Their Role

As pointed out above, it is accepted that mere efficiency considerations may lead to over- or under-protection when efficiency is balanced with the other principles, where these are not incorporated into the broad concept of efficiency.

5.2.3.1 Proportionality

One consideration to take into account is that copyright protection based on mere efficiency may give the right holder 'power beyond what a person rightfully deserves, or beyond what makes sense, given the circumstance'.[25] Proportionality in this sense means that the protection shall not be excessive or disproportionate to what is considered as fair, also taking more indirect effects such as privacy into consideration. This implies that even though efficiency considerations may point in the direction of giving the right holder the right to control a certain kind of behaviour, it should be possible to adjust the outcome with reference to that where, given the circumstances, it would result in disproportionate protection for the right holder, and in principle also the other way around. As an example, the principle of proportionality may speak against using 'small' copyrights as strategic leverage to control large markets.[26] Hence, the proportionality principle may serve as a tool to introduce *fairness* into the right to reasonable exploitation.[27] In addition, proportionality as a 'balancing instrument' implies that values other than efficiency, for example privacy, shall also be taken into account. Thus, 'proportionality' in this sense is the normative idea that a property right ought to be reasonably related to something socially useful and valuable. Where an unregulated market price of a property right moves radically out of alignment

24. Landes & Posner (1989), 343.
25. Merges (2011), 160.
26. *See* Merges (2011), 161.
27. The notion of fairness which may underlie the support for a bestseller clause protecting authors signing away their rights (as discussed in s. 5.2.2 above) could also be argued to justify amending efficiency based considerations under the umbrella of proportionality.

with underlying social utility, an institutional response is called for.[28] The proportionality principle should be taken into consideration ex ante when drafting the catalogue of examples, however without excluding the possibility for courts to also take it into consideration ex post.[29]

5.2.3.2 Public Domain

Reference to the public domain implies that not all information can or shall be protected with IP rights.[30] In copyright law, this is reflected in various kinds of rules, for example the distinction between non-protected ideas and protected expression, the originality criterion and the term limitation. From a utilitarian point of view these limitations to copyright protection may be explained through its efficiency enhancing functions designed to maximize social welfare. In fact, economic studies seem to suggest that the current rules, e.g., on term of protection, are not in full accordance with economic reasoning.[31] Still, preserving the public domain may be claimed to be of concern beyond the question of measurable costs and benefits, and, to the extent that may be the case, the principle of public domain may supplement or adjust the outcome based on efficiency.[32] As regards the scope of the economic rights and thus the right to reasonable exploitation, discussions about the right to public lending and data mining for research purposes are examples where the principle of public domain may play a role even beyond mere efficiency considerations.

5.2.3.3 Dignity

The concept of dignity may from one point of view refer to the interests protected by moral rights in copyright, implying that the creator of the work should be respected and recognized.[33] It is, however, also possible to have a broader take on dignity, referring to the special role copyright works play in relation to the enjoyment of the cultural life of the community, cf. also Article

28. Merges (2011), 181.
29. Cf. Merges (2011), 182–184.
30. Compare Merges (2011), 143–146 ('principle of non-removal').
31. *See* e.g., R. Pollock, 'Forever Minus A Day? Calculating Optimal Copyright Term', *Review of Economic Research on Copyright Issues* 6 (2009): 35–60, who, based on theoretical and empirical grounds, comes to the conclusion that the optimal copyright term from an economic point of view is around fifteen years, i.e., considerably shorter than any current copyright legislation would provide for.
32. Compare Merges (2011), 144.
33. Merges (2011), 157–158. It is to be noted that moral rights have been largely ignored in any economic analysis of copyright, *see* e.g., M. Rushton, 'The Moral Rights of Artists: Droit Moral ou Droit Pécuniaire?' *Journal of Cultural Economics* 22 (1998): 15–32, although there are recent studies of cultural economics that offer a different view from standard copyright economics, *see* Towse (2006).

27(2) of the Universal Declaration of Human Rights (UDHR).[34] Deriving from non-consequentialist natural rights thinking, like the Lockean moral desert and Kantian and Hegelian personality theories,[35] more than utilitarian efficiency based considerations, the concept of dignity may supplement efficiency considerations.[36]

5.2.3.4 Freedom of Expression

Freedom of speech and expression is a fundamental right laid down both in international and transnational human rights instruments and various national laws. Pursuant to the guidelines outlined in the foregoing, it is possible to claim that freedom of expression is implicit in the principles of public domain and proportionality, in the sense that freedom of expression may speak in favour of leaving certain kinds of use of the copyright work to the public domain, and that it also reflects a social value to which the exclusive right must be related. When freedom of expression is enumerated here as a principle on its own, it is under the consideration that copyright also *enhances* cultural expression, not only limits it.[37] Thus, when stating above that other social or legal norms, like freedom of expression, can give reason to amend the position derived from efficiency considerations, the implication is not necessarily that it gives the right holder a weaker position than that which follows from the incentive rationale. The main point here is that freedom of expression is a guiding principle on its own, which although may be included in a welfare economic framework, will serve as an independent argument when assessing the scope of the right to reasonable exploitation.

5.2.3.5 Market Integration

Under EU law, market integration has a similar position to freedom of expression. Market integration concerns may also be included in efficiency considerations, but the way it has been treated under EU law is not necessarily in compliance with the latter. Thus, the market integration

---

34. *See* D.J. Gervais, 'How Intellectual Property and Human Rights Can Live Together: An Updated Perspective', in *Intellectual Property and Human Rights (Third Edition)*, ed. P.L.C. Torremans (Amsterdam: Kluwer Law International, 2015), 3–26, basing a dignity claim on 'refocusing the policy efforts to operationalize the (supposed) value attached to creation in the traditional conceptual edifice of copyright, recognizing that copyright works (arguably with the huge exception of software) have special status because of their cultural resonance' (20).
35. *See* D.J. Gervais, 'Human Rights and the Philosophical Foundation of Intellectual Property', in: *Research Handbook on Human Rights and Intellectual Property*, ed. C. Geiger (Cheltenham UK; Northampton US: Edward Elgar, 2015), 89–97, 94–95; and Merges (2011), 156.
36. *See* examples in ss. 5.4.1 and 5.4.2.3 below.
37. *See* Rognstad (2015), 516, fn. 31.

rationale seems to apply irrespective of whether or not it enhances efficiency. There are reasons to question this policy, but on the other hand it is hard to ignore the significance of a rationale that has been applied more or less consistently by the CJEU for six decades. When discussing the content of 'reasonable exploitation' in a European context, the market integration rationale should at least be taken into account. One of the advantages of the proposed model is that it is aimed at revealing the policy considerations at stake, instead of concealing them within concepts like reproduction, distribution, communication to the public and so on.

5.2.3.6 The Role of the Other Guiding Principles vis-à-vis Efficiency

The outline of the various guiding principles that should contribute to the understanding of the principle of 'reasonable exploitation' underscores the complexity of copyright policy. Rather than taking a pure instrumentalist approach to the purpose of copyright, where everything may be explained through a narrow conception of economic efficiency, it is acknowledged that the basis for modern copyright policy is best found in a mix between consequentialist and non-consequentialist considerations. The various guiding principles, other than efficiency, are meant to reflect this. A problem, however, with the starting point whereby various values are emphasized simultaneously, is that it easily ends up with a 'weighing' exercise – the so-called balancing test – where incommensurable values are held against each other in order to try to reach a compromise based on what seems to be the 'right' balance between various values and interests. It goes without saying that this is an exercise that does not lead to very precise results and much ambiguity exists as to 'how to strike the appropriate balance'. Here, a different method for how to approach the question of what is a 'reasonable exploitation' is proposed.

Following up on what was said about the relationship between efficiency and other values in section 5.2.1 above, the concept of 'reasonable exploitation' will be built on a preliminary presumption that results based on incentive based efficiency considerations will be compatible with the other guiding principles. In other words, these results are presumed to be proportional, in line with the interest of the public domain, in compliance with the principle of dignity in the wider sense, and apt to enhance freedom of expression and market integration. Thus, an adjustment of the efficiency based outcome to account for the other guiding principles will only need to be considered when efficiency and the other principles appear to be in conflict. This method is to be applied both ex ante and ex post, i.e., both when drafting legislation that will implement the right to reasonable exploitation, including the example catalogue that will be further elaborated on in section 5.5 below, and in case law interpreting the legislation. It should be emphasized, however, that the right to reasonable exploitation is only meant as a model for drafting 'internal' copyright rules within a specific copyright regime. It is not the intention to create a system that internalizes 'external norms', like for example international human rights, since this will not be compatible with the current legal order. Thus, even though the ambition with the model is to create an environment that does not conflict with 'external norms', the implication is not that it is immune against 'intervention' from such norms. The case studies in this chapter suggest, however, that in many instances there is no reason to actually adjust the outcome of an efficiency based analysis.

5.3 THE RIGHT TO REASONABLE EXPLOITATION OPERATIONALIZED

5.3.1 Implementation of 'The Alternative Model': Principles and Catalogue Regulation

In the previous article on the right to reasonable exploitation, it was suggested that the model be implemented by way of a combination of general principles and a catalogue of examples demonstrating where the concrete boundaries for what is considered as reasonable exploitation are to be drawn.[38] The idea is that both the general principles and the catalogue should be established in statutory provisions. The purpose of this kind of regulation is to seek an optimal balance between the need for predictability, legal certainty and transparency on the one hand, and the urge for flexibility resulting from the ever-changing technological and economic conditions on the other. This goes into the general discussion about rules versus standards as regulatory instruments, and the method of regulation is supported by studies suggesting that catalogue regulation would be 'preferable to both rules and standards and better enhance the foundational values of the legal system'.[39]

As already indicated above, the scope of the right to reasonable exploitation may be determined with reference to efficiency, proportionality, public domain, dignity, freedom of expression and market integration, which may serve as *guiding principles* both ex ante and ex post. That is, these principles should guide legislators when further specifying the boundaries of

38. Rognstad (2015).

39. *See* G. Parchomowsky & A. Stein, 'Catalogs', *Columbia Law Review* 115 (2015): 165–209. *See also* C. Bousallis, Y. Feldman & H.E. Smith, 'Experimental Analysis of the Effect of Standards on Compliance and Performance', *Regulation & Governance* 11 (2017): *see* http://onlinelibrary.wiley.com/doi/10.1111/rego.12140/abstract (accessed 5 October 2017).

the right to reasonable exploitation, that perhaps being their most important function. They may also play a role ex post for courts applying the rules, although the operationalization discussed below, as well as the 'catalogue of examples', and analogizing from it, will be more instrumental in this respect.

As also pointed out above, efficiency should be the starting point when concretizing reasonable exploitation. And to be sure, creating optimal incentives for creation of works is often cited as the core aim of current copyright law. Our allegation is, however, that this is barely reflected in the way the economic rights are defined and structured today. This is not least so because the economic rights in terms of *reproduction*, *communication to the public* and *distribution* no longer seem to match with the digital environment. Even though these acts are broad and general in the sense that they can be applied to music, books, films, etc., they appear to be more adequate and relevant in an analogue environment than in a digital environment. In EU law one can observe the CJEU struggling with these concepts to take a position on relatively common issues such as linking and embedding, resale of digital content and making copies of digitally acquired content. In an analogue environment, it may have been logical (if only for the sake of enforcement) to make reproduction an important element of the exclusive right of the creator, for instance, but in the current digital environment, this no longer seems the case. Accidental or transient copies of works, for instance, are continually made in the process of consuming or distributing works, but these do not affect the exploitation by the right holder. Reproducing a work without distributing these copies, for instance, seems harmless for the incentives for the creator to create or to exploit a work. Also, it is disputable whether the welfare costs of the protection of economic rights (transaction costs as well as static and dynamic dead-weight losses) in a digital environment are sufficiently taken into account.

Therefore, when operationalizing the right to reasonable exploitation, there is a need for a different take on these problems. For an economic assessment of the exclusive right to reasonable exploitation, one needs to go back to the economic foundation of copyright protection, which is resolution of the 'public good' market failure associated with the creation of works, so as to provide proper incentives for the creation and exploitation of works. As a general principle, one would only want to give a creator exclusive rights with respect to acts that, *as a consequence of this public good market failure, negatively and significantly affect the current or future exploitation opportunities for the right holder* and hence negatively interfere with these incentives. Acts that do not meet this criterion can be considered 'copyright irrelevant' or may even benefit the right holder. Hence, they do not fall within the exclusive right to reasonable exploitation.

Here, it is essential to realize that exploitation can take many forms other than a simple exchange of a physical carrier – a copy of a work – for money. Exploitation can take the form of providing digital access to works on a permanent or temporary basis – for instance in digital download models such as iTunes and streaming models such as Spotify and Netflix. Moreover, a monetary payment by the end user in exchange for a work or access to a work is just one of several possible business models. Others may rely on advertising revenues (e.g., YouTube, Spotify Free, Readfy), collecting data about consumers, creating an environment of cross-selling other works or products, building a fan base or reputation which can be monetized in the future, and whatnot. For the right holders of works on free platforms such as YouTube or SSRN, the number of views or downloads can be an important incentive for creating and posting works, as views or downloads may be monetized directly through a share in advertising revenues, or indirectly as a proof of reputation or fame which contributes to the career opportunities of the right holder. When the challenges of copyright in the digital age became apparent, in particular in the context of unauthorized file sharing, an often-heard recommendation was that the content industry develop new business models.[40] Now that various such business models have emerged, it is important that the existence of a variety of exploitation models is borne in mind when operationalizing reasonable exploitation. This does not imply that any current exploitation model must be respected and protected by copyright. But it does mean that the concept of reasonable exploitation should be broad enough to allow for many of the current exploitation models and general enough to account for new models that are yet to be developed.

5.3.2 Conditional Control as the Operationalization of Reasonable Exploitation

In this section we will operationalize the economic foundation – the efficiency function – of the economic rights. This operationalization, which also is intended to be laid down in statutory provisions, serves to make the economic rationale behind the exploitation rights concrete and to formulate the core of it.

The central notion implicit in the exclusive rights to exploitation of the work, even under the current framework, is that of *control*, which enables the right holder to exchange access to a work for something which has direct or indirect commercial value for him, be it money, website traffic, attention or personal data. A right holder exploiting a work can control who can consume a work and under what circumstances, and choose an exploitation model which seems fit. This ability to control the exclusion of consumers is what is lacking without copyright protection due to the 'public good' nature of a work. However, from an economic incentive perspective, control is only justified to the extent that, due to this public good market failure, a lack of control would negatively and significantly affect the current or future

40. *See* e.g., N. van Eijk, J. Poort & P. Rutten, 'Legal, Economic and Cultural Aspects of File Sharing', *Communications & Strategies* 77 (2010), 35–54.

exploitation opportunities for the right holder and thereby reduce the incentives to create, publish or exploit works.

Still, even if a negative and significant effect may occur, the various 'costs' of copyright protection need to be considered. First, transaction costs may justify curtailing copyright and placing certain acts still outside the realm of copyright, even though they negatively and significantly affect the current or future exploitation opportunities for the right holder.

Dead-weight losses that result from above marginal cost pricing and chilling effects that stem from uncertainty about the scope of copyright are a difficult issue. In theory, the interests of society at large and the right holders to minimize such costs are aligned, but in practice, given the fact that perfect price discrimination is not achievable, a right holder will be inclined to accept such dead-weight losses if it helps to maximize revenues. Thus, reasonable exploitation may involve limits on the ability of right holders to price above marginal costs, in particular vis-à-vis new creators where it will cause dynamic inefficiencies.

Following from the costs of copyright protection outlined in section 5.2.2, four questions can be formulated to assess whether or not a certain act would fall within or outside the realm of copyright as a right to reasonable exploitation:

(1) Does an act relate to the public good nature of works and thereby affect the *control* of a creator over exchanging access to a work for something which has direct or indirect commercial value for him?
(2) If so, does it negatively and significantly affect the current or future exploitation opportunities for the right holder and thereby reduce the incentives to create, publish or exploit works?
(3) If so, are the transaction costs of considering an act to be copyright relevant small in comparison to the benefits to the creator and in particular his incentives for creation and active exploitation?
(4) If so, are the dead-weight losses and chilling effects of considering an act to be copyright relevant small in comparison to the benefits to the creator and in particular his incentives for creation and active exploitation?[41]

The notion that the intervention to introduce copyright is justified by the 'public good' nature of works implies that, as a default, control over a work should not extend beyond its first exploitation any more than what is the case today for tangible copies due to the exhaustion rule: once a digital or physical copy of a work has been sold, the market failure that justified copyright legislation has been resolved with respect to this specific copy. Like for any other product which does not suffer from this market failure, there is in

41. Note that the answers to questions (3) and (4), which balance the costs and benefits of copyright protection, could in theory differ between different kinds of works. This chapter does not elaborate on such potential differences.

general no economic justification for granting the initial creator control over the secondary market or over the value created with the product downstream in the value chain.[42] However, a market failure may exist where the buyer of a copyright work could extend the market by selling multiple copies or by granting several new consumers access to the work. Thus, the initial buyer becomes a new seller, not just of what he bought, who can undercut the original creator because he has no investment in the initial creation to recoup. This reintroduces the initial 'public good' market failure and can in certain circumstances justify intervention for the initial creator to regain control. These mechanisms will be studied in more detail below, in particular when discussing the issue of private copying and digital exhaustion.

Bearing in mind the considerations above, the operationalization of the efficiency principle may be formulated in the legislation as a *right to control the use of the work to the extent necessary to secure current or future exploitation opportunities for the right holder*. This will serve as a starting point which also has to be supplemented by considerations under the other guiding principles. The more concrete implications of the right to reasonable exploitation will have to be laid down in the catalogue of examples, which will demonstrate the outcome of this operationalization of the efficiency principle, along with the guiding principles.

5.4 'CASE STUDIES' THROUGH THE LENS OF REASONABLE EXPLOITATION

In the following sections, some proposals for concretization of the right to reasonable exploitation will be made against the background of an analysis of certain issues that for the most part have been dealt with in recent case law of the Court of Justice of the European Union (CJEU). First, we discuss instances of the use of authorized material, after which we turn to the use of unauthorized content. The analysis will outline how the questions are to be solved by applying the operationalization of efficiency formulated in the preceding section and possible adjustments to it on the basis of other guiding principles. The solution is contrasted with the outcomes of the CJEU case law.

5.4.1 Starting Point: Conditional Control

Conditional control implies that the right holder should be in a position to decide when and under what conditions the work is communicated to the

42. In this context *see also* the discussion of the fallacious concern over 'pecuniary externalities' (as opposed to 'technological externalities') in: J.F. Duffy, 'Intellectual Property Isolationism and the Average Cost Thesis', *Texas Law Review* 83 (2005): 1077–1095.

outside world for the first time. Otherwise, he would be deprived of his current (and most likely also his future) exploitation opportunities. In this respect, the principles of efficiency and dignity go hand in hand.[43] After a work has been made public for the first time, the question is what kind of use should fall under the right holder's control. As pointed out above, the starting point for this analysis should, under the right to reasonable exploitation, be the assessment of whether, against the background of the public good nature of works, the right holder's control is necessary in order to secure the current and future exploitation of the work, where transaction costs, dead-weight losses and chilling effects relating to the control should also play a role as to what kind of solution should apply.

When outlining solutions that are believed to comply with this, a distinction, at least for presentational purposes will be made between exploitation or use of material that has been acquired or accessed with the right holder's consent, and exploitation or use based on unauthorized access. In the latter case, the right holder obviously lacks all control over the access to the work and in many instances there is a strong presumption that the exploitation or use will affect the right holder's current or future exploitation possibilities, so the assessment is likely to be different from situations where the exploitation or use is based on authorized access and control can largely be exercised. In the following section, proposals are made as to how certain situations are to be handled under the right to reasonable exploitation where the exploitation or use is based on authorized access, also taking into account the necessity of adjustments to the outcome based on the guiding principles other than efficiency. Thereafter we will, on the same premises, deal with some (of the same) situations where the exploitation or use is based on unauthorized access.

As pointed out, the main purpose here is to outline possible solutions. As was said in the introduction, the solutions are based on economic considerations that will not be presented in detail here, but in a separate chapter of this volume.[44]

5.4.2 Use of Authorized Material

5.4.2.1 Private Copying

To assess the extent of reasonable exploitation vis-à-vis private copying, it is useful to distinguish different kinds of private copies:[45]

---

43. Cf. the moral right principle of the right to first publication ('droit du divulgation').
44. *See* J. Poort, elsewhere in this volume.
45. The typology here and part of this section are taken from J. Poort & J.P. Quintais, 'The Levy Runs Dry: A Legal and Economic Analysis of EU Private Copying Levies', *Journal of Intellectual Property, Information Technology and Electronic Commerce Law* (*JIPITEC*) 4 (2013): 205–224.

(1) Making 'clone copies' of or 'format shifting' CDs, DVDs and media files, or storing streaming audio and video for offline playback (also known as stream 'ripping' or 'capture').
(2) Making backup copies of works.
(3) Making copies of broadcast works for time shifting, such as storing radio or TV content on a recording device to watch it another time, and repeatedly if desired.
(4) Making clone copies or format shifting to *share* works with family and friends.
(5) Making clone copies or format shifting of works from media rented or borrowed from libraries or commercial renters.

A central parameter for assessing these situations against the background of conditional control is indirect appropriability. The concept refers to the economic mechanism according to which, under certain conditions, the demand for originals will reflect the value that consumers place on both the originals and subsequent copies they may make. As a result, the value of private copying can be priced into the initial purchase and, by doing so, this value is indirectly appropriated.

It is presumed that in situations (1) and (2) the value of private copying can largely be priced into the initial purchase and, therefore, these acts are copyright irrelevant. The reason for this is that in these situations the circle of consumers that derive utility from an original unit is not extended: no 'copying groups' are formed in which copies become competitors to the original. Some occasional additional sales could be foregone as a result of such copying, for instance when a person would have bought his favourite CD twice to play it at home and in his car or to replace a CD which has been damaged. But to the extent that consumers can broadly anticipate their copying behaviour, the option to copy can be *priced into the initial purchase* by right holders. Consequently, making copies for format shifting and backup purposes should not be considered to affect the right holder's current or future exploitation possibilities and hence the incentive to create, publish or exploit works in a negative way and should therefore not fall under any exclusive right or be compensated for by way of a copyright levy. Consideration for the other guiding principles such as proportionality and dignity does not seem to suggest otherwise. To the contrary, they are aligned with this outcome based on efficiency arguments. Moreover, the results should be media neutral and also 'carry over' to situations where copying for the purposes above are made in cloud lockers on the Internet. Also, in the latter situation no harm on the part of the right holder seems to be implied since the benefits of making such private copies can be priced into the purchase and the right holder retains control over who can access the work.

The same arguments largely hold for time shifting copies (situation (3)). However, where time shifting also involves systematically skipping advertisements (or time shifting to a moment in time when the ads surrounding a radio or television broadcast no longer have their initial commercial value), it may undermine the exploitation opportunities for the right holder to some extent. Such a case may be looked upon differently and may justify an alternative way of remuneration for right holders, such as a levy on welfare economic grounds, provided the transaction costs and dead-weight losses of such levies do not outweigh the positive incentive effects and the levy system does not raise concerns in relation to the other guiding principles, such as proportionality with respect to consumers privacy concerns.

For situations (4) and (5) the picture is different in that they extend the circle of consumers who derive utility from an original unit of content. Here, the point may be made that indirect appropriability depends on the ability to price discriminate: charging a higher price for users who are likely to copy extensively while preventing arbitrage through a secondary market or other ways to circumvent price discrimination.[46] With respect to libraries (situation (5)) this can be done by setting a higher price for libraries and a lower price for individuals. The utility of copies of type (5) could in theory be appropriated indirectly by setting the appropriate rental prices, unless restrictions put on the rental price from a public service perspective prohibit doing so. For the right holder, this implies that price discrimination between libraries and commercial renters – who would pay a higher price to account for the utility of subsequent copies[47] – and end consumers will be required. If these markets cannot be separated, copying groups will be too variable in size to adequately price copying into the purchase and a levy will be justified.

Regarding copies shared with family and friends (type (4)), the aforementioned private copying might be harmful to copyright holders even though part of the additional utility can be appropriated indirectly. This is partly due to the fact that the size of such copying groups is variable, while right holders cannot observe this group size and hence cannot price discriminate accordingly.[48] There might therefore be a need for regulating this situation differently.

5.4.2.2 Resale of Digital Content

As pointed out above, an efficiency based approach implies that there is no market failure to justify granting the initial creator automatic control over the secondary market or over the value created from the product downstream in

46. *See* the study of S.J. Liebowitz, 'Copying and Indirect Appropriability: Photocopying of Journals', *Journal of Political Economy* 93 (1985): 945–957.
47. *Ibid.*
48. *See* S.M. Besen & S.N. Kirby, 'Private Copying, Appropriability, and Optimal Copying Royalties', *The Journal of Law & Economics* 32 (1989): 255–280. Like other models discussed in this chapter, the models Besen and Kirby develop ignore possible positive dynamic effects of the consumption of copies on future sales (the so-called sampling effect) and negative effects of lost sales on the future production of content.

the value chain. This gives an economics based justification for what, under current copyright (and other IP rights), we call the exhaustion (or first sale) rule, and the economic rationale applies in principle irrespective of whether or not the content is tied to tangible objects. As for 'ordinary' private goods such as smartphones, cars and jewellery, there is no market failure to justify granting the initial creator automatic control over the secondary market or over the value created with the product downstream in the value chain once a work has been sold. To be sure, the right holder may want to contractually restrict a purchaser's right to dispose of the content he has bought. The validity of such clauses may be subject to scrutiny under contract law and competition law (and in EU law also taking market integration aspects into consideration), but from an incentive based economic perspective, copyright protected works do not seem to deserve special privileges in this respect.[49] The other guiding principles identified in section 5.2, proportionality, public domain, dignity, freedom of expression and market integration, do not relate to resale of digital content in any way that gives reason to adjust this outcome.

A point which is often raised to argue that resale of digital content is different and therefore should not be allowed, is that digital content does not degrade. As a consequence, first and second-hand copies would become perfect substitutes, spoiling the first-hand market. Several points can be made in this respect. First, just as in the case of jewellery, cars and smartphones, the option to resell may be anticipated by the initial buyer, resulting in a higher average willingness to pay (comparable to the concept of indirect appropriability in relation to private copying). Second, copyright works are typically fast-selling products, which generate most of their revenues within a limited time span, before the second-hand market would gather steam. For works such as video games, versioning strategies can be pursued to support this. Third, most buyers will have a preference for the first-hand market over the second-hand market, even for digital content, for fear of buying a faulty product without a right to reclaim their money.

Yet, there is a need for refining the approach with regard to the possibilities for product and price discrimination: it can be welfare enhancing to prevent discounted student licences for software being resold to companies. Also, partial reselling of multi-user licences would constitute a serious threat to price discrimination, as it would undermine volume based (second degree) price discrimination. On the other hand, in digital markets a provider can try to uphold price discrimination without contractual arrangements, for instance by versioning or offering additional services.[50]

---

49. Cf. A. Katz, 'The Economic Rationale for Exhaustion: Distribution and Post-Sale Restraints', in: *Research Handbook on IP Exhaustion and Parallel Imports*, ed. I. Carboli & E. Lee (Cheltenham: Edward Elgar, 2016), 23–43.
50. In the case of software, *see* e.g., O-A. Rognstad, 'Legally Flawed But Politically Sound? Exhaustion of Copyright in the EU After UsedSoft', *Oslo Law Review* 1 (2014): 1–19.

As pointed out above, an obvious problem arises if the secondary market can lead to market extension, where buyers can resell multiple copies or grant several new consumers access to the work, undercutting the original creator because they have no investment in the initial creation to recoup. Therefore, an important precondition for letting the initial purchaser exploit the secondary market will be that he deletes his access to the purchased product, e.g., a software program or an e-book.[51]

Without TPMs a right holder has next to no possibilities to guarantee that such market extension does not occur: He lacks the possibility of monitoring whether the initial version is deleted or uninstalled after resale. There are two ways to deal with this. The first is simply to accept this and still allow digital resale as a general rule. In this approach, right holders can regain control by implementing strong copy protection by TPMs.[52] A disadvantage of this approach is the transaction costs and dead-weight losses it entails, because TPM protected works are in many cases less user-friendly.

A second option, which may be preferable, is only to allow digital resale for works protected by TPMs. As long as this condition is transparent on sale, it need not be an obstacle for consumers, and market places can easily monitor to ensure that only TPM protected works can be resold. For TPM-free material, monitoring the legitimacy of the secondary market is not possible and therefore control is exercised by having exclusive rights to the secondary market.[53]

5.4.2.3 Linking and Embedding

From the efficiency based perspective of conditional control outlined above, a distinction will have to be made between hyperlinking and embedding. This is irrespective of any distinction between various kinds of hyperlinks, e.g., 'reference links' (links to homepages) and 'deep links' (links to subpages). A common trait with hyperlinks and embedding is that the right holder remains in control of the availability and integrity of the content subject to linking and embedding. If the right holder decides to make changes to the content, the changes will immediately extend to the linking or embedding sites. This is a fundamental difference between linking and embedding on the one hand, and emailing documents downloaded from a website or posting them on a different site on the other. In the latter case, the

---

51. Compare the *UsedSoft* decision by the CJEU (*UsedSoft GmbH v Oracle International Corp*, CJEU 3 July 2012, case C-128/11, EU:C:2012:407), *see* further in s. 5.4.4 below.
52. Or by contractually limiting or forbidding such resale, in which case such a contract is subject to general rules concerning fair business practices and antitrust.
53. A solution resembling this has been achieved by the Dutch e-book reseller *Tomkabinet*, which only accepts an e-book for resale if the seller provides the original download link to the original seller via an on-site login. Thus, Tomkabinet can make sure they are only reselling the same book once at a time. However, they cannot verify that a seller actually erases his own copy. *See*: https://www.tomkabinet.nl/en/faq/ (accessed 1 August 2017).

control over the availability and integrity of the content is lost.[54] With respect to the question of whether there is any negative and significant effect on the current or future exploitation opportunities for the right holder, however, there is a substantial difference between linking and embedding.

In the case of linking, the right holder cannot only control the availability and integrity of the work, but also the environment in which the work can be accessed. Moreover, linking has significant and positive effects for the consumption of the work. The right holder remains in control of the information that is made public as well as the conditions under which it is made public (e.g., payment, registration, advertisements). This is also the case for so-called deep links (links to a 'subpage'), which can even be redirected to the home page, and the contextual information and advertisements surrounding a deep link will still be seen. Hence, in the vast majority of cases, linking can only positively affect the current or future exploitation opportunities for the right holder, if it affects them at all, and it seems hard to argue that linking should infringe on the right to reasonable exploitation. This should consequently also be the default rule. It can, on the other hand, not be excluded that links can be used in a way that affects current or future exploitation opportunities for the right holder. This is only presumed to occur in exceptional cases, for which the right holder should have the burden of argumentation.

Embedding and framing are fundamentally different from hyperlinking in respect of the fact that the right holder in such cases has no control over the environment in which the work is accessed. This can negatively and significantly affect the exploitation opportunities for the right holder, as it entails that the right holder's site does not need to be visited and advertisements or other information on this site are not seen. This could deprive right holders of reasonable forms of exploitation.

However, before jumping to the conclusion that embedding might therefore fall within the scope of copyright as a right to reasonable exploitation, the transaction costs and dead-weight losses of doing so need to be taken into consideration.[55] It goes without saying that many right holders

---

54. This should not imply that downloading content and emailing it or posting it on a site should be infringements per se. In many cases, right holders do not depend on copyright for their income or otherwise. Think for instance of an academic author writing a research paper, or a politician writing an essay. Often, he or she would not object to people proliferating such a document by email and might even encourage it. They will just want people to read their work and do not care about an exploitation model other than the attribution of the work, or not even that, if it is purely the message they want to get across. It is undesirable for copyright as a right to reasonable exploitation to also stigmatize such acts which right holders often do not object to as infringements. One way to solve this would be to consider such emailing and posting of works acceptable, unless the environment in which the works can be accessed for free obviously qualifies as an exploitation model, e.g., by using advertisements, requiring registration or counting downloads.
55. *See* questions (3) and (4), s. 5.3.2. above.

do not mind if their content is embedded, or even encourage it. Hence, it would entail enormous transaction costs to require a licence for any such embedding. One possible way to avoid requiring individual licences is to create opt-in or opt-out possibilities, for example by way of some standardized information in the meta-text of a web page which states whether the information can be embedded without consent, either as a 'do not embed'-line (opt-out), or an 'okay to embed'-line (opt-in). The preferable choice between the two from an economic perspective is the one which involves the lowest transaction costs. Taking into account the vast number of web pages that currently exist and assuming that a large majority of the website owners do not mind being embedded, an opt-out would be preferable. If a website were to ignore such an opt-out, it could be held liable for enforcement such as a notice and take down, blocking or fines.[56]

On the other hand, the right holder should not be required to install an effective access restriction whenever he does not appreciate embedding of his content. Even though such restrictions would probably be more effective than a 'do not embed' line in the meta-text of a web page, the transaction costs and dead-weight losses of this suggestion will be very large, making it a less efficient solution: it would deprive the website holder of the possibility to offer users easy access without a requirement to log in.

The solutions advocated here seem to prove that the efficiency principle plays well along with the other guiding principles. The dignity principle would be an argument in favour of securing the right holder's control over the environment in which the work is accessed in the embedding situation, and freedom of expression seems to be sufficiently secured by the solutions advocated here.

5.4.2.4 Data Mining

A much-discussed issue in current copyright law is so-called text and data mining (TDM) which, according to one definition is 'the discovery of interesting, unexpected or valuable structures in large datasets'.[57] The copyright relevance of the current framework is undisputed, since TDM will affect the reproduction right. Whether it should fall within the scope of a right to reasonable exploitation to control such actions is more doubtful. The economic arguments for placing TDM within the scope of the economic

56. In principle, such a solution could also be applied to linking but, as discussed, in the case of linking it is much less likely that a right holder has legitimate reasons to prevent linking on the ground of reasonable exploitation.

57. *See* I. Hargreaves et al., *Standardisation in the Area of Innovation and Technological Development, Notably in the Field of Text and Data Mining. Report from the Expert Group* (EU Commission: Brussels, 2014), available at http://ec.europa.eu/research/innovation-union/pdf/TDM-report_from_the_expert_group-042014.pdf (accessed 1 August 2017). *See also* D.J. Hand, H. Mannilla & P. Smyth, *Principles of Data Mining* (Cambridge MA: MIT Press, 2001).

rights are weak. The possible arguments are that any unlicensed use which has economic significance and generates additional profits as a consequence unreasonably prejudices the legitimate interests of the right holder and therefore should be licensed. Such reasoning resembles the argument criticized in previous sections, i.e., in the case of digital resale, that authors should somehow be entitled to a share of any surpluses created by or with works in downstream markets. However, while in the case of digital resale the market failure can be considered resolved for any physical or digital copy that is sold, in the case of TDM, it can be observed that there never was a market failure in relation to TDM that needs to be resolved, provided *access* to articles to engage in TDM is lawfully obtained.

The additional profits generated by TDM have never been part of the incentive system of the authors. This can be linked to the concept of 'foreseeability', which is proposed by Balganesh to limit the exclusive rights of copyright. Balganesh states that 'creators, like actors elsewhere, are incapable of fully anticipating all future contingencies associated with their actions, which in turn limits the effectiveness of incentives'.[58] Put differently, there is no point in granting rights that provide ineffective incentives or no incentives at all. In this vein, the emergence of TDM can be considered to have been unforeseeable in the past and can have no retroactive incentives. Now that TDM is an emerging field of research, it may have become foreseeable and part of the incentive system for present-day publishers aggregating large databases of articles. But to the extent that TDM was unforeseen in existing contracts for accessing such databases, this can be assumed not to have been the case.[59] In such a case, requiring an additional licence for TDM would give windfall profits to right holders without any incentive effect, while imposing dead-weight losses (as well as transaction costs) on TDM. Turning to the guiding principles other than efficiency, control of TDM may hamper freedom of expression and does not sit well with the principle of proportionality. The copyright relevance of this kind of use can therefore be highly disputed.[60] Thus, controlling it should not be considered as a reasonable exploitation of the work.[61]

58. S. Balganesh, 'Foreseeability and copyright incentives', *Harvard Law Review* 122 (2009): 1569–1633, 1571.
59. For future contracts, the value users derive from TDM can largely be priced into the purchase without specific contractual clauses.
60. Compare the Position Statement of the Max Planck Institute for Innovation and Competition on the Proposed Modernisation of European Copyright Rules, part B (exceptions and limitations), available at http://www.ip.mpg.de/fileadmin/ipmpg/content/stellungnahmen/MPI-Position-Paper_TDM_2017-01-14-corr_def.pdf (accessed 1 August 2017), paras 6–8 and 13.
61. This conclusion is in line with the recommendations in Hargreaves et. al (2014).

5.4.2.5 Access Controls and Protection of TPMs

The right to reasonable exploitation implies that the regulation of access controls and TPMs is integrated in the exclusive rights and not treated as a separate 'layer' of protection.[62] Access controls and TPMs are used by right holders to control the distribution and use of works. They may be used to prevent the unauthorized distribution of works or to bolster price discrimination. The latter is for instance achieved by preventing users from installing software with a single licence on multiple computers, using a basic Netflix subscription on multiple devices simultaneously, or playing DVDs with a US region code in the EU. Also, allowing access to online services from some countries and blocking it from others (geo-blocking) can be argued to fall within this category.

A right holder's commercial interests in controlling such activities by the use of TPMs is easily understood: unauthorized distribution of works undermines the basic control required for reasonable exploitation while price discrimination between, for instance, single and multiple user licences or between regions can be an important instrument for recouping investments in the fixed costs of creating a work.

From the perspective of the right to reasonable exploitation, however, there may be distinctions between different uses of access control and TPMs. It can be argued that as soon as a work on a physical carrier has been sold, or as soon as access to a work on a subscription basis has been licensed, the public good market failure has been resolved and no further protection is required.[63] This implies that there is no reason for *copyright* to protect for instance TPMs that aim to price discriminate between regions. There is no market failure to justify copyright works enjoying a privileged position as compared to other products and services in the legal 'protection' of strategies for price discrimination. On the other hand, there is no reason to treat copyright works more harshly and to forbid price discrimination categorically. Such practices ought to fall outside the scope of copyright and be dealt with through the lens of fair business practices and antitrust, like for other products and services. The principles of proportionality, public domain, dignity and freedom of expression are well-aligned with this position. In the case of geo-blocking, the principle of market integration may be a justification for discouraging or even forbidding such practices, even though the welfare economic rationale in this specific case is disputable.

TPMs that aim to price discriminate between e.g., single and multi-user licences are different, as they aim to address the public good market failure that forms the economic justification for copyright: installing or 'copying' a single licence a large number of times. As a consequence, preventing such

62. *See* Rognstad (2015), 535–540.

63. Compare this with the discussion of redistribution of purchased material, for which exhaustion applies as a basic principle.

multiplication or market extension logically falls within the scope of reasonable exploitation and hence within the scope of copyright, although it could also be dealt with as a breach of a licence contract.

5.4.3 Use of Non-authorized Material

Having dealt with a number of uses of works that are acquired with the authorization of the right holder, we now turn to a few cases of the use of unauthorized content. For this discussion, some general observations are in place on unauthorized up- and downloading, e.g., by downloading from social media or cyber lockers that are open to all or large numbers of internet users, or by sharing content through peer-to-peer networks.

Regarding such activities, the lack of authorization clearly affects the ability of a creator to control access to works and to exchange it for something which has direct or indirect commercial value for him. The second economic question phrased in section 5.3.2, whether unauthorized publication negatively and significantly affects the current or future exploitation opportunities for the right holder, has proven to be more cumbersome. Drawing on the large body of literature on the effect of unauthorized file sharing, a variety of different and opposing interactions may occur.[64] Still, one conclusion drawn is that 'the vast majority of the literature … finds evidence that piracy harms media sales'.[65] Note, however, that this evidence generally suggests a much smaller effect than a one-to-one displacement of sales by illegal copies. According to many studies, the effect is also substantially smaller than the loss of revenues from recorded music that the industry has experienced since the late 1990s. Nevertheless, in general the claim that unauthorized use and exploitation of works negatively and significantly affects the current or future exploitation opportunities for the right holder and may thereby reduce the incentives to create, publish or exploit works seems justified.

5.4.3.1 Private Copying

In line with the general observations above, the economic analysis of making private copies of non-authorized material – which is how downloading from unauthorized sources for private purposes could be construed – differs fundamentally from that of private copies from authorized material in section 5.4.2.1. Copying for private purposes from such unauthorized sources has *constant* (near-zero) marginal costs while the size of copying groups will differ immensely: a first high-quality torrent of a blockbuster movie may be

64. *See* Van Eijk, Poort & Rutten (2010), who distinguish nine different interactions.
65. Smith & Telang (2012).

downloaded thousands or even millions of times, which implies indirect appropriability is not feasible in the face of online file sharing. Since there is no relation between the uploader (including any unlawful content provider) and the downloader, and the number of copies made from an original will vary dramatically, one cannot charge a buyer of a DVD, CD or e-book for the value downloaders attribute to it were she to put it on a file-sharing site. Hence, there are sound economic arguments for such copies to fall within the exclusive right of the creator, or to introduce some compensation system to the extent that such copying cannot be controlled.[66] Privacy concerns and thus the principle of proportionality could here speak in favour of such a compensation system.

5.4.3.2 Linking and Embedding

So far, we have dealt with the cases of linking to and embedding of lawful sources. Turning to the question of how to consider linking to or embedding of *unauthorized* sources, the general observations above about the unauthorized use and exploitation of works need to be borne in mind. As a consequence, linking to content that has been published without authorization can negatively and significantly affect the current or future exploitation opportunities for the right holder, irrespective of the fact that the linking (or embedding) party may not himself be publishing without authorization.

This suggests that linking to or embedding of unauthorized content should be deemed infringing, but on the other hand, holding a linking party liable for infringement in all cases, without prior warning, would entail enormous transaction costs and potential dead-weight losses in terms of chilling effects, as a linking party would have to make sure that he is not linking to content that is published without authorization. Thus, linking to unauthorized content may have a significant negative effect on the exploitation opportunities for creators and hence on creation itself, but making such links ex ante infringements would involve perhaps even more significant welfare costs through transaction costs and dead-weight losses. The principle of freedom of expression supports this conclusion.

A way to partially resolve this dilemma would be a procedure of notice and take down for links to illegal content. The idea would be that in general linking and embedding are acceptable and do not require consent or a licence, nor do they require any ex ante knowledge whether the linked content has been published with authorization. Only if the copyright holder alerts the linking site that the content on the linked site is published without authorization, would there be an obligation to remove the link. For a careful procedure and to make sure links are not removed unjustly, one could require a court order. However, this would increase the transaction costs and the

66. *See* the chapter by Quintais and Hugenholtz in this volume.

response time of such a procedure substantially, and by doing so thwart its effectiveness and efficiency. In practice, a simple procedure without necessary intervention by a court but with a procedure to reinstall links that have been removed unjustly could work – much like the procedure YouTube has for removing unauthorized content.

The suggested approach is primarily ex post, relying on notice and take down in order to avoid undesirable chilling effects and dead-weight losses that would result from a regime which requires a linking party to ascertain the lawfulness of the linked content ex ante. Such an ex post approach has a risk of creating a game of 'cat and mouse' by sites who knowingly link to unlawful content waiting for right holders to give them notice each time. To avoid this, the ex post regime could be supplemented with ex ante liability for linking to 'obviously unlawful sources'.

A final issue remains concerning what can be done about linking sites and linked sites that are outside the jurisdiction of the 'reasonable exploitation copyright legislation'. Taking down such sites has proven to be legally difficult as well as rather ineffective: mirror sites are easily created once a site is taken down. Ordering internet service providers (ISPs) to block access to such individual sites is often proposed and even implemented as a remedy, but – apart from any legal objectives one may have related to e.g., freedom of speech and censorship – is fairly ineffective as well.[67] It can easily be circumvented by using mirror sites and by using VPN connections for instance.

Hence, it is illusory that linking to and (more importantly) downloading and streaming from unauthorized sources can be eradicated entirely. Acknowledging this, several academic authors have proposed introducing some form of 'statutory licensing scheme' with a levy system to compensate for this practice. Such proposals are also known as for instance 'content flat rate' or 'alternative compensation schemes'.[68]

5.4.3.3 Intermediaries' Liability

Unauthorized distribution or exploitation of works undermines the basic control required for reasonable exploitation and, despite the fact that the literature on unauthorized file sharing is less conclusive than one might expect it to be, it is very plausible that it negatively affects the exploitation opportunities for right holders. By doing so, it may reduce their incentives to invest in creating and exploiting works. In the past, unauthorized distribution or exploitation of works occurred on a relatively small scale in the form of

67. J. Poort, J. Leenheer, J. van der Ham & C. Dumitru, 'Baywatch: Two Approaches to Measure the Effects of Blocking Access to The Pirate Bay', *Telecommunications Policy* 38 (2014): 383–392.
68. The chapter by Quintais and Hugenholtz in this volume provides an example of such a proposal. Further references can be found there.

pirated copies in clandestine markets and shops. Since the turn of the century, it happens on a much larger scale and with negligible marginal costs over the Internet, primarily making use of peer-to-peer software, cyber lockers, social media or newsgroups. Like authorized exploitation, part of the unauthorized exploitation has moved from offering downloading services to streaming services.

The existence and anonymity of such unauthorized distribution platforms underline the fact that contractual arrangements (forbidding a customer to put content on a sharing site for instance) and TPMs (making it hard for customers to put content on a sharing site or making it hard to do so without exposing themselves) do not suffice. An additional reason for this is that unauthorized distribution platforms operate internationally and by doing so can relatively easily stay outside the reach of enforcement.

This raises the question of whether internet access providers, being the parties who provide access to the Internet and by doing so enable end users to access unauthorized material, should have a role in enforcing copyright or might even be liable for the copyright infringements of their clients. A role in enforcement could take different forms: software and equipment could be installed to block the unauthorized exchange of content, websites serving as a platform for the unauthorized exchange of content could be blocked, or ISPs could be forced to supply right holders with names and addresses associated with IP addresses which can be shown to have engaged in the use or distribution of unauthorized material.

Assuming that the negative effect of the use and exploitation of unauthorized material on the exploitation opportunities of right holders is beyond doubt, the question from a welfare economic framework perspective would be to what extent the potential benefits of such enforcement actions outweigh the transaction costs and potential dead-weight losses. On the one hand, this requires an assessment of the benefits of such enforcement: is blocking a sharing website or filtering traffic effective towards its aim to diminish the unauthorized use and exploitation of works? Is going after individuals behind IP addresses an effective way to stop them and others from unauthorized use and distribution? In general, the effectiveness of such enforcement seems limited,[69] but more evidence is needed. On the other hand, an assessment of the costs is required, which first of all involves the transaction costs of blocking, filtering or charging customers engaging in unauthorized use. Second, it involves the dead-weight losses which may occur when platforms and users stop any activity which they fear could be infringing and, by doing so, also stop activities which are not (chilling effects). Related are the costs of false positives, when sites are blocked and activities filtered out, which are (partially or wholly) legitimate, and possible chilling effects on legitimate consumption by consumers who are unsure about the legal status of a provider and fear fines or prosecution. It is as yet

69. Poort et al. (2014).

an open question whether the welfare benefits of such interventions outweigh the costs, taking into account such transaction costs and chilling effects.

Still, even if the outcome of such a welfare economic cost-benefit analysis were positive, one needs to consider the other guiding principles set out in this chapter, such as freedom of expression and proportionality on behalf of ISPs. In theory, one could try to assess the wider long-term economic effects of e.g., the monitoring and blocking software on such values to incorporate these in the economic framework, but in practice, these arguments can be used to balance the outcome of the partial welfare economic analysis.

5.4.4 Contrasting the Right to Reasonable Exploitation with Current EU Law

One of the major ideas behind the model predicated on a right to reasonable exploitation is to bring copyright closer to its rationale, the implied allegation being that current copyright has lost touch with this. The further allegation is that one of the reasons for this lies in the structuring of the economic rights in that the right holder as a point of departure holds exclusive rights to all kinds of behaviour that are classified as acts of reproduction, communication to the public, public distribution and so on, concepts that have only broadened over time. Since these broad concepts set the standard for the scope of the exclusive rights, along with notions that exceptions and limitations have to be interpreted narrowly, and in the EU context the fact that Member States' freedom to provide for exceptions and limitations is limited through the exhaustive list in the Infosoc Directive as well, there is obviously a risk of over-protection. On the other hand, the fact that the basic concepts are not (anymore) tied to the economic rationale for copyright, in addition to attempts to narrow down the broad conceptions by way of legal interpretations, may represent certain risks for under-protection too. By introducing a different structure based on what is considered as reasonable exploitation, it should be possible to bring copyright closer to its rationale. In the following section, we will demonstrate the possible differences in outcome when approaching the problems discussed above from the angle of reasonable exploitation on the one hand, and current EU law, including recent case law of the CJEU, on the other.

5.4.4.1 Private Copying

Regarding *private copying*, it is suggested above that it should not be covered by the exclusive right to reasonable exploitation, including an obligation to pay remuneration, to the extent that the possibility to copy may be priced into the initial purchase of access to the work. This contrasts with current EU law, which does not even provide for a mandatory rule on private copying, but a voluntary option for the Member States to introduce an exception or limitation for such purposes upon the payment of fair compensation for *all* kinds of private copying.[70] The rule follows a logical legal rationale based on the fact that private copying is an *exception* to the right holder's exclusive right to reproduction, and the presumption that such copying may harm the right holders' interests, but is not concerned with the potential double compensation implicit in the right holder's opportunity to receive remuneration for private use through payment for the initial access. The latter is underscored by the rulings of the CJEU in the *VG Wort* and *Copydan* cases, where the Court held that payment for a licence to make private copies could have no impact on levies paid under private copying rules, since the user had no obligation to pay for such a licence given that private copying is exempted from exclusive rights under the law of the Member State.[71] This rationale, which is obviously based on the main rule versus exceptions structure of current copyright law, clearly conflicts with the reasonable exploitation approach suggested here. On the other hand, the ruling in the *ACI Adam* case, where the CJEU held that private copying from unlawful sources was not covered by the private copying rule of the Infosoc Directive,[72] is principally in line with the suggestion that the right to reasonable exploitation covers such copying. However, as the consequence of the *ACI Adam* decision was that Member States may not provide for rules that permit private copying from unlawful sources upon remuneration, it is suggested above that the right to control such copies under the right to reasonable exploitation may be replaced by some form of compensation system, to the extent that such copying cannot be controlled. In sum, there are obvious differences between the current EU rules and a right to reasonable exploitation when it comes to private copying.

5.4.4.2 Resale of Digital Content

The current EU rules entail considerable ambiguity as regards exploitation of secondary markets, including *redistribution of purchased material.* On the one hand, it is evident that the right to control secondary markets for tangible copies of copyright works is curtailed by the rule of exhaustion of the distribution right.[73] On the other hand there are clear indications in the

70. Article 5(2)(b) of the Infosoc Directive.
71. CJEU, Joined cases C-457/11 to C-460/11 (*VG Wort*) para. 37 and case C-463/12 (*Copydan*) para. 65.
72. CJEU, Case C-435/12 (*ACI Adam*) para. 41.
73. Infosoc Directive, Art. 4; Computer Program Directive (Directive 2009/24/EC of the European Parliament and of the Council of 23 April 2009 on the legal protection of computer programs (codified version), OJ No. L 111/16, 5 May 2009, (replacing Council Directive 91/250/EEC of 14 May 1991 on the legal protection of computer programs, OJ No. L 122/42, 17 May 1991)), Art. 4(c); Database Directive (Directive 96/9/EC of the

Infosoc Directive that no exhaustion shall apply to the online context.[74] This distinction follows to a large extent a legal logic based on the fact that online exploitation is not to be considered as distribution, but rather affects the right to communication to the public and the reproduction right in combination, and that these rights are not subject to exhaustion by the first sale. In addition, it seems to be predicated on a misconception that exhaustion may only apply to goods, not services.[75] In the *UsedSoft* case, however, the CJEU broke through that logic when it applied the rule of exhaustion of the distribution right in the Software Directive[76] to the resale of software licences.[77] The decision leaves on the one hand much legal uncertainty regarding the scope of the distribution right and the application of the exhaustion rule to other kinds of works.[78] On the other hand, it follows the rationale behind the rule applying to tangible goods, highlighting the lack of justification for controlling secondary markets even with regard to online services.[79] Looking through the lens of reasonable exploitation, the approach of the Court lacks the necessary sophistication to justify the extension of the 'exhaustion rationale' to the digital context.[80] Yet it aligns well with the principle that the right holder's absolute control over secondary markets is not necessary in order to secure current or future exploitation possibilities, even in such a context. The risk that buyers may extend the secondary market is counteracted by the premise that a buyer must make his own copy 'unusable' at the time of the resale.[81] The '*UsedSoft* solution' is thus in line with the first alternative outlined above, namely allowing the resale on this premise and regaining control through TPMs.[82] Again, however, the legal ambiguity surrounding this problem, and the lack of sophistication approaching it, is due to the structuring of the rights blurring the fundamental problems at stake.

5.4.4.3 Linking and Embedding

The same could be said about *linking and embedding*. In the *Svensson* and *BestWater* decisions the CJEU equated the two different situations, treating

---

European Parliament and of the Council of 11 March 1996 on the legal protection of databases, OJ No. L 77/20, 27 March 1996), Art. 7(2).

74. Article 3(3) and Recital 29.
75. Recital 29.
76. Directive 2009/24/EC of the European Parliament and of the Council of 23 April 2009 on the legal protection of computer programs (codified version), OJ No. L 111/16, 5 May 2009, (replacing Council Directive 91/250/EEC of 14 May 1991 on the legal protection of computer programs, OJ No. L 122/42, 17 May 1991).
77. Case C-128/11 (*UsedSoft*).
78. *See* Rognstad (2014), 4–12.
79. This is reflected in particular in paras 45 and 61. *See* Rognstad (2014), 14–15.
80. *See* s. 5.4.2.2 above.
81. *UsedSoft* para. 78.
82. *See UsedSoft* para. 87.

them both under the so-called new public doctrine, and implying that both linking and embedding fall outside the scope of the communication to the public right as long as the linked or embedded work was freely and unrestrictedly made available on the Internet.[83] Again, equating the two seems logical on the basis of the legal regulation and the fact that embedding is based on linking technique, but the rulings are ignorant to the fact that the *effect* of the two is quite different. Thus, although there are some similarities between the *results* of the new public approach and of the approach following conditional control under the proposed right to reasonable exploitation, we claim that the former are based on non-economic and legally inconsistent grounds.[84] Comparing the results, conditional control implies that there should be an opening for banning links that, exceptionally, affect current or future exploitation possibilities, irrespective of the new public rationale. Furthermore, there is a difference in the approach to embedding, as we suggest an 'opt out procedure' for securing the right holder's right to control, instead of creating incentives to impose access restrictions, which would be the result of the new public approach.[85]

Third, the right to reasonable exploitation opens the way for different solutions for links to unauthorized material. To be sure, even under the apparently objective concept of 'communication to the public', the CJEU has in the *GS Media* case attempted to distinguish between links to authorized and unauthorized content and in addition also by contrasting certain situations.[86] Thus, according to the logic of the CJEU, posters of links who did not know, or have reason to know, about the lack of authorization, are not communicating the work to the public, while those who have such knowledge, or ought to have it, do and consequently also infringe copyright.[87] In addition, the CJEU also introduced a rebuttable presumption of knowledge on the part of those posting hyperlinks 'for profit'.[88] And in any case, the CJEU 'noted that … rightholders, in all cases, have the possibility of informing [posters of hyperlinks] of the illegal nature of the publication of their work on the Internet and of taking action against them if they refuse to remove that link',[89] prescribing a sort of notice and take down procedure. Contrasting the approach of the CJEU with our discussion in section 5.4.3.2 above, the approach coincides with the right to reasonable exploitation on two points: (1) that links to obviously unlawful sites should be deemed

83. *See* CJEU case C-466/12, (*Svensson*) paras 24–32 and case C-348/13 (*BestWater*) paras 14–19.
84. As to the former, *see* s. 5.4.2.3 above, as to the latter, *see* O-A. Rognstad, 'Linking – A Gordian Knot of Copyright Law', in *Liber Amicorum Jan Rosén*, ed. G. Karnell et al. (2016), 681–689.
85. *See Svensson* para. 31.
86. CJEU case C-160/15 (*GS Media*) paras 46–53.
87. *Id.* paras 47–49.
88. *Id.* para. 51, and *a contrario* para. 47.
89. *Id.* para. 53.

infringing, and (2) that the poster of the links should act upon received knowledge about the unauthorized content. On the contrary we believe that including the 'ought to know' standard and, not least, the presumption based on the highly ambiguous 'for profit' criterion, is likely to have undesirable chilling effects and cause net dead-weight losses, in addition to freedom of speech concerns.

In addition, we will point to the fact that solutions based on subjective criteria, like knowledge, fit well with the concept of a right to reasonable exploitation, but are conceptually incompatible with the notion of 'communication to the public' and overlook current distinctions between primary and secondary infringements. Thus, the approach of the CJEU in *GS Media* appears – like those of *Svensson* and *BestWater* – as a strained effort to reach prima facie reasonable results on the basis of legal criteria unfit for the purpose, and also without having a yardstick for reasonableness, like our operationalization of the efficiency principle in terms of conditional control.

5.4.4.4 Text and Data Mining

The treatment of TDM also highlights the difference between the current rules and the reasonable exploitation approach. Even though there are no precedents yet from the CJEU regarding this matter, the current legal regime implies that there is a copyright problem on the basis of the reproduction right.[90] Against this background the European Commission has launched a proposal for an exception for TDM as part of its Single Digital Market Agenda, which is limited to TDM for the 'purposes of scientific research'.[91] In other jurisdictions the problems concerning the scope of the reproduction rights may be remedied through more flexible justification rules, like the fair use doctrine in the US. Under the reasonable exploitation approach, however, the fact that TDM may involve acts of reproduction of the work is irrelevant, and there is consequently no need for any *justification* for placing TDMs outside the scope of copyright. As pointed out above, neither the efficiency principle nor any of the other guiding principles speak in favour of leaving TDM within the scope of the economic rights. Consequently, there is no reason for including TDM in the right to reasonable exploitation.

5.4.4.5 TPMs and Intermediary Liability

Under current copyright regimes, the legal protection of copy and access controls (TPMs), as well as the question of intermediaries' liability, are to a

90. Infosoc Directive Arts 2 and 5(1), cf. decisions in CJEU case C-5/08 (*Infopaq I*) and case C-302/10 (*Infopaq II*).
91. Proposal for a Directive of the European Parliament and of the Council on copyright in the Digital Single Market, COM(2016)593, Art. 3.

large extent handled by way of special rules or doctrines outside the right holders' exclusive rights. The concept of reasonable exploitation implies, on the contrary – due to its simplification of the structure of the economic rights – that legal protection of TPMs and intermediary liability may also be covered by the right holder's exclusive right, but only on condition that the right holder's control be *reasonable*. As far as TPMs are concerned, this means that, unlike current rules in the EU and the US, there will be no tension between the limits to the copyright protection and the legal protection of TPMs.[92] Moreover, whereas the current rules on protection of TPMs may prohibit the circumvention of TPMs that aim to price discriminate between markets, it follows from the analysis above that such practices do not necessarily amount to a reasonable exploitation, discrimination between single and multi-user licences being an important exception. When it comes to the question of intermediary liability, the regulation within the framework of the economic rights is not intended to grant right holders a stronger position than under current doctrines of secondary liability. From an economic point of view, the liability should depend on whether the benefits outweigh the transaction costs and the dead-weight losses. Apart from such efficiency considerations, other guiding principles such as freedom of speech are also at stake here. This provides for a careful approach to intermediary liability under the concept of reasonable exploitation, but again the concept will provide for a simpler and more transparent structure for dealing with the problems than the current 'patchwork' of different (and partly divergent) doctrines of secondary liability.[93]

5.5 IMPLEMENTATION OF THE RIGHT TO REASONABLE EXPLOITATION: CATALOGUE REGULATION

A general, and much debated, issue in law concerns the style of regulation, i.e., whether provisions should be formulated in broad and general terms or by use of more specific language and detailed regulation.[94] Typically the discussion revolves around two prototypes, *rules* that safeguard the need for specificity ex ante and *standards* that leave much to ex post assessments and

92. *See* Rognstad (2015), 537, with reference to the fact that '[a]lthough there *are* limits to the legal protection both U.S. and EU law, these legislations put the right holder in the position to control and condition access beyond the express limits of copyright law', whereas on the other hand it would be a logical impossibility under the concept of reasonable exploitation 'to permit a certain kind of use in the first place only to prohibit circumvention of technological measures that prevent the permitted use in the second. That would be equal to saying that what is not reasonable, namely imposing restrictions on the use in question, is reasonable after all.'
93. *See also* Rognstad (2015), 542–543.
94. *See also* Stefan Bechtold, in this volume.

are therefore able to meet the need for flexibility but may provide less legal certainty ex ante. In the copyright field, it may be considered that on the one hand rule-style regulation is called for, in particular as regards actions that are carried out frequently and by a large number of people,[95] such as private copying and hyperlinking. On the other hand, there is a need for flexibility due to the rapid changes in technology, which may call for the use of standards.[96] In the current state of copyright law, the regulation may be held to be somewhat asymmetric as the exclusive rights are regulated by rules, which on the other hand are getting quite blurry and 'standard-like' in the digital environment, while the exceptions and limitations to a variable degree are based on standards, although more so in the US than in the EU due to the standard-like fair use doctrine (section 107 of the US Copyright Act).

The alternative model based on the right to reasonable exploitation aims to do away with this asymmetry.[97] By abandoning the 'six stage structure' the aim is to achieve a more coherent regulation. It is important to remember, however, that the complexity inherent in the countless ways of exploiting a work does not disappear as a result of simplifying the structure. Instead, the complexity must be handled within the one stage structure based on the right to reasonable exploitation. It is believed that a catalogue regulation is the most appropriate way of handling the complexity, as this 'third category' styled regulation entails the benefits of both rules and standards, and thus is apt to balance the needs for predictability and flexibility.[98] A typical catalogue comprises 'two or more enumerated instances (or items) followed by a general provision that empowers courts to recognize other unenumerated instances (or items) that have the same key characteristics as the enumerated ones'.[99] Although regulating the entire exclusive rights regime in copyright, including features that are currently regulated by adjacent rules or principles,[100] involves much greater complexity than for example a provision under criminal law prohibiting dangerous weapons,[101] the structure implicit in the right to reasonable exploitation is a catalogue structure. On the face of it the proposed model may look like a standard regulation, but the intention is to regulate a number of enumerated instances in order to concretize the

95. *See* L. Kaplow, 'Rules Versus Standards: An Economic Analysis', *Duke Law Journal* 42 (1992): 557–629.
96. *See* R. van der Noll, et al., *Flexible Copyright: The Law and Economics of Introducing an Open Norm in the Netherlands* (Amsterdam: SEO Economic Research/IViR, 2012).
97. Compare also J.S. Horowitz, 'Copyright's Asymmetric Uncertainty', *The University of Chicago Law Review* 79 (2012): 331–385.
98. Cf. Parchomowsky & Stein (2015), 186: 'catalogs can integrate the advantages of rules and standards while minimizing its shortcomings'.
99. *Ibid.* 181–182.
100. Such as doctrines on secondary infringements and protection of technical protection measures.
101. *See* the example by Parchomowsky & Stein (2015), 191 on the provision in D.C. Code § 22-4502(a). On the other hand, the authors also consider parts of the fair use provision in US Copyright Act § 107 as a catalogue regulation, *see* pp. 189–190.

content of 'reasonable exploitation' against the background of the guiding principles, starting from the concept of conditional control. As demonstrated above, the latter may give considerable guidance as to how the line between reasonable and non-reasonable control is to be drawn with respect to concrete instances and this wisdom may in its turn be implemented into the statutory provisions as enumerated catalogue examples. Thus, the catalogue will give further and more precise guidance as to how not only the enumerated but also unenumerated instances are to be solved, through assessments of 'family resemblance' with the enumerated examples.[102]

It goes without saying that when drafting the catalogue of examples the legislator cannot and shall not predict all conceivable or inconceivable situations that may occur. First, it is obvious that the catalogue will have to reflect the current, or at least the foreseeable, state of technological development, and that it is practically impossible, and undesirable from a cost perspective, to amend the legislation every time new problems occur. The very idea of the proposed regulation should be that existing examples, along with the guiding principles and the operationalization of efficiency in terms of conditional control, give sufficient guidance to predict the outcome of emerging problems, at least for a foreseeable period of time. From thereon, legal certainty will increase as the body of case law builds. To be sure, it will still be necessary to carry out periodic law revisions under this kind of legislation, but the claim is that the task of amending and adding to the catalogue should be easier and less costly than introducing new rights and exceptions under the current regulation.

Second, the legislator will in any case have to make a selection of examples that give guidance as to how similar cases are to be solved. There should be a number of possible criteria for selecting such examples, but it is obviously important how frequently an example is expected to occur. The cases discussed in this chapter clearly fulfil this criterion and, given the current technological state of the art, the solutions outlined in section 5.4 could be implemented in the catalogue.

To illustrate how the catalogue regulation could work in comparison with current law, consider the state of technology some years ago when illegal downloading – but not streaming – was a regular problem (e.g., around the turn of the century when the Infosoc Directive was adopted). In light of the model advocated in this chapter, private copying should be lawful insofar as it is indirectly appropriated in the pricing of the original copy or the online service. Therefore the catalogue might state that copying for personal purposes falls outside the scope of the right to reasonable exploitation. Copying from unauthorized sources could, on the same basis, be subject to a compensation system. When streaming became normal, the logic behind conditional control along with the solutions enumerated in the catalogue for private copying, should tell us that the same should apply to

102. *Ibid.* 185 et seq., drawing on Ludwig Wittgenstein's ideas in the philosophy of language.

streaming. There is certainly no case for controlling streaming from lawful sources, while streaming from unlawful sources may affect current or future exploitation possibilities, at the same time as privacy concerns implicit in the principle of public domain would speak against a control right. Under the current EU copyright rules, the situation has been far more ambiguous as the downloading from unlawful sources is covered by the right holder's exclusive right, while at least not until recently it was clear how streaming on the part of the end user is to be treated in the equivalent situation.[103]

We also claim that it would be much easier to solve the question of 'digital resales' by way of a catalogue regulation of redistribution of tangible copies of works, than to tackle this problem under the current rights regime that distinguishes between a distribution right subject to exhaustion and rights of communication to the public and reproduction that are not subject to exhaustion.

It is submitted that under this model, the question of who has the 'burden of proof'[104] as to whether there is a violation of the right to reasonable exploitation – the 'right holder' or the 'user' – is not intended to shift beyond what should follow from general procedural principles. In our model, whether or not an exploitation is 'reasonable', is a legal – not a factual – question, to be answered by interpreting the 'catalogue rules' on the basis of the guiding principles. The 'burden of proof' question simply misses this point. Thus, a more appropriate question would be to ask who has the 'burden of argument' as to whether a certain conduct falls within or outside the scope of the exclusive rights. The answer to this question seems to be 'no one', as the interpretation of the right to reasonable exploitation should depend on ordinary legal methods and not some construed principles. Nonetheless, both parties may provide factual evidence for the occurrence or absence of harmful effects, which courts may take into consideration. In addition, parties could be asked to provide evidence, for instance about prior notices or consent, but this also puts no specific burden of proof on any one party. It should be borne in mind that a core feature of the concept of 'reasonable exploitation' is that it is not biased. Thus, the starting point is neither that the right holder holds exclusive rights to 'exploitation' of the work, such that users will have to prove that it does not, nor the other way around. In our model, right holders hold exclusive rights to *reasonable* exploitation, and what has been suggested here is a method for how to delineate the scope of these rights.

---

103. As pointed out above, it follows from the *ACI Adam* decision (2013) that private copies from unlawful sources are not covered by the private copying provision in Art. 5(2)(b) of the Infosoc Directive, and do therefore conflict with the exclusive right to reproduction. Whether streaming from unlawful sources conflicts with the exclusive rights depends on whether temporary copies reproduced in the user's browser are made with the purpose of enabling lawful use pursuant to Art. 5(1), *see* now case C-527/15 (*Filmspeler*) paras. 60–67.
104. *See* Bechtold in this volume.

5.6 CONCLUSION

In this chapter, we have elaborated on the model of copyright as a right to reasonable exploitation by 'filtering' the content of 'reasonable exploitation' through the utilitarian goal of social welfare maximization (efficiency). Unlike hard-core economists who would hold that the welfare economic framework includes any norms other than equity (or fairness) through their welfare effects, we take a more pragmatic approach by opening up room for guiding principles other than efficiency, to give reason to amend the normative economic stance. Proportionality, public domain, dignity, freedom of expression and market integration are identified as norms that may give reason to adjust the outcome of a welfare economic analysis of copyright issues to the extent that it does not monetize these norms.

Towards the economic goal of efficiency, a key consideration is that it is the non-excludability or 'public good' market failure of the rents of creating a work of art, literature or science that justifies intervention on economic grounds. Through the decreased costs of copying in the digital realm, this market failure may well have increased over the last decades, but at the same time the costs of copyright protection in terms of transaction costs, dead-weight losses and chilling effects need to be taken into account.

Implementing the aforementioned efficiency approach to reasonable exploitation, it should be acknowledged that exploitation of works can take a wide variety of forms, the exchange of a copy of a work for a sum of money being just one of them. This implies that the concept of reasonable exploitation should be broad enough to allow for many of the current exploitation models. At the same time, it ought to be general enough to account for new models that are yet to be developed. Starting from that notion, we operationalize the efficiency principle by the concept of conditional control: acts can only be considered copyright relevant if, against the background of the public good character of works, they affect the ability of a creator to control access to a work and exchange it for something which has direct or indirect commercial value for him, and do so by negatively and significantly affecting the current or future exploitation opportunities for the right holder. But even with respect to copyright relevant acts, the positive effect of protection on the exploitation opportunities, and eventually the incentives to create for the right holder, need to be balanced against any transaction costs, dead-weight losses and chilling effects. Moreover, the primary aim of copyright should remain to resolve the public good market failure inherent in creative works, and not exceed this goal by protecting price discrimination or control of secondary markets beyond what is considered acceptable in other markets. This implies that many issues related to price discrimination and contractual arrangements should not be dealt with in the context of copyright but instead in the context of contract law, competition law and EU law on market integration.

This approach to reasonable exploitation has subsequently been applied to a number of prominent present-day copyright issues: private copying, redistribution of purchased material, downloading from illegal sources, data mining, access controls and protection of TPMs, intermediaries' liability, and linking and embedding. Across this diverse set of cases studies, it was shown to lead to consistent and converging outcomes. However, these outcomes were also shown to differ in a number of respects from the formalistic approach followed by the CJEU. In line with the alternative model for restructuring the economic rights in copyright we propose that a catalogue style of regulation is the optimal way of balancing predictability and flexibility under the right to reasonable exploitation.

Chapter 6

Realigning Economic Rights with Exploitation of Works: The Control of Authors over the Circulation of Works in the Public Sphere

Séverine Dusollier*

6.1 INTRODUCTION

Economic rights have lost their meaning and their efficiency. Reduced to technical notions that are applied to uses that seem harmless, and whose interpretation is all but certain, they cannot ensure the legitimate control by authors of the exploitation of their works. Economic rights are organized around two key notions: reproduction and communication to the public, which formed the backbone of copyright in its early age and accompanied its evolution and its gradual inscription in international treaties and European law. For that reason, both rights seem immovable, forged in the fabric of the Berne Convention[1] and of the *acquis communautaire*. Reconstructing economic rights in copyright could employ two strategies. The first would be to

* Successive versions of this chapter were discussed in a series of workshops. I am grateful for productive comments from participants in those events, and in particular, beyond the participants in the project, to Valérie-Laure Benabou, Lionel Bently, Sari Depreeuw, Daniel Gervais, Jonathan Griffiths, Matthias Leistner, Alexander Peukert, Martin Senftleben and Hanns Ullrich.

1. Berne Convention for the Protection of Literary and Artistic Works.

adapt the rights to the digital environment, by trying to reform their interpretation and application in a more balanced and consistent manner. A second move would be more radical and consist of setting aside the ill-adapted notions of reproduction right and communication right to devise a new concept delineating the control a copyright owner should have over her work.

The approach of this chapter is based on such a principle of *tabula rasa*. What would we do with exclusive rights in copyright if we had to start from scratch, with the experience of the last twenty years, but unencumbered by the Berne Convention, the WIPO Treaties and the EU InfoSoc Directive?[2] Could we define the control of copyright owners on the exploitation of their work by purifying this very notion of exploitation from its legal translations into reproduction and communication?

This question will be answered in four parts. The first will argue that the notion of exploitation was the guiding principle of the rights of reproduction and communication – acts that were only means to help such exploitation. The second part will explore the increasing disconnection between economic rights and actual exploitation. I will then propose replacing the current system by a broad and unique right of exploitation, related to the function of copyright, which is to grant to authors control over the public circulation of their works. The details of this exploitation right will be developed and applied to certain types of use in the final part.

The model proposed here will focus on copyright, leaving aside neighbouring rights and the specific protection of software. It will also be limited to economic rights, although a brief reflection on moral rights will be made at some point.

6.2 THE CONTROL OF COPYRIGHT OWNERS OVER THE EXPLOITATION OF THEIR WORKS

A. Lucas wrote that 'what triggers the application of the exclusive right is an act of exploitation'.[3] This is a strong affirmation that deserves to be repeated and sacred as a key principle of copyright. It means that the ultimate objective of the control granted to copyright owners in the form of economic rights pertains to the exploitation of the work as an end, not to individual and specific acts of use that could constitute the many steps of a process. This also entails that the exploitation could be seen as the source of the exclusive rights, each of them being conceived as a part of the exploitation of creative works.

2. Directive 2001/29/EC of 22 May 2001 on the harmonisation of certain aspects of copyright and related rights in the information society, OJ No. L 167/10, 22 June 2001.
3. A. Lucas, H.-J. Lucas & A. Lucas-Schloetter, *Traité de la propriété littéraire et artistique,* 2012, Lexis/Nexis, §263 (my translation).

This equation between economic rights and the concept of exploitation can be found in some copyright laws as an overall concept for economic rights. This has been the case in French copyright law since the 1957 reform. The French law regroups its two principal rights, reproduction and communication, under a single umbrella: the right to control exploitation of the work. In a simple formula, Article L.122-1 of the Code de la Propriété Intellectuelle (CPI) states that 'le droit d'exploitation appartenant à l'auteur comprend le droit de représentation et le droit de reproduction' (the right of exploitation belonging to the author includes the right of communication and the right of reproduction[4]).

However the notion of exploitation referred to is rather empty as it is not defined,[5] but is explained by reference to the two key economic rights of reproduction and communication. Thereby, the economic rights, as defined by law, inform the concept of exploitation, instead of the 'exploitation' informing the scope of the exclusive rights.

In the early days of copyright, economic rights were defined to encompass what counted then as ways of exploiting a creation. The bundle of economic rights granted by copyright reflected the many means by which a work used to be exploited. Historically the reproduction right enabled the author to control the number of copies that could be made and sold to readers, thereby giving a sense of the size of the potential public getting access to the work.

On the other side, the right of communication, or right of public performance in the early copyright texts, covered the performance of literary and dramatic works in theatres, then later with the development of communication technologies, the transmission of the work. Both were means to achieve some control over the exploitation of a work and were 'taken as the suitable anchor points for the protection of the exploitation'.[6]

The economic rights hence aligned rather directly with the sectors of the cultural economy that relied on exploitation of creative works: reproduction for the book publishing industry; communication for the performance of plays; and both rights for the exploitation of musical and audiovisual works. Other economic rights, such as the distribution right, the rental right and the right of (re)transmission by cable or satellite, have been progressively added to the bundle when new technologies or ways of exploitation required new

4. My translation.
5. *See ibid.*, p. 252, §255, regretting however that the notion of 'exploitation' is not defined and remains rather vague. ('L'essentiel, dira-t-on, est que, dans tous les cas où elle est le siège d'une exploitation économique, l'auteur puisse la maîtriser. Reste que le terme "utilisation" (comme d'ailleurs celui d'exploitation utilisé par l'article L. 122-1) n'est pas assez chargé de signification juridique pour délimiter la portée du monopole de l'auteur et qu'il faut bien préciser quelles sont les modalités concrètes de cette utilisation qui sont soumises à autorisation').
6. S. Depreeuw, *The Variable Scope of the Exclusive Economic Rights in Copyright*, Kluwer Law International, 2014, p. 493.

control by copyright owners. The resale right was then conceived to address one specific means of exploitation of artistic works[7] that was not relevant to other forms of expression.

The copyright system was then primarily a form of regulation of the trade in physical products, with some subsidiary attention for the public performance of creative works, this second activity gaining in significance with the development of communication technologies. Copyright rules also intervened between authors and the first exploiters (publishers, producers, theatres etc.) to entitle them to produce and distribute products or to provide the work to the public.

It entailed that the mere reception or use of a copyrighted work was never considered to be a prima facie infringement. Nor were acts of reading or processing the information carried by the work. They are not part of exploitation but rather activities on the receiving end of the trade in copies or the public performance of works, which escape copyright control altogether.

6.3 THE DISCONNECTION BETWEEN ECONOMIC RIGHTS AND EXPLOITATION OF WORKS

6.3.1 An Obsessively Technical Definition of Economic Rights

With the advent of digital formats and networks, reproduction and communication have become technically defined standards of use, thereby evolving from means to ends. The link between the act of reproduction or communication and its purpose has now been severed.

6.3.1.1 The Right of Reproduction

The right of reproduction is one of the oldest rights in copyright. Making copies of works was considered early on as being one of the major ways in which a work could be exploited. Copies were needed to print a work, sell it and distribute it to the public. The right of reproduction hence constituted one of the pillars of copyright from its foundation.

There is an evident link between the making of copies and the distribution thereof to the public. The reproduction right is a means to control

7. Considering the resale of artistic works as an act of exploitation might be disputed, as the sale of a painting generally occurs between private persons, the link with the diffusion of the work to a public being absent. However, one could say that the successive acts of resale of a work amongst public art dealers and art buyers repeatedly increases the value of the work. *See* section 6.5.4.1 *infra* for a discussion on droit de suite.

the number of copies circulating in the market, hence the extent to which the public have access thereto.

That link between the reproduction right and the ultimate circulation of such copies to the public is sometimes reflected in its definition. For instance, the French definition of the reproduction right is 'the material fixation of the work by all means that *enable to communicate it to the public* in an indirect way' (Article L. 122-3 CPI, emphasis added). Similarly the US definition of copies (as the copyright includes the right to reproduce the work in copies) refers to 'material objects in which a work is fixed … and *from which the work can be perceived, reproduced, or otherwise communicated*, either directly or with the aid of a machine or device' (section 101 US Copyright Act, emphasis added).

By contrast, the definition of the reproduction right that appears in the EU regulatory framework is disconnected from the purpose of the copies. The approach is instead strictly technical, as any copy of a copyright work is said to be prima facie infringing. Indeed, Article 2 of the InfoSoc Directive states that 'Member States shall provide for the exclusive right to authorise or prohibit direct or indirect, temporary or permanent reproduction by any means and in any form, in whole or in part.'

As a consequence, any fixation of a work, any duplication, even fugitive and merely technical, falls within the scope of the right. That explains the European treatment of temporary reproductions in Article 5(1) of the InfoSoc Directive, which are considered to be covered by the exclusive right, but partially exempted via an exception under strict conditions. The Court of Justice of the European Union (CJEU) has construed the notion of temporary reproduction as covering any technical copy, including a copy on a computer[8] or television screen,[9] copies on a set-top box during a transmission,[10] and copies made during digital processing of works.[11] This technical approach has been reinforced by the requirement for automatic deletion of the incidental copies in order to be eligible for the exception.[12]

In theory, this could entail a right of control for authors over the mere reception or reading of a work, despite the largely agreed-upon principle that copyright does not control the enjoyment of a work.[13] The question of the

---

8. CJEU, 5 June 2014, *Public Relations Consultants Association Ltd v. Newspaper Licensing Agency Ltd*, C-360/13.
9. CJEU, 4 October 2011, *Football Association Premiere League*, joined cases C-403/08 and C-429/08.
10. *Ibid.*
11. ECJ, 16 July 2009, *Infopaq International*, C-5/08 & CJEU, 17 January 2012, *Infopaq International II*, C-302/10.
12. *See Infopaq II*, C-302/10, §30.
13. A. Lucas et al., n. 3, n°243; P.B. Hugenholtz, 'Adapting Copyright to the Information Superhighway', in P.B. Hugenholtz (ed.), *The Future of Copyright in a Digital Environment*, Kluwer, 1996, p. 93 ('The mere reception or consumption of information by

possible control of copyright owners over the reception and reading of news articles by subscribers to a news review service has been subject to the scrutiny of the CJEU, which had to assess it under the limited conditions of the temporary copying exception,[14] demonstrating that such consumptive activities are now within the ambit of copyright.

The CJEU has followed an economic approach when interpreting the condition of independent economic significance: 'the economic advantage derived from [the implementation of acts of temporary reproduction] must not be either distinct or separable from the economic advantage derived from the lawful use of the work concerned and it must not generate an additional economic advantage going beyond that derived from that use of the protected work'.[15] There is such an additional economic advantage 'if the author of that act is likely to make a profit due to the economic exploitation of the temporary reproductions themselves'.[16] What enables the application of the exception, hence the removal of the act of copying from the scope of exclusive rights, is thus the absence of independent exploitation. This partial reconnection to the nexus of exploitation is nevertheless twisted as it applies through the operation of the conditions of an exception, not as an element defining the perimeter of the right.[17] As a consequence, the link with exploitation will be strictly defined and subject to the additional application of the three-step test, which is rather unsatisfactory. What is shielded from the exclusive right by the exception is not equivalent to what is positively defined as belonging within the control of copyright owners. It also subjects the interpretation to uncertainty and to a fragmented scrutiny dividing a single process into multiple copies.[18]

Beyond the exception for temporary reproduction, the technical approach dominating the right of reproduction has also been confirmed by the CJEU in the *Art and Allposters* decision that held that a transfer of a work from one embodiment to another, the first one disappearing in the process, is an act of reproduction.[19] The copy itself triggers the exclusive right, with no consideration of the number of copies subsisting after the process that could

the end user has traditionally remained outside the scope of the copyright monopoly'); in US law, J. Litman, 'The Exclusive Right to Read', *Cardozo Arts & Ent. L.J.* 1994, Vol. 13, p. 43.

14. CJEU, 5 June 2014, *Public Relations Consultants Association Ltd v. Newspaper Licensing Agency Ltd,* C-360/13.
15. *Infopaq II*, n. 11, §50.
16. *Ibid.*, §52.
17. S. Dusollier, 'Technology as an Imperative for Regulating Copyright: From the Public Exploitation to the Private Use of the Work', *E.I.P.R.*, 2005, pp. 201–204.
18. V.-L. Benabou, '*Jurisprudence Infopaq: que reste-t-il au juge national pour dire le droit d'auteur?*', *R.D.T.I.*, 2009, n°37, p. 71.
19. CJEU, 22 January 2015, *Art & Allposters*, C-419/13, §43.

be then offered to the public.[20] This demonstrates that the process of making a copy is in itself sufficient.

6.3.1.2 The Right of Communication

The technical feature of the right of communication is less visible in EU law and jurisprudence. Aligning the scope of the communication right with the transmission to a new public arguably follows the notion of exploitation, as works are exploited when they reach different publics that can hence enjoy, view or listen to the content received. It can also serve to determine, from the many technical acts involved in the transmission of a work to its final public, which ones should be covered by the exclusive right.[21] The dividing line in recital 27 of the InfoSoc Directive between acts of transmission to the public and the provision of physical facilities for enabling or making a communication demonstrates as well that the notion of communication to the public should not be grounded on purely technical features.[22]

The *SBS Belgium* judgment of the CJEU may imply a shift towards a more technical approach to the right. The question referred to the court was whether the transmission of broadcasts through a technique of direct injection amounts to an act of communication to the public. Such a technique consists of transmitting the signal via a private line to the distributors, whether satellite operators, cable distributors or internet access providers. With the advent of digital television, the initial wireless (over-the-air) transmission of programme-carrying signals has given way to direct transmissions by formerly secondary transmitters, such as cable operators and satellite platforms – no primary wireless transmission being necessary anymore.

The CJEU held that the transmission of the signal from the broadcaster to the operators that then transmit it to the public are acts of communication but that the 'public' element was missing. As the term 'public' refers to a fairly large number of persons, it considered that the limited number of specified individual distributors to whom the broadcasting organization transmitted their signals does not constitute a public.[23] The only public is composed of the subscribers of each distributor and is the same as that covered by the broadcasting organization when transmitting the signal to the

20. On similar facts, the Canadian Supreme Court decided otherwise, considering that mechanical transfer with no multiplication of copies did not amount to an act of reproduction under copyright law. *See Théberge v. Galerie d'Art*, 2002 SCC 34.
21. For an application to technical acts required by broadcasting, *see* the Opinion of the Advocate General, 17 March 2011, *Airfield*, C-431/09 & C-432/09.
22. *See also* CJEU, 19 November 2014, *SBS Belgium*, C-325/14, §31; CJEU, 13 October 2011, *Airfield*, C-431/09 & C-432/09, §79, which held that a transmission that is just a technical means of ensuring or improving reception of the work does not amount to an act of communication.
23. CJEU, 19 November 2014, *SBS Belgium*, C-325/14, §23.

distributors.[24] This results in broadcasters not being considered to carry out an act of public communication, despite the undisputed fact that they economically exploit copyright works in their programmes.

The Supreme Court of Norway reached a similar outcome in holding that a TV cable distributor did not carry out an act of retransmission as the signal it received in an encrypted format had not been previously broadcast to the public.[25] In other words, there could be no retransmission without a first transmission. This ruling testifies both to a literal reading of the definition of the cable retransmission right in Norwegian law (and for that matter in the EU SatCab Directive[26]) and to a technical approach to the acts that should be included in the process. The requirement of a secondary transmission made perfect sense at a time when TV signals transmitted over-the-air were picked up by a cable operator for retransmission in another country. It no longer does with the digital evolution of broadcasting. In a dissenting opinion, one Norwegian Justice considered that such technological change was not a sufficient reason to discriminate between different modes of transmission, at the risk of copyright losing its technological neutrality.

Similar cases that raise the issue of direct injection of TV signals have been decided all over Europe. They underline the defeat of the technological neutrality principle due to a technically obsessed definition of exclusive rights, but with a different outcome than with the reproduction right. While a technical definition of copy, irrespective of the public exploitation made thereof or of its duration or permanence, resulted in excessive control over mere uses or technical and ancillary manipulations of works, the focus on retransmission in the cable context implies that the control by copyright owners over the economic operators exploiting their works rather precariously depends on the techniques put in place to transmit the works to the public. The disconnection between the definition of exclusive rights and the reality of the exploitation of works is thus harmful for both users and copyright owners. It is mostly damaging for the consistency of copyright.

6.3.2 The Consequences of a Technical Definition of Economic Rights

Beyond the failure of the principle of technological neutrality, the technical approach to the rights will have a supplementary effect, for it will split the exploitation into many fragments corresponding to separate acts of

24. *Ibid.*, §§27–28.
25. Norwegian Supreme Court, 10 March 2016, *Norwaco v. Get AS*, HR-2016-00562-A.
26. Council Directive 93/83/EEC of 27 September 1993 on the coordination of certain rules concerning copyright and rights related to copyright applicable to satellite broadcasting and cable retransmission, OJ No. L 248/15, 6 October 1993.

reproduction or communication. In the digital environment, any act of use requires the clearance of at least two rights: reproduction and communication to the public. As those distinct rights might be owned or managed by different entities (rights owners or collective management organizations) in different countries, getting clearance for exploiting copyright works is revealed to be an intricate process. The case law that starts to emerge about direct injection also fragments the process of transmitting the works to the public into different actors each responsible, or not, for the technical acts that accompany their exploitation of content.

This is detrimental both to providers of copyright works, who face a cumbersome process of copyright clearance, and to copyright owners themselves. Indeed, as the outcome of the *SBS Belgium* and *Norwaco* decisions shows, copyright owners' revenue will be the sum of the remuneration collected for each fragment and any change in the legal interpretation of a right might result in copyright owners losing one share of the pie, without being able to reconstitute the whole pie.

Such fragmentation paradoxically takes the focus away from core exploitation activities carried out by some operators. As the exploitation is only defined by reference to technically defined acts and not in terms of benefit or value, the scope of the economic right can equally be underreaching. Many internet actors today capture the value of copyright works either to provide a service, get the attention of users or monetize the browsing by users through advertisement, while avoiding the radar of copyright control.

For instance, YouTube has become the primary source for obtaining access to musical and audiovisual works, way beyond paid streaming services such as Netflix or Spotify or illegal sharing sites; four hundred hours of videos are uploaded every minute to its platform. Largely immunized by the safe harbour provisions of the E-commerce Directive,[27] Google, the company operating this service, is not liable for any copyright clearance of content or copyright infringement appearing on the site. The questions of reproduction (there are many on Google servers) or communication to the public (which is the core service that it offers) are not even raised.[28] While Google sometimes agrees to provide remuneration to collective management

27. Directive 2000/31/EC of the European Parliament and of the Council of 8 June 2000 on certain legal aspects of information society services, in particular electronic commerce, in the Internal Market (Directive on electronic commerce), OJ No. L 178/1, 17 July 2000.
28. Save for the disastrous *GS Media* decision of the CJEU, which seems to consider that search engines are liable for hyperlinking to unauthorized content, based on the criterion of for-profit purpose that is normally irrelevant in copyright law. *See* CJEU, 8 September 2016, *GS Media*, C-160/15; *see also* the Opinion of Advocate General Szpunar, 8 February 2017, *Stichting Brein v. Ziggo BV*, C-610/15, §49 ff. (confusing the lack of intervention that prevents the application of the safe harbour principle and the necessary intervention required for an act of communication according to CJEU case law).

organizations in contractual negotiations, it carefully avoids linking it to relevant acts falling within the scope of copyright economic rights.[29]

Scrutinizing the service provided by such intermediaries or platforms, through the lens of exploitation, could change this status quo. Video-sharing platforms or search engines are benefiting from the value of copyright works that constitute their very activity. The works increase the attractiveness of their service and generate their own audience in an economy of attention.[30] More convincingly, the fact they are able to monetize the works by advertising and revenue sharing demonstrates that they directly participate in the value chain. Indeed, when audiovisual content is posted on YouTube without the consent of copyright owners, the latter can react and notify Google to take it down. Google then offers them two possibilities: either removing the illicit content, or inserting advertising whose revenues will be shared between the US enterprise and the copyright owner. As 90% of Google's revenue comes from selling advertising online, it is difficult to argue that the way it monetizes creative works posted on YouTube is not an economic exploitation.

I will come back to the position of such intermediaries in the proposal for a revised model.

6.4 REALIGNING ECONOMIC RIGHTS WITH EXPLOITATION DEFINED AS CIRCULATION OF WORKS IN THE PUBLIC SPHERE

This chapter suggests a new model, or rather a return to the original conception of economic rights in copyright. The approach proposed here is more functional as it would align the delineation of the control of copyright owners on the exploitation of works, such control of exploitation being the function of the copyright grant. It would consist of the following.

A use of a work would be considered as infringing copyright when two conditions are met: (1) the work is used as a work, i.e., for its expressive content, and not as information or reference; and (2) the use harms the function of copyright, that is to ensure the control of right holders over the exploitation of their works. This two-prong infringement test resembles what has been gradually developed in trademark law, as will be explained.

29. A recent study (J. Farchy, *L'économie numérique de la distribution des œuvres et le financement de la création,* Etude CSPLA, Septembre 2016, p. 45) estimates the remuneration that Google pays to rightholders under such contracts at EUR 5 million for France in 2014, to which one could add the revenues from monetization schemes developed by the US firm in response to notices and take down requests, which were about EUR 15 million in 2014. This is not much compared to the EUR 548 million euros paid by other music or video providers to French copyright owners.

30. *See* V.L. Benabou & J. Rochfeld, *A qui profite le clic?*, Ed.Odile Jacob, 2015.

The notion of exploitation, at the crux of the infringement test and of the function of the right, will be defined by reference to a paradigm of copyright based on the notion of public sphere. Copyright aims to provide creators with the rights to control the circulation of their works in the public sphere. Basing our model on the concept of the public sphere is grounded on communication theories developed by copyright scholars under a Kantian influence, and on the historical coincidence between the legal recognition of copyright and the emergence of a public sphere as theorized by Jürgen Habermas.

Defining exploitation by circulation of works in the public sphere will mean that:

(1) exploitation is not purely an economic concept and is not defined by the possibility of trading the work on a market;
(2) exploitation is rather related to any activity that disseminates the work to the public;
(3) relevant means of such dissemination need to be defined, without being reduced to an exhaustive list of acts of exploitation; and
(4) the object of the circulation is the work as a communicative act, not as a commodity or as an item of information (which brings us back to the beginning of our argument).

My argument will proceed in several steps as follows. First, the choice of a functional approach and a reconnection to the notion of exploitation will be briefly justified. Then, the paradigm of the public sphere will be explained as an alternative theory of copyright and of its function. Thereafter, the economic rights of the author will be delineated, based on the public sphere paradigm thus defined.

6.4.1 The Function of Copyright: Control over Exploitation of Works

The technical and autonomous definition of exclusive rights in copyright significantly contrasts with other intellectual property rights. In trademark law, the standard of infringement is the use in the course of trade. Some examples of the types of use that are relevant are given by trademark laws (e.g., affixing the sign to the goods, importing the goods under that sign, etc.), but they are illustrative and amount to infringement only if they harm one of the functions of the trademark. The scope of patent protection might be seen as being broader as any *making* and any *use* of the invention is considered an infringement. Neither trademark law nor patent law define the rights granted to the right owners by reference to technical acts of use, or only by way of examples.

In trademark law, more emphasis has been put on the function of trademark protection in recent years. The CJEU is now systematically insisting on the function(s) of trademark protection as a compass for any rule applicable in trademark law, from the conditions of protection to the scope of infringement.[31] In several decisions the European Court has required as a condition for trademark infringement that the use of the protected sign has harmed one of the functions of the trademark.[32] By establishing a link between the scope of protection and the very objective of the trademark grant, it indirectly installed the notion of exploitation on the throne of protection. Indeed, the control of the trademark owner will be limited to cases where the trademark has been exploited without any authorization, and not merely used. The difference between exploitation and use in trademark law is that for a trademark to be exploited, the capacity of the trademark to accomplish one of its functions through the use made by a third party would be affected.[33] Contrary to the protection of trademarks as a mere property right, which could lead to any use or reference to a protected trademark being infringing, such a functional approach limits the intellectual property right to a purpose-bound property right that only confers on its owner a right to control the exploitation of the right, defined as what the grant of the right aims at, i.e., in the case of a trademark, serving as a sign distinguishing goods and services of one undertaking from another or guaranteeing the goodwill, reputation or quality of the products bearing the sign.[34]

The story is slightly different in patent law, where any use of the invention is deemed to be infringing with no consideration of the harm to a yet-undefined function of the patent right. The only reference in patent case law to a functional approach appears in the CJEU *Monsanto* decision of 2010. The CJEU refused the protection of the patent for 'a patented DNA sequence which is not able to perform its function'.[35] The key question here

31. From the vast array of CJEU decisions using the function of a trademark as a key factor, *see* in particular ECJ, 12 November 2002, *Arsenal v. Reed*, C-206/01; ECJ, 25 January 2007, *Adam Opel*, C-48/05; ECJ, 18 June 2009, *L'Oréal v Bellure*, C-487/07; CJEU, 23 March 2010, *Google*, C-236/08, C-237/08, C-238/08; CJEU, 22 September 2011, *Interflora*, C-323/09 (all on the harm to the function of trademark as a factor for infringement); CJEU, 19 July 2012, *Pie Optiek*, C-376/11 (notion of licensee eligible for registration of a.eu domain name); CJEU, 19 December 2012, *Leno Merken,* C-149/11 (notion of genuine use in the EU).
32. *See* the decisions referred to in n. 31 *supra.*
33. Our satisfaction with the insistence on the function of a trademark might be tempered by some valid criticism that has been voiced against this evolution and that reproached the vagueness of the many functions, the inadequacy in double identity cases of infringements (i.e., use of a sign similar to the registered trademark for similar products) and the protection of the function of quality or goodwill beyond the trademark with a reputation. For a critical comment, *see* M. Senftleben, 'Adapting EU Trademark Law to New Technologies – Back to Basics?', in C. Geiger (ed.), *Constructing European Intellectual Property: Achievements and New Perspectives*, Edward Elgar Publishing, 2011; Max Planck Institute for Intellectual Property and Competition Law, *Study on the Overall Functioning of the European Trade Mark System*, February 2011, pp. 103 et seq.
34. Those functions can be discussed, as not all seem relevant for trademarks, despite the case law of CJEU, but here is not the place for such a discussion.
35. CJEU, 6 July 2010, *Monsanto*, C-428/08, §49.

was to decide whether the detectable presence of a patented DNA sequence in flour produced from genetically modified soy plant was sufficient to consider that the flour itself was a product infringing the patent. Customs authorities in many EU countries had seized the shipments of soy meal, alerted by the patent owner to a possible infringement of its patent for the soy plant.

The case rather focused on the subject-matter of protection, not on the scope of patent protection of the invention. By refusing to extend the patent to non-organic products derived from the biological invention, the CJEU insisted that the patent only covered the invention 'in action', i.e. the invention performing its technical function. Therefore the patent protection cannot cover inventions when they are not operating as technical mechanisms. Interrogated on the scope of protection of a patent in a biotechnological invention,[36] the court held that the patent cannot extend to a DNA sequence that 'is not able to perform its function when it is incorporated in a dead material such as soy meal'.[37] The protection was aligned with the capacity of the invention to perform its function and could lapse depending on the products of which the invention formed part, as patent protection should not be conferred on 'the patented product … contained in the soy meal, where it does not perform the function for which it was patented, but did perform that function previously in the soy plant, of which the meal is a processed product, or would possibly again be able to perform that function after it had been extracted from the soy meal and inserted into the cell of a living organism'.[38]

This does not say anything about the scope of the economic rights granted to the patent owner and the decision only concerns biotechnological inventions where the delimitation of the invention itself is challenging due to its automatically reproducible nature. However, this decision hints at the need to limit patent protection to inventions whose technical teaching is exploited, and to exclude uses of products that do not exploit as such the patented product or process.

By contrast, copyright does not follow a functional approach, except in cases of abuse under competition law.[39] In one such decision, the CJEU has ruled that 'the specific subject-matter of the intellectual property is intended in particular to ensure for the right holders concerned protection of the right to *exploit commercially the marketing or the making available of the*

36. Article 9 of Directive 98/44/EC of the European Parliament and of the Council of 6 July 1998 on the legal protection of biotechnological inventions, OJ L 213/13, reads: 'The protection conferred by a patent on a product containing or consisting of genetic information shall extend to all material … in which the product is incorporated and in which the genetic information is contained and performs its function.'
37. CJEU, 6 July 2010, *Monsanto*, C-428/08, §49.
38. *Ibid.*, §50.
39. *See* the early ECJ case law relating to competition law in copyright, such as ECJ, 8 June 1971, *Deutsche Grammophon*, C-78/70.

protected subject-matter, by the grant of licences in return for payment of remuneration'.(emphasis added)[40] It has hence anchored the function of copyright to the commercial marketing or making available of works and the possibility of obtaining adequate remuneration therefor. In two other decisions, the EU judges have related acts of public performance or of reproduction and marketing of the copies of works to the exploitation.[41] The specific rights of communication or reproduction were then considered as means to achieve exploitation, not ends in themselves. Advocate General Kokott, in the *FAPL* case, has perhaps expressed the relationship with exploitation in the most convincing way. Indeed, she considered that the exemption of temporary copying allowed under Article 5(1) of the InfoSoc Directive is precisely 'to permit acts of reproduction which are the condition for actual exploitation',[42] thereby anchoring the right of reproduction not to a technical act but to exploitation, which, in the case of broadcasts, she defines as the possibility of reception of the work by a public. To this end, an act of reproduction can only enter the scope of copyright if it is carried out with a view to transmission.[43] The CJEU has not however followed its Advocate General in this view.

The notion of exploitation is also present in the conditions of the three-step test, borrowed from the Berne Convention and the TRIPS agreement, not as a standard for economic rights, but instead as a counter-argument to the admissibility of exceptions. In one WTO Panel decision, the notion of exploitation has been defined as follows: 'the ordinary meaning of the term "exploit" connotes "making use of" or "utilising for one's own ends". We believe that "exploitation" of musical works thus refers to the activity by which copyright owners employ the exclusive rights conferred on them to extract economic value from their rights to those works'.[44]

This interpretation refers to what is generally understood by 'exploitation', as referring to the extraction of economic value from something, as using for one's advantage, as yielding some benefit out of its use. The Oxford Dictionary defines exploitation as 'the action of making use of and benefiting from resources'. All definitions insist on the economic dimension of the notion.

My view on exploitation as the underlying concept of the economic rights will be slightly different as it integrates the cultural and communicative dimension of copyright.

---

40. CJEU, 4 October 2011, *Football Association Premiere League,* joined cases C-403/08 and C-429/08, §107.
41. CJEU, 22 September 1998, *Foreningen af danske Videogramdistributører*, C-61/97, §14; CJEU, 22 January 2015, *Art & Allposters*, C-419/13, §36.
42. Opinion of the Advocate General, 3 February 2011, *Football Association Premier League Ltd and Others v. QC Leisure and Others*, C-403/08 and C-429/08, §92.
43. *Ibid.*, §§92–93.
44. WTO Report Panel, *US 110(5),* §6.165.

6.4.2 Copyright and the Public Sphere

Many theories of copyright have been advanced over the years, from a Lockean justification of property on the fruits of creative labour, to utilitarian economic insights or personality theories inspired by Hegel or Kant, but few are deployed to the extent they could serve as paradigms explaining the conditions and extent of copyright. The property theory for example only grounds the grant of the exclusive right to the creator who reaps thereby the fruits of his labour, without deciding what scope that property right should have.[45] Proponents of the utilitarian theory have developed views on the proper scope of economic rights that would judge the legitimacy of a control over some uses of the work by an argument of economic efficiency and wealth maximization. As they base their utilitarian approaches on a classical law and economics perspective[46], they usually rely on price discrimination or market failure arguments, even though the legitimacy of these could be disputed, to justify an expansive reach of copyright into all avenues where a work can be used.[47]

In recent years, a number of scholars have developed an argument of copyright as a regulation of an act of speech and of the participation in the democratic dialogue.[48] Most of these communication theories find their source in the concept of the public use of reason as developed by Kant. This concept, resulting from the Enlightenment and Kant's writings, insists on the need to keep free the public use of one's reason. That public use of reason is

---

45. Considering that copyright is a property right, and thereby holding that the owner has an absolute right over all possible uses of the work is a different thing, as it starts from the property right as a specific legal protection, not as the theory of property as justifying the grant of copyright in the first place.
46. Note that law and economics are not free from criticism and has been welcomed with not much reservation in IP law. For a valid critique of the law and economics tenets, *see* D. Kennedy, 'Cost-Benefit Analysis of Entitlement Problems: A Critique', 33 *Stanford L. Rev*. 387 (1981).
47. For law and economics analysis of copyright law, *see* for instance W.M. Landes & R.A. Posner, 'An Economic Analysis of Copyright Law', *The J. Leg. Stud.*, June 1989, Vol. 18, no. 2, pp. 325–363; N. Elkin-Koren & E. Salzberger, *The Law and Economics of Intellectual Property in the Digital Age: The Limits of Analysis*, Routlege, 2012. *Arguing in Favor of Price Discrimination and Extensive Scope of Copyright*, T. Bell, 'Fair Use v. Fared Use: The Impact of Automated Rights Managements on Copyright's Fair Use Doctrine', *N. C. L. Rev.*, 1998, Vol. 76, p. 589; M. Meurer, 'Copyright Law and Price Discrimination', *Cardozo L. Rev.*, 2001, Vol. 23, pp. 55–148. For a critique, *see* J. Cohen, 'Copyright and the Perfect Curve', *Vand. L. Rev.*, 2000, pp. 1799–1819; W. Gordon, 'An Inquiry into the Merits of Copyright: The Challenges of Consistency, Consent, and Encouragement Theory', *Stanford L. Rev.*, 1989, Vol. 41, pp. 1343–1469.
48. *See* for instance, N. Elkin-Koren, 'A Democratic Approach to Copyright Law in Cyberspace', *Cardozo Arts & Ent. L.J.*, 1996, Vol. 14, pp. 215–295; A. Barron, 'Kant, Copyright and Communicative Freedom'. *L. & Phil.*, 2002, Vol. 31, pp. 1–48; N. Netanel, 'Copyright and a Democratic Civil Society', *Yale L.J.*, 1996, Vol. 106, pp. 283–387; A. Drassinower, *What's Wrong with Copying?*, Harvard University Press, 2015.

defined by the German philosopher as 'the use which a person makes of it as a scholar before the *reading* public' (my emphasis).[49] The specific relationship between an author and her readers is particularly emphasized without any reference to copyright.

In another text, Kant has more explicitly addressed the need to protect the author against the unauthorized reproduction of his writings and elaborates on the relationship between the author and his publisher in respect to the communication of the work to the public:

> In a book as a written work the author is speaking to his reader; and he who has printed it speaks by his copies not for himself but entirely in the name of the author. He gives public representation to the latter's speaking and facilitates merely the delivery of this speech to the public. Now, the copy of this speech - be it in handwriting or in print - may belong to whom it will, yet the use of a copy for oneself or in order to circulate it is a business which every owner of such a copy can conduct in his own name and at his own discretion. However, to let someone speak publicly, to deliver his speech as such to the public, that means to be speaking in that person's name and to effectively be telling the public the following: 'Through me a writer is having this or that brought to your attention, for your information etc. I answer for nothing, not even for the liberty which the former is taking in speaking publicly through me; I am just the mediator of how this is transmitted to you.'[50]

The work as a public discourse disconnects the protection of creation from the only property that could result from labour and could then be transferred to the publishers (which was one argument of publishers at that time to benefit from legal protection).[51] In a Kantian perspective, the right of the author is a personal right, not a property right; the publisher is a mere 'transmitter' of her discourse and the publicity of the discourse requires its protection.[52] The presence of the *public* in the argumentation of Kant is fundamental as it enables the imposition of an obligation of publication on the publisher 'for the publisher possesses the manuscript only on the condition that he uses it for a business of the author with regard to the public'.[53] Elsewhere, Kant considers that publishing is not a usual trade, as reading has become a universal and indispensable need.[54]

49. I. KANT, '*Beantwortung der Frage: Was Ist Aufklärung?*', *Berlinische Monatschrift*, 1784 (my translation).
50. I. KANT, '*Von der Unrechtmäßigkeit des Büchernachdrucks*', *Berlinische Monatschrift*, 1785, 5, available in English as 'On the Unlawfulness of reprinting', at http://www.copyrighthistory.org/cam/index.php (accessed 1 October 2017).
51. *See* the argumentation of Diderot supporting the rights of publishers on the ground of a property right of the authors that would be totally transferrable.
52. *See* the analysis of A. BARRON, n. 48, pp. 16 et seq.
53. I. KANT, 'On the Wrongfulness of Unauthorized Publication of Books', p. 31.
54. I. KANT, *On Turning Out Books. Two Letters to Mr. Friedrich Nicolai*, 1798.

The emphasis put on the public speech of authors could be enriched by the study of the public sphere carried out by Jürgen Habermas in 1962.[55] Starting from the public expression of reason that Kant related to the production of writings and to the relationship between an author and a public,[56] the German philosopher theorizes the *Öffentlichkeit* ('publicity') as a 'liberal model of bourgeois public sphere',[57] historically rooted in the evolution of industry and trade, development of the press and of the bourgeois class,[58] and constituted of private persons gathered in a public who use their reason, as stated by Kant.[59] The Kantian individuals constitute a public and take part in a discourse in a public space supported by the societal infrastructure of the eighteenth century. The public sphere creates a new political space that subjects the authority of the state to a public and rational critique.

What Habermas adds to the Kantian perspective of a public sphere related to cultural production, is the development of a market for cultural commodities that engenders a public of 'recipients, consumers and critics of art and literature'. The culture, increasingly accessible by the development of the printing technique and industry, and the emergence of a trade in literary and cultural goods, is considered as the matrix of the political public sphere but is also developed for the first time in history in an economic market. Readers emerge as buyers of books and other cultural products; the influential courtly and ecclesiastical patronage that had so far sustained the economy of cultural production is increasingly substituted by publishers, which demonstrates that a market for books, enabled by the development of the printing press,[60] is now possible and could support the creation and production of cultural goods.[61] Works become marketable commodities and objects of discussion at the same time, losing their uniqueness or sacred character:

> To the degree, however, to which philosophical and literary works and works of art in general were produced for the market and distributed through it, these culture products became similar to that type of

55. J. Habermas, *Strukturwandel der Öffentlichkeit*, 1962, published in English as *The Structural Transformation of the Public Sphere: An Inquiry into a Category of Bourgeois Society*, Polity Press, 1989.
56. I. Kant, 'What Is Enlightenment?'.
57. J. Habermas, n. 55.
58. *Ibid.*, p. 31.
59. *Ibid.*, p. 38.
60. R. Chartier, *Les origines culturelles de la Révolution Française*, Paris, L'univers Historique, Seuil, 1990, p. 45.
61. P.E. Geller, 'Copyright History and the Future: What's Culture Got to Do With It', *J. Copy. Socy USA*, 2000, Vol. 47, p. 223; F. W. Grosheide, 'Paradigms in Copyright Law', in B. Sherman et A. Strowel (eds), *Of Authors and Origins*, Clarendon Press, 1994, p. 205.

> information: as commodities they became in principle generally accessible. They no longer remained components of the Church's and court's publicity of representation; that is precisely what was meant by the loss of their aura or extraordinariness and the profaning of their once sacramental character. The private people for whom the cultural product became available as a commodity profaned it inasmuch as they had to determine its meaning on their own (by way of rational communication with one another), verbalize it, and thus state explicitly what precisely in its implicitness for so long could assert its authority.[62]

I have developed elsewhere my belief in the public sphere theory as a relevant paradigm for copyright law.[63] The emergence of copyright in the eighteenth century in Europe is contemporary with the birth of the *public sphere* as described by Jürgen Habermas. This is no coincidence, as this historical moment explains not only the legal recognition of the protection of authors, but also its epistemology. The increasing trade in books, associated with the growing financial and political autonomy of readers, and the substitution of publishers for patrons and sponsors has pushed the claim for the suppression of printing privileges and for protection of authors, now released from the benevolence of the King and the Church, but subjected to the taste and approval of the public and to the rules of the market. Paradoxically, under the Habermas perspective, it is when works of art enter the market that they simultaneously eschew it. The public sphere is indeed distinct from the private sphere, which encompasses the family's internal place and the civil society that is the realm of commodities exchange and social labour.[64]

Early debates on the recognition of legal protection of authors and writings show some elements borrowed from the public sphere and public use of reason thinking. This communicative and democratic dimension of copyright influenced the debates surrounding its enactment, the copyright regime being a creature of the same historical and political period. For copyright is contemporary with this public sphere development; its purpose is both the protection of the author, in order to confer on her the autonomy to create and to take part in the public discourse, and the protection and autonomy of the public. The paradigm of the public sphere posits a normative model of copyright that purports to contribute to the constitution of a public space for discussion and creation.[65] It supplements the Lockean

62. J. Habermas, n. 55, pp. 36–37.
63. S. Dusollier, *Droit d'auteur et protection des œuvres dans l'univers numérique*, Bruxelles, Larcier, 2005, pp. 220 et seq.
64. J. Habermas, n. 55, *see* the table on p. 30. The work also gets out of the sphere of public authority (i.e., the state and the Court) where it was before.
65. Habermas also studies the transformation of the public sphere (and its decline) in the twentieth century. The development of mass media and communication technologies have, in his view, transformed the public into passive readers and public opinion is shaped

justification of a right grounded in the labour of the author, but qualifies an overly strict property right by inserting a public dimension therein. In France, Condorcet pleaded for the abolition of publishers' privileges by referring to Enlightenment, whose progress would depend on printing regulation.[66]

Many copyright scholars have developed a justification of copyright based on the communicative theory and public discourse under the influence of Kant.[67] They all insist on the way copyright needs to promote discursive production of works and social dialogue for democratic purposes. The nineteenth century French copyright scholar Renouard also insisted on the social objective of copyright in a spirit influenced by Enlightenment views.[68] A few scholars have explored the implications of the public sphere of Habermas for copyright, like M. Rose[69] or R. Coombe in cultural study and anthropology.[70]

---

instead of being enlightened by a discursive process. That does not disqualify the application of the public sphere model to copyright, as his vision might be a bit exaggerated, the public sphere having survived the evolution of media and having subsisted in other forms, particularly on the internet, and as copyright could still be considered as an appropriate legal framework to protect and enhance the autonomy of authors and readers in such a public sphere. For a development of that point, *see* S. Dusollier, n. 63, pp. 226 et seq.

66. M. J.-C. Condorcet, *Œuvres*, Paris, Firmin Didot Frères, 1847, t. II, p. 312, in A. Strowel, '*Le droit d'auteur et le copyright entre histoire et nature*', in Ph.Gerard, F. Ost & M. van de Kerchove (eds), *Images et usages de la nature en droit,* Facultés Universitaires St Louis, 1993, p. 147. *See also* a Bill on freedom of the press prepared by Condorcet that insisted on 'the progress of enlightenment, and hence, of public interest, associated with the idea of distributive justice, to require that the property of a work be ensured to author by law' (in J. Ginsburg, 'A Tale of Two Copyrights: Literary Property in Revolutionary France and America', *R.I.D.A.*, Janvier 1991, n. 147, p. 174).
67. On Kant and copyright, *see* A. Barron, n. 48; L. Biron, 'Public Reason, Communication and Intellectual Property', in A. Lever (ed.), *New Frontiers in the Philosophy of Intellectual Property*, Cambridge Intellectual Property and Information Law, 18, Cambridge University Press, 2012, pp. 225–260; N. Netanel, 'Copyright and a Democratic Civil Society', n. 47; N. Elkin-Koren, 'A Democratic Approach to Copyright Law in Cyberspace', n. 47. *See also* P. E. Geller, 'Toward an Overriding Norm in Copyright: Sign Wealth', *R.I.D.A.,* Avril 1994, pp. 3–109; F.W. Grosheide, in B. Sherman & A. Strowel (eds), *Of Authors and Origins*, Clarendon Press, 1994, pp. 210–211.
68. A.-C. Renouard, *Traité des droits d'auteurs dans la littérature, les sciences et les beaux-arts*, Paris, Jules Renouard et Cie, 1838, Tome I, p. 433 et suiv.; A. Strowel, '*Considérations sur le droit d'auteur à la lumière des intérêts sous-jacents*', in Ph. Gérard, F. Ost, M. van de Kerchove (ed.), *Droit et Intérêt*, Facultés Universitaires St-Louis, Bruxelles, 1990, Vol. 3, p. 257.
69. M. Rose, 'The Public Sphere and the Emergence of Copyright: Aeropagitica, the Stationers' Company, and the Statute of Anne', in R. Deazley, M. Kretschmer & L. Bently, *Privilege and Property: Essays on the History of Copyright*, Open Book Publishers, 2010.
70. R. Coombe, *The Cultural Life of Intellectual Properties – Authorship, Appropriation and the Law*, Duke University Press, 1998, p. 5 (who develops a critique of the public sphere as theorized by Harbermas, notably for its gender and minorities bias). *See also*, for a

All share the view that the author's creation is a public act of speech initiating a dialogue with the public, conceived as other speakers, and that copyright law should be part of the legal framework facilitating that dialogue.[71] Works are not mere commodities but are acts of speech[72] and copyright should secure equal and reciprocal freedoms for both authors and users and readers of copyright works.[73] That idea has been developed particularly by A. Drassinower in a recent publication, *What's Wrong with Copying?*. He posits that 'because a work of authorship is a communicative act, copyright infringement is a wrong to an author's autonomy as a speaking being'.[74] I beg to differ slightly here. Communicating a work to the public, thereby infringing copyright, is not only, as Drassinower argues, harming the autonomy or dignity of the author as a speaker, by speaking on her behalf in the public sphere, it also deprives the author of the means to be associated with the public circulation of her creations to enable her to participate thereto and hence to sustain an active public sphere. As explained by A. Barron, by reference to Kant's writings, copyright is 'a systematic legal structure for the protection of communicative freedom',[75] this structure being constituted by the rights of authors, publishers and the reading public in relation to authorial communications, and not only protecting the right to speak as authors and the reciprocal right of readers.

Considering writings, and more generally creative expression, under the epistemology of the public sphere has many effects on copyright. It centres the right on the head of the author, the publisher being only a transmitter of the speech of the author. Copyright should aim at ensuring the autonomy of the author by giving her the means to control the circulation of works in the public sphere and to obtain revenue from it. It should also foster the participation of the public in cultural life and access to works, for the public is a central actor in copyright, as a recipient and possible discussant of the works.

The circulation of works is necessarily linked to the public sphere, even if it is mediated by the market. As far as the definition of economic rights is concerned, it prevents the definition of the rights in such a way that the copyright owners would be able to control any individual act of transmission or reception of the work, for example through a technical approach to the reproduction, which transforms the relationship between the author and the public to a relationship between the author and a consumer in substitution for the public sphere.

---

more positive reception of the public sphere argument, R. Coombe, 'Left Out on the Information Highway', *Or. L. Rev.,* 1996, Vol. 75, pp. 239–240.

71. A. Barron, n. 48, p. 3.
72. A. Drassinower, n. 48.
73. *Ibid.*
74. *Ibid.*, pp. 13–14.
75. A. Barron, n. 48, pp. 22–23.

Finally, the moral right is not absent from the public sphere, but could be seen as its precondition. The right of divulgation, where it is recognized by law, is the act that puts the work in the public sphere and inaugurates the discursive relationship between the author and the public. It could even be said that divulging the work creates the public. It is the act of publicity (*Öffentlichkeit*) as meant by Kant.

6.5 ECONOMIC RIGHTS INFORMED BY THE PUBLIC SPHERE EPISTEMOLOGY

6.5.1 The Non-market Dimension of the Exploitation

Exploitation is generally made synonymous with economic value and with the fructification of a resource. It alludes to the possibility of extracting revenues from property (the *fructus* in the civil notion of *propriété*). This is not the mere use of a resource, which is a first distinction between property and intellectual property: in property, any use of the resource without authorization will be considered as trespassing and infringing the right; in intellectual property law everyone agrees that not all acts of use are infringing and that the intellectual property realm is limited to the control of some activities only. As the owned thing is intangible, not all uses of the work can be controlled by lack of physical possession. The exclusive right created by law to remediate the non-exclusive feature of the work, would only grant a limited control defined by the contours of the rights granted.

Traditionally, a for-profit purpose is not a condition for copyright infringement and the divide between commercial and non-commercial purposes is irrelevant.[76] The economic approach is nonetheless gaining momentum in EU case law, as demonstrated by the reference to for-profit purpose in interpreting the communication right[77] or the equation made by the CJEU between the remuneration due to authors and the economic value of the exploitation.[78] National courts sometimes rely on the capturing of the economic value of creative works to rule that an act of exploitation has occurred. For instance, a French court has decided, without bothering to scrutinize the precise definitions of the reproduction right and its exceptions,

76. Despite CJEU, 8 September 2016, *GS Media*, C-160/15.
77. *See* ECJ, 7 December 2006, *SGAE*, C-306/05, §44; CJEU, 15 March 2012, *Phonographic Performance (Ireland) Limited*, C-162/10, §§36–37; CJEU, 15 March 2012, *SCF v. Marco del Corso*, C-135/10, §88; CJEU, 7 March 2013, *ITV Broadcasting*, C-607/11, §43.
78. CJEU, 4 October 2011, *Football Association Premiere League,* C-403/08 & C-429/08, §109 ('In order to be appropriate, such remuneration must be reasonable in relation to the economic value of the service provided. In particular, it must be reasonable in relation to the actual or potential number of persons who enjoy or wish to enjoy the service').

that an internet-based service for recording TV programmes (nPVR) infringes copyright as it 'creates and captures an economic wealth by a service of copying of works or audiovisual programs avoiding the remuneration of copyright holders'.[79]

Nevertheless, the economic perspective should not be the only factor to define exploitation of copyright works. If copyright is an act of communication, exploitation can be dissociated from its economic dimension and related to the circulation of works in the public sphere. Remember that Habermas explained that the public sphere emerged from the development of a market for cultural artefacts, even though the importance of the public access to works requires dissociating the public sphere from the market. Works are not commodities. Therefore, exploitation is not synonymous with trade in the market, but incorporates some public dissemination of the work, which borders the control by copyright owners. A Belgian scholar, writing before the advent of the internet, had already explained that the different prerogatives of copyright 'are not simple powers of exploitation, strictly limited to the use of some process, but they aim at ensuring, within their own field, the control of the author on the communication or diffusion of her work. The recognition of this common purpose to the discrete attributes of copyright enable to safeguard its internal coherence, the many rights being the different manifestations of a fundamental mastery of the author over the diffusion of her creation'.[80]

The public sphere includes the circulation of embodiments of works in the market and it is a necessary condition to sustain the economic wealth of authors, but also preserves non-market circulation in the public interest, including for example provision of works by libraries and for educational purposes.[81] Economic rights should then refer to any activity enabling the work to be made available to a public. The perimeter of exploitation should be drawn by reference to the public dimension of the use of works. The bundle of rights gathered under the notion of exploitation should enable the author to enjoy an economic reservation of her work and to associate her with the constitution of a public space where works circulate.[82] In other words, the rights granted to the author do not entitle her to oppose all uses of her work, nor to control all segments of or activities in the market but they

79. TGI Paris, 6 August 2008, available at http://www.legalis.net/spip.php?page=breves-article&id_article=2405 (accessed 1 October 2017, my translation).

80. J.-G. Renauld, '*Les destinées récentes du droit de reproduction mécanique et le droit d'auteur*', *R.C.J.B.*, 1956, p. 196 (my translation).

81. *See* on the necessity to preserve some space non-mediated by the market in copyright, P. Lescure, *Mission 'Acte II de l'exception culturelle', Contribution aux politiques culturelles à l'ère numérique*, 2013, p. 185; Opinion of the CJEU Advocate General, 16 June 2016, *Vereniging Openbare Bibliotheken*, C-174/15.

82. A. Strowel, *Droit d'auteur et copyright – Divergences et convergences*, Bruxelles/Paris, Bruylant/LGDJ, 1993, p. 65.

should give an author enough autonomy (including financial means) to associate her with its dissemination on the market.

6.5.2 The Public Dimension of the Exploitation

My starting point to define economic rights in copyright being the public sphere and public circulation of works begs for a clear definition of what 'public' is and covers. This is a tricky exercise in the contemporary world where the boundaries between private and public are blurred and merging.

Habermas discussed the transformation of the public sphere in the twentieth century in a world where mass media started to emerge and concluded that the public sphere was in decline. That was one of the most criticized points in his argumentation, for many scholars in political theory contested the contemporary disappearance of the public sphere, the public discussion having moved to other spaces instead. The internet age has certainly multiplied the spaces where public discussion takes place and blurred the divide between public and private. The exact location of public spheres in the twenty-first century with its many technologically-mediated spheres is a question of political theory, but its implication for copyright control is significant, as copyright has always operated on the division between public and private. The only positive definition of 'public' we have today results from the case law of the CJEU on the communication right that defines the 'public' as referring to 'an indeterminate number of recipients, … and [implying], moreover, a fairly large number of persons'.[83]

In lieu of a quantitative assessment by the CJEU, the public sphere mandates a qualitative assessment: what is public is what can result in public discussion, outside the private or family sphere. In other words, it is the 'publication' of the work that matters, in the sense of its being made publicly available.[84] Let's take the examples of Facebook, Instagram, Twitter and other social networks, where the public/private dimension might be blurred. Even though users might consider they are involved in a community of friends where they act in a private capacity, such social networks are instituting, in my view, a contemporary public sphere where public discussion and exchanges take place, perhaps in a renewed form that is more comparable to the eighteenth century public sphere described by Habermas, than to the mass media that tended to stifle public discussion and made people inactive and silent. What is posted or communicated on internet social

83. CJEU, 19 November 2014, *SBS Belgium*, C-325/14 §21; CJEU, *SGAE*, C-306/05, §§37 and 38; CJEU, *ITV Broadcasting and Others*, C-607/11, §32.

84. *See also* A. Drassinower, n. 48, p. 9: '"publication" rather than "reproduction" is the central organizing principle of copyright law' (even though Drassinower seems to employ a definition of publication referring to both rights of divulgation and rights of public communication).

networks, irrespective of the number of followers or friends, is an act of speech and public communication.

This is not to say that copyright should cover all postings made on social networks, as some might be only referential or not constitute an act of circulation of the work, as will be discussed later on. Most of the time, content appearing on social networks is taken from other website locations, through hyperlinks or references. For that reason, such hyperlinks should be left outside copyright control for they only consist of references to copyright works already in the public sphere. The work is not re-communicated to the public but the user engages in the public discussion initiated by the first circulation of the work by referring others to its location on the web and thereby bringing them into the discussion.

The 'publicity' of the exploitation does not exclude acts of communication of works to individuals that are each located in their private sphere either. Making works available by broadcasting, streaming or downloading to readers, viewers or consumers who are not at the same place at the same time, has a public dimension as works are destined for the public sphere constituted by the individuals to whom works are distributed. That might be a slight deviation from the public sphere described by Habermas, who insisted on public spaces, such as French *salons*, or theatres, forming the public sphere and where the discussion actually took place between conversing individuals.

Conversely, personal uses are excluded from exploitation. Reading, viewing, receiving or enjoying a work are not exploitation activities as they lack any public dimension. The same is true of copies made for personal use. As a consequence, private copying should not be covered by a copyright exception but be exempt from copyright control altogether, as it is not aimed at a public. By losing its current status of exception in most EU Member States, no right to remuneration or levy would be due. This is not a minor change, as many authors and performers benefit from significant revenue from private copying levies and would be suddenly deprived of such benefit. Under the current private copying regime, the exception is limited to copies made from a lawful source, which prevents acquisition of a work through the process of copying it for one's own benefit. As a consequence, private copying as authorized by law and compensated by remuneration only occurs when making multiple copies of legitimately acquired works (e.g., burning a CD of an album bought online, downloading a favourite song with a streaming subscription on a few devices). In such cases, the remuneration that is due under the levy system might be disputed as it complements the remuneration the user has already paid for the service or acquisition. Time-shifting copies are another example of exempted private copying, but they are increasingly carried out by economic operators in nPVR services and hosted on servers on which no remuneration is collected. This makes the private copy and levies system less meaningful or less harmful for copyright owners.

The importance of private copying levies in the revenue of the authors and performers should not supersede the need to justify the legitimacy of covering private copies by copyright in the first place or to prove the harm suffered by rightholders due to such copies. There is some ambiguity in compensating the decreasing revenues of creators by rights to remuneration, thereby transforming copyright into a hidden form of rent or cultural subsidy. More effort should be made to ensure fair remuneration of creators and participation in the benefits engendered by the actual exploitation of their works. The loss of private copying levies should be significantly compensated by better protection of the remuneration for creators for acts of exploitation.

6.5.3 The Communicative Dimension of the Exploitation

Defining exploitation by the circulation of works in the public sphere entails a communicative dimension: the exploitation is a communicative act that has the work as object.[85] Therefore, the work itself, as a creative expression, should be presented to the public and the purpose of the act should be communicative, not merely technical. Both dimensions are emphasized by A. Drassinower: 'paradigmatic instances of nonuses involve use of a work's material form not as a work but as a tool, not communicatively but technically'.[86]

What is being communicated to the public is the creative expression, not the tangible item that incorporates it nor the information, ideas and mere data it conveys. In trademark law too, the reference to the harm to one of the functions of the trademark as a test for infringement has excluded cases where the protected sign was used not as an indication of origin but in any other way. For example, affixing the trademark of a car brand on a toy replica of the car is only replicating the sign to be faithful to the original, not to identify the origin of the product or service.[87] Likewise, there might be cases where copying a work or communicating to the public does not pertain to the creative expression itself but disseminates some unprotected information or data. In other words, works are sometimes exploited for purposes other than conveying the copyright expression.

Two examples can illustrate that requirement. The French *Cour de cassation* once refused to consider the repeated inclusion of drawings hanging on the walls of a classroom in a documentary film as an infringement, for they were 'not represented for themselves' but as accessories to the

85. This is further elaborated by A. Strowel in his chapter elsewhere in this volume.
86. A. Drassinower, n. 48, p. 183.
87. ECJ, 25 January 2007, *Adam Opel*, C-48/05.

scene that was filmed.[88] The decision however ruled on the admissibility of an exception for an incidental use of the work, and did not consider whether the economic rights in reproduction and communication of the work were implicated by the use.

At the EU level,[89] a television broadcast of the graphic user interface of a computer program was not deemed by the CJEU to be an act of communication covered by copyright, as the interaction with the user, deemed to be an essential element of such interface, was impossible. This might look like a puzzling condition for the communication right and in blatant contradiction with the refusal of the CJEU to qualify the user interface as a computer program (which conversely could have explained the requirement for an interaction). The only way to understand and accept this element might be to link the ruling to the notion of exploitation. Should communication to the public not be restricted to cases where the work is indeed achieving its purpose of being transmitted to the public, and effectively received by the public? The graphic user interface was in that case only represented as mere data, not as an expressive work.

What should count, in my opinion, is that the communication permits the exploitation of the creative content, i.e., its transmission to the public and exploitation as a work, and not only its transmission as data. By that token, search engine results should avoid copyright control as they indicate references to works but do not communicate them as works, except when they make the works themselves directly visible to the public. This will be developed later on.

The second element of the communicative dimension is that the use should aim at public dissemination of the work. It should not be merely technical. In other words, a technical and ancillary copy would not be covered by copyright if it is not a vehicle for a public communication of the work or is only a necessary part thereof. Mere technical copies of works that are not transmitted or are only incidental to reception or use of works are not normatively relevant. In comparison to the current treatment of temporary reproduction in EU copyright law, merely technical uses of a work would not be covered by an exception, but treated as 'non-use'[90] not actionable under copyright.

---

88. Cour de cassation, Arrêt n°453, 12 May 2011 (08-20.651), this argument was mostly developed in the decision of the Court of Appeal, Paris (4th ch.), 12 September 2008, 07/00860, available at www.legifrance.fr (*'dès lors que le réalisateur n'a pas eu la volonté de représenter et de divulguer une oeuvre figurant dans un espace public ou dans l'environnement quotidien de la personne filmée et que sa présence à l'écran est fortuite, il ne peut être question d'avoir à demander une autorisation'*).

89. CJEU, 22 December 2010, *Bezpečnostní softwarová asociace*, C-393/09, §57.

90. A. Drassinower, n. 48, p. 88.

6.5.4 The Means of Exploitation Today

If exploitation is the umbrella notion determining the scope of economic rights, the precise rights that its bundle contains are still to be identified. I already posited that the rights are means to serve the end of exploitation, not self-operating notions. As reproduction, distribution and communication were illustrative of the means of exploitation in pre-internet times, a similar exercise should be carried out to single out types of use that exploit the creative value of works and participate in the public circulation of works today.

I would propose categorizing, based on the function of copyright, the different ways a work is disseminated or transmitted to the public as a whole or to members of the public as a communicative act, into three groups of uses that are illustrative of exploitation but in no way exhaustive.[91]

The three categories of relevant acts of exploitation would be:

(1) marketing a good embodying a protected work;
(2) providing a service or an experience of a work; and
(3) exploiting a derivative work.

Each category would be defined broadly and examples of current modes of exploitation included in the category could be listed, without being exhaustive. It would be a matter for the courts to consider whether a new mode of exploitation is to be covered by the economic rights as defined. An exploitation would not be fragmented into a number of technical acts: the process of exploiting the work would be considered as a whole for its ultimate end.

The economic rights as we know them today would no longer be relevant. There would be no need to characterize an act of reproduction, communication or distribution in order to trigger the application of copyright. Instead, many uses of works previously consisting of communication or distribution would remain covered. That might not be true for reproduction. Save where covered by an exception, any copy of a work currently infringes copyright, whether independently or through involvement in a broader process of communication. In our revised model, acts of reproduction could be considered as exploitation reserved to copyright owners only where they entail an act of transmission of the work to the public. Rather, they will be absorbed in a process of exploitation that will be the very object of the right. Control of copies as such would lose its central role and might eventually disappear, at least for digital exploitation.[92] An exception could be

91. This is similar to what O.A. Rognstad & J. Poort and A. Ohly propose, in different ways, in their contributions to the present volume.
92. Compare with D. Visser, *Auteursrecht op toegang – De exploitatierechten van de auteur in het tijdperk van digitale informatie en netwerkcommunicatie,* VUGA Uitgeverij, 's-Gravenhage, 1997, who similarly argued for the abolition of the right of reproduction.

reserved for first acts of copying by the publisher or producer who transforms the work into a marketable product, whether tangible or intangible. To maintain some power for the author in the negotiation transferring her rights to such first exploiters and determining the number of copies that will be produced for exploitation, such reproductions should count as acts of exploitation, separate even from further acts of provision of those copies to the public.

The first two groups of acts of exploitation aim at including the operations that make a work available to the public. Instead of relying on making works available, directly or indirectly, by tangible copies, as it is currently framed in copyright law, our distinction draws a line between the reception of a good by the public for permanent use, and access to and reception of a work as an ephemeral experience, without the user keeping a permanent copy of the content.

6.5.4.1 Marketing a Good Embodying a Protected Work

A first type of exploitation would consist of any act of 'distribution' of a work that could enable its permanent use by the public, whatever the channel of distribution and regardless of whether the good is in tangible or intangible form. When copies of the work are transmitted to members of the public, in such a way that the acquirers of said copies could enjoy the work as their own and with no limitation in time, authors and copyright owners should be able to control such acts of exploitation.

That would include sale or any other transfer of tangible copies of works (e.g., books, DVDs, CDs or video games), or making works available for irreversible download (e.g., 'sale'[93] of ebooks, music or video files, or software by dedicated platforms, or file-sharing on peer-to-peer platforms). In line with the CJEU decision in *UsedSoft*, the reality of the transfer, i.e., the reception of the work for permanent use, and not the tangible or intangible dimension[94] of the product received, will be relevant. Without having to resort to a fragile and contested definition of sale, as the CJEU did, the transfer of a copy of a work, irrespective of its embodiment, but with the intention that the user will own this copy and does not have to return it, will be the defining feature of this first cluster of exploitation acts.

---

93. The legal qualification of the operation is not relevant at this stage. It could be a sale or a licence. As observed by the CJEU (3 July 2012, *UsedSoft*, C-128/11), a licence providing software for a price and for a use unlimited in time can be considered as a sale, which can be followed perfectly economically speaking (one can still challenge this equation on legal grounds).
94. A digital file has a physical dimension too. Tangible refers here to a hard copy, a physical product, whereas 'intangible' refers to the provision of a digital file that has no fixed or permanent embodiment.

The making of the copy in itself will not be considered as an infringement of copyright, but any exploitation of copies and their distribution will be. This is another justification for the disappearance of the private copy exception.

The *droit de suite* could enter in this category. Even though the resale of an original work of art occurs between two persons, it is mediated by the intervention of an art market professional and is an act of further circulation of the work in the art market sphere that could be equated to a part of the public sphere. Each sale of a work for a higher price captures some value of the work for the benefit of the seller. Successive sales of a painting or any other type of artistic work constitute the usual way of transmitting the creative value of this type of work to the public. For the sake of clarity, the *droit de suite* could alternatively be maintained as a separate act of exploitation as it presently stands.

6.5.4.2 Providing a Service or an Experience of a Work

The second type of operation would encompass the provision of a work in a non-permanent way, enabling the public to gain access to the work and its creative content or to experience the work in any way. This might be the biggest change to copyright brought about by the digital age, where provision of temporary or limited enjoyment of creative content prevails over sales of copies.[95] In such cases, the user does not get access to a permanent copy of the work from which she could enjoy the work with no limitation in time. She would instead get access to the experience of the work, being able to read, view, listen to or play with it for a limited time or even, in subscription-based models of circulation of works, for a time determined by the duration of the subscription (which could potentially be unlimited).

This would include many acts of exploitation: traditional analogue communications or performances such as dramatical or musical performances in theatres or concert halls, film screenings in movie theatres, as well as broadcasting, cable or satellite transmission, occurring either in an analogue mode or in a digital one. Making works available on information networks would be covered, such as the posting of a work online without a download option, or streaming services such as Spotify, Deezer or Apple-Play. The rental or lending rights would be integral to that category of exploitation and would apply independently of their brick-and-mortar or online environment (such as Netflix-type VOD services), due to the limited-in-time enjoyment of the work they allow. Likewise, the provision of

95. T. Dreier, 'L'analogue, le digital et le droit d'auteur', in *Propriétés Intellectuelles-Mélanges en l'honneur d'André Françon,* Paris, Dalloz, 1995, p. 119. *See also* the 'shift to trade in normative positions' mentioned by J. Bing, 'Convergence and Some Possible Consequences for Copyright and Right Holders', in *Copyright, Related Rights and Media Convergence in the Digital Context*, ALAI Conference 2000, Stockholm, p. 43.

a computer program or a video game for online and remote use (e.g., software-as-a-service) falls within that type of exploitation, as it does not transfer ownership of a copy of the work to the user.

6.5.4.3 The Making of a Derivative Work

A final type of exploitation activity would consist of exploiting the creative value of a work in a derivative creation. The right to make derivative works, which is not harmonized at EU level but exists in many national copyright legislations, is a hard case to define and limit, as it might be difficult to draw a line between adaptations, transformations or reworkings of works that should be deemed to be infringing, and derivative uses that are privileged under an exception.[96]

The public sphere paradigm and the communicative focus it has on copyright is ambiguous in that regard. The control it should grant to the author over the circulation of her creation entails on the one hand that a re-circulation of the work adapted for a new genre, or in an amended or a modified version, requires her prior authorization, for the author should be able to oversee how her expression is conveyed. Adapting a work in another medium or genre, translating it, rearranging it or novelizing it, could certainly count as a new circulation of the creation in the public sphere. This is an important prong in the bundle of exploitations that the author should be able to control or obtain remuneration for. It is not the mere making of a derivative work that would trigger the exclusive right of copyright owners but only the fact that the derivative work is a new vehicle to publicly disseminate the expressive elements of the underlying work. Consequently, purely technical adaptation of works in another format should not be covered by the exploitation right, for only data are exploited here and not the creative work itself. Abridgments or condensations of works might be considered as derivative works if they go beyond mere development of the unprotectable ideas and content of the work and copy substantial parts of the original work and act as substitutes thereof.[97] Also, acts of adaptation carried out in the private sphere with no intention of public dissemination should not be encompassed by the right of making derivative works.

On the other hand, the same public sphere paradigm begs for the public to be given an autonomous voice and some discursive empowerment, which would allow use of the work in new expressions. For that very reason, A. Drassinower considers that the right of making derivative works is an oddity in copyright law and should be suppressed. In his view, the concept of a work

96. *See* for a reflection on US law, the excellent article by P. Samuelson, 'The Quest for a Sound Conception of Copyright's Derivative Work Right', *Geo. L. J.*, Vol. 101, no. 6, pp. 1505–1564; *see also*, M. van Eechoud, 'Adapting the Work', in *The Work of Authorship*, Amsterdam University Press, 2014.

97. *See* P. Samuelson, n. 96, p. 1518.

as a communicative act cannot tolerate the 'derivative work right', for this right denies the recognition of the defendant's authorship that is irreducibly integral to the copyright system in his paradigm.[98] In his view, the making of derivative works should then not be discussed as fair use, but should be recognized as a non-infringing use, as they are equal and autonomous acts of speech.[99] I would disagree here, as it presumes that all adaptations of works are discursive answers to communications initiated by the underlying work. Besides, copyright is not about allowing or enabling anyone to speak (as freedom of speech is protected for that very purpose), but is about associating the one who speaks with the circulation of her speech (both by recognizing who speaks and enabling her to control to some extent such circulation).

True, not all transformative uses of a copyright work should be covered by copyright and the line might be thin between derivative works exploiting an existing creation (e.g., an adaptation of a literary work into a motion picture version, a remix of a musical work or a translation of a work into another language) and mere references to works, follow-on innovation and creation or free expression. But there is in my view a difference between the screen adaptation of a novel, which is faithful to its plot and characters and even makes literal copies of parts of its text, and an integration of a work into a new creation for parody, critique, appropriation art or experimentation (as in a musical remix). All these examples are to be placed on a line separating exploitations considered to be making a derivative work from reworkings of the work either not considered to be such exploitations, or excused by fair use or exceptions.

For example, the adaptation of a work into a parody or to make a critique or a political statement should be preserved for obvious freedom of expression reasons, and fundamentally to preserve the agency of the public in a public sphere justification of copyright. To the extent copyright is justified as allowing the creator to disseminate her creation and discourses in the public sphere as well as enabling the public to engage in critical discussion of works, copyright should equally protect the emergence of counter-discourses in the public sphere. A perfect example is the US case of the retelling of *Gone with the Wind* from a slave's viewpoint in Alice Randall's novel *The Wind Done Gone.*[100] Commenting on an existing work or using it for referential purposes should equally escape copyright's control, which would include fan fiction,[101] many cases of user-generated works,[102]

98. A. Drassinower, n. 48, p. 222.

99. *See infra.*

100. *Suntrust v. Houghton Mifflin Co.*, 252 F. 3d 1165 (11th Cir. 2001).

101. *See* R. Tushnet, 'Legal Fictions: Copyright, Fan Fiction, and a New Common Law', *Loy. L.A. Ent. L.J.* 1997, Vol. 17, pp. 651, 654; A. Chander & M. Sunder, 'Everyone's a Superhero: A Cultural Theory of 'Mary Sue' Fan Fiction as Fair Use', *Calif. L. Rev.* 2007, Vol. 95, pp. 597, 600.

102. V.-L. Benabou, *Rapport de la mission du CSPLA sur les œuvres transformatives*, 2014.

as well as parodies using underlying works as means of critique and not objects thereof.[103]

Digital technologies have also accelerated playful uses of creative content in new works or performances. Copyright works are increasingly used as primary material for new creation (and not only as sources for imitation or copying). User-generated content is an obvious example as a product of democratization of means of creation and of the transformation of creative content in cultural signifiers. Many forms of appropriation art incorporate existing works of art or copyright protected forms of expression through collages or copies as representations of their times, as cultural signs. Musical remixes could also be described as creations using existing songs or musical tunes as one would use letters, notes or paint.

For all these examples, drawing a line between what could count as exploitations that should remain within the control of copyright owners and legitimate uses that would either stay outside the exclusive right or be excused by a copyright exception will not be an easy task.

6.5.5 Some Consequences of the Revised Model

Aligning economic rights of exploitation would leave some uses of copyright works outside the control of copyright owners. We have already considered uses for personal purposes, such as private copying, and temporary and incidental reproductions. Reproduction as such will not be actionable if it is not part of a process of transmission or adaptation of the work.

This proposal merely defines the scope of the economic rights and does not exclude exempting certain valuable forms of exploitation by way of exceptions or limitations. Second-hand resale, not-for-profit sharing of works, provision of access to works by libraries or educational establishments and provision of experiences of works by museums could be considered, in our model, as means of exploitation as they circulate the work to the public. Recourse to exceptions and limitations, on the ground of the need for balance and preservation of important social, cultural and democratic values, should leave such spaces uncontrolled, under certain conditions. The impact of our revised model of exclusive rights on exceptions to copyright should be carefully assessed. Evidently, a revision of economic rights by a *tabula rasa* strategy bears a risk of removing valuable spaces for uncontrolled and uncompensated uses of creation while trying to get the table clean to start all over. This is a risk of which one should be particularly aware.

---

103. This refers to works using existing creation as primary material to criticize or comment on a topic other than the work itself. This has been authorized by the CJEU, 3 September 2014, *Deckmyn*, C-201/13, at 21.

Finally, the concept of exploitation, if it indicates which uses of works deserve to be covered by the rights granted to copyright owners, does not impose the extent of control they would benefit from. Rightholders can enjoy exclusive rights enabling them to authorize or not the exploitation in question or they could only claim compensation. The criteria for deciding which would be relevant for each exploitation could be further discussed.

My proposal does not explore the modifications the model would necessarily bring to collective management, which is heavily structured today around rights of reproduction and communication to the public. This is not a minor consequence of any restructuring of economic rights in copyright and more attention should be paid to it.

The revision of economic rights proposed here has been anchored to the function and justification of copyright. Neighbouring rights are younger in the history of intellectual property and do not answer to a similar objective nor relate to a communication or public sphere argument. Their justification has rather been the protection of an artistic contribution to creation or of an investment. When introducing neighbouring rights in the system of intellectual property, no consideration was given to crafting the economic rights the new regime would grant to fit the specificities and justifications of this new species of intellectual property rights. The rights granted by neighbouring rights have been simply shaped in the same mould.

It might seem artificial to transpose the rights based on a notion of exploitation rooted in the specific history of copyright to related rights. Yet, one advantage thereof is that it aligns copyright and related rights clearance for the same exploitation of content around the same economic rights. That could be one argument to apply our exploitation model to both types of rights indiscriminately, despite its disconnection from the justification and epistemology of neighbouring rights. For the sake of consistency and legal certainty for the users of creative content, I propose to apply the same scheme to copyright and related rights.

The realignment of economic rights to the circulation of works in the public sphere might be difficult to transpose for copyright in computer programs. Indeed, when software entered the copyright realm, reproduction and distribution were the key activities deemed to be infringing with no attention being paid to communication. That could be explained by the modes of exploitation that were then specific to computer programs. As this was the pre-internet era, no copies of software were made available online, instead software was copied or distributed in tangible form. Current modes of disseminating software, such as distribution of tangible copies, making software available for download, and providing access to software functions as a service, could still be encompassed in my revised model. Copying a program would no longer be covered by a suppressed reproduction right, but could be covered under a derivative work right if the copy results in a new version or adaptation. That being said, it is true that the peculiar subject-matter of software, which is more a tool than an expression, might elude a public sphere reasoning. Most copyright rules applied to computer programs are merely aimed at protecting their distribution to and use by customers, and do not reflect a public sphere justification of copyright. Reconciling computer program protection with a revised model of economic rights might require a more profound change.

6.5.6 Application to Test Cases

6.5.6.1 Text and Data Mining

Text and data mining operations are easily excluded from a redefined scope of exploitation for two reasons. The first is that, absent the inclusion of mere technical copies in the economic rights, no exploitation activity could be found in the mere analysis and processing of data and texts implied by TDM. There is no public circulation of the processed works through an operation of text and data mining.

A second reason is that the mining operation only aims at exploiting the data and information contained in the analysed material. The exploitation, if any, is not about communicating works, but only deals with data and underlying information.

In conclusion, text and data mining should not be considered as infringing economic rights under copyright. Therefore, treating it as a privileged use under an exception, as envisaged in the proposed EU Directive on copyright in the Digital Single Market (proposed DSM Directive),[104] is not necessary. Nor should it be limited to researchers or research organizations, non-commercial purpose or to works to which lawful access is proven.

6.5.6.2 Hyperlinking

Hyperlinking to a copyright protected work will in most cases not amount to an act of exploitation, as a hyperlink only sets up a reference to the location of a work, an indication of where to find the work. The hyperlinked work is already part of the public sphere and the act of referring thereto does not amount to a new circulation, even though it may contribute to generating new public discussion about the work.

Such analysis is not derived from the technique of hyperlinking but from its context. A hyperlink that makes the work visible as embedded in the referring website, or a framing technique, could in my view, be further discussed. To some extent, the work is then presented to the public in a renewed way and it could qualify as an act of providing the experience of a

104. Proposal for a Directive of the European Parliament and of the Council on copyright in the Digital Single Market, 14 September 2016, COM(2016) 593 final, Art. 3.

work. For instance, the pictures that are indexed by Google Images are made directly viewable on the search outcomes page and the internet user can download a copy of any image by a mere click without any need to visit the original location of the image.

6.5.6.3 Exploitation by Internet Platforms

A revised notion of exploitation might also result in inclusion of activities related to copyright works that used to be immune to the application of economic rights. While preserving the principle of exemption from liability for intermediaries for illicit content posted online by users, the reality of the exploitation of creative content carried out by some of them should be acknowledged.

The most obvious example is video-sharing platforms such as YouTube or Dailymotion. The qualification of YouTube or the like as mere hosting providers is increasingly challenged. Technically the audiovisual platform hosts content posted by its users on its servers and is incapable of checking the lawfulness of such content, as it has no editorial liability. Seen through the lens of exploitation however its principal purpose is to provide access to and make available the videos posted by users to the general public, and it organizes the stored content, by automatic means or algorithms, used to display, tag, search and sequence the videos. Those two elements are defining features of a 'video-sharing platform service' referred to by the proposal to revise the Audiovisual Media Services Directive[105] with the purpose of imposing new obligations on services storing large numbers of programmes or videos regarding the protection of minors and prohibition of hateful content.[106] The proposal to extend the scope of the Directive to include video-sharing platforms is one of the two prongs of a Commission initiative to 'ensure that online platforms act responsibly'.[107] The other is the 'allocation of revenues for the use of copyright-protected content' and a fair sharing of the value generated, which has been eventually conveyed in the fiercely contested Article 13 of the proposed Directive on Copyright in the DSM. This Communication insists that the content posted on such platforms is made widely available and yields economic benefits.[108]

105. Proposal for a Directive of the European Parliament and of the Council amending Directive 2010/13/EU on the coordination of certain provisions laid down by law, regulation or administrative action in Member States concerning the provision of audiovisual media services in view of changing market realities, 25 May 2016, COM(2016) 287 final; definition of 'video-sharing platform service' in Art. 1.

106. *See* Art. 28a & 28b of the draft Directive.

107. Communication from the Commission, *Online Platforms and the Digital Single – Market Opportunities and Challenges for Europe*, 25 May 2016, COM(2016) 288 final, p. 7.

108. *Ibid.*, p. 8.

The proposed DSM Directive has somewhat shied away from a qualification of the activities of video-sharing platforms as exploitation triggering economic rights under copyright, as it only requires concerned platforms either to give effect to contracts possibly entered into with rightholders (though with no obligation to do so[109]) or to implement content recognition technologies. Only one recital implies that when service providers store and provide access to the public to copyright works and other subject-matter uploaded by their users they are 'going beyond the mere provision of physical facilities and performing an act of communication to the public'.[110] At the same time, the safe harbour regime laid down by the E-commerce Directive would be left untouched, using the disputed 'active role' standard[111] to refuse its protection to some intermediaries.

The EU lawmaker should do better and create a certain legal framework for the activities of video-sharing platforms, as it has done in the revision of the Audiovisual Media Services Directive (AVMS Directive).[112]

Under a public sphere paradigm, video-sharing platforms make the works uploaded by their users available to the general public, and enable their circulation in the public sphere. Contrary to simple hosting of content on servers, hence made available online, they engage in determining the organization of the content, thereby providing it to the public. Economically speaking, one could add that the actual exploitation notably results from the capacity of YouTube and others to monetize the content by general advertising included on its website as well as by the insertion of ads before the work can be viewed. In a way, these platforms could be compared to cable distributors who are considered to exploit copyright works, who provide a flow of works and audiovisual programmes to the public without

109. Recital 38 of the draft Directive is bolder as it requires rightholders to enter such agreements without specifying the cause thereof, or the fact that such licences aim at getting an authorization under the communication right. Art. 13 is more ambiguous and unclear as to its exact scope.

110. Recital 38.

111. That criterion was first used by the CJEU in the Google case (CJEU, 23 March 2010, *Google*, C-236/08 & C-238/08, §120), but was later criticized by its Advocate General (*see* Opinion of Advocate General Jääskinen, 9 December 2010, *L'Oréal v. eBay*, C-324/09, §§139–142) on the basis that the condition for the intermediary to keep a passive position was only required by one recital of the E-commerce Directive for mere transport activities and not for hosting service providers. The active-passive division has nonetheless been repeatedly used by the CJEU and the European Commission as a decisive factor in the application of the exemption of liability to host services.

112. Directive 2010/13/EU of the European Parliament and of the Council of 10 March 2010 on the coordination of certain provisions laid down by law, regulation or administrative action in Member States concerning the provision of audiovisual media services (Audiovisual Media Services Directive) (codified version), OJ No. L 95/1, 15 April 2010, codifying Council Directive 89/552/EEC as amended by Directives 97/36/EC and 2007/65/EC. The analysis is further developed in S. Dusollier, Intermédiaires et plateformes de l'Internet, cet éléphant dans le salon du droit d'auteur, in *CERDI Conference Proceedings*, forthcoming.

being aware of the actual content or having selected it. Cable operators and new digital platforms both provide an experience of the works to users. In reference to what Kant has written about the role of publishers, platforms contribute to the circulation of the work and intervene as intermediaries that publish the author's speech for the public to gain access thereto.

Including the provision of works by video-sharing platforms within the newly defined economic rights does not necessarily imply an exclusive right. In the case of platforms where the content is uploaded by users, the exclusive right could be transformed into a remuneration right that might be sufficient to compensate copyright owners for the capture of the value of their works by such audiovisual services, completed by a possibility for copyright owners to have recourse to a notice and take down procedure to remove the content they do not want publicly communicated.

This combined remuneration right/take-down notice approach departs from the French government's proposal, based on a report by P. Sirinelli, A. Bensamoun and M.J. Benazeraf, to apply the exclusive right to public communication to video platforms,[113] which inspired recital 38 of the proposed DSM Directive. It is closer to the ideas developed by a group of German scholars in the *Berlin Gedankenexperiment,*[114] that suggest applying a remuneration right to intermediaries whose services would compete with or substitute products or services offered by authors and exploiters. This 'substitution' factor in my view borrows too much from an economic analysis that might vary according to the maturity of a market or the size of the platforms analysed and lead to indefinite conclusions.

6.5.6.4 Digital Resale

The application of the exhaustion principle is currently dependent on the technical notion of distribution defined as a transfer of property in the tangible embodiment of the work. Does it really make sense that the possibility to dispose of one's property and sell it to someone else depends on the nature of the object of property (tangible or not) and on the channel of its first acquisition?

Shifting the definition of economic rights to a notion of exploitation based on transmission of the work to the public should include a new approach to distribution and its corollary, the exhaustion principle. The right of distribution itself would disappear and be absorbed by the prong of the exploitation right that targets any transfer of a copy of work, in any form, for a permanent use. If the exhaustion rule still plays a role (and it should, for

---

113. P. Sirinelli, A. Bensamoun et J.A. Benazeraf, *Rapport du CSPLA sur l'articulation des directives 2000/31/CE et 2001/29/CE*, 2015.
114. *Berlin Gedankenexperiment on the Restructuring of Copyright Law and Authors Rights*, *JIPITEC*, 2016, n° 7, p. 76. *See also* J. Griffiths, 'Proposals from Berlin and Paris – Intermediary Liability in European Copyright Law', *JIPITEC,* 2016, no. 7, p. 70.

property reasons as well as for internal market motives), it should apply irrespective of the format of the work and of the way it has been transmitted to the individual wishing to resell it. Nonetheless, it should be limited to genuine transfers of a copy, with proof that the 'seller' does not conserve the work in any way. Otherwise, it would amount to an act of re-circulation of the work that should be captured by economic rights. Nowadays, it might be difficult to establish sound evidence of the deletion of any copies by the 'seller', but technologies or exploitation models might be developed to remedy that obstacle.

6.6 CONCLUSION

Copyright is a legal intervention structuring the way creation circulates in the public sphere. It should be about giving authors enough protection and autonomy to enable them to make that circulation possible in the first place and to give them some control over the dissemination of their works, while recognizing and encouraging public discussion and enjoyment of creation by the public. This is not only a matter of striking a balance with more or less weight on one side or the other. The right granted by copyright is not a reservation granted to authors, who will then transfer it to economic operators, that only needs proper checks and limitations to accommodate other interests. The realm of exclusivity it confers should be conceived instead as a set of entitlements to enjoy the value of the work, some reserved to authors, others offered to the public, seen equally as recipients, readers and follow-on creators, as a system distributing the enjoyment of creation and circulating it to enhance its protection.

Economic rights define what the author and the ensuing copyright owners could control and prohibit, as well as for what uses the author can be remunerated. If we want to preserve the cultural dimension of copyright, they should not extend to every corner of the market and they should not be defined mechanically but in relation to their purpose. Copyright's economic rights have become a train without a driver, lacking direction or measure, only gaining speed at an exponential pace. Reproduction and communication rights are applied as technical notions, being triggered by a mere act of 'use' corresponding to a copy or to a transmission, without any consideration of its objective.

The present chapter has proposed reconnecting economic rights with the function of copyright, which should be to ensure the circulation of the work in the public sphere. The notion of exploitation in copyright should be rediscovered and be given meaning. Three types of exploitation of works, that each aims at transmitting the work, as a communicative act, to the public sphere, could constitute new anchor points for acts of use to be considered as entering the exclusive reservation of authors: (1) the provision of copies to the public for a permanent use, (2) the provision of access to or experiences of the work, and (3) the making of derivative works. Any use of a work, currently existing or to be developed, that would fall under one of these forms of exploitation could be controlled by the copyright owners or be compensated for. Personal uses, technical copies and mere uses of the informational content of the work should remain free.

My proposal to revise the economic rights in copyright might appear utopian and abstract, I agree. This is a candid way of looking at the current mess of the scope of copyright and an attempt to try and cleanse it with ideas, more than with empirical evidence. You may think that I have provided a romanticized narrative of copyright history and foundation, that does not stand against economic reasoning or utilitarian objectives. True, it is overly abstract to some extent, excessively simplified and obviously incomplete. And yes, it starts from intuition and perceptions that the ultimate objective of copyright is to provide works to the public and give authors the means to be protected in such a process. But have revolutions not sometimes started with ideas, utopias and intuition?

Chapter 7

Reconstructing the Reproduction and Communication to the Public Rights: How to Align Copyright with Its Fundamentals

Alain Strowel

7.1 INTRODUCTION

The gap between the delineation of the economic rights within copyright law and copyright's objectives and principles has been a topic of discussion since the advent of the Internet and the digitalization of works, thus for about twenty-five years.[1] The 'digital crisis of copyright'[2] has led to paradoxical consequences: a serious weakening of copyright's effectiveness and

1. *See* in Europe: P.B. Hugenholtz, Adapting copyright to the information superhighway, in P.B. Hugenholtz (ed.), *The Future of Copyright in a Digital Environment*, Den Haag/London/Boston: Kluwer Law International 1996, pp. 81–102; D. Visser, *Auteursrecht op toegang. De exploitatierechten van de auteur in het tijdperk van digitale informatie en netwerkcommunicatie*, VUGA Uitgeverij, 1997; A. Quaedvlieg, Authorship and Ownership: Authors, Entrepreneurs and Rights, in: Tatiana-Eleni Synodinou, *Codification of European Copyright Law. Challenges and Perspectives*, Kluwer, 2012, pp. 197–232; S. Depreeuw, *The Variable Scope of the Exclusive Economic Rights in Copyright*, Wolters Kluwer, 2014. Similar criticisms were made in the US (*see*: J. Litman, *Digital Copyright, Protecting Intellectual Property on the Internet*, Prometheus Books, 2001; P. Samuelson, Does Copyright Law Need to Be Reformed?, 50 Comm. ACM, 2007, pp. 19–23, in particular p. 22).
2. P. Samuelson, Does Copyright Law Need to Be Reformed?, n. 1, p. 19.

legitimacy on one side, and a vigorous reinforcement of copyright's domain and scope on the other. With the digitalization of many works, from music to films and books, and their online dissemination, rightholders and their supporters often rightly complain about the difficulty of controlling the spread of unauthorized copies, the possibilities for pirates to move to haven countries, the inadequacies of civil enforcement (too slow and expensive), the fact that criminal enforcement is a low priority for judicial authorities, and the systematic hacking of digital rights management technologies (DRMs), etc. On the other side, users' groups and their allies, as well as many academics, rightly explain that new items, including short extracts of works and user-generated content,[3] are now subject to copyright control, that copyright's duration and remedies have been expanded over time, that additional remuneration rights (and levies) have multiplied, that DRMs override fair use and exceptions, that media industry consolidation is growing, and that the scope of copyright's exclusivity has been significantly broadened.

Without ignoring the big picture, I focus here on the last issue, i.e., the broadening of copyright's exclusive rights following an inadequate definition of those rights.

7.1.1 The Mismatch of the All-Encompassing and Formalistic Notion of Reproduction

Let's start with the example of reproduction. The concept can be traced back to the regulation of the printing press[4] and the analogue world of paper or other tangible media. Once digital, works are subject to numerous acts of reproduction which are required by the inner workings of the 'digital machine'.

By 'digital machine', I mean the various technologies that allow the making, use, and dissemination of multiple copies. On top of the digital copies that the end-users can use and enjoy, the digital machine generates numerous *intermediate* copies, most of which should not require the right owner's authorization. This is for instance the case for:

- the numerous temporary copies (e.g., on the RAM memory of a computer) required to use a work or repair software;[5]

3. User-generated content relying on existing works existed well before the appearance of the web 2.0 platforms. However, this never led to homeric copyright clashes because of the limited possibilities for further distribution in the pre-YouTube and Facebook era.
4. *See* on the origin of copyright: L.R. Patterson, *Copyright in Historical Perspective*, Vanderbilt University Press, 1968.
5. As illustrated by the US Court of Appeal decision in *MAI Systems Corp. v. Peak Computer, Inc.*, 991 F.2d 511 (9th Cir. 1993) described as 'outrageously wrongheaded' by P. Samuelson, Does Copyright Law Need to Be Reformed?, n. 1.

- the transitory and cache copies (on the Internet servers and routers) required to transmit a work on the telecom networks;
- the non-transitory copies made by Content Delivery Networks (CDNs)[6] on the proxy servers located in data centres;
- the copies made for indexing images, and searching the Internet or big data aggregates;
- the copies needed to conduct text and data mining (TDM);
- the copies made for checking mistakes and plagiarism;
- the copies made for automatic translation.

The term (digital) 'machine' is used here as in the formula attributed to Charles Clark:[7] 'the answer to the machine is in the machine'. I doubt that the answer is in the machine,[8] it lies rather at the core of copyright as shown below. Thus, my motto is 'the answer to the machine is in the mechanics of copyright law'. 'Mechanics' refers here to the fundamentals (or basic principles) of copyright law.

Digital technologies have expanded the scope of copyright without much help from the legislator,[9] it has just happened through the extension of the existing synthetic and technology-neutral notion of reproduction.[10]

---

6. A content delivery network or content distribution network (CDN) 'is a globally distributed network of proxy servers deployed in multiple data centers. The goal of a CDN is to serve content to end-users with high availability and high performance … . Content providers such as media companies and e-commerce vendors pay CDN operators to deliver their content to their audience of end-users. In turn, a CDN pays ISPs, carriers, and network operators for hosting its servers in their data centers' (*see* https://en.wikipedia.org/wiki/Content_delivery_network (accessed on 27 September 2017)).
7. Ch. Clark, The Answer to the Machine is in the Machine, in: P. Bernt Hugenholtz (ed.), *The Future of Copyright in a Digital Environment*, Kluwer Law International, 1996, p. 139. Charles Clark was a British publisher and lawyer, who worked for the International Publishers Copyright Council when the Internet became prominent in the mid-nineties.
8. Indeed, 'code (in the sense of computer code, which is part of the "machine") should not make law' to paraphrase another well-known formula coined by L. Lessig (*Code and Other Laws of Cyberspace*, Basic Books, 1999) referring to the role of technology (and mainly software) in shaping what is allowed or not in the digital age.
9. In many jurisdictions, the notion of reproduction came to cover many ephemeral and transitory copies just by application of the existing law. Sometimes, as in Art. 2 of the InfoSoc Directive, the legislator has made it clear that reproduction encompasses 'temporary' reproductions, thus contributing to the expansion of copyright's reach in the technological environment.
10. The principle of technological neutrality relies on the text of Art. 2 InfoSoc Directive, which refers to copies 'by any means and in any form'. The technology-neutral definition of reproduction has allowed its application outside the printing press context where it originated. In parallel to the expansion of the notion of work, which applies to new products of technology and creativity (films, computer games, etc.), the notion of copy was able to adapt to new technologies so that it now applies to new ways of making copies (e.g., to various digital copies, but also non-digital copies such as canvas transfer). In that sense, the legal notion is neutral or independent from the technology involved. There are, however, other ways to define the principle of technological neutrality. For a short and recent discussion of its meanings, *see* K. Lo, What is Technological Neutrality (in

Technological neutrality in the field of copyright requires that all copies, whether analogue or digital, must be treated equally as reproductions under copyright.[11] It is probably time to differentiate between copies, and not only for the application of the copyright exceptions. Many widespread copies, such as the non-transitory copies made by CDNs, cannot qualify under the existing exceptions. Rather than trying to add new exceptions to exempt the massive digital copies, it appears essential to revise the notions of reproduction and infringement. Otherwise copyright will continue to lose touch with reality.

At the same time, the development of the digital world, where reproductions are ubiquitous, has raised the expectations for economic return for rightholders in a manner that is not commensurate with the economic fundamentals that apply to digital uses, especially on the Internet. The explosion of digital copies cannot translate into the same increase of value that would be generated by additional non-digital copies: first, the inflation of copies and content reduces the value of each copy or single content item (for instance, the spreading of news on the Internet makes it possible to find substitutes, such as alternative sources of news, and thus reduces the willingness to pay for news); second, many copies have no value in themselves and are solely the tools or basic ingredient for value-adding services (for instance, copies made for detecting meaningful occurrences of words). The notion of reproduction is ill-suited to the digital realm because of the massive technology-driven copies that lack any commercial value and the inflated hopes generated by the expectations of right owners who tend to believe that reproduction, even without economic reason, should be covered by copyright.

On the other hand, there are some 'value gaps' along the chain of digital exploitation which should fall within copyright. In particular, the communication to the public right, which, as shown below, relies on economic criteria (in particular the 'profit-making nature' of the exploitation) could help to cover the uses that extract some value from the protected works.

7.1.2 The Need to Reconnect with the Fundamentals of Copyright

We rely here on two fundamentals of copyright: the first relates to the economics of copyright and the well-known, but often wrongly conceived, incentive-and-remuneration rationale; the second refers to the underlying, and often hidden, foundation of copyright as a way to encourage and protect

Copyright) Anyway? Revisiting *CBC v. SODRAC*, 1 August 2017, accessible on http://canliiconnects.org/en/commentaries/46245 (accessed 27 September 2017).

11. As flagged in section 7.4.1 below, the same technological neutrality principle is embedded in the communication to the public right which covers all forms of transmission.

a form of speech aimed at enhancing the spread of original ideas and the enlightened communication between human beings.

First, copyright might be seen as an instrument for controlling the true exploitation of works and ensuring that authors (and, indirectly, publishers and distributors) enjoy a reasonable remuneration for this exploitation. Yet many acts falling within copyright's categories (such as reproduction) do not involve a real economic exploitation. Many digital uses cannot adequately be qualified under the notions inherited from the analogue era: if, in the analogue world, a reproduction corresponds more or less with an exploitation, this is no longer the case with the numerous technical copies.

Second, copyright, as an institution, relies on a philosophical justification: a copyright work is an elaborate way for speakers to communicate with an audience (sometimes at distance and over time). A work revolves around expressive and valuable speech, allowing humans to share ideas, thoughts, feelings, etc. According to this view, the author-audience nexus is one of the fundamentals of copyright. Copyright is therefore justified as long as it fosters this communicative dimension.[12] Significantly, many intermediate (and transient) copies in the digital machine do not fit with the philosophical underpinning of copyright which involves authors as speakers and works as instances of communication between humans. From this angle, it appears difficult to reconcile the control on the myriads of technical copies with the overall objective of the system, i.e., to promote the ongoing conversation between creative humans and their public.

To bridge the growing discrepancy between the fundamentals of copyright and its legal scope, the interpretation of the statutes and the legal reasoning on copyright must be informed by economic and principled considerations. Other contributors, including to this project, have explored several ways to reconnect copyright with the economic rationale, for instance by putting forward the notion of 'use'[13] or of '(reasonable) exploitation'[14] as the controlling concepts for copyright (rather than 'reproduction'). Less frequently, commentators have discussed the shape of copyright's exclusivity by relying on its philosophical root (the author-audience nexus).

12. *See* A. Drassinower, *What's Wrong with Copying?*, Harvard University Press, 2015.
13. *See* D. Visser, n. 1.
14. *See* O.-A. Rognstad, Restructuring the Economic Rights in Copyright – Some Reflections on an 'Alternative Model', Journal of the Copyright Society of the U.S.A., 2015, vol. 62(4), pp. 503–544; *see also* Rognstad & Poort, elsewhere in this volume; S. Dusollier, L'exploitation des oeuvres: une notion centrale en droit d'auteur, in *Mélanges en l'honneur du professeur André Lucas*, LexisNexis, 2014, pp. 263–275; *see also* her contribution to this volume. However, other commentators are putting forward the 'exploitation' concept to support a rather extensive view of copyright's exclusivity: *see* for example S. Carré and G. Vercken, Google et la fortune du droit d'auteur, in *Mélanges en l'honneur du professeur André Lucas*, LexisNexis, 2014, pp. 135–137. This last example points to a risk inherent in any conceptual reconstruction of copyright notions.

The reconstruction process is a promising exercise, but at the same time it is largely utopian because of the strong constraints on the shape of copyright imposed by its international sources[15] and the *acquis communautaire*. I will stick with the utopian line of the essays contained in the present volume, but I propose a copyright utopia *for the present time*, which means that my proposal for reconstructing copyright could fit with the existing framework for copyright. I thus claim to propose a realistic utopia!

7.2 TAKING THE SPIRIT OF THE ECONOMIC RIGHTS SERIOUSLY

7.2.1 The Two Main Economic Rights: Reproduction and Communication to the Public

In Europe, the building blocks of copyright lie in the reproduction and communication to the public rights defined in Articles 2 and 3 of the InfoSoc Directive[16] respectively[17]. Article 2 defines the reproduction right as 'the exclusive right to authorize or prohibit direct or indirect, temporary or permanent reproduction by any means and in any form, in whole or in part' of the authors' works. Article 3 requires Member States 'to provide authors with the exclusive right to authorize or prohibit any communication to the public of their works, by wire or wireless means, including the making available to the public of their works in such a way that members of the public may access them from a place and at a time individually chosen by them'. This wording is close to the language used in the post-Berne international instruments, for example in Article 8 of the WIPO Copyright

15. As a reminder, the Berne Convention defines the minimum economic rights that the Union countries must grant, and this includes the right of translation (Art. 8), the right of reproduction (Art. 9), the right of public performance and of communication to the public of a performance for dramatic and musical works (Art. 11), the broadcasting and related rights (Art. 11*bis*), the right of public recitation and of communication to the public of a recitation for literary works (Art. 11*ter*), and the right of adaptation (Art. 12). This list, which offers a piecemeal framework according to the type of work involved, is arguably not fit for the digital economy where many rights overlap and the need for a fast clearing of the rights is difficult to reconcile with complex systematics.
16. Directive 2001/29/EC of 22 May 2001 on the harmonisation of certain aspects of copyright and related rights in the information society, OJ No. L 167/10, 22 June 2001.
17. Also, we can presume that this European framework respects the international obligations, including those defined by the 1886 Berne Convention for the Protection of Literary and Artistic Works (Berne Convention), the 1994 Agreement on Trade-Related Aspects of Intellectual Property Rights (TRIPS Agreement), and the 1996 World Intellectual Property Organisation Copyright Treaty (WIPO Copyright Treaty).

Treaty for communication to the public and in the recently signed Trans-Pacific Partnership (known as TPP) for defining the two main rights.[18] Reconstructing those two rights within the constraints of those legal definitions could thus have an impact at EU level but also at a global level.

The terminology and wording used to define those two rights is strikingly different: in order to fall under copyright, a communication must be addressed 'to a public'; a reproduction, in contrast, could happen in the absence of any public. This puts the audience or the reception of the work by individuals at the centre of the communication to the public and shows the communicative nexus of this economic right. A communication to the public according to Article 3 InfoSoc Directive requires an act of outreach towards a public. Judge Malenovsky, who appears as the *judge-rapporteur* in most copyright cases before the CJEU, considers that a communication to the public includes two cumulative elements, i.e., an 'act of communication' of a work and the transmission of this work to a 'public'.[19] The broad notion of 'communication to the public' is illustrated by, and contains, the 'making available to the public' characterized by the fact that 'members of the public may access' the works from a place and at the time they choose.

This reference to an audience and the possibility for it to access the work is not expressly part of the legal concept of reproduction. Rather, the application of the reproduction right is triggered by an operation of 'copying' on a tangible medium. While the communication to the public is less tangible, and is based on a dialogue with a public, or at least on a transmission between a sender and a human receiver, the reproduction right results in a tangible change (new copy on a disc or on a server), possibly without any direct intervention from, or reception by, a human being. For this reason, the reproduction right is more likely to overreach in the context of the digital machine. Also, the absence versus presence of the 'public' in the specific wording used to define those two rights points to the need to reconstruct the two rights differently, as proposed below. My thesis is that we need to rethink the reproduction right in more depth than the communication

---

18. The final version of the TPP as released by New Zealand defines the right of reproduction (Art. 18.58) as follows: 'Each Party shall provide to authors, performers and producers of phonograms the exclusive right to authorise or prohibit all reproduction of their works, performances or phonograms in any manner or form, including in electronic form'. Article 18.59 on the right of communication to the public is close to the European text: 'Each Party shall provide to authors the exclusive right to authorise or prohibit the communication to the public of their works, by wire or wireless means, including the making available to the public of their works in such a way that members of the public may access these works from a place and at a time individually chosen by them'.
19. J. Malenovsky, La contribution de la Cour de justice au droit d'auteur en droit de l'Union européenne, in Annual ERA Conference on European Copyright Law 2015: Recent Case Law from the CJEU, 2015, unpublished (speaking about the 'communication au public', J. Malenovsky writes that 'selon une jurisprudence constante, cette notion associe deux éléments cumulatifs, à savoir un "acte de communication" d'une œuvre et la transmission de cette dernière à un "public"').

to the public right. Reconstructing the reproduction right requires relying on the principle embedded in copyright rules, and in particular on the nexus between an author and an audience. This, in turn, requires revisiting the standard for copyright infringement (*see* section 7.3.2 below). On the contrary, reconstructing the communication to the public right only involves a fine-tuning in light of an economic analysis.

7.2.2 The Construction of the Main Rights by the Court of Justice of the EU

The Court of Justice of the European Union (CJEU or Court) has contributed to the delineation of the external borders of these two economic rights. Under the CJEU reading, the InfoSoc Directive has evolved towards 'a genuinely horizontal instrument' which harmonizes various concepts, including the bundle of core rights within copyright, 'beyond an area-specific, piecemeal approach'.[20] In a 2011 article on the economic rights, A. Ohly concluded that: 'The most important effect of the [InfoSoc] Directive, at least with respect to the scope of the economic rights, is that it enables the ECJ to clarify some fundamental concepts of copyright law on a step-by-step basis … . If the court takes this task seriously, copyright law could become a model for a future European private law methodology which combines broad statutory definitions familiar to Continental lawyers with the careful analysis of precedent known from common law.'[21] The CJEU has taken this task seriously, but unfortunately, it has not always managed to conduct a careful analysis, and this has led to some inconsistencies in its interpretation of the rights defined by the InfoSoc Directive.[22] However, the general approach followed by the CJEU for communication to the public tends to align with

20. M. Leistner, Europe's Copyright Law Decade: Recent Case Law of the European Court of Justice and Policy Perspectives, Common Market Law Review, 2014, vol. 51, p. 560. For M. Leistner, the harmonization of the exclusive rights 'follows a concept of full harmonization, i.e., provides for an autonomous, uniform and conclusive European definition of the rights' (p. 568). This is probably true, but the CJEU harmonization effort does not lead to a clearly enclosed copyright domain, as the Court combines various factors to outline the limits of the rights, leaving considerable room for further determination of their boundaries.
21. A. Ohly, Economic Rights, in E. Derclaye (ed.), *Research Handbook on the Future of EU Copyright*, Edward Elgar, 2009, p. 232.
22. I am thus not sure that I can share A. Ohly's optimism when he wrote in 2009 that '(o)ne does not have to be a prophet to predict that in some years or perhaps decades the concepts of reproduction, distribution or communication to the public will be entirely "Europeanised"' (*Id.*, pp. 232–233). It is true that the CJEU has had to rule on many situations, but its interpretation still leaves many gaps for the national judges, which means that the Europeanization or harmonization is still incomplete. I tend to consider this as bad, but there are also some good arguments for limiting the degree of harmonization and leaving some room for national approaches.

the economic rationale. M. Leistner even concluded that 'in the realm of exclusive exploitation rights, the Court follows an *essentially "economic"*, rather flexible approach, focusing on the need to ensure an appropriate remuneration for any independent (economic) exploitation of the work by a respective user' (emphasis added).[23]

7.2.3 In Search of the Spirit of the Main Exclusive Rights

Sections 7.3 and 7.4 of this chapter – which will review the scope of the reproduction and communication to the public rights – will first rely on the CJEU reading of the existing copyright framework. After a critical review of the CJEU case law, each section will propose a new way to best assess the limits of the right. We will see that the CJEU interpretation and application of the communication to the public right is more satisfactory than its broad reading of the reproduction right.

Because the overall project leading to the present chapter focuses on a 'reconstruction of the economic rights' within copyright, I deliberately exclude here the reverse approach that would focus on the right delineation of the exceptions to reshape copyright.[24] However, the European legislator seems to favour an approach based on adding new exceptions. This is illustrated by the September 2016 proposal of the European Commission for a directive on copyright in the digital single market[25], which for instance introduces a TDM exception[26] (rather than carving out those acts from the reproduction right). To ensure text and data research in protected corpuses is allowed, I would prefer to rely on the fundamental principle underlying the reproduction right, i.e., that the work be used *as a work*. To use a work for TDM arguably is not a use as a work (*see* section 7.3.3 below).

The reconstruction exercise must be conducted in light of the *spirit* of copyright law. The spirit of copyright law commands a more restrictive view of copyright's boundaries than an interpretation based on the black letter of the law. This is counter-intuitive: the spirit of the law is commonly invoked by lawyers to make the law more flexible, and to encompass new situations that the legislator could not have conceived of. The letter of the law is commonly seen as stuck in the past, while the unexpected future requires a

---

23. M. Leistner, n. 20, p. 569 (referring to von Ungern-Sternberg, Urheberechtliche Verwertungsrechte im Lichte des Unionsrechts, GRUR, 2012, p. 1198 and ff.).
24. This is my response to the fair criticism of M. Leistner who invited me to redesign the exceptions, rather than the economic rights. M. Leistner pointed to interesting sources which could be used if this reverse exercise is conducted (E.T. Wang, The Line Between Copyright and the First Amendment and Why Its Vagueness May Further Free Speech Interests, 13 Journal of Constitutional Law, 1471 (2011) and S.J. Horowitz, Copyright's Asymmetric Uncertainty, University of Chicago Law Review, 331 (2012)).
25. Proposal for a Directive of the European Parliament and of the Council on copyright in the Digital Single Market, 14 September 2016, COM(2016) 593 final.
26. *See* Art. 3 of the Proposal for a Directive on Copyright in the Digital Single Market.

reversion back to the spirit of the law, sometimes illustrated by the open debates in the *travaux préparatoires*.

The so-called synthetic approach [27] or 'broad definition'[28] of the economic rights known and commonly defended in the *droit d'auteur* countries, starts in reality with the opposite point of view, i.e., that the literal text itself commands a broad reading and that the rights should have a wide coverage. This assumption reverses the complex relation between the letter and the spirit of the law. For instance, the reproduction right has been considered as encompassing all material exploitations of an intellectual work, independently from the medium used for the copy or the duration of the copy. The notion of reproduction under copyright law has evolved towards a catch-all concept that blurs the instances where a copy is made in the course of an economic exploitation or in the course of a technological and incidental use of the work.[29] To reconstruct the economic rights within copyright it is necessary to better distinguish real economic uses from other uses and therefore to take the *spirit* of the rights seriously.

7.2.3.1 The Communication Nexus Behind the Reproduction Right

Reconstructing the reproduction right will draw on the *philosophical spirit* of the copyright system. Copyright is about works and works have a

27. *See* the traditional French approach summarized by A. Kerever, Le droit d'auteur: acquis et conditions du développement de la culture juridique européenne, Droit d'auteur, 1990, pp. 138–147 in particular p. 142; F. Gotzen, Le droit de destination et son fondement juridique, in L'importance économique du droit d'auteur. Problèmes posés par la distribution d'exemplaires d'oeuvres protégées par le droit d'auteur, Paris, ALAI, 1989, p. 61 ff and discussed among others by A. Strowel, *Droit d'auteur et copyright, Convergences et divergences*, Bruylant, 1992, pp. 144 ff. This view is confirmed by the leading commentary on French copyright law: according to A. Lucas, H.-J. Lucas and A. Lucas-Schloetter, both the reproduction right and the representation (or communication to the public) right are designed 'in a synthetic way' under French law. This approach for instance 'has allowed to deduct the "destination right" from the reproduction right'. In addition, under French law, the translation and adaptation rights are conceived as 'corollaries of the reproduction right' and thus not viewed as 'distinct rights'. A. Lucas a.o., *Traité de la propriété littéraire et artistique*, LexisNexis, 2012, 4th ed., p. 251, nr. 254.
28. S. Carré and G. Vercken, Google et la fortune du droit d'auteur, in *Mélanges en l'honneur du professeur André Lucas*, LexisNexis, 2014, p. 136.
29. Similarly, on the Continent, the representation right (in France) has evolved towards an all-encompassing notion that covers all immaterial exploitation of the work. It thus corresponds to the communication to the public right (known in other European countries). The copyright countries have somewhat better resisted such broadening by interpretation, in part because of the constraining definitions and rules contained in the long copyright statutes. The rhetoric of ownership and the romantic vision of authorship which both command a broadening of the rights were also more prominent in the continental *droit d'auteur* systems (*see* A. Strowel, n. 27, pp. 130 ff.).

communicative dimension. When the copy of a work (as in the case of purely technical copies) is just a tool in a digital machine, there is no use of the work *as a work*, meaning as a nexus for a communication between an author and a public.[30] When this communicative dimension is lacking, there is no dialogue between humans (only steps in a digital process). In the absence of an expressive use (a use *in the copyright sense*), it is fair and consistent to conclude that no infringement of the reproduction right takes place.[31]

7.2.3.2 The Economic Spirit of the Communication to the Public Right

In order to reconstruct the communication to the public right, while respecting at first sight the letter of the law, the *economic spirit* of the right will be made more prominent. My chapter is built on the presumption that the communication to the public right should allow the author to reap some value from the for-profit exploitation of her work on the relevant market when there is a negative impact on the market for the copyright work and/or a positive impact on the user's services. The requirement that the use be '*for profit*' and other criteria having an essentially economic meaning (such as the criterion of the 'new public') are already embedded in the CJEU case law on the right of communication to the public, but the analysis of the double market impact (on the author's work and on the user's service) is not expressly articulated. Bringing the economic reasoning into the centre of the definition of the right of communication to the public will help us find the right balance.

Final warning: the reconstruction proposed below aims to address the digital crisis of copyright and the 'border(on)line' cases. It is thus only meaningful for realigning the scope of copyright in digital contexts.

7.3 BACK TO THE FUNDAMENTALS OF COPYRIGHT FOR DEFINING THE REPRODUCTION RIGHT AND ITS INFRINGEMENT

In contrast to its interpretation of the communication to the public right (*see* section 7.4.1 below), the CJEU case law largely ignores the economic dimension when dealing with the reproduction right. Reproduction is mainly interpreted with reference to a basic and conceptual notion of reproduction and an underlying presumption about the need for a technology-neutral approach covering all copies.

30. This will be further explained in section 7.3 (below).
31. *See* below in section 7.4.2.2 the developments based on the similar requirement of a use *in the trademark sense* as a condition for trademark infringement.

After summarizing the CJEU view on the reproduction right and its exceptions, this section will propose a forward-looking reconstruction requiring that for the reproduction right to be infringed the work should be used *as a work*. This requirement is rooted in the fundamental aim of copyright, i.e., to foster the communication of an original speech to a public.[32] (The philosophical idea of a communication to a public used here does not correspond to the copyright notion of 'communication to the public' discussed below.) Because of this aim, copyright is relying on a philosophical point of view on what a work is (i.e., a truly expressive speech by which someone aims to express and transmit some view), who is the originator of a work (an author), and to whom a work is addressed (a public). The reproduction right today is disconnected from this copyright rationale. The reconstruction exercise is thus quite sweeping.

7.3.1 The Boundaries of Reproduction under Existing EU Law

7.3.1.1 The Broad Scope and Technical Approach to Reproduction in the CJEU Case Law

The CJEU has developed 'a consistently broad interpretation of the reproduction right'.[33] In *Infopaq*, the Court considered that several reproductions occur during a data capture process, such as the creation of a TIFF file by scanning, the conversion into a searchable text file (by an OCR or Optical Character Recognition process), the storing of an extract, and the printing of that extract on a paper medium.[34] Under *Infopaq*, partial reproductions may be prohibited insofar as the part of the work reproduced fulfils the condition of copyright protection, i.e., reflects the author's own intellectual creation.[35] Similarly, in *Premier League*, the Court held that 'the reproduction right extends to transient fragments of the works within a satellite decoder and on a television screen, provided that those fragments contain elements which are the expression of the author's own intellectual creation'.[36] That 'transient fragments' of works are covered shows how encompassing the right of reproduction is. In those two cases, the operations discussed by the Court (i.e., within the data capture and conversion process or within the satellite transmission process) are essentially technical. Therefore, the Court appears to support a technical view of reproduction, but, in reality, it applies a highly

32. This section largely relies on the illuminating book by A. Drassinower, *What's Wrong with Copying?*, Harvard University Press, 2015.
33. M. Leistner, n. 20, p. 569.
34. CJEU, 16 July 2009, C-5/08, ECLI:EU:C:2009:465 (*Infopaq I*), §51.
35. *Infopaq I*, §32 and ff.
36. CJEU, 4 October 2011, C-403/08 & C-429/08, ECLI:EU:C:2011:631 (*Premier League*) §159.

conceptual (if not metaphysical) and very broad notion of reproduction to various technical processes and their outcomes: many technical processes could fall under the reproduction umbrella because of the technological neutrality principle embedded in its definition (*see* above). Even for software, a highly technical item that raises issues when subsumed under copyright, the Software Directive[37] proposes an undefined and neutral notion of reproduction without giving it a technical content. Indeed, Article 4(a) of the Software Directive does not say that loading, displaying, running, transmission, or storage of a computer program are (technical) reproductions, it just states that 'in so far as' those acts of loading, etc. 'necessitate such reproduction, such acts shall be subject to authorisation by the rightholder'.

If the application of the reproduction notion to the processes under scrutiny in *Infopaq* and *Premier League* appears very technical (and if lawyers are expected to analyse complex technical processes to identify each reproduction), this is made possible by the broad and formalistic notion of reproduction, completely disconnected from the real context of the process and from the requirement of having acts of (economic) exploitation.[38] Formalism definitely prevails over substance, and the absence of any requirement to make a substantial analysis of the situation facilitates the extension of the legal concept.

More significantly, in order to delineate the reproduction right, the CJEU does not refer to the presence of a 'public' which might be a proxy for an economic exploitation; neither does it put forward the condition that the use should be commercial or have a for-profit nature, as underlined in the decisions on communication to the public (*see* section 7.4.1 below).

In general, the reproduction, especially in the context of digital technologies, is disconnected from the real enjoyment of the work. 'The

37. Directive 2009/24/EC of the European Parliament and of the Council of 23 April 2009 on the legal protection of computer programs (codified version), OJ No. L 111/16, 5 May 2009, (replacing Council Directive 91/250/EEC of 14 May 1991 on the legal protection of computer programs, OJ No. L 122/42, 17 May 1991).

38. I thus partly follow the thorough analysis developed by S. Depreeuw in her excellent book (n. 1): the reproduction right appears general and technology-neutral (pp. 65 and 67), not only under the Berne Convention, also under the InfoSoc Directive. Thus, Art. 2 InfoSoc Directive does not offer a technical notion. In addition, I do not think that 'the general reproduction right' (under EU law) is 'substantially extended compared to the general reproduction right in the Berne Convention'. Rather, in the digital context (starting with software), the application of this broadly designed right requires dissection of the analysed processes into discrete technical acts. For J. Griffiths as well (The Role of the Court of Justice in the Development of European Union Copyright Law, in I. Stamatoudi and P. Torremans, *EU Copyright Law. A Commentary*, Edward Elgar, 2014, p. 1106), the Court's interpretation reveals a 'highly technical understanding of the concept of "reproduction"'. I prefer to conclude that the Court's interpretation remains very conceptual, broad, and synthetic, and therefore all the (technical) processes (whatever their input and output) can be sliced into many highly specific reproductions.

reproduction right does not distinguish according to the ways the works are enjoyed'.[39] More fundamentally, a reproduction can exist whether or not the works are enjoyed. The public remains completely irrelevant and singularly absent in the common analysis of what a reproduction covers.

While the CJEU case law on the communication to the public, although convoluted, is heading in the right direction, the EU approach to the reproduction right,[40] illustrated by the CJEU case law, needs to be more fundamentally reassessed.

7.3.1.2 A Marginal Role for the Economic Reasoning in the Delineation of the Exceptions

The broad scope of reproduction is not really balanced by the effective application of the InfoSoc Directive's exceptions, which are not interpreted in the light of an economic criterion. Nevertheless, the wording of several exceptions points at the economic importance of the use for deciding whether it should be exempted (or not). For example, Article 5(1) exempts some reproductions if: (1) they are temporary, (2) transient or incidental, (3) an integral and essential part of a technological process, (4) their sole purpose is to enable a transmission in a network between third parties, and (5) they have *no independent economic significance*. The CJEU however has not taken this last condition seriously, for instance in *Infopaq II* and *Premier League*. According to *Infopaq II*, temporary reproductions 'aim to make access to the protected work and their use possible' and as the works 'have a specific economic value, access to them and their use necessarily has economic significance'.[41] This economic value is *not independent* if the person carrying out the temporary reproductions 'does not enable the generation of an additional profit',[42] i.e., a benefit that, in the satellite transmission process, goes 'beyond the advantage derived from the mere picking up of the broadcast and its visual display'.[43] Thus, under the CJEU case law, the exploitation of the work is 'at no point a factor in the application of the reproduction right'.[44] Other exceptions that take into account the 'non-commercial purposes' of the use (Articles 5(2)(c), (d) and

39. S. Depreeuw, n. 1, p. 67.
40. But the same criticism could be addressed to the Berne notion of reproduction revisited in 1967. S. Depreeuw (n. 1, pp. 73 ff) refers to the definition of reproduction proposed by M. Fabiani in an article of 1964, while the Stockholm revision conference was under preparation, aimed at giving some substance to the notion by adding the requirement that the act 'causes an economic harm to the author'. This proposal was discussed and rejected by other scholars at the time.
41. CJEU, 17 January 2012, C-302/10, ECLI:EU:C:2012:16 (*Infopaq II*), §48.
42. *Infopaq II,* §54.
43. *Premier League,* §175.
44. S. Depreeuw, n. 1, p. 240.

5(3) (a), (b) InfoSoc Directive) have not been interpreted by the CJEU in a way that underlines the economic rationale underpinning the reproduction right.

A solution for resizing the reproduction right could consist of adding new exceptions excluding technical copies disconnected from the economic exploitation,[45] but it is doubtful whether the European and national legislators will be able to achieve this. Until such legislative change occurs, one must rely on the courts and their interpretation of the existing framework. This framework can be reconstructed through a renewed analysis of the infringement test.

7.3.2 Reconstructing the Infringement Test: The Requirement for a 'Use as a Work'

The infringement test helps define the scope of copyright protection: when the conditions for infringing copyright are not met, the exclusive right cannot result in an injunction or a grant of damages, even if the act involved falls within the scope of the right. For instance, the reproduction right clearly covers reproduction 'in part' (Article 2 InfoSoc Directive), but not all partial reproductions are infringing because courts in several jurisdictions have imposed a 'substantial similarity' and a 'taking' test. That the infringement analysis contributes to the delineation of copyright's scope is often overlooked by commentators who instead focus on the statutes as interpreted by the courts (e.g., the economic rights listed in the InfoSoc Directive as interpreted by the CJEU).

It is worth recalling the typical sequence of issues that a court successively has to go through in a standard copyright infringement case:

45. This approach was proposed by the so-called Wittem group in its proposal for a *European Copyright Code* (2010), available at https://www.ivir.nl/copyrightcode/european-copyright-code/ (accessed 27 September 2017).

Figure 7.1 Proposal of Title Standard Copyright Enforcement Issues and Broad View on the Notion of Copyright's Scope

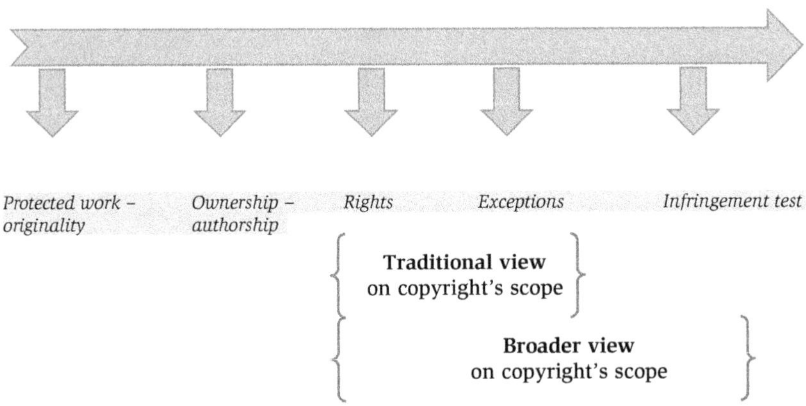

While EU copyright law provides for a definition of the main rights and offers a limited list of optional exceptions, the EU directives do not contain any provision that directly deals with the test for copyright infringement.[46] The EU *acquis* therefore does not provide much guidance for the assessment of this last step in a copyright infringement case. At the same time, the EU *acquis* does not constrain national copyright laws and national courts on how to design the infringement test. The standard for determining copyright infringement that will be developed below may thus be implemented within the existing EU copyright framework. For this reason, the proposal outlined below is less utopian than other attempts to revisit the building blocks of copyright.

After recalling the basic conditions imposed by case law for concluding that a copyright infringement has taken place, I will show how an additional requirement, to use the work 'as a work', modelled on the requirement for trademark infringement (to use a sign as a trademark), could be embedded in the copyright infringement analysis.

46. On the contrary, the EU legislation defines the conditions for a design (or trademark) infringement. For example, Art. 10 of the Design Regulation (Council Regulation (EC) No. 6/2002 of 12 December 2001 on Community designs, OJ No. L 3/1, 5 January 2002) provides that 'The scope of the protection conferred by a Community design shall include any design which does not produce on the informed user a different overall impression.' There is no similar provision on infringement in the copyright directives. However, as suggested by M. Leistner, whom I thank for this comment, *Infopaq* and other decisions of the CJEU could be read as providing some indications as to when there is a copyright infringement. *See also* Julien Cabay, L'objet de la protection du droit d'auteur, unpublished PhD thesis, Bruxelles, 2016, pp. 299 ff. But this case law leaves enough room for adding (and proposing) a requirement to use the work as a work.

7.3.2.1 Standard Copyright Infringement Test

The infringement test in copyright commonly requires proving: (1) substantial similarity, and (2) copying. First, substantial similarity entails identifying the boundary of the work, and whether parts of a work qualify as a work (and what parts are original). This assessment is sometimes difficult as the case law does not offer clear guidance as to how the boundary of a work is to be determined and how the unprotected ideas should be filtered and discarded.[47] Second, the infringement analysis requires a comparison of the protected work (adequately identified and filtered) with what the defendant has taken. In the case of identity or sufficient (substantial) similarity[48] between the two, copying must still be established as independent creation lies outside copyright's scope. The copying requirement may be satisfied even though the defendant did not consciously copy. Copying is often difficult to prove directly, and it is usually indirectly established by showing that the defendant could have accessed the work. This derivation or 'causal connection'[49] between the work and what is used by the alleged infringer must be shown, and this is complex.

7.3.2.2 Implicit Requirement to 'Use the Work as a Work'

The requirement for trademark infringement that the mark be used as a trademark is still debated, but it can work as a source of inspiration for constructing the condition of 'use of the work as a work' under copyright law.

7.3.2.2.1 Requirement to 'Use a Sign as a Trademark'

Debate on Trademark Use under UK and US Trademark Law

Under old UK trademark law, this requirement clearly existed. According to Bently and Sherman, 'in order for a mark to be infringed under the 1938 Act [predating the implementation of the Trademark Directive], it was necessary to show that the mark had been used as a mark. That is, the mark had to be used in the course of trade to indicate a connection with the owner of the trademark'.[50] As a consequence, other uses such as descriptive or decorative uses could not fall within the trademark right's scope. Dillon L.J. put that

47. L. Bently and B. Sherman, *Intellectual Property Law*, Oxford University Press, 2001, 1st ed., pp. 160–162 (point 5.1.1.).
48. This assessment is of course left for the discretion of the courts and has led to complex case law.
49. L. Bently and B. Sherman, n. 47, p. 158.
50. *Id.*, p. 867.

clearly: 'it stands to reason that a Trade Marks Act would only be concerned to restrict the use of a mark *as a trademark or in a trademark sense*, and should be construed accordingly. If descriptive words are legitimately registered … there is still no reason why other people should not be free to use the words in a descriptive sense and not in any trade mark sense' (emphasis added).[51]

In the US, authors such as Dogan and Lemley have defended the view that US law only makes actionable the 'uses' of the plaintiff's (famous) trademark when the defendant uses the trademark to identify and distinguish its own goods and services, in other words, when there is a trademark use. On the contrary, all uses of a trademark in a non-branding way – for example, by comparing, describing, criticizing, informing, presenting in proximity, learning, commenting, reporting, or simply poking fun[52] – remain outside the trademark's realm. The requirement of trademark use has helped to keep various uses at bay, for example descriptive and nominative fair uses, and, according to Dogan and Lemley, has contributed to the protection of comparative advertising, parody, news reporting, commentary, and criticism, which all make non-trademark use of the protected sign.

Trademark Use under EU Trademark Law[53]

According to EU trademark law, a trademark infringement clearly exists if there is a use 'in the course of trade',[54] but there is only an implicit requirement that the protected sign be used *as a trademark*. A use of a trademark constitutes a use in the course of trade where it occurs 'in the context of commercial activity with a view to economic advantage and not as a private matter'.[55] This express condition of use 'in the course of trade'

51. *Mothercare v. Penguin Books* [1988] RPC 113, 119.
52. *See* S.L. Dogan and M.A. Lemley, The Trademark Use Requirement in Dilution Cases, Santa Clara Computer & High Technology Law Journal, 2008, vol. 24, pp. 541–557, in particular p. 542 (*see also*: S.L. Dogan and Mark A. Lemley, Grounding Trademark Law Through Trademark Use, Iowa Law Review, 2007, vol. 92, p. 1669). However, other leading commentators (G.B. Dinwoodie and M.D. Janis, Confusion Over Use: Contextualism in Trademark Law, Iowa Law Review, 2007, vol. 92, pp. 1597 ff) doubt that the constant extension of trademarks, similar to the broadening of copyright, can be solved by recalibrating the requirement of trademark use.
53. For an overview on this issue under EU law, *see* A. Kur, Confusion over Use? Die Benutzung 'als Marke' im Lichte der EuGH-Rechtsprechung, GRUR Int., 2008, 1, p. 11.
54. *See* Art. 9(1) of the EUTM Regulation which refers to the possibility of preventing third parties 'from using in the course of trade'; *see also* the same language in Art. 10(2) of the Trademark Directive (Directive (EU) 2015/2436 of the European Parliament and of the Council of 16 December 2015 to approximate the laws of the Member States relating to trade marks, recasting Directive 2008/95/EC).
55. CJEU, 15 November 2002, C-206/01, ECLI:EU:C:2002:651 (*Arsenal v. Matthew Reed*), §40; CJEU, 23 March 2010, C-236/08 to C-238/08, ECLI:EU:C:2010:159 (*Google France v. Louis Vuitton Malletier*) §50.

thus refers to the economic or commercial nature of the use. (Under copyright, this economic requirement is not express, but could be derived from the case law, as shown in section 7.4.1 below for the communication to the public right).

The implicit requirement of trademark use developed by case law in the UK and other EU Member States was only partly codified by way of some statutory exclusions in trademark law. Some *descriptive uses*, for instance a use in a dictionary, encyclopaedia, or similar reference work, are expressly exempted under the Trademark Directive[56] (Article 12) and the EUTM Regulation[57] (Article 10). Similarly, EU law excludes *(indicative) uses* defined as 'indications concerning the kind, quality, quantity, intended purpose, value, geographical origin, the time of production of the goods or of rendering of the service, or other characteristics of the goods or service' (Article 12 EUTM Regulation[58]) provided that these are in accordance with honest practices. In all those instances, the sign (its material form) is used, but *not as a trademark*, i.e., not to indicate the origin of goods and services. The distinction between the sign (the letters or visual elements of the sign visible on paper or on any medium) and the trademark value of the sign or its use as a trademark must be preserved to avoid trademark law from overreaching. Confusing the intellectual subject matter of an intellectual property right with its material embodiment[59] is a common mistake in dealing with intellectual property. It commonly leads to what is called the 'propertization' of intellectual property. Propertization extends the scope of control and brings the position of the intellectual right owner closer to the power of an owner with regard to tangible objects.[60]

By underestimating the implicit requirement of trademark use and neglecting the risk of propertization, the CJEU arguably 'has constantly

---

56. Directive 2008/95/EC of the European Parliament and of the Council of 22 October 2008 to approximate the laws of the Member States relating to trade marks (codified version), OJ No. L 299/25, 8 November 2008 (replacing Council Directive 89/104/EEC of 21 December 1988 to approximate the laws of the Member States relating to trade marks, OJ No. L 40/1, 11 February 1989, as amended).
57. Council Regulation (EC) No. 207/2009 of 26 February 2009 on the Community trade mark.
58. *See also* Art. 6(1)(b) of the Trademark Directive (Directive 2008/95/EC of the European Parliament and of the Council of 22 October 2008 to approximate the laws of the Member States relating to trade marks (codified version), OJ No. L 299/25, 8 November 2008 (replacing Council Directive 89/104/EEC of 21 December 1988 to approximate the laws of the Member States relating to trade marks, OJ No. L 40/1, 11 February 1989, as amended)).
59. When a sign is protected independently from its environment and context, the trademark right risks extending to each appearance or material embodiment of the sign (e.g., an embodiment of the verbal trademark in the word included in a dictionary, etc.).
60. For a critique of propertization in another context, *see* A. Ohly, The Freedom of Imitation and Its Limits – A European Perspective, IIC, 2010, p. 506, in particular p. 511.

weakened' the general protection requirement of trademark use,[61] considering for instance that several *informational and referential uses* are to be considered as trademark uses. For the Court, use for informing the public about repair and maintenance services, as well as use in comparative advertising, imply a use of the sign as a trademark. Similarly, parodic or decorative uses of protected signs have been considered as trademark use by several national courts. As a result, M. Senftleben concludes that 'the basic requirement of trademark use does not prevent trademark owners from asserting their rights against references to the trademark even though the public does not perceive these references as an indication of commercial source'.[62] I share this reading, but this is not a reason to abandon the criterion of the use as a trademark in contexts other than referential uses. The trademark use requirement could still work as a useful filter for *technical uses* (as opposed to referential uses) of trademarks. If, as some trademark experts are inclined to think, the use as a trademark is an outdated doctrine, the existing function theory might similarly help to distinguish some purely technical uses of trademarks. [63]

Today, technology makes it possible for trademarks to be used, more often than in the past, in a non-trademark sense (i.e., beyond the functions of a trademark as distinguished by the CJEU). In particular, several online uses of protected signs do not qualify as uses in a trademark sense. The issue was for instance discussed in the CJEU decisions on keyword selling by search engines, in particular in *Google France* and *Interflora v. Marks & Spencer*.[64] According to the Court, when the advertiser selects a keyword identical to a trademark in order to display an ad linking to the site on which he offers his goods, he uses the trademark in the course of trade (it is a commercial activity) and as a trademark (to indicate a connection with goods and services and their origin). On the contrary, the referencing service (Google) uses the protected sign in the course of trade *but not as a trademark*: for the Court, the referencing service is carrying out a commercial activity when it stores as keywords signs for its clients (the advertisers) and displays the ads on the basis of those keywords, but it cannot be inferred that the service provider 'itself "uses" those signs within the terms of Article 5 of [the Trademark]

61. M. Senftleben, Adapting EU Trademark Law to New Technologies – Back to Basics?, in C. Geiger (ed.), *Constructing European Intellectual Property: Achievements and New Perspectives*, Edward Elgar, 2013, pp. 137–176, in particular p. 147.
62. *Id.*, p. 147.
63. If the trademark use test is no longer applied by the courts, at least the theory of trademark functions underlined by the CJEU has replaced it as a filter. *See* the contribution of A. Ohly in the present volume at [pp. 94–95]: 'Rather than requiring use "as a mark", the Court enquires whether … the use is likely to affect the protected functions of the mark … . The function analysis plays a different role in each of the three categories of infringement'.
64. CJEU, 23 March 2010, C-236/08 to C-238/08, ECLI:EU:C:2010:159 (*Google France v. Louis Vuitton Malletier*); CJEU, 22 September 2011, C-323/09, ECLI:EU:C:2011:604 (*Interflora v. Marks & Spencer*).

Directive and Article 9 of [the EUTM] Regulation'[65] (the Court expressly highlights the notion of 'use' by putting it between quotation marks[66]). For the Court, 'the fact of creating the technical conditions necessary for the use of a sign and being paid for that service does not mean that the party offering the service itself uses the sign' (§57).[67]

The confusion between a use in the common sense and the use as specified under trademark law[68] explains why some courts have overlooked the fact that Google, in the keyword selling cases, does not use the trademarks as such, i.e., as trademarks. There is a technical use of the sign by the referencing service (the reservation of the keyword in the 'digital machine' triggers a process and an output, the appearance of an ad), but not a use as a distinctive sign. Because the use of the sign by a referencing service is technical rather than distinctive, it therefore cannot constitute a direct trademark infringement, although the activities of the service provider could be subject to other rules, for instance on the indirect liability of a hosting provider.[69]

Similar reasoning can apply in the field of copyright law to exclude certain technical reproductions that do not involve a use of the work *as a work.*

7.3.2.2.2 The Requirement of 'Use of a Work as a Work'

There is no explicit CJEU case law explaining what a use 'as a work' means for assessing direct copyright infringement.[70] Copyright law however entirely relies on the notion of a work and the principle of authorship.

---

65. *Google France,* §55.
66. *See also Google France*, §56: 'A referencing service provider allows its clients to use signs which are identical with, or similar to, trade marks, *without itself using those signs*' (emphasis added).
67. Similarly, in *L'Oréal v. eBay*, the Court found that the use of third party trademarks in offers for sale on the eBay platform did not amount to a use of the trademarks by eBay (as it was not used by eBay 'in its own commercial communication'), but it is a trademark use by eBay's customers placing their offer on the platform. *See*: CJEU, 12 July 2011, C-324/09, ECLI:EU:C:2011:474 (*L'Oréal v. eBay*), §§101–105 (stressed by M. Senftleben, n. 61, p. 160). However, this illustration is less relevant for dealing with the many invisible and technical copies that should remain out of the reach of copyright.
68. This confusion would also exist if one considers that I use the verbal trademark 'Google' in the present chapter of this book: the use and appearance of the trademark sign ('Google') embodied in this chapter is not a use as a trademark.
69. *Google France,* §107 referring to Art. 14 of the e-Commerce Directive.
70. However, some national decisions could be read as requiring use of a work 'as a work' (or 'in a copyright sense') for a copyright infringement to take place. For example, a leading decision of the French Supreme Court back in 1987 (*Microfor*) had recognized that the titles of the articles of the newspaper *Le Monde* could be protected by copyright, but that their use in an index to identify the classified articles 'did not violate the exclusive right of exploitation of the author', arguably because their function was purely to search for the articles (Cass. ass. pl., 30 October 1997, JCP E, 1998, II, 15093, nr 4, obs. M.

The Protected Work as a Nexus Between an Author and an Audience

A work exists where an individual becomes an author by creating a form of expression which shows the imprint of her personality. There is no work without an original expression.[71] A work is not a thing, even less a tool, it is 'an act whereby a person addresses others through speech'.[72] Immanuel Kant's piece, 'On the Wrongfulness of Unauthorized Publication of Books'[73] has developed the idea that the work of an author is the speech of a person. It is the nexus for a communication between the author and a public. From this perspective, copyright law appears as a form of speech regulation, since it 'protects the integrity of the work as a communicative act'.[74]

Copyright law, at its inception, was a way to empower authors and grant them rights for their original expression, but at the same time it was a means for achieving some State control over the author's expression by making authors liable with regard to their speech.[75] The first copyright laws were not separate from laws regulating speech, and copyright law should thus be considered and interpreted in this context.[76]

Vivant and A. Lucas). This decision involving a database could be compared with the discussion on text and data mining (*see* below): in such case, the work arguably serves as a raw material from which to extract relevant information, but is not read, copied and used as a work. In another decision, the French Supreme Court considered that the reproduction of the illustrations of a reading method used in school classes as a background in a documentary film devoted to a great school teacher were not used 'for themselves' or as protected works (they were totally incidental in the film). *See* Cass., 12 May 2011, JurisData nr. 2011-008403 and the observations of M. Vivant, Droit d'auteur et théorie de l'accessoire: et si l'accessoire révélait l'essentiel?, La Semaine juridique, éd. G., nr 28, 11 July 2011, p. 1360; M. Vivant, Objet juridique, objet social. Réflexion sur la propriété intellectuelle, P.I., April 2012, nr 43, pp. 269–272. I thank Julien Cabay for pointing me to these sources.

71. I do not want to discuss the concept of work here, but this definition directly derives from the CJEU case law on originality which is intertwined with the work notion. *See*: CJEU, 16 July 2009, C-5/08, ECLI:EU:C:2009:465 (*Infopaq I*); CJEU, 1 December 2011, C-145/10, ECLI:EU:C:2011:798 (*Painer*).
72. A. Drassinower, n. 12, p. 8.
73. I. Kant, Von der Unrechtmäßigkeit des Büchernachdrucks (1785), Gesammelte Schriften, Berlin, Walter de Gruyter, 1968 Ak. VIII, pp. 77–88, translated as On the Wrongfulness of Unauthorized Publication of Books, in *Practical Philosophy*, Cambridge University Press., 1996, pp. 27–35.
74. A. Drassinower, n. 12, p. 8. Other commentators have stressed this communicative dimension: C.J. Craig, *Copyright, Communication and Culture – Towards a Relational Theory of Copyright Law*, Edgar Elgar, 2011; R. Coombe, *The Cultural Life of Intellectual Properties – Authorship, Appropriation and the Law*, Duke University Press, 1998. *See also* the view of S. Dusollier, Realigning economic rights with exploitation of works, in the present volume.
75. On the link between the early copyright laws and censorship (or State control of speech) *see* the numerous historical studies (including L. R. Patterson, n. 4).
76. In the US, N. Weinstock Netanel claims that copyright should be 'located' or understood 'within the First Amendment skein' (N. Weinstock Netanel, Locating Copyright Within the First Amendment Skein, Stanford Law Review, vol. 54, nr 1 (2001), pp. 1–86). Other

The Copyright Infringement Test and the Communication Dimension

This should influence the condition of copying in the assessment of a copyright infringement. According to Drassinower, '[b]ecause a work is a communicative act, to reproduce it is to recommunicate it. To copy is to repeat an author's speech as such. Uses of the work as a mere pattern of ink, so to speak, in the absence of recommunication, are not uses of the work *as a work*.' (emphasis added)[77] Under this view, non-communicative uses are thus not actionable.

Yet, many technical reproductions constitute non-communicative uses: they are only needed for the 'digital machine' to function. The copy is just a tool, not an expression addressed to other humans. This applies to uses such as copying a text or corpus for a data mining exercise, making a technical copy on a router for the transmission of content on the Internet, or making a copy of a student's papers for the purposes of detecting plagiarism,[78] etc.[79] In all those cases, the digital embodiment of the work (as a series of bits) is indeed reproduced, but there is no use as a work in the absence of a human public to hear and decipher it.

For Drassinower, when a work is not used for a communicative use, it should not be qualified as a *fair* use, but simply a *non-use* of the work.[80] Case law shows however that courts in the US tend to apply the fair use provision (section 107 of the US Copyright Act) to exclude such *non-uses*. In the EU, there is no similar open formula to exclude fair uses, and many technical and intermediate copies do not fit within the closed list of exceptions (Article 5 of the InfoSoc Directive). Therefore, at least until the InfoSoc Directive list of exceptions is adequately adapted to the digital machine, recasting the copyright infringement test as requiring a communicative use of the work seems appropriate.

---

authors, including Drassinower (n. 12) and Patterson n. 4), have stressed the speech dimension of a work and the speech regulation aspect of copyright.

77. A. Drassinower, *supra.*, p. 87 (emphasis of the author on the requirement 'as a work').
78. *See* the illustration proposed by A. Drassinower: *A.V. v. iParadigms LLC*, 562 F.3d 630 (4th Cir. 2009), 640: 'iParadigms' use of these works was completely unrelated to the expressive content and was instead aimed at detecting and discouraging plagiarism'.
79. M. Leistner kindly alerted me to the fact that the situation is a bit more complex with a thumbnail reproduction for searching images on the web. The copy undoubtedly has an indexing function, but the thumbnail image is seen by the Internet user before accessing the full image and this intermediate copy already 'speaks' to the person searching images and thus has a communicative value, contrary to other intermediate copies. *See* the reasoning of several courts which have exempted thumbnail reproductions because those copies are a tool to find information, rather than a presentation of the expressive works: *Kelly v. Arriba Soft Corp.* 336 F.3d 811 (9th Cir. 2003), 818; *Perfect 10 Inc. v. Amazon.com Inc.*, 508 F.3d 1146 (9th Cir.); Bundesgerichtshof, 29 April 2010, I ZR 69/08 (*thumbnail bei Google*).
80. A. Drassinower, n. 12, pp. 13 and 87.

Of course, other theories could help too. For instance, an economic analysis of the impact of those uses (*see* section 7.4 below) could be useful.[81] Relying, as I do here, on the fundamental objective of copyright is more radical. In other words, as with some technical uses of trademarks (e.g., when a trademark is used to reserve a keyword), there is a use of the material form (the digital embodiment). The digital embodiment however is used as a tool for a technical process or for achieving a function, but not as a work for reaching out towards a public. Those intermediate copies should not fall within the copyright realm properly conceived. Reconstructing the reproduction right by taking into account the fundamental communicative aspect of a copyright work automatically limits its scope to cases where a work is used as an expressive work.

7.3.3 The Reconstructed Right Applied to TDM: The Work as a Tool or Data, Not as a Work

TDM is a form of research that extracts data and patterns from large datasets[82] and identifies word frequencies, syntactic patterns, and thematic markers in a corpus of documents. When asked if TDM should fall under copyright, many copyright scholars until recently would have doubted copyright's relevance. That copyright might extend to the TDM process does not appear legitimate: no author of literary or artistic production in the past has conceived her copyright as a way to limit the use of her work as a source of useful information, for instance for discerning fluctuations in interest in a particular subject or for determining fashionable expressions. No author, while producing a work, has seriously relied on the possibility of earning revenues from the derivative use related to searching and indexing a corpus that includes her work.[83] Such use is far removed from the core exploitation field of most works. In addition, when it appeared more than two centuries ago, copyright was not only intended to remunerate authors (and publishers) for creating (and disseminating) works, but was also promoted to expand public learning. This is not only true for the US copyright system, as the same rationale is at the origin and core of the continental *droit d'auteur* system.[84]

Yet there are good arguments to conclude that the all-encompassing notion of reproduction, as delineated by EU law (*see* section 7.3.1 above), is broad and sufficiently undetermined to cover the TDM (re)search process,

81. *See* J. Poort, in this volume.
82. R. Kitchin, *The Data Revolution*, Sage, 2014, p. 104.
83. *See also* J. Poort, in this volume.
84. *See* my review of the history and principles of copyright in both legal traditions: *Droit d'auteur et copyright*, Bruxelles and Paris, 1993; more recently, A. Strowel, Droit d'auteur et copyright. Convergence des droits, régulation différente des contrats, in *Mélanges en l'honneur d'André Lucas*, Paris, 2014, pp. 699–717 at pp. 701–703.

involving various processing of data and works. Copyright can thus be used to block the spread of relevant information extracted from protected corpuses. If this is possible, then copyright law is working against copyright's aim, which is a reason for concern.[85]

In the US, the fair use provision can function as a way to delineate the boundaries of the author's exclusive right with a view to its final objectives. In the *Google Books* case (*Authors Guild v. Google, Inc.*), the US Court of Appeals for the Second Circuit decided that the various acts committed by Google in reproducing books, including for searching and TDM, are to be considered as fair use.[86] We do not have the same legal tool under EU law. Of course, it is in principle possible to add a specific exception to the exclusive reproduction right. Following some Member States (including the UK), the European Commission, in its proposal of 14 September 2016, advocates the adoption of a TDM exception.[87] The envisaged exception would not allow research conducted in a commercial context as it is limited to (public interest) 'research organisations' and 'for the purposes of scientific research' (*see* Article 3 of the proposed directive on copyright in the Digital Single Market).

In the absence of such an express exception, it is perhaps possible to rely on the implicit requirement that the reproduction involves a use as a work. Such use as a work does not exist in the case of TDM, nor in other cases involving copying for deriving information or checking conduct (e.g., to identify plagiarism). As put by the Court in *Authors Guild v. Google, Inc.*, 'the purpose of Google's copying of the original copyrighted books is to make available significant information *about those books*, permitting a searcher to identify those that contain a word or term of interest' (emphasis added).[88] This purposive analysis of the act of copying strongly weighs in favour of fair, because highly transformative, use. In the EU, the requirement of use as a work can help to reach the same outcome. Indeed, when acts of reproduction are carried out for the purpose of search and TDM, the work is not used as a work, it only serves as a tool or data for deriving other relevant

85. In 2011, the Hargreaves Report mentioned TDM as 'one current example of a new technology which copyright should not inhibit, but does' (*Digital Opportunity. A Review of Intellectual Property and Growth*, p. 48). I prefer to refer to TDM as a practice of finding and spreading useful information that copyright was supposed to encourage.

86. *Authors Guild v. Google, Inc.* 804 F.3d 202 (2d Cir. 2015). To make available parts of the corpus of books, Google has scanned the digital copies and established a publicly available search function, the ngrams tool.

87. *See* Art. 3 of the Proposal for a Directive on Copyright in the Digital Single Market. *See also* European Commission, Towards a modern, more European copyright framework, COM(2015) 626 final, 9/12/2015, p. 7 ('The need to better reflect technological advances and avoid uneven situations in the single market is also clear with text and data mining (TDM), through which vast amounts of digital content are read and analysed by machines in the context of science and research. The lack of a clear EU provision on TDM for scientific research purposes creates uncertainties in the research community.').

88. *Authors Guild v. Google, Inc.*(n. 86).

information. The expressive features of the work are not used, and there is no public to enjoy the work, as the work is only an input in a process for searching a corpus and identifying occurrences and possible trends or patterns.

Even if the EU Parliament and Council decide to include an exception for TDM that is broad enough (this would require some commercial research to be exempted), the analysis based on 'the use of the work as a work' condition for copyright infringement remains necessary to address other types of copying for the purpose of providing information, such as copies for checking mistakes and plagiarism, copies to use or repair a protected work with a utilitarian function, non-transitory copies made on proxy servers, and many other similar uses that cannot be anticipated.[89]

7.4 PUTTING FORWARD THE ECONOMIC DIMENSION OF THE COMMUNICATION TO THE PUBLIC RIGHT

7.4.1 The Economic Parameters of Communication to the Public According to the CJEU

The CJEU definition of communication to the public[90] is complex and relies on a sliding scale of criteria.

89. The following US decisions quoted in *Authors Guild v. Google, Inc.* have, for instance, exempted several uses that, without the application of the work use requirement, cannot escape copyright's exclusivity in the EU: *A.V. ex rel. Vanderhye v. iParadigms, LLC*, 562 F.3d 630, 638–640 (4th Cir. 2009) (justifying as transformative fair use purpose the complete digital copying of a manuscript to determine whether the original included matter plagiarized from other works); *Perfect 10, Inc. v. Amazon.com, Inc.*, 508 F.3d 1146, 1165 (9th Cir. 2007) (justifying as transformative fair use purpose the use of a digital, thumbnail copy of the original to provide an Internet pathway to the original); *Kelly v. Arriba Soft Corp.*, 336 F.3d 811, 818–819 (9th Cir. 2003) (same); *Bond v. Blum*, 317 F.3d 385 (4th Cir. 2003) (justifying as fair use purpose the copying of author's original unpublished autobiographical manuscript for the purpose of showing that he murdered his father and was an unfit custodian of his children).

90. The case law comprises the following decisions: CJEU, 7 December 2006, C-306/05, ECLI:EU:C:2006:764 (*SGAE v. Rafael Hoteles)*; 22 December 2010, C-393/09, ECLI: EU:C:2010:816 (*Bezpečnostní softwarová asociace*); 4 October 2011, C-403/08 & C-429/08, ECLI:EU:C:2011:631 (*Premier League)*; 13 October 2011, C-431/09 & C-432/09, ECLI:EU:C:2011:648 (*Airfield*); 24 November 2011, C-283/10, ECLI: EU:C:2011:772 (*Circul Globus*); 15 March 2012, C-135/10, ECLI:EU:C:2012:140 (*Societa Consortile Fonografici (SCF) v. Del Corso*); 15 March 2012, C-162/10, ECLI:EU:C:2012:141 (*Phonographic Performance Ltd*); 7 March 2013, C-607/11, ECLI:EU:C:2013:147 (*TVCatchup*); 27 February 2014, C-351/12, ECLI:EU:C:2014:110

Any Technical Means of Transmission

The technical means used for the transmission do not matter (*SGAE,* §46; *Premier League,* §193). This is derived directly from recital 23 of the InfoSoc Directive: 'This right should cover *any* such *transmission* or *retransmission* of a work to the public by wire or wireless means, including broadcasting' (emphasis added). A principle of technological neutrality, as defined above (*see* section 7.1), seems to be acknowledged. However, each technically independent (re)transmission does not automatically imply that a communication to the public takes place.[91]

Two Main Conditions

In its 2016 *Reha Training*[92] judgment, the Grand Chamber of the CJEU considered that two basic cumulative elements, i.e., an 'act of communication' of a work and the transmission of this work to a 'public', are required.[93] The 'act of communication' means that the user has an 'indispensable role' to play: some action or intervention by the user is needed, but the Court has always been vague about what this means, and the threshold seems low. The notion of 'public' is mostly defined by reference to a quantitative criterion (indeterminate but *de minimis* number of persons who are the potential recipients of the communication). The qualitative criterion (such as the private bond between the members of the public[94]) is not relevant.

Two Additional Parameters

In *SGAE v. Rafael Hoteles*, a case involving the use of television sets and the distribution of broadcast music in hotel rooms, the Court had already distinguished, on top of the two main conditions (a communication and a public), two other parameters:[95] (1) the transmission to a *new* public (i.e., the requirement that there is a broadening of the audience), and (2) the user's profit motives in transmitting the work. In *SGAE*, the 'act of communication' was established because of the user's active role in the transmission (the

---

(*OSA*); 31 May 2016, C-117/15, ECLI:EU:C:2016:379 (*Reha Training v. GEMA*). The cases involving hyperlinking are treated separately below when I analyse the borderline cases.

91. This differs from the analysis of the reproduction right: each technical copy is presumptively covered by the reproduction right (but can be exempted under an exception).
92. CJEU, 31 May 2016, C-117/15 (*Reha Training v. GEMA*), §37.
93. The judge-rapporteur in most copyright cases decided by the CJEU, J. Malenovsky, has confirmed this; J. Malenovsky, La contribution de la Cour de justice au droit d'auteur en droit de l'Union européenne, n. 19.
94. For the Court, the qualitative nature of the public is not taken into account. Therefore the private nature of hotel rooms is for instance not relevant. A new public might be reached, even if the members of the public will remain in an otherwise 'private' space.
95. *See also* J. Griffiths, n. 39, p. 1109.

installation of the TV sets in the hotel rooms so as to retransmit the TV signals to the hotel guests). The *SGAE* ruling also offers an economic interpretation of the condition of 'public': as users quickly succeed each other in hotel rooms, 'taken separately, they are of limited economic interest for the hotel' (*SGAE* §39), but not when aggregated. The presence of such a public over time generates an economic return. The 'for-profit' motive of the user shows that the legal notion is linked to the commercial or economic nature of the use.

Subsequent decisions of the Court also consider the outreach towards a 'new public' and the profit-making nature of the use as decisive parameters.

Premier League involves the transmission of broadcast works via a television screen and loudspeakers to the customers of a pub. The Grand Chamber of the CJEU defines the 'new public' as 'an additional public' 'which was not taken into account by the authors of the protected works when they authorized their use by the communication to the original public' (*Premier League* §§197 and 198; *see also OSA*, §31).[96] The Court, using a double negation, adds that 'it is *not irrelevant* that a "communication" within the meaning of Article 3(1) of the Copyright Directive is of a profit-making nature' (emphasis added) (*Premier League,* §204) and concludes that the pub owner transmits in order 'to benefit therefrom' (*Premier League,* §205). In *TVCatchup* and subsequent decisions, the Court uses the same double negation ('not irrelevant') about the profit-making nature of the act and adds that it is 'not necessarily an essential condition' (*TVCatchup*, §44).[97] With *GS Media*[98], as shown in section 7.4.3.2 below, the Court puts the profit-making nature of the act at the centre of the communication to the public.

Airfield concerned the communication to the public by satellite. Again, the expansion of the public (or market) by a specific service, together with the fact that the service is performed with the aim of making a profit (*Airfield*, §§76 and 80), are the crucial parameters for concluding that a communication to the public took place.

In *Phonographic Performance Ltd* (hereafter *PPL)*, the issue was whether a hotel can be exonerated from the payment of the equitable remuneration when using phonograms in the hotel bedrooms. Decisive here is the fact that the hotel operator 'derives economic benefits' from the transmission (*PPL*, §51) and intervenes actively in the process. The intervention of the hotel 'constitutes an additional service' which has an influence 'on the hotel's standing and, therefore, on the price of the rooms'

96. Referring also to the order of 18 March 2010 in Case C-136/09 *Organismos Sillogikis Diacheirisis Dimiourgon Theatrikon kai Optikoakoustikon Ergon*, §38.
97. In *TVCatchup,* the Court concludes that there is a communication because of the use of a different and independent means of transmission, without enquiring whether there is a 'new public'.
98. CJEU, 8 September 2016, C-160/15, ECLI:EU:C:2016:644 *(GS Media).*

(*PPL*, §44). The reference to the impact on the price illustrates again the economic reasoning of the Court.[99] The Court even stresses that the requirement of 'a profit-making nature' is more important for a right to equitable remuneration than for an exclusive right (*PPL*, §36).

This – possibly too flexible – method of weighting different criteria, without considering all of them as cumulative and without clearly classifying them by order of importance, was applied in *Reha Training*. To assess whether there is a communication to the public in a concrete situation, 'several complementary criteria' have to be taken into account. As those criteria may be 'present to widely varying degrees', 'they must be applied individually in their interaction with one another' (*Reha Training*, §35).[100] No certainty can be derived from this view, and the case law of the Court definitely shows an ad hoc application of the various criteria.

The CJEU case law has thus managed to somewhat take into account the economic realities by using a sliding scale of four criteria, with three of them having an economic component (in particular the profit-making nature of the act). As underlined by M. Leistner, the focus of those CJEU decisions 'is no longer on the legal monopoly of the authors, but rather on the question of whether the concrete user *economically exploits* the copyright protected subject matter with regard to a (new) public' (emphasis added).[101] However,

99. *PPL* contrasts with the Court's opinion in *Del Corso* involving the free broadcasting of phonograms in a dentist practice. In *Del Corso*, the Court puts forward two main criteria: the requirement of a public and the profit-making nature of the act. Several individuals will not necessarily constitute a public, the communication must be directed 'to persons in general, that is, not restricted to specific individuals belonging to a private group'. In the case of a dental practice, the patients constitute 'a determinate circle of potential recipients' and are not 'persons in general'. Besides, the number of persons present in the practice at the same time is very limited (*Del Corso*, §85 and §§95–96). As the dentist cannot 'expect a rise in the number of patients because of that broadcast alone or increase the price of the treatment', the communication has no 'impact on the income of that dentist' and is 'not of a profit-making nature' (*Del Corso*, §§97–99). The Court *en passant* adds its view on what a dental treatment should include: 'the broadcasting of phonograms is in no way a part of dental treatment' (*Del Corso*, §98)! The possibility (or not) to pass the value (added by the use of the phonograms) into the price of the services (the price of the room or dental treatment) is the conclusive factor in those cases.

This justification was restated in the *OSA* judgment (§§34–35): the intervention by a spa establishment distributing a signal by means of TV sets in the bedrooms differs from the use of phonograms in a dental practice. The communication in spa bedrooms has an economic effect on the price of the bedrooms, not the communication within a dentist practice (as the added value cannot translate into a higher price for the dentist service, in part because the price of the dental treatment is fixed by the public authorities).

100. *See also PPL*, §30 and *Del Corso*, §79: 'account has to be taken of several complementary criteria, which are not autonomous and are interdependent. Consequently, they must be applied individually and in their interaction with one another, given that they may, in different situations, be present to widely varying degrees'.

101. M. Leistner, n. 20, p. 570.

the economic thinking behind the application of the right could be made clearer and better articulated. The proposal below aims to achieve that.

7.4.2 Reconstructing Communication to the Public by Adding a Double Market Analysis

True Exploitation Must Be Authorized and Remunerated

The European Commission is aware of the difficulties in applying the communication to the public right in the online environment. As put by the European Commission in its December 2015 Communication for 'achieving a well-functioning marketplace for copyright':

> [a]n important aspect is the definition of the rights of communication to the public and of making available. These rights govern the use of copyright-protected content in digital transmissions. Their definition therefore determines what constitutes an act on the Internet over which creators and the creative industries can claim rights and can negotiate licences and remuneration. There are contentious grey areas and uncertainty about the way these concepts are defined in EU law in particular about which online acts are considered 'communication to the public' (and therefore require authorisation by the rightholders) and under what conditions. These questions create on the one hand uncertainty in the market and, on the other, put into question the ability of these rights to transpose into the online world *the basic principle of copyright that acts of exploitation need to be authorised and remunerated.* (emphasis added)[102]

I agree with the basic principle that *acts of exploitation need to be authorized and remunerated*, but how to define what is a (true) 'exploitation'? Other scholars have attempted to reconstruct the economic rights by substantiating the notion of 'exploitation'.[103] To use a formal or technical criterion for the communication to the public no longer seems possible because there is no clear correspondence between a particular type of '(re)transmission' and a mode of exploitation. To put the basic principle into practice, one has to offer a clearer economic standard for a true act of exploitation. This approach will not remove uncertainty, but should not increase the existing uncertainty either. A relative uncertainty also prevails in the US case law on 'fair use' which aims to define the (economic) scope of copyright, but from the perspective of copyright's limitations.

---

102. European Commission, Towards a modern, more European copyright framework, 9/12/2015, COM(2015) 626 final, point 4.
103. *See* the contributions of O.-A. Rognstad, J. Poort, and S. Dusollier elsewhere in this volume.

– The economic analysis is needed for the border(on)line cases

In the proposal below, the focus is on the *border(on)line* cases. There is no need to use this approach for settled situations, such as an additional performance or recitation in front of a (new) public or a broadcast, cable retransmission, or satellite transmission which broadens the public. Those situations fall within the legal monopoly and automatically trigger the application of the right of communication to the public (or the performance right). The legal standard is clearly sufficient here.

For the *border(on)line* cases, such as those envisaged in the CJEU case law on catch-up TV and hyperlinking, the impact of the act on: (1) the marketing of the copyright work, and (2) the user's service, must be taken into account for assessing whether a new communication to the public takes place. In my view, this double market analysis should complement the application of the existing parameters developed by the CJEU, in particular the for-profit nature of the act, which already shows an economic understanding of the legal exclusivity. The analysis of the impact on the two markets (the market for the work and the market for the user's service) is based on economic data and tends to be objective, while (some of) the conditions put forward by the CJEU (in particular the 'profit-making nature' of the act) involve a more subjective approach, which requires investigation of the intention and motive of the person transmitting the work. The CJEU reasoning puts too much weight on the subjective factors, and does not constitute a real economic analysis of the situations. In particular, the impact of the use on the market for the copyright work is not expressly articulated in the Court's reasoning on communication to the public.

7.4.2.1 Impact on the Market for the Work

In the US, the fair use provision for determining when a use falls outside the realm of copyright refers expressly to the factor of 'the effect of the use upon the potential market for or value of the copyrighted work' (Article 107(4) of the US Copyright Act). This criterion was described by the US Supreme Court as 'undoubtedly the single most important element of fair use'[104] and has been applied in most fair use cases. It focuses on whether the use 'brings to the marketplace a competing substitute', 'so as to deprive the rights holder of significant revenues'[105] derived from the initial use. Applying this notion to the snippet function (allowing access to short extracts of scanned books) in the *Google Books* case, the US Court of Appeals of the Second Circuit concluded that this function in fact 'does not give searchers access to effectively competing substitutes' and 'does not threaten the right holders

104. *Harper & Row*, 471 U.S. at 566.
105. *Authors Guild v. Google Inc.*, 13-4829-cv, US Court of Appeals (2d Circ.), 16 October 2015 (under point D. Factor Four).

with any *significant* harm to the value of their copyrights or diminish their harvest of copyright revenues' (emphasis added), although it acknowledges that '*some* loss of sales' (emphasis added)[106] might occur. The reasoning that not *all* losses of revenue, but only the significant ones leading to an 'effectively competing substitute' must be prevented by the application of copyright is essential.

The CJEU follows a similar approach when defining the ultimate objective of copyright. The CJEU indeed has not recognized that authors should enjoy maximal protection, but only an appropriate one and *in relation to the economic value*. In several decisions, the Court stressed that the right of communication to the public should be interpreted broadly because of the objective of the InfoSoc Directive 'to establish a high level of protection' (*SGAE*, §36; *Premier League*, §183). Commentators, however, tend to overlook the fact that this does not imply that the protection should be maximized; on the contrary, the Court considers that this objective translates into the possibility for authors 'to obtain an appropriate reward for the use of their works' (*SGAE*, §36; *Premier League*, §186). 'Appropriate' means 'reasonable *in relation to the economic value* of the service' (emphasis added) (*Premier League*, §109). To follow the economic reasoning of the Court does not lead to the maximization of protection as 'the specific subject-matter of the intellectual property does not guarantee the right holders concerned the opportunity to demand *the highest possible remuneration ... only appropriate remuneration* for each use of the protected subject' (emphasis added) (*Premier League*, §108). This is in line with older decisions stressing that copyright and the related rights are 'economic in nature, in that they confer the right to exploit commercially' the works.[107]

Therefore, not all transmissions which have a negative effect on the market for the work should result in a communication to the public; only those creating competing substitutes and significant harm or loss of revenues. Economic analysis could help define a 'competing substitute'. Informed by such an analysis, courts could better define the scope of the communication to the public right.

To assess the degree of substitutability, economic analysis first aims to define the 'relevant market' for the work. In the copyright analysis, the notion of relevant market is broader than the existing market on which competition law analysis usually focuses. Copyright and other intellectual property rights

106. *Id.*
107. CJEU, 20 October 1993, C-92/92 and C-326/92, ECLI:EU:C:1993:847 (*Phil Collins v. Imtrat*) §20: 'The specific subject matter' of copyright and related rights 'is to ensure the protection of the moral and economic rights of their holders. The protection of moral rights enables authors and performers, in particular, to object to any distortion, mutilation or other modification of a work which would be prejudicial to their honour or reputation. Copyright and related rights are also economic in nature, in that *they confer the right to exploit commercially* the marketing of the protected work, particularly in the form of licences granted in return for payment of royalties.' (emphasis added).

are indeed supposed to incentivize an investment by allowing it to be recouped in the future, so that a future market is taken into consideration when the initial investment is made (and the US fair use provision also rightly refers to the effect on the 'potential' market for the copyright work). Once the relevant market (taking into account the expectations of the copyright owner when investing in the work) is defined, the economic impact of the act of transmission on this relevant market might then be assessed. With this information in mind, the courts could better assess the need for subordinating the envisaged use to the authorization of the copyright holder. Of course, this would require that economic experts provide the right information to the courts. The way copyright cases are heard is different from in the field of competition law, where a specialized agency (the competition authority) comprising skilled economists is able to provide the necessary market analysis before a decision is taken. Nevertheless, one could conceive of the EU Intellectual Property Office or national offices, together with competition authorities, being tasked with such a role in the border(on)line copyright cases.

7.4.2.2 Impact on the Market for the User's Service

The impact on the user's service and the boost that the use of the work(s) has on the competitiveness of the service must also be factored in. The CJEU is inclined to consider this aspect. For instance, the Court stresses in *Reha Training* that it is important that the public in the rehabilitation establishments (such as Reha Training) 'is not merely "caught" by chance, but is targeted by their operators' (*Reha Training,* §48). The broadcast of the programme in those establishments has a profit-making nature where the user can 'obtain an economic benefit' (*Reha Training,* §51). This is the case where the broadcasting of the TV programmes, 'intended to create a diversion for the patients of a rehabilitation centre' in reality constitutes a new service which 'does have an impact on the establishment's standing and attractiveness, thereby giving it a competitive advantage' (*Reha Training,* §63). The Court's analysis fails however to explain what this 'competitive advantage' is. As for the condition relating to the market for the copyright work, the input of economists or market experts could be valuable to substantiate this advantage. I therefore advocate supporting the legal analysis by a thorough market analysis on the competitive advantage that the use of the work(s) confers.

One particular way to assess the impact on the user's service is to check whether the transmission of the protected work(s) allows the user to extract some value and to pass it on by adjusting the price of its service. In *PPL, Del Corso* and *OSA* (*see* section 7.4.1 above), the CJEU shows some sympathy for this controlling factor. Where the price of the user's service is not flexible (as for a dental treatment which is partly/largely defined by the health insurance or reimbursement authority), there is no possibility for the user down the transmission chain to earn extra money from the use of the works. This has prompted the Court to conclude that no communication to the public took place in the circumstances of *Del Corso*.

However, one should not conclude that no communication to the public takes place each time the user benefits from the work without being able to adjust the price of the service or when the service is free. Most of the time, the use of the work (such as the broadcasting of TV programmes) will offer a positive for the user's service. In certain instances, this advantage might constitute attracting and retaining clients (or the patients of a rehabilitation centre). Nevertheless, not all uses reinforcing the attractiveness of the user's service should lead to the conclusion that a relevant copyright act (a communication to the public) took place. If this becomes the rule, the copyright protection would probably tilt too much in favour of the copyright owner. Therefore, the existence of a 'bounty' for the user is not a sufficient condition for concluding that some control should exist for the right owner over the use. Economic analysis could help to draw the line here.

The teaching that judges should keep in mind when dealing with those border(on)line cases is the same as for other areas of creation or innovation: because earlier creators and innovators provide benefits to later creators and innovators, they should be compensated for their contributions by being granted 'some' right in respect of subsequent creations and innovations. But that right should not go too far: if all subsequent creations and innovations were considered as infringing, later innovators would have no incentive to invest if they might be barred from offering a new service or from implementing the follow-on innovation (or from marketing the derivative creation). Or they might only have a reduced incentive if a significant part of the revenues they can anticipate would go to the creator or innovator further up the chain. The greater the rights granted to the initial creators, the lower the incentives for subsequent creators, and vice versa. When applying this, courts should take into account all the economic circumstances of the case. Granting an injunction based on the exclusive right is only one option among several.

7.4.3 The Reconstructed Right Applied to Two Digital Cases

As for the reconstructed right of reproduction in relation to TDM (*see* section 7.3.3 above), I now apply the right of communication to the public, interpreted in light of its economic rationale and reconstructed through the additional double market test in two situations: aggregation of works by online platforms and hyperlinking to works.

7.4.3.1 Platform Aggregation

Economists such as the Nobel Prize winner Jean Tirole[108] emphasize that digital platforms[109] are substantially modifying the value chain in many economic sectors. Whether the law should intervene to address some of those changes in the value chain raises huge debate at national and European levels.[110]

Regarding content platforms, such as YouTube and Dailymotion (video), Flickr and Instagram (photos), and Facebook and LinkedIn (various content), the Commission had already expressed a concern about the allocation of revenues between the platforms and the rightholders for the use of copyright content in December 2015.[111] On 14 September 2016, the Commission proposed a far-reaching copyright package containing several provisions affecting content platforms.[112] The Commission does not attempt to harmonize the definition of, or to codify, the right of communication to the public.[113] Rather, it focuses on facilitating the licensing of content by

108. *See* J. Tirole, *Economie du bien commun*, PUF, 2016, chap. 14 (entitled 'Quand le digital modifie la chaîne de valeur'), pp. 497 ff.
109. There is no single definition of what a platform is, but the Commission considers that 'platforms are generally known as "two-sided" or "multi-sided" markets where users are brought together by a platform operator in order to facilitate an interaction' such as the provision of goods, services, capital or content. Here we focus on the (1) online and (2) content platforms. *See* the discussion on the platform notion in the Commission Staff Working Document, Online Platforms, Accompanying the Communication on Online Platforms and the Digital Single Market, SWD(2016) 172, pp. 1 ff. and p. 31 ff for the content platforms. As stressed by the Commission, online platforms have 'the capacity to facilitate, and extract value, from direct interactions or transactions between users' (p. 2).
110. European Commission, Online Platforms and the Digital Single Market. Opportunities and Challenges for Europe, 25/5/2016, COM(2016) 288/2.
111. European Commission, Online Platforms and the Digital Single Market. Opportunities and Challenges for Europe, n. 110, p. 8: 'there is a growing concern as to whether the value generated by some of these new forms of online content distribution is fairly shared between distributors and rights holders'. *See also* European Commission, Promoting a fair, efficient and competitive European copyright-based economy in the Digital Single Market, 14/9/2016, COM(2016) 592 final, p. 7 (referring to 'a growing concern about the equitable sharing of the value generated by some of the new forms of online distribution along the value chain').
112. *See* the Commission's proposal for a directive on copyright in the Digital Single Market, COM(2016) 593 final.
113. On this point, the September 2016 Commission package does not go as far as the December 2015 Communication (*see* the quote in section 7.4.2 above, where the Commission stresses that 'the definition of the rights of communication to the public and of making available' is important to determine 'what constitutes an act on the Internet over which creators and the creative industries can claim rights and can negotiate licences and remuneration').

mandating the information society service[114] providers to take measures such as the use of effective content recognition technologies and by imposing transparency obligations in favour of rightholders.[115] Recital 40 of the draft Directive stresses that rightholders 'need information to assess the continued economic value of their rights, compared to the remuneration received for their licence or transfer'. The draft Directive thus hints at what certain rightholders have called the 'value gap', defined as a market distortion resulting from the discrepancy between the revenues from paid services (e.g., Netflix) and the revenues from free-to-consumer services (e.g., YouTube).

The economic parameters put forward by the CJEU (in particular the profit-making nature of the user's act of communication and its deliberate aspect) combined with the double market analysis proposed above (in section 7.4.2) help to assess whether platforms such as YouTube and Facebook use protected works in a copyright sense. The application of those parameters leads to the conclusion that, when the role of those intermediaries goes beyond technical support (beyond the provision of physical facilities for storing content), they are performing an act of communication to the public. We saw above (in section 7.4.1) that the CJEU has emphasized several economic parameters to determine whether there is communication to the public: (1) the deliberate intervention of the service provider for making the works available (in the case of platforms, the intervention relies on the optimization of the presentation of the uploaded works); (2) the role of the service provider in expanding the public for the works (the promotion of some pages/channels by the platform); and (3) the profit-making nature of the act of communication. Those parameters in fact reflect the conditions for assessing the active/passive role of the platforms. For those service providers to be shielded by the liability exemption of the e-Commerce Directive[116] (Article 14), they must play a passive role.[117] The active role of the content platform can also be assessed through an analysis of the impact of the online aggregation on the market for the copyright work and on the user's service. Concerning this last aspect, the content aggregation platforms are economically benefiting, through their advertising revenues, from the value of the copyright works that are shared by the platforms' users.[118] Reconstructing the

114. The proposal for a directive on copyright in the Digital Single Market (COM(2016) 593 final) still uses the terminology used in the e-Commerce Directive, and thus envisages the online platforms as 'information society service providers'.
115. *See* Art. 13 and recitals 38 ff of the Proposal for a directive on copyright in the Digital Single Market.
116. Directive 2000/31/EC of the European Parliament and of the Council of 8 June 2000 on certain legal aspects of information society services, in particular electronic commerce, in the Internal Market (Directive on electronic commerce), OJ No. L 178/1, 17 July 2000.
117. *See* among the CJEU case law: CJEU, 12 July 2011, C-324/09, ECLI:EU:C:2011:474 (*L'Oréal v. eBay*).
118. *See also* S. Dusollier in the present volume.

communication to the public right (by relying on, and complementing, the CJEU approach) thus also contributes to the delineation of the liability exemption when applied to content aggregation platforms.

7.4.3.2 Hyperlinking

Prior to the *GS Media* decision of September 2016, the CJEU hyperlinking decisions,[119] in particular *Svensson,*[120] did not expressly rely on the profit-making nature of the act of retransmission.

For the Court, hyperlinking is a form of retransmission, but not to a 'new public', and there is thus no communication to the public in addition to the first making available online by the linked-to site. The notion of a new public means that more people will benefit from, and enjoy, the work, and some economic reasoning thus underlies the criterion of the 'new public'. By denying the existence of a new public in the case of hyperlinking to a page containing authorized content, the *Svensson* decision already incorporates some economic reasoning, although not in an express way.

With *GS Media*, the Court puts the economic parameter at the forefront: after having underlined that 'it is relevant[121] that a "communication" ... is of a profit-making nature' (*GS Media*, §38), the Court establishes a new theory based on whether the hyperlink is posted for-profit (financial gain) or not. While the Court's approach blurs the distinction between direct and indirect liability, the circumstances under which the link is established now appear decisive, in particular whether there is some knowledge of the illicit nature of the linked-to content and whether the posting is carried out for-profit (*GS Media*, §49 ff). When the hyperlink is provided for 'the pursuit of financial gain' (*GS Media*, §55), there is a presumption of knowledge as to the illicit nature of the linked-to content.[122] The Court then considers that a communication to the public takes place.[123] For the Court, commercial or

119. The four hyperlinking decisions are: CJEU, 13 February 2014, C-466/12, ECLI: EU:C:2014:76 (*Svensson*); 21 October 2014, C-348/13, EU:C:2014:2315 (*BestWater*); 26 March 2015, C-279/13, ECLI:EU:C:2015:199 (*C-More Entertainment*); 8 September 2016, C-160/15, ECLI:EU:C:2016:644 (*GS Media*).
120. Contrary to *Svensson, GS Media* involves a link to a protected work (photo) which was made available on another website *without* the consent of the rightholder.
121. Note that in the previous decisions on the communication to the public (*see* above), the Court used the double negation in the English version: 'it is not irrelevant'.
122. The for profit provider of the link is supposed to carry out advance 'checks to ensure that the work concerned is not illegally published on the website to which those hyperlinks lead' (*GS Media*, §51).
123. While we can agree with the conclusion that the provider of the link is liable in those circumstances, the liability is indirect, not direct. On the important distinction between direct and indirect liability, *see* A. Strowel (ed.), *Peer-to-Peer File Sharing and Secondary Liability in Copyright Law*, Edward Elgar, 2009, in particular A. Strowel and V. Hanley, Secondary liability for copyright infringement with regard to hyperlinks, pp. 71–109.

for-profit transmissions of works by hyperlinking to unauthorized content can presumptively be considered as falling within copyright's scope.

By focusing its analysis on the pursuit of financial gain (and the presumed knowledge), the Court seems to embrace, more than in the past, an economic vision about the right of communication to the public. It would however be preferable for the Court to conduct a thorough analysis of the impact of the linking act on the market for the protected work and on the user's service before concluding that a communication to the public occurs. Such analysis would be helpful in other CJEU cases involving hyperlinking and additional acts, such as *Filmspeler* and *Ziggo*.[124] An economic analysis leads to the conclusion that there is a true exploitation of the works in those two cases. The CJEU came to the same conclusion, but did not rely on economic reasoning, and even less on a double market test. While the outcome of those cases is fine, the Court's reasoning is not satisfactory and blurs the legal concepts, including the notion of communication to the public (and the distinction between direct and indirect liability). Putting forward the economic dimension of communication to the public would help in achieving a reasonable application of copyright.

7.5 CONCLUSION

The chapter proposes reconstructing the two main rights within copyright and it thus helps to redefine the boundaries of copyright's exclusivity. By adequately redesigning copyright's boundaries, one can solve some difficult border(on)line cases. Sometimes, as in the case of TDM, the use of the works should remain outside the ambit of copyright. Sometimes the use, such as by aggregation platforms, deserves to fall under copyright. By reconstructing the two main rights as proposed here, a balanced application of copyright could arguably be reached.

124. *See* CJEU, 26 April 2017, C-527-15, ECLI:EU:C:2017:300 *(Stichting Brein v. Jack Frederik Wullmens, acting under the name of Filmspeler)* and 14 June 2017, C-610/15, ECLI:EU:C:2017:456 (*Stichting Brein v. Ziggo BV and XS4ALL Internet BV)* as well as the Opinions of the Advocate Generals in those two cases.

Chapter 8

Towards a Universal Right of Remuneration: Legalizing the Non-commercial Online Use of Works

P. Bernt Hugenholtz & João Pedro Quintais

8.1 INTRODUCTION

The digital revolution has brought advanced information technology and broadband connections to the average household. Ever since, the law of copyright has been in a state of deep crisis. Despite vigorous efforts by the copyright industries to enforce their rights against individuals, or against online intermediaries and platforms, copyright content is routinely being illegally reproduced and 'shared' by hundreds of millions of users worldwide.[1] This strongly suggests a growing gap between copyright norms and social norms in the digital environment.[2] The exclusive right that allows right holders to make access to a work conditional upon prior authorization and payment is increasingly perceived not as an incentive to produce and

1. J. Poort, J. Leenheer, J. van der Ham & C. Dumitru (2014), 'Baywatch: Two Approaches to Measure the Effects of Blocking Access to the Pirate Bay', *Telecommunications Policy*, 38(4), 383–392.
2. *See* D. Gervais (2004), 'The Price of Social Norms: Towards a Liability Regime for File-Sharing', *Journal of Intellectual Property Law*, 12, pp. 39–73; N. W. Netanel (2003), 'Impose a Noncommercial Use Levy to Allow Free Peer-to-Peer File Sharing'. *Harvard Journal of Law & Technology*, 17(1), pp. 1–84; J.-J. Vallbé, B. Bodó, C. Handke & J. P.

disseminate creative works, but as an obstacle to cultural freedoms and the principle of unlimited access.[3]

As empirical research points out, the overall welfare effects of mass unauthorized uses may be positive rather than negative,[4] particularly in digital networked environments where costs of distribution are close to zero.[5] This runs counter to the logic of copyright, i.e., to foster the production and dissemination of creative content by granting creators a temporary monopoly over their works. Thus technological change challenges not only the legal and economic landscape of copyright, but also its moral and socio-cultural underpinnings. However, as surveys also indicate, the idea that creators deserve a just reward for their creative endeavours is still generally endorsed.[6] In sum, while the exclusive right that has always been an essential feature of copyright has become practically unenforceable and is losing moral ground, the rights of creators to fair remuneration retain public support.

The spectacular market success of recently introduced *all-you-can-eat* content services, such as Spotify and Netflix, illustrate the need for non-exclusive approaches towards copyright. However, these business models appear to be flawed insofar as the revenue they generate is not fairly distributed among authors and artists.[7] More importantly, as empirical research also reveals, the introduction of these and similar new services has not eliminated the market for illegal sharing or streaming services.[8] While Spotify and its competitors seem to have somewhat reduced digital 'piracy' in the music sector, general levels of copyright infringement online have remained stable.[9] And despite the enormous market penetration of Netflix and similar audiovisual subscriber services in recent years, online piracy of audiovisual content, in particular television series, is still on the rise.[10]

Despite immense enforcement efforts by rights holders and their enforcement agents which have, at times, resulted in financial penalties and

---

Quintais (2015), 'Knocking on Heaven's Door. User Preferences on Digital Cultural Distribution'. Amsterdam: IViR, available at https://ssrn.com/abstract=2630519 (accessed 13 December 2017).

3. L. Lessig (2004), *Free Culture: The Nature and Future of Creativity*, The Penguin Press.
4. J. Karaganis (2011), *Media Piracy in Emerging Economies*. Brooklyn, SSRC.
5. Y. Benkler (2006), *The Wealth of Networks: How Social Production Transforms Markets and Freedom*, Yale University Press; A. Huygen et al. (2009), *Ups and Downs. Economic and Cultural Effects of File Sharing on Music, Film and Games*, TNO Report, Delft.
6. B.W. Schermer & M. Wubben (2011), *Feiten om te delen. Digitale contentdistributie in Nederland*. Amsterdam; Vallbé et al., 2015.
7. R. Kain (2016), 'Wat de opbrengsten van "Drank & Drugs" leren over de muziekindustrie van nu', *De Correspondent*.
8. TNS/Kantar Media (2017), *Online Copyright Infringement Tracker. Latest wave of research (March 2017) Overview and key findings*, UK IPO (July 2017), available at https://www.gov.uk/government/uploads/system/uploads/attachment_data/file/628704/OCI_-tracker-7th-wave.pdf (accessed 13 December 2017).
9. *Ibid.*
10. *Ibid. See also* Poort et al. 2014.

criminal sanctions for individual infringers, court-ordered injunctions against file-sharing facilitating platforms, and site-blocking orders against internet access providers, online piracy has by no means disappeared.

In fact, there is little conclusive evidence that enforcement effectively and significantly reduces online infringement.[11] True, rights holders have over time managed to shut down numerous illegal sharing platforms. However, as the recent take-up of web browser-integrated torrent-based sharing and streaming platforms such as 'Popcorn Time' illustrates, more than fifteen years after the emergence of Napster, unauthorized peer-to-peer (P2P) file sharing seems to thrive as ever before.[12] Empirical evidence suggests that litigation has at best a short-term deterrent effect before demand and supply relapse into infringing practices through alternative channels.[13] Furthermore, complex enforcement approaches, such as graduated-response systems, are costly and rarely efficient.[14] Perhaps the time has come to accept that file sharing will never go away.

Strict copyright enforcement may also be undesirable. On the one hand, it is now apparent that these measures alienate consumers and erode respect for and public legitimacy of copyright law.[15] On the other hand, strict

---

11. *See*: R. Giblin, 'Evaluating Graduated Response', *Columbia Journal of Law & the Arts*, 37(2), 147–210; C. Handke, B. Bodó & J.-J. Vallbé (2015), 'Going Means Trouble and Staying Makes It Double: The Value of Licensing Recorded Music Online', *Journal of Cultural Economics*; G.S. Lunney (2014), 'Copyright on the Internet: Consumer Copying and Collectives'. In Susy Frankel & D. Gervais (eds), *The Evolution and Equilibrium of Copyright in the Digital Age* (pp. 285–311), CUP; Poort et al., 2014; J. Poort & J. Weda (2015), 'Elvis Is Returning to the Building: Understanding a Decline in Unauthorized File Sharing', *Journal of Media Economics*, 28(2), 63–83.
12. *See*: D. Gervais (2010), 'Collective Management of Copyright: Theory and Practice in the Digital Age'. In D. Gervais (ed.), *Collective Management of Copyright and Related Rights* (2nd ed., pp. 1–28), Kluwer Law International, p. 16, arguing that mass-scale use has brought about a reshaping of the copyright landscape, making it apparent that, short of expelling users from the internet there is no effective way to prevent these practices; and A. Bridy (2009), 'Why Pirates (Still) Won't Behave: Regulating p2p in the Decade after Napster'. *Rutgers Law Journal*, p. 604, noting that '[a]s an empirical matter, the mass lawsuits appear to have had only a transitory deterrent effect'.
13. Poort et al. 2014, pp. 2–4, with further references.
14. *See*: C. Geiger (2014), 'Challenges for the Enforcement of Copyright in the Online World: Time for a New Approach'. *Max Planck Institute for Innovation and Competition Research Papers*, (14), pp. 5–11; R. Giblin, 'Beyond Graduated Response'. In S. Frankel & D. Gervais (eds), *The Evolution and Equilibrium of Copyright in the Digital Age* (pp. 81–112), CUP; Hadopi Drev – Département Recherche Etudes et Veille (2013), *Accès aux œuvres sur Internet*, 1–14, available at https://hadopi.fr/ressources/etudes/etude-acces-aux-oeuvres-sur-internet-inventaire-et-analyse-des-usages (accessed 13 December 2017); and P. Lescure (2013), *Mission 'Acte II de l'exception culturelle': contribution aux politiques culturelles à l'ère numérique*. Direction de l'information légale et administrative.
15. A. Peukert (2012), 'Why Do "Good People" Disregard Copyright on the Internet?'. In C. Geiger (ed.), *Criminal Enforcement Of Intellectual Property: A Handbook of Contemporary Research* (pp. 151–167), Edward Elgar Publishing.

enforcement of copyright risks impinging on fundamental rights and freedoms of both individuals and intermediaries. In several cases before the Court of Justice of the European Union (CJEU), various enforcement measures such as filtering, blocking, and disclosing internet service providers' (ISP) subscribers' information have been held to potentially conflict with fundamental rights and freedoms protected by the Charter of Fundamental Rights of the European Union (EU Charter),[16] such as freedom of expression and information, privacy in telecommunications, protection of personal data, and freedom to conduct a business.[17] The CJEU's jurisprudence requires that a 'fair balance' be reached between protecting copyright as a right of property and competing fundamental rights, sometimes giving primacy to the latter.[18] At the political level, similar considerations have led the EU legislature to reject systems of graduated response.[19]

This chapter assumes that unauthorized content sharing by individual users on a substantial scale is an inherent feature of the open internet, and will not disappear. It therefore proposes a system that legalizes such exchanges while guaranteeing fair remuneration to creators and other right holders. This is by no means a novel idea. Since the 2000s a rich body of academic literature has proposed and examined mechanisms that would legalize unauthorized P2P file sharing, while ensuring compensation to the authors and right holders concerned.[20] Recent years have seen various such proposals being advocated in the political realm, under various labels such as tax-and-royalty systems, '*licence globale*', content or culture flat-rate, file-sharing levy, sharing licence, or alternative reward systems.[21] These

16. Charter of Fundamental Rights of the European Union, OJ C 364/1, 18.12.2000.
17. *See*, e.g. Case C-275/06, *Productores de Música de España (Promusicae) v. Telefónica de España SAU*, 29.01.2008, ECLI:EU:C:2008:54; Case C-70/10, *Scarlet Extended SA v. Société belge des auteurs, compositeurs et éditeurs SCRL (SABAM)*, 24.11.2011, ECLI:EU:C:2011:771; Case C-360/10, *Belgische Vereniging van Auteurs, Componisten en Uitgevers CVBA (SABAM) v. Netlog NV*, 16.02.2012, ECLI:EU:C:2012:85; Case C-314/12, *UPC Telekabel Wien GmbH v. Constantin Film Verleih GmbH and Wega Filmproduktionsgesellschaft mbH*, 27.03.2014, ECLI:EU:C:2014:192.
18. In Europe, the legal basis for the cited rights is found in Arts 8 and 10 of the European Convention on Human Rights, and Arts 7, 8, 11, and 16 of the EU Charter.
19. *See* Art. 1(3)(a) of Council Directive 2002/21 of 7 March 2002 on a common regulatory framework for electronic communications networks and services as amended by Directive 2009/140/EC and Regulation 544/2009. *See also* European Parliament, Resolution on the transparency and state of play of the ACTA negotiations, P7_TA(2010)0058, 2010, para. 11.
20. *See*: W.W. Fisher (2004), *Promises to Keep: Technology, Law, and the Future of Entertainment*. Stanford University Press; Gervais, 2004; Netanel, 2003; A. Peukert (2005), 'A Bipolar Copyright System for the Digital Network Environment', *Hastings Communications & Entertainment Law Journal*, pp. 1–80.
21. J.P. Quintais (2014), *Legalizing File-Sharing: An Idea Whose Time Has Come Or Gone? Report from the Information Influx Conference 2014*, Amsterdam: IViR, available at https://ssrn.com/abstract=2510545 (accessed 13 December 2017).

proposals have at times received considerable political support, especially in Germany and France, although they have failed to make it into law.

Alternative compensation systems such as these, however, have an even longer history, and can be traced back to earlier times when low-cost reproduction technologies made mass unauthorized use viable, and copyright difficult or even undesirable to enforce. Drawing on these earlier precedents this chapter proposes a *universal* remuneration scheme that would generally allow reproducing and communicating works of authorship to the public over the internet, by individual users acting without commercial purpose, subject to a right of remuneration. As this chapter will argue, such a scheme would serve the main normative aims of copyright, i.e., to foster the dissemination of cultural works and to reward authors, while protecting users' privacy and freedom of expression and preserving the integrity of the internet. It would most likely also find favour with a majority of consumers.

The outline of this chapter is as follows. After a short glance in the rear-view mirror of copyright history in section 8.2, the contours of the proposed universal right of remuneration are outlined in section 8.3. As this section demonstrates, the proposed model of legalization might take on different legal forms – from voluntary collective agreements to a statutory (legal) licence. Section 8.4 thereafter discusses normative aspects of the proposed model, and queries to what extent the model would fit the general rationales of copyright, as expressed in EU secondary law. Section 8.5 speculates on the economic and social impact of the model, on the basis of recent empirical work carried out at the University of Amsterdam's Institute for Information Law (IViR). Section 8.6 offers conclusions.

8.2 LESSONS FROM THE PAST

The archetypal alternative compensation system is that of the private copying levies that emerged in Europe during the second half of the twentieth century. Not unlike file sharing in the early twenty-first century, private copying arose on a mass scale as reproduction technology (particularly tape recording equipment) became widely available and affordable for general consumer use in the course of the 1950s and 1960s. As attempts by the copyright industries to enforce copyright against consumers proved deeply unpopular, and risked impinging on citizens' rights of privacy and data protection, levy systems that compensated right holders while permitting private copying emerged as a socially viable and fair alternative legal solution.[22]

---

22. P.B. Hugenholtz (2012), 'The Story of the Tape Recorder and the History of Copyright Levies'. In B. Sherman & L. Wiseman (eds), *Copyright and the Challenge of the New* (pp. 179–196), Kluwer Law International.

The latter part of the last century also witnessed the emergence of several other new communication technologies that have similarly challenged traditional models of copyright exclusivity and enforcement, such as reprography and cable retransmission. This section briefly examines these precedents. Can the solutions developed for these problems of the past be applied *mutatis mutandis* to the problems of the digital future?

8.2.1 Private Copying Levies

As one of the authors of this chapter has described elsewhere in some detail, the emergence of tape recorders as a consumer product in the 1950s and 1960s gave rise to a range of problems that have haunted the law of copyright until today.[23] With the introduction of recording technology in private homes, which allowed normal consumers to produce high-quality copies of musical works with the proverbial 'push of a button', copyright law for the first time entered the private sphere.

In response to the early copyright claims made in Germany against manufacturers and owners of tape recording equipment, the *Bundesgerichtshof* (German Federal Court of Justice) produced an impressive body of case law that directly dealt with, and anticipated, many vexing questions that persist in the field of copyright until this day. Should copyright extend to, and be enforceable in the private sphere? Are copyright management systems compatible with privacy protection? Can manufacturers of reproduction technology be held accountable for facilitating copyright infringement, or is such technology essentially 'neutral'? How to fairly compensate authors for unauthorized use that is difficult or impossible to monitor and prohibit?

While some may disagree with the way the German Federal Court of Justice mediated between the competing claims of copyright and privacy, the tape recorder case law that the Court produced between 1953 and 1965 is remarkable, and deserves praise for the way the Court has attempted to reconcile the seemingly irreconcilable. Whereas the Court held that copyright protection does not stop short of the private sphere, and that authors deserve remuneration for home copying, it would not accept that copyright be enforced at the expense of the end users' right to informational privacy. Whereas the Court held manufacturers of recording equipment liable for facilitating copyright infringement without 'GEMA notice', the manufacturing of tape recording equipment was never actually prohibited. In retrospect, the Court's 'invention' of a levy scheme in its final and most famous tape recorder decision – *Personalausweise* of 1964 – was the logical consequence of its previous rulings: a pragmatic compromise between protecting authors'

23. *Ibid.*

interests, respecting consumers' privacy, and allowing a prosperous electronics industry to flourish.[24]

Following this series of remarkable judicial decisions, the German legislator introduced a statutory licence for private copying in the new copyright act of 1965. The new provision allowed private users to copy works for personal use subject to a levy. Initially, the statutory licence was aimed at home taping of sound recordings and audiovisual works. However, the system eventually extended to private copying of works on any medium, including digital media. As a consequence, a growing array of devices and media eventually became targets of the levy. Manufacturers and importers of these devices and media were made debtors of the levy, but were expected to pass it on to consumers. Due to the transaction costs of managing the system, the right to remuneration was subject to mandatory collective management.[25]

Having been 'invented' by the German Federal Court of Justice in 1964 and adopted into law in Germany in 1965, private copying levies became a staple of copyright law in most Member States of the EU, and many countries outside Europe. At EU level, an optional private copying limitation, combined with a right of 'fair compensation', eventually made its way into Article 5(2)(b) of Directive 2001/29/EC on the harmonization of certain aspects of copyright and related rights in the information society ('InfoSoc Directive'). With the notable exception of Cyprus, Malta, and the common law countries of the UK and Ireland, where private copying has never been fully legalized, most Member States gradually introduced a system of private copying levies and implemented the InfoSoc Directive's limitation.[26] Levies are imposed on the importation and manufacture of copying equipment, blank media, or both, collected by collective rights management organizations (CMOs) representing authors, performing artists, film producers and publishers, and ultimately paid for by consumers.

Aggregate private copying levy income in the EU has gradually risen over time, to more than EUR 700 million for the year 2014.[27] As tape recorders were replaced by digital recording and reproduction devices, levies have gradually spread into the digital realm, and thereby rekindled old

24. *Ibid.*
25. J.P. Quintais (2017), *Copyright in the Age of Online Access: Alternative Compensation Systems in EU Law*, Kluwer Law International.
26. *See* European Commission, 'Copyright and the Challenge of Technology', Green Paper, COM (88) 172 final, Brussels, 7.06.1988, pp. 102 et seq.; Hugenholtz, 2012, pp. 191–192; WIPO & Stichting de Thuiskopie (2016), *International Survey on Private Copying Law & Practice 2015*, Geneva. The UK introduced the limitation in 2014, but it was overturned during the course of 2015 due to issues with the lack of a fair compensation requirement in the national implementing regulations. *See* High Court of Justice of England and Wales, 17.07.2015, Case No. CO/5444/2014, [2015] EWHC 2041 (Admin).
27. WIPO & Stichting de Thuiskopie 2016, pp. 14–16.

discussions.[28] An example is the current debate on applying levies to cloud services.[29] With the scope of the private copying regime constantly expanding, the levy scheme has come to approximate a general compensation scheme for digital copying.[30] Private copying levies, it is noted, remain on the Commission's agenda to this very day as an 'on-going initiative'.[31]

8.2.2 Reprography

Another 'copyright crisis' of the past was prompted by the rise of photocopying in the 1970s.[32] In many countries this has similarly led to levy schemes on reproduction equipment,[33] ranging from traditional photocopying and fax machines to digital scanners and printers. In other countries reprography was legalized by way of a variety of legal mechanisms. At EU level, Article 5(2)(a) of the InfoSoc Directive allows Member States broad

28. P.B. Hugenholtz, L. Guibault & S. van Geffen (2003), *The Future of Levies in a Digital Environment*, Amsterdam: IViR.
29. *See* European Parliament resolution of 27 February 2014 on private copying levies (2013/2114(INI)), paras 28–30. On the private copying issues associated with cloud-based services, *see* M. Senftleben (2013), 'Breathing Space for Cloud-Based Business Models Exploring the Matrix of Copyright Limitations, Safe Harbours and Injunctions', *Jipitec*, 4(2), pp. 91–93. On stakeholders' concerns surrounding the interaction between cloud services and private copying, *see* Report on the responses to the Public Consultation on the Review of the EU Copyright Rules, Directorate General Internal Market and Services, Directorate D – Intellectual property, D1 – Copyright, July 2014, available at http://ec.europa.eu/internal_market/consultations/2013/copyright-rules/docs/contributions/consultation-report_en.pdf (accessed 13 December 2017), pp. 72–77. *See also* Case C-265/16, *VCAST Limited v. R.T.I. SpA*, 29.11. 2017, ECLI:EU:C:2017:913, on the application of the private copying exception to cloud services for the remote video recording of works.
30. The Draft Report on private copying levies, 2013/2114(INI), Committee on Legal Affairs (Rapporteur: Françoise Castex), para. 27, mentioned the need to 'examine the possibility of legalizing works sharing for non-commercial purposes so as to guarantee consumers access to a wide variety of content and real choice in terms of cultural diversity'. This paragraph was dropped in the final version of the document.
31. *See* M. van Eechoud, P.B. Hugenholtz, S. van Gompel, L. Guibault & N. Helberger (2009), *Harmonizing European Copyright Law: The Challenges of Better Lawmaking*, Kluwer Law International, p. 7; and J. Poort & J.P. Quintais (2013), 'The Levy Runs Dry: A Legal and Economic Analysis of EU Private Copying Levies', *Jipitec*, 4(3)3, 205–224. *See also* European Commission, *The EU Single Market, Copyright and Neighbouring Rights, Private copying levies*, available at http://ec.europa.eu/internal_market/copyright/levy_reform/index_en.htm (accessed 13 December 2017).
32. P.E. Geller (1991), 'Reprography and Other Processes of Mass Use', *Journal of the Copyright Society of the U.S.A.*, 38(21), 21–40.
33. A 2014 WIPO/IFFRO report identifies twenty-nine such countries worldwide. *See* WIPO & IFRRO (2014), *International Survey on Text and Image Copyright Levies*, Geneva.

freedom in legalizing reprography exemptions, subject to the provision of fair compensation for authors and other holders of the reproduction right.[34]

For example, Germany has established a legalization cum remuneration system for photocopying similar to the levy model developed for home taping, imposing a levy on both manufacturers of photocopying equipment and those who operate the equipment – educational and research institutions including schools, universities, and vocational training institutions and public libraries, as well as copy shops.[35]

France, on the other hand, has subjected the exercise of reprography rights to a system of compulsory collective rights management,[36] while the Nordic countries (unsurprisingly) apply their oft-praised system of extended collective licensing to photocopying by schools, government, and businesses.[37]

In the Netherlands, state entities, such as schools and libraries, and commercial enterprises, benefit from a statutory licence that allows these entities broad freedoms to make photocopies of news articles and scientific works, against a state-determined tariff of 4.5 Eurocents (formerly, 10 Dutch cents) per photocopy of copyright protected text. [38]

Finally, the UK permits educational photocopying by prescribing limited exemptions in default of negotiated licences; subjecting licences to review by the Copyright Tribunal; and authorizing the Secretary of State to expand the licence to encompass similar works.[39]

Like the rules on private copying, the EU reprography regime has gradually spread into the digital realm. In the *VG Wort* case, the CJEU validated this development by clarifying that the notion of 'reproductions effected by the use of any kind of photographic technique or by some other process having similar effects' within the meaning of Article 5(2)(a) of the InfoSoc Directive extends to digital copying processes, and 'must be

34. Article 5(2)(a) reads: 'Member States may provide for exceptions or limitations to the reproduction right provided for in Article 2 in the following cases: (a) in respect of reproductions on paper or any similar medium, effected by the use of any kind of photographic technique or by some other process having similar effects, with the exception of sheet music, provided that the rightholders receive fair compensation'.
35. WIPO & IFRRO 2014, pp. 69–77.
36. Articles L. 122-10 through L. 122-12, French Intellectual Property Code.
37. T. Koskinen-Olsson & V. Sigurdardottir (2016), 'Collective Management in the Nordic Countries'. In D. Gervais (ed.), *Collective Management of Copyright and Related Rights* (3rd ed., pp. 243–262), Kluwer Law International, p. 246.
38. D. Visser (2012), 'Private Copying'. In P.B. Hugenholtz, A.A. Quaedvlieg & D.J.G. Visser (eds), *A Century of Dutch Copyright Law: Auteurswet 1912-2012* (pp. 413–441), DeLex, pp. 424–428.
39. UK Copyright, Designs and Patents Act 1988 §§36, 136–137, 140–141. *See also* P. Goldstein & P.B. Hugenholtz (2013), *International Copyright. Principles, Law, and Practice* (3rd ed.), OUP, pp. 382–383.

interpreted as including reproductions effected using a printer and a personal computer, where the two are linked together'. [40]

8.2.3 Cable Retransmission

Yet another noteworthy precedent for de facto legalization is the special copyright regime for cable retransmission that has existed in the EU since 1993. During a large part of the 1970s and 1980s retransmission of television programmes by (then emerging) cable networks was carried out without permission, until courts gradually confirmed that cable retransmission was a restricted act.[41] The ensuing complexities of rights clearance eventually led to Directive 93/83/EEC of 27 September 1993 on the coordination of certain rules concerning copyright and rights related to copyright applicable to satellite broadcasting and cable retransmission ('SatCab Directive').

Articles 9–12 of the SatCab Directive contain a special regime for the cable retransmission right. The right applies only to simultaneous, unaltered, and unabridged retransmissions by cable of television or radio programmes originating in another Member State (thus excluding purely national retransmissions) following an initial broadcast over the air or by wire.[42] The definition of the right thus requires a primary transmission and the use of the specific technology of cable as the means for the secondary transmission.[43]

The regime is unique in EU law as it is the only case of mandatory collective management of an *exclusive right.* Article 9 of the SatCab Directive elucidates that CMOs manage the right to refuse or grant authorization to a cable operator for cable retransmission, even if rights holders have not transferred the management of their rights to a CMO. In this case, the CMO managing rights in the same category is deemed mandated to manage the rights of non-members. If more than one such CMO exists, rights holders may freely choose between the authorized CMOs. Only the original broadcasting organizations themselves are exempt from this system. [44]

Even before the SatCab Directive was adopted, collective management of cable rights had already become normal practice in many EU Member

40. Case C-457/11, *Verwertungsgesellschaft Wort (VG Wort) v. Kyocera and Others* (C-457/11) *and Canon Deutschland GmbH* (C-458/11), *and Fujitsu Technology Solutions GmbH* (C-459/11) *and Hewlett-Packard GmbH* (C-460/11) *v. Verwertungsgesellschaft Wort (VG Wort)*, 27.06.2013, ECLI:EU:C:2013:426.
41. M. de Cock Buning (2012), 'Cable Retransmission and Other Secondary Use'. In *A Century of Dutch Copyright Law: Auteurswet 1912–2012*, De Lex; S. Depreeuw (2014), *The Variable Scope of the Exclusive Economic Rights in Copyright*, Kluwer Law International, pp. 309–318.
42. Articles 1(3) and 8 SatCab Directive.
43. On the requirements of initial transmission and retransmission by cable, *see* Depreeuw 2014, pp. 393–400.
44. Article 9(1) and (2) SatCab Directive. Art. 10 SatCab Directive exempts broadcasting organizations from this regime.

States. In some cases, this practice was aided by (the threat of) compulsory licensing, as permitted under Article 11*bis* of the Berne Convention for the Protection of Artistic and Literary Works (BC). The directive would eventually reject the possibility of compulsory licensing for cable retransmission, in favour of its system of mandatory collective rights management.[45]

The SatCab Directive's regime of mandatory collective rights management seeks to ensure that cable operators are in a position to acquire all rights necessary to allow cable retransmission of broadcast programmes, and to avoid a situation in which holders of rights in parts of broadcast programmes who are not represented by a CMO enforce their exclusive rights individually vis-à-vis cable operators, thereby causing 'black-outs' in retransmitted programmes.[46] For all practical purposes, the SatCab Directive's special regime has created a situation whereby cable retransmission of broadcast television programmes is effectively legalized, subject to permission of the broadcasting organization and payment of remuneration to the rights holders through a CMO.

8.2.4 Lessons from the Past

What the legal models discussed in this brief historical account have in common is that they reconcile several competing social and economic goals: (1) facilitating rights management in situations where effective individual licensing and enforcement are difficult, impossible, or undesirable; (2) promoting access and use by private and institutional users to extensive catalogues of culturally and/or scientifically important works; (3) respecting rights to privacy and data protection by avoiding undue monitoring and enforcement within the private sphere; and (4) guaranteeing fair remuneration to authors and other right holders.

The result has been restriction of the nature or exercise of the exclusive right in favour of non-voluntary licensing regimes. In that process, remuneration and access have replaced exclusivity and enforcement at the centre of the regulation of mass use of copyright works.

Another common thread is that while these models of legalization were originally designed for 'analogue' uses of works, most if not all of these

45. On the rationale for the rejection of compulsory licensing of the cable retransmission right in the SatCab Directive, *see* Proposal for a Council Directive on the coordination of certain rules concerning copyright and neighbouring rights applicable to satellite broadcasting and cable retransmission, COM(91) 276 final – SYN 358, 11 September 1991, pp. 22–23 (paras 35, 36), and Recital 21 SatCab Directive. *See also* Depreeuw 2014, pp. 387–405.
46. *See*: Depreeuw 2014, pp. 402–406; Explanatory Memorandum SatCab Directive (n. 45), pp. 20, 24, 32; J. Rosén (2014), 'The Satellite and Cable Directive'. In I. Stamatoudi & P. Torremans (Eds.), *EU Copyright Law. A Commentary*, Edward Elgar, pp. 234–235.

regimes have proliferated into the digital domain. Viewed in this light, consolidating the existing array of use-specific systems, such as private copying, reprography, and cable retransmission, into a more general legalization and compensation scheme would not be a revolutionary step.

8.3 DRAWING THE CONTOURS OF A UNIVERSAL RIGHT OF REMUNERATION

The scheme proposed in this chapter would permit acts of reproducing and making available to the public online works of authorship *by individual users acting for non-commercial purposes*, while guaranteeing remuneration from intermediaries (e.g., ISPs and/or other platforms) to authors and other right holders through a CMO. Under the proposed system such acts would no longer infringe relevant rights of reproduction and communication to the public/making available, while eliminating secondary liability for facilitating such acts. Conversely, intermediaries would be obliged to fairly remunerate authors, performing artists, and (other) affected right holders (e.g., film producers, phonogram producers, and broadcasters).

8.3.1 Legal Qualification and Structure

The proposed model would permit qualifying users to use eligible content without the prior authorization of the right holders. Drawing inspiration from the schemes briefly discussed in section 8.2, one could imagine such a model taking on different legal forms, subject to varying degrees of legislative intervention: (a) voluntary collective licensing; (b) extended collective licensing; (c) mandatory collective management; (d) statutory licensing combined with a copyright limitation; and (e) tax models. These schemes would impose gradually increasing restrictions on the exercise and nature of the exclusive rights of reproduction and communication to the public, as currently designed and adopted in international treaties and EU law, most notably in Articles 2 and 3 of the InfoSoc Directive.

8.3.1.1 Voluntary Collective Licensing

The least interventionist model would be that of a voluntary collective licence. This is also the least restrictive form of collective rights management.[47] In this system, a CMO enters into a contract with users for the rights it represents. Depending on how the system is set up, a commercial user (e.g., an ISP) may contract directly with a CMO and obtain the right to sublicense

47. Gervais 2010, p. 26.

its customers, or act as a mere intermediary obtaining licences for the benefit of clients or subscribers, i.e., the actual end users of works.[48] It is possible to envisage a system where agreements are entered into by a consortium of CMOs and other (major) individual right holders on the one hand, and internet intermediaries and platforms, on the other.[49]

Depending on the subject matter and scope of the agreement, this collective licence would contractually legalize a variety of online consumptive and distributive uses of, e.g., musical works, phonograms, audiovisual works, and books, by the subscribers of these platforms. Note that since under prevailing copyright doctrine passive intermediaries are not deemed to commit acts of direct copyright infringement, the intermediaries would not – technically speaking – be the licensed agents. Instead, they would be entering into the licensing arrangement *on behalf of* their subscribers. Assuming *arguendo* that (most or all) holders of rights affected by such online uses would be represented in such voluntary agreement(s), no need for legislative intervention would arise. In other words, and in theory, this model could be realized immediately – if and when all parties concerned were to reach agreement.

In most EU Member States, voluntary collective licensing has been a common phenomenon for nearly a century, particularly in the area of music.[50] For example, the two main modes of (primary) exploitation of musical works – mechanical reproduction and broadcasting – have been licensed collectively since virtually the introduction of these technologies. In practice however, these voluntary collective licensing schemes closely resemble a model of statutory licensing.

National laws on the collective administration of rights, as recently harmonized by Directive 2014/26/EU on collective management of copyright and related rights and multi-territorial licensing of rights in musical works for online use in the internal market ('CRM Directive'), and general rules of competition law, have left CMOs little room to refuse licences to users willing to pay a fair price. The directive, for instance, requires that

48. C. Colin (2011) (sous la supervision et avec la participation de la Prof. Séverine Dusollier), *Etude de Faisabilité de Systèmes de Licences pour les Echanges d'Oeuvres sur internet. Rapport pour la SACD/SCAM – Belgique*, CRIDS, Facultés Universitaires Notre-Dame de la Paix – Namur, pp. 64–77. *See also* S. Dusollier & C. Colin (2011), 'Peer-to-Peer File Sharing and Copyright: What Could Be the Role of Collective Management?', *Columbia Journal of Law & the Arts*, 34, 823–824, arguing that the later use is known in civil law jurisdictions as a 'stipulation for another person'. It is also conceivable that certain licence agreements qualify ISPs as sub-licensors with the authority to license end users.

49. Gervais 2004.

50. *See* Commission Staff Working Document Impact Assessment Accompanying the document Proposal for a Directive of the European Parliament and of the Council on collective management of copyright and related rights and multi-territorial licensing of rights in musical works for online uses in the internal market, SWD(2012) 204 final, Brussels, 11.7.2012, pp. 2–7, on the use of voluntary licensing in the field of music.

negotiations with users for the purposes of licensing be carried out in good faith, in a timely manner, with disclosure of the necessary information, and that licensing terms be subject to objective and non-discriminatory criteria. In the same vein, refusals to license a particular service must be presented to users in a reasoned statement.[51] Moreover, collective rights management is subject to ever-intensifying government oversight and transparency rules, especially in the EU.[52]

Although organizations, of authors and performing artists in particular, have lobbied for the extension of this broadcasting model ('radio model') to the online world,[53] it seems unlikely that all stakeholders concerned would buy into such a voluntary arrangement in the foreseeable future, even if empirical research does suggest that such a system could significantly enhance royalty income for all right holders.[54] The current state of the online management of music rights in the EU is illustrative of this, showing that for certain rights, rights holders (in this case phonogram producers) are unwilling to entrust CMOs with their rights, preferring to manage them directly or through other vehicles, such as independent management entities.[55]

The participation problem is compounded for sectors of the content industry where – unlike the music, visual arts, and photography sectors – collective management of online rights is not common practice.[56] Examples include 'film producers, book publishers, journal and magazine publishers or games publishers', who typically handle mono- and multi-territorial licensing of online rights in Europe without the intervention of CMOs.[57] In the audiovisual sector, for instance, collective management is an accepted practice only for cable retransmission of audiovisual works.[58] It is therefore

51. *See*, e.g., Art. 16(1)–(3) and Recital 32 CRM Directive.
52. In this respect, *see* e.g., the rules on transparency and reporting in Arts 18–22 of the CRM Directive.
53. *See* e.g., letter of the Dutch Consumers' Union, NTB and FNV/KIEM to the Dutch Parliament (Second Chamber), 12 May 2014, available at http://goo.gl/Kbm2i4 (accessed 13 December 2017).
54. *See infra* 8.5.
55. The CRM Directive (Arts 23–32) prescribes a special regime for multi-territorial licensing of authors' online rights in musical works, which can be viewed as a model of reinforced voluntary collective licensing. Art. 3(b) CRM Directive defines 'independent management entity' as 'any organisation which is authorised by law or by way of assignment, licence or any other contractual arrangement to manage copyright or rights related to copyright on behalf of more than one rightholder, for the collective benefit of those rightholders, as its sole or main purpose, and which is: (i) neither owned nor controlled, directly or indirectly, wholly or in part, by rightholders; and (ii) organised on a for-profit basis'.
56. SWD CRM Directive 2012 (n. 50), p. 12.
57. *Ibid.* (& n. 50).
58. *See* AGICOA: Association of International Collective Management of Audiovisual Works, *Frequently asked questions*, available at http://www.agicoa.org/english/tools andhelp/faq.html#1c (accessed 13 December 2017). *See also* SWD CRM Directive

unlikely that a sufficiently high number of copyright owners in this sector would entrust the management of their online rights to CMOs.

In light of these challenges, this chapter proceeds on the assumption that legislative change is required for such a model to be put in place.

8.3.1.2 Extended Collective Licensing

An alternative that would require only modest legislative intervention would be to implement the proposed scheme under a system of extended collective licensing (ECL). This is a type of collective management that allows the offering of blanket licences for the entire repertoire(s) represented by a CMO.[59] In this system, a CMO first enters into voluntary agreements with rights holders. When the organization meets a representativeness criterion – meaning that it is authorized to manage a category of rights by a substantial number of domestic and foreign right holders – a statutory presumption extends its representation powers to non-member rights holders. This de jure extension increases the organization's repertoire and simplifies acquisition of rights.[60] In this way, ECL aims to solve the problem of providing 'fully covering licenses in cases of mass uses'.[61]

This legal mechanism was first developed and applied successfully in the Nordic countries (Denmark, Finland, Iceland, Norway, and Sweden) from the 1960s,[62] and is rapidly gaining popularity in other regions.[63] At EU

2012 (n. 50), p. 57 ('Collective licensing of film is essentially limited to cable retransmissions. These are licensed for each territory in which a cable network operates.')

59. SWD CRM Directive 2012 (n. 50), p. 197, defining blanket licence. *See also* T. Riis & Jens Schovsbo (2010), 'Extended Collective Licenses and the Nordic Experience: It's a Hybrid But Is It a Volvo or a Lemon?', *Columbia Journal of Law & the Arts*, 33(4), 473 & n. 4, noting that the first proposal for an ECL model is attributed to the Swedish law professor Svante Bergström.
60. SWD CRM Directive 2012 (n. 50), p. 45. *See also* D. Gervais (2016), 'Collective Management of Copyright: Theory and Practice in the Digital Age'. In D. Gervais (ed.), *Collective Management of Copyright and Related Rights* (3rd ed., pp. 3–30). Kluwer Law International, p. 24, and Riis & Schovsbo 2012, pp. 935–939.
61. Koskinen-Olsson & Sigurdardottir 2016, p. 250.
62. Riis & Jens Schovsbo 2010, pp. 472–474, noting that ECL was initially developed to respond to administration of broadcasting rights in 1961 and in 1974 begun to be used in a coordinated way for the management of copyright.
63. Gervais 2010, p. 21, 2016, pp. 23–24; Riis & Jens Schovsbo 2010, pp. 472, 478; SWD CRM Directive 2012 (n. 50), pp. 45–46. On the proposed application of ECL in the US, *see* P. Samuelson (2016), 'Extended Collective Licensing to Enable Mass Digitisation: A Critique of the US Copyright Office Proposal', *European Intellectual Property Review*, 38(2), 75–82. For central and Eastern Europe, *see* M. Ficsor & M. Chatalbashev (2016), 'Collective Management in Central and Eastern Europe'. In D. Gervais (ed.), *Collective Management of Copyright and Related Rights* (3rd ed., pp. 111–138), Kluwer Law International, pp. 130–133. Remarkably, a new copyright act of 2015 in Slovakia contains an ECL mechanism that applies *inter alia* to the making available right. *See* M. Gera (2016), 'Extended Collective Licensing under the New Slovak Copyright Act', *Journal of Intellectual Property Law & Practice*, 11(3), 170–171.

level, the SatCab Directive permits ECLs between CMOs and broadcasting organizations in respect of the exclusive right of communication to the public by satellite. The regime, which does not cover cinematographic works, requires that the act of communication simulcasts a terrestrial broadcast by the same broadcaster, and that the unrepresented rights holder has the right to opt out of the system.[64]

As noted, an ECL extends by operation of the law the terms of a voluntary collective licence to right holders not directly or indirectly represented by the licensing CMO. An ECL-based model thus presupposes the existence of a voluntary licence agreed between a CMO and one or more users. Likewise, the amount of remuneration would be contractually negotiated. It also assumes the presence of a CMO sufficiently representative for the category of rights and rights holders involved in the licence agreement.

A necessary prerequisite for the scheme proposed in this chapter to operate under an ECL would therefore be a mature and functional rights management infrastructure in all creative sectors concerned. While such an infrastructure is already in place for music, and rapidly developing for literary, journalistic, and visual works, this might be more problematic in the realm of audiovisual production, where copyright in respect of online uses is commonly owned by film producers who are generally unwilling to have their online rights collectively managed.[65]

Another likely requisite is the adoption of secondary EU law imposing an ECL framework for non-commercial acts of reproduction and communication to the public online, including a country of origin rule to enable cross-border effect for the national licences.[66] It would also have to address the possibility for rights holders to opt out of the system. Most, but not all, ECL provisions currently in force allow non-represented right holders to opt out of the collective licence. The opt-out consists of a declaration from rights holders to the CMO managing the ECL to the effect that they do not wish the organization to represent them. The declaration will come into effect after a reasonable deadline, following which the CMO will exclude the represented works or subject matter from its repertoire. As a whole, the procedure should be simple and not burdensome.[67]

---

64. Article 3(2)-(4) SatCab Directive.
65. *See supra* 8.3.1.1.
66. *See* L. Guibault (2015), 'Cultural Heritage Online? Settle It in the Country of Origin of the Work', *Jipitec* (6), 173–191, proposing the establishment of ECL systems as a solution for the clearance of rights for the digitisation and making available of works contained in the collection of a cultural heritage institution. Guibault argues 'that the only workable solution to the problem of extra-territorial application of ECL schemes would be to formally establish a "country of origin" principle'.
67. M. Ficsor (2016), 'Collective Rights Management from the Viewpoint of International Treaties, with Special Attention to the EU Acquis'. In D. Gervais (ed.), *Collective Management of Copyright in Europe* (3rd ed., pp. 31–79), Kluwer Law International, p. 68.

For the system to work, rights holders would have to, in the first place, adhere to collective management in large enough numbers to meet a representativeness threshold sufficient to trigger the extension effect. As noted above for voluntary collective licensing, the challenge is particularly great in sectors that do not have an established practice in collective rights management of online rights. Even if the challenge is met, the possibility of opting out is a constant threat to the viability of the system. Although in Nordic practice opt-outs rarely occur,[68] the question arises whether a universal remuneration scheme crafted in the form of an ECL including an opt-out could lead to a massive withdrawal of rights by reluctant holders, such as film producers, and thus undermine the entire scheme.

8.3.1.3 Mandatory Collective Rights Management

A variant of the ECL approach would be to subject the exercise of relevant rights in respect of acts of non-commercial reproduction and communication to the public to a system of mandatory collective rights management. Mandatory collective management is the most restrictive model of collective licensing. It prevents rights holders from directly exploiting their works, imposing by law the transfer or assignment of the exercise of rights to a CMO, which will act on their behalf.[69]

Mandatory collective management aims 'to ease copyright clearance, to reduce transaction costs for users and to limit fragmentation of copyrights'.[70] Due to the restrictions it imposes, the application of mandatory collective management to *exclusive* rights is subject to strict requirements and should be considered only when voluntary models prove unsuitable for exercise of the right.[71]

This variant of a legalization scheme would resemble the existing system of mandatory collective exercise of cable retransmission rights imposed by the SatCab Directive, explained above. Like the ECL model, this variant would build on existing structures of collective rights management. Likewise, the amount of remuneration would be negotiated between CMOs and intermediaries. A major difference however is that the mandatory collective management model would not allow any opt-outs, making this

---

68. P.B. Hugenholtz, S. van Gompel, L. Guibault & R. Obradović (2014), *Extended collective licensing: panacee voor massadigitalisering?*, Onderzoek in opdracht van het Ministerie van OCW. Amsterdam, p. 33.
69. L. Guibault (2002), *Copyright Limitations and Contracts: An Analysis of the Contractual Overridability of Limitations on Copyright*, Kluwer Law International, p. 26.
70. Dusollier & Colin 2011, p. 819.
71. *See* D. Gervais (2001), *Collective Management of Copyright and Neighbouring Rights in Canada: An International Perspective*, Canadian Heritage, available at http://works.bepress.com/daniel_gervais/28/ (accessed 13 Dec. 2017), pp. 37–38, and D. Sinacore-Guinn (1993), *Collective Administration of Copyrights and Neighboring Rights: International Practices, Procedures, and Organizations*, Little, Brown, p. 379.

model more akin to the system of statutory licensing discussed below. The similarities extend to procedural aspects, such as the determination of remuneration.[72]

However, these similarities do not necessarily result in identical legal qualification or effects on the exclusive right. In particular, it is often debated whether the application of mandatory collective management to exclusive rights affects their nature, turning them into remuneration or compensation rights, and thus justifying the analogy to a limitation-based statutory licence.[73] Although it is impossible for this chapter to address the issue in depth, some general remarks are justified.

Proponents of the broader applicability of this regime to exclusive rights argue that the effect of a statutory licence is to place copyright uses 'outside the field of exclusiveness',[74] meaning that the permission to use a work does not flow from the rights holder but from the law. In contrast, in mandatory collective management, the powers to authorize and enforce copyright shift from the authors to their representative – the CMO – whose sole purpose is to act for the collective benefit of its members; these, furthermore, have a say in defining the terms and conditions of licensing and distribution.[75] As a result, the argument goes, mandatory collective management merely modulates the options for exercise of copyright.[76]

Article 9(1) SatCab Directive is a case in point: the positive dimension of the right (to grant an authorization) remains intact, but there is some regulation of its exercise.[77] While moral rights are left untouched, the economic right remains transferable by contract or legal presumption. This

72. Guibault 2002, p. 26, noting that the process is analogous in mandatory collective management and compulsory licences, insofar as it relies on negotiation between all stakeholders involved and, failing an agreement, is subject to fixation by an administrative or judicial body.
73. *See* Quintais 2017, pp. 118–124, for a summary of this discussion.
74. C. Geiger (2007), 'The Role of The Three-Step Test in the Adaptation of Copyright Law to the Information Society', *UNESCO E-Copyright Bulletin* (January-March), p. 10.
75. *Ibid. See also* S. von Lewinski (2004), 'Mandatory Collective Administration of Exclusive Rights – A Case Study on its Compatibility with International and EC Copyright Law' *UNESCO E-Copyright Bulletin*, pp. 1–14.
76. *See* Geiger, 2007, p. 10, citing *IFPI Simulcast* (Commission Decision 2003/300/EC) and *Uradex* (Case C-169/05, *Uradex SCRL v. Union Professionnelle de la Radio et de la Télédistribution (RTD) and Société Intercommunale pour la Diffusion de la Télévision (BRUTELE)*, 1.06.2006, ECLI:EU:C:2006:365, where in relation to Art. 9(2) SatCab Directive the CJEU 'reaffirms that the Directive has, for legal certainty and simplification of procedures, implemented a mandatory collective management of the exclusive right of cable retransmission'. *See also* T. Dreier (2010), 'Satellite and Cable Directive'. In M. Walter & S. von Lewinski (eds), *European Copyright Law: A Commentary*, OUP; P.B. Hugenholtz (2006), 'Satellite and Cable Directive'. In T. Dreier & P.B. Hugenholtz (eds), *Concise European Copyright Law*, Kluwer Law International; Dusollier & Colin 2011, p. 827.
77. Dreier, 2010, p. 451. *See also* Hugenholtz 2006, pp. 280–281.

can happen for example in the case of a 'broadcasting organization initially transmitting the subject matter', provided no prior transfer of the right was made to a CMO. Where a transfer to the broadcaster occurs, the right cannot be subject to collective exercise.[78]

This view would be consistent with Recital 12 of the CRM Directive, which lists mandatory collective management as a type of arrangement 'concerning the management of rights', along with individual management or ECL.[79] It would also be consistent with the fact that this model of collective rights management is left out of the exhaustive menu of limitations and exceptions in Article 5 of the InfoSoc Directive.[80] In this light, from a legal-technical standpoint, to qualify it as a limitation appears inconsistent with the *acquis*.[81]

The 2016 decision of the CJEU in *Soulier and Doke* could, however, call into question this interpretation. The case concerns Articles L. 134-1 to L. 134-9 of the French Intellectual Property Code, which impose a hybrid model of mandatory collective management for certain acts of digital exploitation of out-of-print books.[82]

According to the CJEU, authors have an exclusive right to authorize or prohibit the use of their works, subject to the exhaustive list of limitations in the InfoSoc Directive. This exclusive right is preventive in nature, and therefore requires prior consent for the use of works.[83] Still, under certain conditions, that consent may be expressed implicitly.[84] For the implicit consent to be valid 'every author must actually be informed of the future use of his work by a third party and the means at his disposal to prohibit it if he so wishes'.[85]

In light of *Soulier and Doke*, the policy space available for mandatory collective management of exclusive rights under the InfoSoc Directive seems

78. Dreier 2010, pp. 451–452; Hugenholtz 2006, pp. 280–281. This interpretation is confirmed by Recital 28 SatCab Directive.
79. *Contra* Ficsor 2016, pp. 56–57.
80. von Lewinski 2004, pp. 13–14. *See also* G. Mazziotti (2008), *EU Digital Copyright Law and the End-User*, Springer, p. 265 & n. 872.
81. *See*: C. Bernault & A. Lebois (2005), *Peer-to-peer File Sharing and Literary and Artistic Property A Feasibility Study regarding a system of compensation for the exchange of works via the Internet*, Institute for Research in Private Law, University of Nantes (Translated from the French by Leigh Smith and Cedric Palazzetti), p. 67; Colin 2011, p. 44; Geiger 2014, p. 19 (& 81); Guibault 2002, pp. 26–27; P.B. Hugenholtz & R. L. Okediji (2008), *Conceiving an International Instrument on Limitations and Exceptions to Copyright*, Study supported by the Open Society Institute (OSI), available at https://ssrn.com/abstract=2017629 (accessed 13 December 2017); von Lewinski, 2004, p. 6. Reaching a similar conclusion with regard to the SatCab Directive, *se* A. Modot et al. (2011), *The 'Content Flat-Rate: A Solution to Illegal File-Sharing?'* Brussels, p. 121.
82. *See* Case C-301/15, *Marc Soulier and Sara Doke v. Premier ministre and Ministre de la Culture et de la Communication*, 16.11. 2016, ECLI:EU:C:2016:878, paras 14–16.
83. *Ibid.*, paras 33–34.
84. *Ibid.*, para. 35.
85. *Ibid.*, para. 38.

fairly limited. However, it is noted that the judgment does not address non-commercial use, or even clearly qualify mandatory collective rights management as a per se copyright limitation. As such, it is unclear whether a legalization proposal based on this rights management scheme would need to pass the three-step test, as would be the case for a limitation-based statutory licence.

8.3.1.4 Statutory Licensing Based on a Copyright Limitation

The most interventionist approach would be to structure the scheme in the form of a statutory licence combined with a compensated limitation or exception, similar to the above-mentioned rules on private copying and photocopying that exist in multiple Member States.

In this option, the exclusive rights of reproduction and making available to the public in Articles 2 and 3 InfoSoc Directive would be subject to one or more limitations covering the relevant online use of works by individuals. These limitations would be combined with a remuneration or compensation right, and complemented by rules setting up a system to administer and enforce the right, including the calculation, collection and distribution of compensation.

Following this approach, the law would precisely define the scope and subject matter of the legal authorization, designate the CMO charged with receiving remuneration on behalf of the rights holders, and identify the intermediaries that would be liable for payment of the remuneration/compensation. The law might also set the tariff, delegate this to a government or independent authority, or leave the tariff setting to a tripartite negotiation process between the CMO, intermediaries, and consumer representatives.[86]

The main benefit of a limitation-based statutory licence in this field is that it would efficiently solve most challenges associated with territorial and substantive fragmentation, as well as legal uncertainty, representing a comparative advantage in relation to pure collective management systems. However, in light of the limited scope available for statutory licensing in international law, a legalization model of this type would affect the nature of the exclusive rights of reproduction and communication to the public, transforming them (for the licensed uses) into non-exclusive rights of remuneration or compensation. Thus, in contrast to the legal structures discussed above, a limitation-based statutory licensing model would clearly need to comply with the 'three-step test' enshrined in EU law and various

86. *See* SWD CRM Directive 2012 (n. 50), p. 197, with a definition of compulsory licence that includes many of these elements.

international treaties.[87] Such issues of compliance are, however, outside the scope of this chapter.[88]

Also largely outside the scope of this chapter, but discussed briefly in section 8.3.2 below, are other aspects that should be addressed in the event a new copyright limitation is included in the *acquis* in the terms proposed above. These include, but are not limited to: the optional or mandatory nature of the proposed limitation; its articulation with existing (compensated and non-compensated) limitations to the affected exclusive rights, namely temporary and transient copying, private copying, quotations, incidental inclusion, caricature, parody, and pastiche[89]; the design of the remuneration or fair compensation right; and its relation to the right of fair compensation for digital private copying and to pre-existing contractual licences. [90]

8.3.1.5 Tax Model

Assuming the overall positive welfare effect of a combined system of legalization of content sharing and fair remuneration of creators, one might also consider a tax-based legalization system. Precedents for tax models in the field of copyright can be found in the fields of private copying and public lending.

Although most EU Member States have implemented Article 5(2)(b) InfoSoc Directive with device or media based levy systems, at least three countries – Norway (since 1995), Spain (between 2012 and 2016), and Finland (since 2015) – have adopted systems whereby fair compensation to rights holders is paid out of the state budget.[91] The Norwegian Copyright Act, for example, states that authors shall receive fair compensation through annual grants via the state budget.[92] The fair compensation is 'funded by the Norwegian Government, as a post on the national budget', and subsequently collected by an umbrella CMO (Norwaco), which then distributes it to member (secondary) organizations representing national and foreign categories of rights holders.[93]

There are doubts as to whether such schemes are compatible with EU law. In the recent *EGEDA* case, for instance, the CJEU noted that under the

87. *See*: Art. 9(2) Berne Convention for the Protection of Literary and Artistic Works; Art. 10(1) and (2) WIPO Copyright Treaty; Art. 16(2) WIPO Performances and Phonograms Treaty; Arts 13, 17, 26(2), and 30 TRIPS Agreement; Art. 5(5) InfoSoc Directive.
88. For an analysis of the compliance of such a limitation-based system with the three-step test Quintais 2017, pp. 263–315.
89. Article 5(1), 5(2)(b), 5(3)(d), (i), and (k) InfoSoc Directive.
90. *See* Quintais 2017, for an analysis of these aspects.
91. WIPO & Stichting de Thuiskopie, 2016, p. 8. *See also* Opinion of Advocate General Szpunar delivered on 19.01.2016, Case C-470/14, *EGEDA and Others v. Administración del Estado and Others*, ECLI:EU:C:2016:24, para. 16.
92. *See* Art. 12 Norwegian Copyright Act.
93. WIPO (2012), *International Survey on Private Copying. Law & Practice 2012*, Geneva, pp. 102–103. A more recent WIPO survey on private copying confirms that '[t]he

Spanish law at issue the revenue allocated to the payment of fair compensation was financed from the general budget resources, i.e., by all taxpayers, including legal persons.[94] Furthermore, the law did not contemplate exemptions for legal persons in this respect, or allow for their reimbursement.[95] Therefore, because it failed to 'guarantee that the cost of compensation is ultimately borne solely by the users of private copies', the Spanish scheme was deemed incompatible with Article 5(2)(b) of the InfoSoc Directive.[96] However, this judgment does not preclude a system that finances fair compensation for private copying through the state budget, provided the same ensures payment of fair compensation to rights holders and guarantees its actual recovery, while excluding payments from legal persons. [97] Be that as it may, the *EGEDA* ruling in fact led the Spanish Supreme Court to annul some of the controversial provisions of the Spanish law at issue.[98]

Similar tax-based remuneration schemes exist in the field of public lending. Over the course of the twentieth century, the increase in lending activities by public libraries caused several European countries to introduce a public lending right for authors.[99] In most cases, national laws' initial implementation of this right was done outside the copyright system.[100] This

remuneration is funded by the Norwegian government as an item on the national budget' and '[t]he rate is set unilaterally in the national budget each year'. *See* WIPO & Stichting de Thuiskopie 2016, p. 123.

94. Case C-470/14, *EGEDA and Others v. Administración del Estado and AMETIC*, 09.06.2016, ECLI:EU:C:2016:418, para. 39.
95. *Ibid.*, para. 40.
96. *Ibid.*, paras 41–42. On this point the CJEU strays from the AG's Opinion, according to which financing the compensation from the General State Budget is consistent with the InfoSoc Directive, 'since this is not a matter of extending the scope of a levy to all taxpayers, but of a system of financing based on a different rationale'. *See Opinion AG in EGEDA*, para. 52.
97. *EGEDA*, para. 37. For example, national laws could provide for a scheme for exempting legal persons' taxes from inclusion in this budgetary item or, alternatively, allow legal persons to seek reimbursement of their taxes used for this purpose. Another possibility, briefly addressed by the AG, would be to introduce a specific tax or duty on natural persons to finance fair compensation. *See Opinion AG in EGEDA*, para. 51. Whether any of these variants is practical or cost-effective is, of course, a separate empirical question.
98. Supreme Court Spain, 10.11.2016, Case No. 4832/2016, ECLI:ES:TS:2016:4832.
99. Report from the Commission to the Council, the European Parliament and the Economic and Social Committee on the Public Lending Right in the European Union, COM (2002) 502 final, Brussels, 12.09.2002, p. 3.
100. *Ibid.*, pp. 3–4. *See also* ALAI (1983), *Public Lending Right. Reports of an ALAI-Symposium and Additional Materials*, H. Cohen Jehoram (ed.), Amsterdam: Kluwer Law and Taxation Publishers: 'it is possible to distinguish two main groups: countries that do not recognize and those that apply the public lending right. Among the latter, some have sought a solution outside the province of copyright, and in fact only one, the Federal Republic of Germany, has accepted public lending right as an integral part of its copyright law'. Countries that did not recognize any public lending right were Italy, France, and Belgium (to the extent that the existing law was considered a 'dead letter'). For a description of the UK example of the 1979 Public Lending Right Act, *see ibid.*

occurred through multiple mechanisms, including national funds constituted by library subscription taxes, and direct budget allocation of taxes. Only later was the public lending right incorporated into national copyright laws and, eventually, into EU law through a harmonized exclusive or (optional) remuneration right.[101]

For mass online use of works, a tax-based scheme would have the clear advantage of reduced transaction costs compared with the collective licensing models discussed above. No requirement for negotiating tariffs between CMOs and intermediaries would arise. Tariffs could be simply set by the state.

Like the statutory licensing model discussed above, a tax-remunerated legalization scheme would need to pass the 'three-step test'. This would, *inter alia*, require that the state funds allocated to the scheme are clearly earmarked, and that a link between the permitted use of works and remuneration paid to rights holders is preserved.

In terms of political viability this model clearly ranks lower than the models previously discussed. Allocating general state funds to compensate creators is hardly a popular proposition in times of economic crisis and budgetary restraints.

8.3.2 Scope of the Proposed Scheme

What uses of which types of content would be allowed under the proposed scheme?

8.3.2.1 Authorized Non-commercial Use

A first question concerns the scope of the scheme. Should the model be technology-neutral, and therefore apply to all acts of reproduction and making available to the public, or should it be limited to online uses? While a truly 'universal' scheme would imply its technology-neutral application to all kinds of copyright-relevant use, whether online or 'in the analogue world', the main *raison d'être* of the scheme would not necessitate such an all-encompassing reach. Given the scheme's underlying premise, i.e., that copyright is no longer effectively and efficiently enforceable in the online world, it would be disproportionate to extend it beyond the digital realm. The scheme would, therefore, only apply to digital content exchange and use of

101. Articles 2(1)(b) and 6 of Council Directive 92/100/EEC, of 19 November 1992 on rental right and lending right and on certain rights related to copyright in the field of intellectual property, 1992 O.J. (L 346/61) as republished and amended by Directive 2006/115/EC of the European Parliament and of the Council of 12 December 2006 (codified version), 2006 O.J. (L 376/28). For an analysis of the public lending right in several countries prior to the implementation of this directive, *see* ALAI, 1983.

works over the internet, including other interconnected wired or wireless networks.

The proposed scheme would distinguish between *non-commercial* uses that would be permitted, and other uses for which the exclusive rights remain intact. While distinguishing a commercial motive (subjective aspect) or nature (objective aspect) of an act may not always be an easy task, a test of 'commerciality' is not unknown in copyright law or in the law of intellectual property generally.

For example, Article 5(2)(b) of the InfoSoc Directive permits exceptions or limitations:

> in respect of reproductions on any medium made by a natural person for private use and for ends that are neither directly nor indirectly commercial, on condition that the rightholders receive fair compensation [...].

The term 'commercial' also regularly occurs elsewhere in Article 5 of the directive, be it a test of 'commercial nature', 'commercial purpose', or 'commercial advantage'.[102]

Moreover, Article 5(3) of the recently adopted CRM Directive mandates that CMOs ensure rights holders have:

> the right to grant licences for non-commercial uses of any rights, categories of rights or types of works and other subject-matter that they may choose.

For another example, Article 61 of the Agreement on Trade-Related Aspects of Intellectual Property Law (TRIPS) uses the objective concept of 'commercial scale', which has been interpreted as referring to 'counterfeiting or piracy carried on at the magnitude and extent of typical or usual commercial activity with respect to a given product in a given market'.[103]

Like the existing regime for private copying, the proposed scheme would allow individual users to reproduce and make available content without direct or indirect commercial motive. To be sure, the notion of 'commercial' is a much narrower concept than – and should not be confused with – the notion of 'economic'. Whereas non-commercial acts of file sharing or streaming would be exempted under the proposed scheme, they would likely have an economic impact.

Thus, the concept of 'non-commercial' use should refer to online activities carried out by individuals for personal enjoyment/consumption of works and outside the market sphere. The concept should exclude online use of a work for profit, within the context of a business activity of an individual,

102. *See* Art. 5(2) and (3) InfoSoc Directive.

103. WTO, China – *Measures Affecting the Protection and Enforcement of Intellectual Property Rights*, WT/DS362/15, 26.01.09, para. 7.577.

or directed at a commercial advantage or monetary compensation.[104] For example, such a licence would not cover online use of works combined with advertisement or similar activities intended to generate income for the user or for him and a third party.[105] The third parties here are digital platforms, like Google, whose main business model is online advertisement.[106] The proposed scheme would also not extend to content services provided by entrepreneurs, either because they are not individuals or because their use triggers the application of an exclusive right and does not qualify as non-commercial. As presently, these service providers would, therefore, require licences from right holders.

8.3.2.2 Subject Matter Covered

A second question is whether the model should be applied to all types of content, including content categories that to date have remained largely exempt from statutory or collective licensing, such as software, databases, and video games.

Considering the model's main aim of providing wholesale legalization, one would ideally envisage a licence covering a broad spectrum of copyright protected works. On the other hand, one could justify a more limited, category-based approach given the fact that the scale of online 'piracy' differs markedly per sector. For example, while piracy is (and remains) rampant for audiovisual content and – to a more limited extent – also for music, illegal exchanges of software, databases, and games seem to be less pervasive.[107]

These diverging piracy rates are due to a number of factors, including the effectiveness and consumer acceptance of digital rights management, and in particular the gradual shift towards service-based models in sectors such as software, databases, and games, making them less vulnerable to piracy.[108]

Moreover, a category-based approach could more easily build on infrastructures of collective rights management that have developed and matured in certain sectors, such as music and literature, but are less advanced or even non-existent in others.

---

104. Quintais 2017, pp. 391–394. Note that such a design would correspond well with the current case law of the CJEU on the online right of communication to the public, which relies on a 'for-profit' condition to determine whether a user has knowledge of the unlawful nature of the source of a work to which he is linking, and whether such act is ultimately restricted by copyright. Cf. Case C-160/15, *GS Media BV v. Sanoma Media Netherlands BV and Others*, 8.09.2016, ECLI:EU:C:2016:644, paras 47–52.
105. Quintais 2017, pp. 391–394.
106. N. van Eijk et al. (2015), *Digital Platforms: An Analytical Framework for Identifying and Evaluating Policy Options*. TNO, IViR, and Ecorys, available at http://hdl.handle.net/11245/1.504534 (accessed 13 December 2017), pp. 12–13.
107. TNS/Kantar Media, 2017.
108. *Ibid. See also* Quintais 2017, pp. 388–389, with further references.

In sum, a more proportionate approach would be to limit the model to traditional categories of copyright and neighbouring rights protected creations: music, text, visual, and video.

The scheme should certainly only apply to works lawfully published or made available online. It would not however impose a requirement of lawfulness of source of the copy of a work for its subsequent online use by individuals, or else the model's aim of general legalization would be defeated. This would be a marked difference from the current approach of CJEU case law on exclusive rights, which imposes liability for private reproductions made from unauthorized sources and for the posting of hyperlinks to works made available online without the consent of copyright holders.[109]

8.3.2.3 Intermediaries

Perhaps the most vexing issue is to define the categories of intermediaries that would be obliged to remunerate creators. This enquiry does not require a preliminary analysis of the liability of intermediaries – whether primary or secondary – for acts of copyright infringement committed by individuals using their services. Like with existing private copying levy models, the obligation to pay remuneration could be largely separated from copyright liability issues. In the online context, such separation would be inevitable anyway, given the safe harbours established for these actors in Directive 2000/31/EC on certain legal aspects of information society services, in particular electronic commerce, in the Internal Market ('E-Commerce Directive').[110]

What is more important is to designate intermediaries that are capable of efficiently and reliably paying remuneration to right holders or their CMOs, and of subsequently passing on the costs to the users. Another pragmatic (and political) factor could be to look for the types of intermediary that currently 'suffer' most from enforcement actions on the part of the right holders, and would therefore be inclined to commit to a compensation model.

All this makes broadband ISPs the obvious candidates,[111] since they: (1) have 'deep pockets', (2) have an existing billing relationship with users/ consumers, and (3) are increasingly targeted by copyright holders – and in

109. On the reduction of the scope of the private copying limitation, *see* C-435/12, *ACI Adam BV and Others v. Stichting de Thuiskopie and Stichting Onderhandelingen Thuiskopie* vergoeding, 10.04.2014, ECLI:EU:C:2014:254, and its progeny. On hyperlinking to unauthorized sources, *see GS Media.*

110. *See* Arts 12–15 E-Commerce Directive.

111. ISP involvement in such a system would be economically efficient. Not only would a (flat or metered) surcharge on the internet subscription payment for households reduce transaction costs among users, but it would also facilitate the provision of adequate compensation to rights holders. *See* Handke, Bodó & Vallbé 2015, analysing the recorded music market in the Netherlands.

future policy scenarios might be legally charged with increasing degrees of 'responsibility' for copyright compliance. For instance, the current policy orientation of EU institutions and industry stakeholders is towards increasing the role and collaboration of online intermediaries in enforcement measures, such as filtering and blocking, which entail costs and additional liability exposure for these intermediaries.[112] Together, these factors might inspire ISPs to more easily buy into a future model of alternative compensation.

Other possible candidates are content sharing platforms such as YouTube or Facebook. While the pockets of these platforms may be even deeper, these intermediaries are not as well-positioned to transfer the costs of the licence to the end users, since they do not usually have a direct billing relationship with consumers. Moreover, in recent years, YouTube, Facebook and similar platforms have invested in and developed sophisticated automated content filtering and identification systems to reduce the amount of unauthorized content uploaded by their users, further offering different modalities of individual content licensing.[113] In addition, many platforms have entered into collective licensing agreements. [114] All this would appear to make these platforms less likely candidates, despite increasing calls to that

112. At institutional level, *see*, e.g.: Communication from the Commission to the European Parliament, the Council, the European Economic and Social Committee and the Committee of the Regions, *on a Single Market for Intellectual Property Rights boosting creativity and innovation to provide economic growth, high quality jobs and first class products and services in Europe*, COM(2011) 287 final (24.05.2011), pp. 22–23; Commission Staff Working Document *E-commerce Action plan 2012-2015 – State of play 2013*, SWD(2013) 153 final, 23.04.2013, pp. 17–18; Communication from the Commission to the European Parliament, the Council, the European Economic and Social Committee and the Committee of the Regions, *A Digital Single Market Strategy for Europe*, COM(2015) 192 final (6.5.2015), pp. 7–8 (discussing a novel 'duty of care' on intermediaries), pp. 11–12; Commission Staff Working Document *A Digital Single Market Strategy for Europe – Analysis and Evidence*, SWD(2015) 100 final (6.5.2015), pp. 55–57; European Parliament resolution of 9 July 2015 on the implementation of Directive 2001/29/EC of the European Parliament and of the Council of 22 May 2001 on the harmonisation of certain aspects of copyright and related rights in the information society (2014/2256(INI)), para. 66 ('stresses the need to adjust the definition of the status of intermediary in the current digital environment'); Communication from the Commission to the European Parliament, the Council, the European Economic and Social Committee and the Committee of the Regions, *Towards a modern, more European copyright framework*, COM(2015) 626 final (9.12.2015), pp. 10–11. *See also* Giblin, 2014 (n. 11), pp. 58–59, describing the enforcement strategy of the content industries since 2007 against online intermediaries.
113. *See*, e.g., YouTube, *How Content ID Works*, available at https://support.google.com/youtube/answer/2797370?hl=en (accessed 13 December 2017); and Facebook, Rights Manager, available at https://rightsmanager.fb.com (accessed 13 December 2017).
114. *See*, e.g., N. Rauer (2016), 'Germany: YouTube and GEMA reach a licensing agreement on music videos', *Lexology*, available at https://www.lexology.com/library/detail.aspx?g=4446f517-d42c-4ccd-8d15-8f67c2b70f4e (accessed 13 December 2017).

effect and legislative proposals to increase their liability for acts of end users.[115]

Prima facie, file sharing facilitators such as The Pirate Bay (TPB), Popcorn Time, and similar torrent-based platforms seem to be the prime candidates for paying remuneration. Upon further reflection, however, they are not. Rogue operators such as TPB are clearly not bona fide and reliable debtors, nor are they in a position to directly pass on the costs of remuneration to consumers. In fact, whether these operators actually exist de jure as natural or legal persons is doubtful. More likely, these actors are merely 'brands' used by fluid groups of loosely organized individuals – an important reason why legal actions against TPB and its offspring have remained largely ineffective.[116]

Past experience with private levying schemes teaches us another lesson. For an alternative compensation scheme to operate successfully, it should be targeted and not proliferate indiscriminately across all media.[117] This is yet another powerful argument to impose the universal compensation scheme obligation on ISPs, and not extend it to providers of value-added services at higher levels in the communications hierarchy.

To make this system effective, ISPs should be allowed to pass on the 'broadband levy' to end users in the price of their household (but not professional) subscriptions. As a matter of transparency, this surcharge should be visible to end users, as is the levy in existing private copying systems.[118]

8.3.2.4 Compensation

A fourth question concerns the issue of compensation. Under this heading, at least two main topics should be addressed. The first relates to the basic

115. *See* recent proposals to subject YouTube and similar platforms to a statutory remuneration right. *See* P. Sirinelli, J.-A. Benazeraf & A. Bensamoun (2015), High Council for Literary and Artistic Property (France), *Mission to Link Directives 2000/31 and 2001/29: Report and Proposals*. On legislative efforts at EU level, note the so-called value gap proposal in Art. 13 and Recital 38 of the Proposal for a Directive of the European Parliament and of the Council on copyright in the Digital Single Market, COM(2016)593. Art. 13 aims to regulate the use of protected content by information society providers giving access to large amounts of works and other subject matter uploaded by their users. For criticism, *see* S. Stalla-Bourdillon et al. (2016), 'A Brief Exegesis of the Proposed Copyright Directive', available at https://ssrn.com/abstract=2875296 (accessed 13 December 2017).
116. Poort, Leenheer, van der Ham & Dumitru 2014.
117. Hugenholtz, Guibault & van Geffen 2003.
118. As with certain debtors of the private copying levy, ISPs may choose to compete on price by absorbing the broadband levy. *See* A. Roßnagel, S. Jandt, C. Schnabel & A. Yliniva-Hoffman (2009), *The Admissibility of a Culture Flat-Rate under National and European Law,* Saarbrücken/Kassel, p. 22.

operation and management of the system, including the calculation, collection, and distribution of the compensation. The second refers to the nature of the universal remuneration or compensation right. As we shall see, the two topics are intertwined.

The main questions regarding the management of the system are how to determine: (1) the total amount of compensation generated by the proposed system; and (2) the specific amount paid by the users for the authorized use.

So far as the total amount generated by the system is concerned, in collective rights management models that quantum is determined through contractual negotiation and tariff setting by CMOs, and is usually not too problematic. In statutory licence or tax-funded models, the determination of the level of the tariffs is imposed by law, subject to a general standard of 'fair' compensation or 'equitable' remuneration. This process could include intervention by a government agency and/or stakeholder negotiations (involving right holders, intermediaries, and consumers), subject to judicial or administrative review.[119]

In this regard, the aforementioned empirical work carried out by IViR may be helpful. This research suggests a general consumer preference for a flat fee structure, and a willingness to pay a substantial monthly fee for the right to download and exchange a wide range of works. More specifically, the research concludes that a limitation-based statutory licence for the rights of reproduction and communication to the public applying to online recorded music has the potential to fully compensate rights holders. For instance, EUR 1.74 surcharge on the ISP subscription for all households with internet connection would equate to the entire revenues in the Dutch physical and digital market for recorded music in 2012, including all conventional purchases of recorded music, of approximately EUR 144 million.[120] As users are willing to pay a monthly amount well above that price point, this system would be welfare increasing, even after correcting the results for overestimation.[121]

Collection of compensation is usually the competence of a CMO designated in the system. For example, the law may mandate an umbrella CMO to administer the system, including collection and subsequent distribution to second-level organizations that represent different categories of

119. Quintais 2017, pp. 143–150.

120. Revenues are calculated by resorting to industry statistics, such as IFPI (2013), *IFPI Digital Music Report 2013: Engine of a digital world*, available at http://www.ifpi.org/downloads/dmr2013-full-report_english.pdf (accessed 13 December 2017), which estimates rights holders' revenues in the Dutch recorded music market at EUR 143.6 million. The focus is on revenues rather than profits due to the lack of reliable information on costs. Data on private copying levies collected in the Netherlands was taken from WIPO, 2013. The results assume the unlikely scenario that an alternative compensation system substitutes all current sales of recorded music (perfect substitution) and provides no cost savings. *See* Handke et al. 2015.

121. *Ibid.*

rights holders. As noted above, the CMO will collect the amount from an intermediary debtor (an ISP or online service provider), who may then have the right to pass it on to the final user.

The distribution of the compensation involves several elements familiar to collective rights management. First, it is necessary to define the beneficiaries of the compensation, namely the categories of rights holders entitled to it. Assuming the universal remuneration right is designed as a compensated limitation to the rights of reproduction and communication to the public in the InfoSoc Directive, it would make sense to design it as a fair compensation right benefiting the rights holders identified in Articles 2 and 3 thereof.[122] This qualification also has implications for the calculation of amounts, as fair compensation should reflect the *harm* suffered by creators and other holders of the affected exclusive rights.[123]

The allocation of the sums collected to each category is determined by law or stakeholder negotiation. Here, again, if we follow the *Luksan* and *Reprobel* approach, creators should be allocated a fixed share due to the unwaivable nature of their fair compensation rights. [124]

The subsequent issue is how to divide the compensation between individual rights holders within a category. Individual distribution could be the competence of second-level CMOs representing each category or even, if judged efficient, the umbrella organization administering the system. It is common in proposals for the legalization of file sharing to suggest distributing the compensation based on measurements of online use, surveys, contingent valuation methods, or negotiated distribution keys.[125]

Methods for measurement of online use include anonymous monitoring, sampling, tracking, census, or a combination thereof. Proposals that rely on monitoring online use typically require some type of registration of works or rights management information in a central registry to enable this measurement. More sophisticated proposals consider the length of works and trace units of consumption (e.g., download or stream counts), or use decentralized metrics or contingent valuation surveys (e.g., by having end users assume a role in distribution through voting mechanisms or user

122. Case C-462/09, *Stichting de Thuiskopie v. Opus Supplies Deutschland GmbH and Others*, 16.06.2011 ECLI:EU:C:2011:397, para. 34; and Case C-572/13, *Hewlett-Packard Belgium SPRL v. Reprobel SCRL*, 12.11.2015, ECLI:EU:C:2015:750, paras 44–49. *See also* European Copyright Society (2015), Position paper on the Opinion of the Advocate General in the case *HP Belgium v. Reprobel* pending before the Court of Justice of the EU (*Hewlett-Packard Belgium SPRL v. Reprobel SCRL*, C-572/13), available at https://europeancopyrightsocietydotorg.files.wordpress.com/2015/12/opinion-in-case-c572_13-hp-belgium-reprobel-2015.pdf (accessed 13 December 2017).
123. Case C-467/08, *Padawan SL v. Sociedad General de Autores y Editores de España (SGAE)*, 21.10.2010, ECLI:EU:C:2010:620, paras 40–42; *Reprobel*, paras 36, 48–49.
124. Case C-277/10, *Martin Luksan v. Petrus van der Let*, 9.02.2012, ECLI:EU:C:2012:65, paras 88 et seq.; *Reprobel*, paras 44–49.
125. Quintais 2017, pp. 146–150.

sampling).[126] Whatever the method, it should by design ensure protection of the right to privacy and personal data of end users, as that constitutes a core normative justification for legalization as an alternative to copyright enforcement. For the same reason, the system should also restrict the possibility for end users to 'pay' with personal data as a counter-performance or consideration for the licence to use works, a payment method expressly recognized in the proposed Digital Content Directive.[127]

8.4 NORMATIVE CONSIDERATIONS

Whereas alternative compensation schemes such as the one explored in this chapter are on the fringes or beyond the exclusivity paradigm of classic copyright law, the model proposed here would not necessarily run counter to the normative considerations (the rationales) underlying EU copyright law. Judging from the preambles of the ten copyright directives currently in place – in particular the InfoSoc Directive–,[128] and from the growing body of case law of the CJEU, copyright law in the EU is based on an amalgam of utilitarian (i.e., economic) and moral considerations – reflecting the main traditions of copyright law in Europe: British *copyright* and continental *authors' rights*. In the EU, copyright is also informed by the economic freedoms of the Treaty on the Functioning of the European Union (TFEU), and by the fundamental rights and freedoms enshrined in the EU Charter.[129]

The mixed foundations of EU copyright law do not, therefore, present a single benchmark against which the proposed model can be unequivocally tested. Rather, the rationales of EU copyright law are multi-layered, and at times seem contradictory.

---

126. For an example of the first, *see* Fisher, 2004. For examples of the second, *see* P. Aigrain (2008), *Internet & création: comment reconnaître les échanges hors-marché sur internet en finançant et rémunérant la création?* In Libro Veritas; D. Baker (2003), *The Artistic Freedom Voucher: An Internet Age Alternative to Copyrights*, CEPR – Center for Economic and Policy Research; P. Eckersley (2012), *Digital Copyright & The Alternatives. An Interdisciplinary Inquiry*, University of Melbourne.

127. *See* Arts 3 and 13 of the Proposal for a Directive of the European Parliament and the Council on certain aspects concerning contracts for the supply of digital content, COM/2015/0634 final – 2015/0287 (COD). *See also* A. Metzger (2016), 'Dienst gegen Daten: Ein synallagmatischer', *Archiv für die Civilistische Praxis, 216*, pp. 817–865.

128. The InfoSoc Directive is of particular importance as it is based on principles and rules already laid down in the directives in force in the area of intellectual property. *See* Recital 20 InfoSoc Directive, and Joined Cases C-403/08 and C-429/08, *Football Association Premier League Ltd and Others v. QC Leisure and Others* (C-403/08) *and Karen Murphy v. Media Protection Services Ltd* (C-429/08), 4.10.2011, ECLI: EU:C:2011:631, para. 187 (and case law cited). For our purposes, it is particularly relevant because it harmonizes the exclusive rights and limitations that form the framework in which a legalization scheme would integrate.

129. The EU Charter, of course, has 'the same legal value as the Treaties'. Cf. Art. 6(1) first subpara. of the Treaty on European Union.

For example, Recital 4 of the InfoSoc Directive seems to espouse a utilitarian policy of industrial development. According to this recital, EU copyright is to 'foster substantial investment in creativity and innovation, including network infrastructure', which 'will safeguard employment and encourage new job creation'.[130] By contrast, Recitals 10 and 11 primarily reflect the rationales of traditional *droit d'auteur*, focusing on the material interests of authors and performers, in particular the need to receive an 'appropriate reward', 'safeguarding the independence and dignity of artistic creators and performers'.[131] Recital 9 for its part confirms that harmonization of copyright and related rights should guarantee 'a high level of protection' (an oft-repeated mantra in the case law of the CJEU), while at the same time mentioning the interests of 'consumers' and 'the public at large'.[132]

Interestingly, nowhere in these foundational recitals is there mention of exclusive rights as an essential feature of the system of EU copyright. Rather, the system of exclusive rights and corresponding limitations is seen as the primary instrument for achieving the various goals set out in the preamble.

The EU Charter has become the primary source of fundamental rights law in the EU since its adoption in 2000. Its Article 17(2) expressly recognizes that '[i]ntellectual property shall be protected', as part of the Charter's general guarantee of property in Article 17(1). In the landmark *Luksan* case the CJEU applied Article 17 to a film director's claim for fair compensation in the following way:

---

130. Recital 4 InfoSoc Directive states: 'A harmonised legal framework on copyright and related rights, through increased legal certainty and while providing for a high level of protection of intellectual property, will foster substantial investment in creativity and innovation, including network infrastructure, and lead in turn to growth and increased competitiveness of European industry, both in the area of content provision and information technology and more generally across a wide range of industrial and cultural sectors. This will safeguard employment and encourage new job creation.'
131. Recital 10 InfoSoc Directive reads: 'If authors or performers are to continue their creative and artistic work, they have to receive an appropriate reward for the use of their work, as must producers in order to be able to finance this work. The investment required to produce products such as phonograms, films or multimedia products, and services such as "on-demand" services, is considerable. Adequate legal protection of intellectual property rights is necessary in order to guarantee the availability of such a reward and provide the opportunity for satisfactory returns on this investment.' Recital 11 InfoSoc Directive reads: 'A rigorous, effective system for the protection of copyright and related rights is one of the main ways of ensuring that European cultural creativity and production receive the necessary resources and of safeguarding the independence and dignity of artistic creators and performers.'
132. Recital 9 InfoSoc Directive: 'Any harmonisation of copyright and related rights must take as a basis a high level of protection, since such rights are crucial to intellectual creation. Their protection helps to ensure the maintenance and development of creativity in the interests of authors, performers, producers, consumers, culture, industry and the public at large. Intellectual property has therefore been recognised as an integral part of property.'

> 68 Finally, it should be pointed out that, under Article 17(1) of the Charter of Fundamental Rights of the European Union, everyone has the right to own, use, dispose of and bequeath his or her lawfully acquired possessions. No one may be deprived of his or her possessions, except in the public interest and in the cases and under the conditions provided for by law, subject to fair compensation being paid in good time for their loss. The use of property may be regulated by law in so far as is necessary for the general interest. Article 17(2) provides that intellectual property is to be protected.

Importantly, the CJEU does not interpret Article 17 of the EU Charter as an unqualified guarantee of an absolute, exclusive right. Rather, the Court accepts that 'in the public interest and in the cases and under the conditions provided for by law' exclusive rights of authors may be substituted by a right to 'fair compensation being paid in good time for their loss'.

Note that *Luksan* and later *Reprobel* also imply that the economic rights protected under EU copyright, and any rights of remuneration derived therefrom, belong *ab origine* to the authors, not to film producers or other 'right holders', such as publishers.[133]

Of course, the EU Charter also recognizes important fundamental rights that provide additional, and powerful, justifications for replacing exclusive rights with rights of remuneration, notably freedom of expression and information (Article 11) and rights to privacy (Article 7) and protection of personal data (Article 8).

Indeed, the law of copyright and neighbouring rights in the EU is already rife with instances where exclusive rights have made way for rights of remuneration for creators, as previously discussed.[134] Examples abound. The public lending right harmonized by the 1992 Rental and Lending Directive, while conceptualized as an exclusive right similar to the right of commercial rental, is subject to such wide-ranging (optional) compensated exceptions that it is, for all practical purposes, reduced to a right of remuneration.[135] Private copying, an optional exception under Article 5(2)(b) of the InfoSoc Directive, although technically subject to the exclusive right of reproduction, is similarly legalized and replaced by a right to 'fair compensation' in nearly all Member States. By the same token, reprographic reproduction, which according to the case law of the CJEU also includes certain acts of digital copying,[136] is broadly permitted subject to the payment of 'fair compensation' under Article 5(2)(a) of the InfoSoc Directive.

The law of neighbouring rights in the EU offers even more examples, the most wide-ranging of which is the absence of an exclusive right for

133. *Luksan*, para. 67; *Reprobel*, paras 44–49.
134. *See supra* 8.2 and 8.3.1.
135. Article 6 Rental and Lending Directive.
136. *VG Wort*, paras 68–72 (as regards the *means* of reproduction).

performers and phonogram producers to oppose the broadcasting of their recorded performances. Instead, Article 8(2) of the Rental and Lending Directive provides for the right to 'a single equitable remuneration', to be paid by the broadcasters and to be shared between performers and phonogram producers.[137]

As this brief excursion into substantive EU copyright law illustrates, substituting an exclusive economic right with a right to remuneration can hardly be called exceptional in EU secondary law. Moreover, in addition to the compensated limitations and exceptions that EU law allows, various other legal mechanisms of de facto legalization, such as mandatory collective rights management and ECL, are explicitly or implicitly recognized in EU law.[138]

Would a universal right of remuneration as proposed in this chapter stand up against the various normative goals of EU copyright identified above?

One might easily argue that by replacing copyright's exclusive right with a right to remuneration for non-commercial online use of works rights holders are not granted a sufficiently 'high level of protection' as envisaged in the preamble of the InfoSoc Directive. Considering, however, that the exclusive rights of authors to oppose digital file sharing and similar online uses by private individuals have proven to be largely unenforceable, while not generating any income from these large-scale illegal uses, this objection becomes less convincing. Would an enforceable right of remuneration not be more effective than an unenforceable exclusive right in safeguarding a 'high level of protection' for authors?

In fact, a high level of protection cannot mean an 'absolute' level of protection. Such an interpretation would support broadening of exclusive rights *ad infinitum* irrespective of the possibility and desirability of individual management and enforcement of copyright. From the economic perspective, '"excessive protection" may have a negative impact on creativity and innovation'.[139] Thus, a 'high level of protection' should best be understood as an *optimal* level of protection of rights holders. In this light, a right of remuneration for mass non-commercial online use by individuals

137. It is noteworthy that the concepts of equitable remuneration and fair compensation are considered distinct autonomous concepts of EU law. On the one hand, the CJEU interprets the concept of equitable remuneration as based on the 'value of the use in trade' and following a logical balance between competing interests. *See*, e.g.: Case C-245/00, *Stichting ter Exploitatie van Naburige Rechten (SENA) v. Nederlandse Omroep Stichting (NOS)*, 6.02.2003, ECLI:EU:C:2003:68, paras 36–37; and Case C-192/04, *Lagardère Active Broadcast v. Société pour la perception de la rémunération équitable (SPRE) and Gesellschaft zur*, 14.07.2005, ECLI:EU:C:2005:475, para. 50. On the other hand, fair compensation is based on the notion of 'harm'. *See*, e.g., *Padawan*, paras 39–40.
138. *See supra* 8.2.3 and 8.3.1.
139. T. Dreier (2016), 'Thoughts on Revising the Limitations on Copyright under Directive 2001/29', *Journal of Intellectual Property Law Practice*, 11(2), 1, 140.

would likely provide more adequate protection for the material interests of rights holders than a largely unenforceable exclusive right.

By legalizing the mass copyright infringement that has plagued the creative sector and the internet for decades, the proposed scheme would likely 'foster substantial investment in creativity and innovation, including network infrastructure', as envisaged in Recital 4 of the InfoSoc Directive. Legalization would obviate or at least substantially reduce the need for costly and inefficient copyright enforcement measures, and take away the significant burden on internet intermediaries to remove or block access to infringing content, or otherwise cooperate with copyright enforcement strategies. The result would be to free up valuable resources for both creators and network providers to invest in creativity and innovation, assisting in the promotion of technological development and the information society – public interest goals undeniably served by a well-functioning internet.[140]

The proposed universal right of remuneration would, most likely, be highly beneficial to authors and performing artists who until now have only marginally profited from 'legal' all-you-can-eat online business models, such as Spotify and Netflix,[141] and have not been compensated at all by hosts of illegal services, such as TPB and Popcorn Time. While the meagre income that authors and artists currently derive from existing legal services is at least partly due to unfair contractual practices, the study of which is outside the scope of the present chapter, it is important to realize that remuneration schemes have an obvious potential to outperform exclusive rights in terms of actually rewarding authors and artists.[142]

Legalization of non-commercial digital exchanges of copyright protected works would surely also benefit 'consumers' and 'the public at large', who would be given legal access to an unlimited catalogue of works (for the subject matter covered by the licence) at modest additional cost.[143]

Most importantly, legalization would be consistent with fundamental rights and freedoms. On the one hand, it would foster freedom of expression and information, by preserving an open internet, which has become an essential medium for the enjoyment and effective exercise of this fundamental freedom.[144] This freedom includes the right to impart, seek, and receive

140. A. Peukert (2015), 'Copyright and the Two Cultures of Online Communication'. In P.L.C. Torremans (ed.), *Intellectual Property Law and Human Rights* (3rd ed., pp. 366–395), p. 380, citing BGH, 17.07.2003, I ZR 259/00 ('Paperboy'), which identifies search engines and hyperlinking as essential components to secure the proper functioning of the internet.
141. Flowers 2015; Vallbé, Bodó, Handke & Quintais 2015, pp. 1–4.
142. Geiger 2010.
143. Note that the proposed remuneration scheme would apply to intermediaries, and not directly charge consumers, although it is likely that these costs would be passed on directly to consumers.
144. Article 19 (2013), *The Right to Share: Principles on Freedom of Expression and Copyright in the Digital Age*, available at https://www.article19.org/data/files/

information and ideas online,[145] and extends to the enjoyment of digital cultural goods, including reading, listening to, viewing, browsing, hyperlinking, and sharing works online.[146]

On the other hand, legalization would better protect privacy and personal data, by not subjecting individual citizens to modalities of copyright enforcement that encroach upon the private sphere, such as individual content use monitoring. This is especially true if a legalization scheme respects the privacy of users in electronic communications, prohibiting the unjustified processing of personal data in this context, ensuring anonymous monitoring of online exchanges for purposes of collection and distribution of rights revenue, and avoiding the payment of data as consideration for the licence to use works.[147]

Additional normative underpinnings could be derived from various other sources of law and doctrine external to EU law, such as the doctrine of '*Sozialbindung*' (social function) of property rights in Germany, or the cultural rights and freedoms framed in international human rights treaties.[148] In this line, Geiger suggests rethinking copyright as an access (rather than prohibition) right. To do so would require adapting the rules of copyright 'to its initially dual character: (1) of a right to secure and organize cultural participation to creative aspects (access aspect); and (2) of a guarantee that the creator participates fairly in the fruit of the commercial exploitation of his works (protection aspect)'.[149]

In sum, while the proposed scheme would probably be difficult to implement within the framework of existing EU copyright law,[150] it would probably not run counter to the various normative considerations underlying EU and national copyright law.

---

medialibrary/3716/13-04-23-right-to-share-EN.pdf (accessed 13 December 2017), p. 7. *See* European Court of Human Rights, *Ahmet Yıldırım v. Turkey* (App. No. 3111/10), 10.12.2012, ECLI:CE:ECHR:2012:1218JUD000311110, para. 54.

145. Article 19, 2013, p. 13.
146. European Copyright Society (2013). *The Reference to the CJEU in Case C-466/12 Svensson*, available at https://ssrn.com/abstract=2220326 (accessed 13 December 2017); Y. H. Lee (2015), *Copyright and Freedom of Expression: A Literature Review*, CREATe Working Paper Series No. 4, pp. 16–17. On hyperlinking, *see GS Media*, para. 45.
147. *See supra* 8.3.2.4 *See also* Quintais 2017, pp. 306, 405.
148. *See* e.g.: Art. 15(1)(c) International Covenant on Economic, Social and Cultural Rights, 16 December 1966, United Nations, Treaty Series, vol. 993, p. 3; Art. 27 Universal Declaration of Human Rights, adopted in Paris on 10 December 1948. *See also* C. Geiger (2015), 'Copyright as an Access Right, Securing Cultural Participation Through the Protection of Creators' Interests'. In R. Giblin, K. Weatherall (eds.), *What if We Could Reimagine Copyright?,* ANU Press, 2017, pp. 73–109.
149. Geiger 2015, pp. 75–76.
150. This compliance analysis is outside the scope of this chapter. On this topic, *see* Quintais, 2017.

8.5 ECONOMIC AND SOCIAL IMPACT

Responses to proposals such as the scheme presented in this chapter – i.e., to legalize non-commercial digital uses subject to a right to remuneration – are often predictably negative. Such a scheme would undermine the exclusive right that is the main driver and backbone of the copyright industries; would legalize piracy; would cannibalize emerging 'legal' business models offering 'all-you-can-eat' content services; and would more generally harm the economic interests of authors and right holders. Moreover, consumers want all content to be free, and would probably not be willing to bear the costs of such a scheme. [151]

The results of empirical work conducted by IViR in recent years, however, strongly suggest otherwise. [152] From 2013 to 2015 IViR conducted a large-scale empirical study of legalization systems that, for a small monthly fee, would authorize non-commercial online uses by individuals, including the downloading and sharing of protected works (such as music, films, and books), while compensating rights holders. The results of the research, which included a survey among a large sample (N = 5,000) of Dutch consumers, indicate that respondents are generally dissatisfied with the currently available legal content channels, and regularly resort to illegal channels. As the research suggests, a majority of Dutch consumers would support the introduction of, and would be willing to pay for, a model of legalization cum remuneration. The results also show that such a legalization system, if implemented, would generate significant additional revenue for the content industries, even assuming that the scheme would lead to complete substitution of existing legal services (which seems unlikely). [153]

The main aim of the survey and study was to determine consumers' willingness to pay (WTP) for a legalization scheme that would be limited to musical recordings. This was done in the form of a discrete choice experiment among a large sample of Dutch households. Different types of compensation scheme were offered as a choice to the sample, with a distinction being made between mandatory participation, voluntary participation, and voluntary participation with stricter copyright enforcement.

---

151. *See*, e.g., S.J. Liebowitz & R. Watt (2006), 'How Best to Ensure the Remuneration of Creators in the Market for Music? Copyright and its Alternatives' *Journal of Economic Surveys,* 20(4), 513–545; Handke et al., 2015, pp. 232–233; and ALAI (2016), Resolution following the 2015 Bonn Congress of ALAI concerning proposals to base the exploitation right on a comprehensive system of remunerations (Rome, 14 September 2016), available at http://www.alai.org/en/assets/files/resolutions/20160914-resolution-Bonn_en.pdf (accessed 13 December 2017).
152. Handke et al. 2015; Vallbé et al. 2015.
153. Handke et al. 2015; Vallbé et al. 2015. *See also* J.P. Quintais, (2016), 'Alternative Compensation Models for Large-Scale Non-Commercial Online Use of Works'. In S. von Lewinski (ed.), *Remuneration for the Use of Works – Exclusivity vs. Other Approaches* (pp. 298–306), De Gruyter.

Variations were possible as to the allowed uses, catalogue completeness, monitoring, and price. The results of the survey indicate broad popular support for a scheme permitting both downloading and sharing as allowed uses, with only temporal restrictions applying to the catalogue of available works, and without individual monitoring. The results show that the mean WTP for such a scheme amounts to EUR 9.25/month, while right holders in the Dutch music industry are already fully compensated at EUR 1.74/month, assuming perfect substitution.[154]

With well over 75 million broadband-connected households in the entire EU, the proceeds of EUR 9.25 compensation scheme for the right holders (12 x 9.25 x EUR 75 million = EUR 8.325 million) would far exceed the amount of revenues lost to the consumption of recorded music from illegal sources in the EU, which the European Union Intellectual Property Office (EUIPO) recently estimated at EUR 170 million for the year 2014.[155] Based on these figures, right holders in the EU music sector would be fully compensated by an alternative compensation scheme (for music exchanges only) set at a measly EUR 0.19/month, again assuming perfect substitution.

These results strongly suggest that consumers, creators, and other right holders would benefit enormously from the introduction of a legalization scheme, even in a sector such as music where 'legal' all-you-can-eat models have already very successfully penetrated the market.

The survey's results, as indicated, assume full substitution of currently legal content services by (currently illegal) content sharing that would become legal under the proposed model. Complete substitution is, however, highly unlikely – for multiple reasons. For one, the current market situation suggests that licensed content services can actually co-exist, and compete, with illegal (and free) sharing models.[156] Apparently, illegal sharing does not fully substitute legal offerings. By implication, it is unlikely that legalized (remunerated) content sharing would crowd out licensed services entirely.

As various economic studies on illegal file sharing have demonstrated, unauthorized file sharing may affect legal markets in both negative and positive ways. While a measure of substitution is likely to occur, file sharing also has beneficial effects on the market in that it allows consumers to 'sample' new content, i.e., it may introduce consumers to works, artists, and genres which increases their demand for these or other works by the same artists or in the same genre.[157] This sampling effect will also occur where legalized content sharing allows consumers to access works not (yet) available through licensed content services.

---

154. Handke et al. 2015.
155. EUIPO, N. Wajsman, C. Arias Burgos & C. Davies (2016). The Economic Cost of IPR Infringement in the Recorded Music Industry, Alicante: EUIPO.
156. Vallbé et al. 2015.
157. *See* the chapter by J. Poort elsewhere in this volume.

While it is therefore plausible that the introduction of a legalization system would have an overall positive welfare effect, and would directly benefit creators, right holders, and consumers engaging in or keen on content sharing, requiring all internet households/subscribers to pay lump-sum remuneration could be deemed unfair for those not interested in content sharing. Similar arguments have been made in the past, and continue to be made against private copying levies imposed on reproduction equipment and media that can, and will, be put to uses other than reproducing works for private purposes.[158]

This problem could be approached in different ways. One would be to simply accept the 'roughness' of the justice, as one generally accepts the inherent unfairness of non-negotiable commercial tariffs of, e.g., cable operators for a package of television programmes. Here too, low-volume users are subsidizing high-volume consumers.

Another approach would be to allow subscribers to opt out of the legalization scheme. For example, professional users and other non-consumers having broadband connections could be permitted to withdraw from the scheme, on the condition of proof of their non-consumer status. Allowing consumers to opt out might however severely undermine the system; if large volumes of subscribers leave the system right holders could feel compelled to reinstate copyright enforcement measures against them and their network providers. A variant of this approach could be to combine an opt-out with content filtering; users opting out of the scheme would have to accept that content flowing through their broadband connections is monitored for copyright infringement. This would however put users' privacy rights at risk, again defeating the purpose of legalization.

Yet another approach would be to exempt from payment certain categories of end users, thereby increasing the fairness of the system. It is a well-known fact that not all users engage in file sharing or consume digital culture online to the same extent. For example, a recent study in the Netherlands shows that 49% of Dutch consumers, including those without internet access, do not access digital channels to consume music, audiovisual content, or books.[159] Therefore, similar to the payment of utilities, the proposed scheme could differentiate between users and targeted households. Using the cited study as an indicator, an alternative compensation system in the Netherlands could include exemptions or reductions of the broadband levy for certain categories of household, such as households whose residents are above a certain age or below a pre-defined income level. The levy could also be lower for slower internet connections. In the future it could even be

158. Hugenholtz et al. 2003, p. 40.

159. Vallbé et al. 2015, attributing this result to holdout groups, characterized by older, less educated people who predominantly use TV and radio ('non-consumers'), and older, educated people who prefer books ('bookworms'). The non-consumers amount to c.a. 29%, whereas bookworms amount to 20%.

possible to vary the levy based on the number of residents per household, and introduce the possibility for users to choose between fixed or metered surcharges (dependent on internet speed and usage).[160] These variations could lead to a fairer system that better approximates actual use and leverages consumers' willingness to participate and pay for this alternative.[161]

Assuming that the applicable tariff could indeed be set at a very modest level, its overall beneficial effects for society would justify a measure of 'rough justice' inherent to the system, combined with empirically justified exemptions or reductions of the levy for certain categories of household.

8.6 CONCLUSION

This chapter proposes the introduction of a universal right of remuneration to replace exclusive rights in respect of currently illegal online content sharing between individuals. As this chapter argues, despite over twenty years of vigorous copyright enforcement online content sharing still persists on a massive scale. Assuming that online piracy will not substantially decrease in the near future, this chapter proposes legalizing non-commercial content sharing, subject to a right to remuneration. The scheme proposed would permit acts of reproducing and making available to the public of online works of authorship by individual users acting for non-commercial purposes, while guaranteeing remuneration from ISPs to right holders through a CMO. Under the proposed system such acts would no longer infringe relevant rights of reproduction and communication to the public, while eliminating secondary liability for merely facilitating such acts. ISPs would be obliged to fairly remunerate authors, performing artists, and other rights holders.

Although this chapter presents several alternative ways of implementing the proposed legalization scheme, it could be based on a carefully crafted copyright limitation to the relevant exclusive rights, and be modelled after existing statutory licence schemes, such as those for private copying and reprography. In delimiting its scope, the scheme would distinguish between permitted 'non-commercial' uses, and other uses for which the exclusive rights remain intact. The scheme would not apply to all categories of copyright protected content, but be limited to traditional categories of creation: music, text, visual works, and video. Other content sectors, such as software, databases, and video games, are less vulnerable to piracy, and therefore less in need of the proposed solution.

The proposed scheme would impose the obligation to fairly remunerate creators upon broadband internet providers, since they have sufficiently

160. This general approach is envisaged by multiple legalization proposals. *See*, e.g., Colin 2011, p. 99.
161. Vallbé et al. 2015. *See also* Handke et al. 2015, regarding recorded music.

'deep pockets' and can easily pass on the costs of the remuneration to consumers. Moreover, ISPs have much to gain from legalization, since this would avoid the high costs of copyright compliance and – more importantly – leave intact their role as neutral conduits.

While the proposed scheme would probably be difficult to implement within the framework of existing EU copyright law, it would conform to most, if not all, of the normative considerations underlying EU copyright law. It would guarantee substantive direct income streams to currently disenfranchised authors and performers, while keeping the internet open, and thus fostering innovation and the circulation of culture, as well as freedom of expression and information online. It would also benefit consumers and the general public, by avoiding potentially privacy-invasive copyright enforcement strategies.

As recent empirical research suggests, such a scheme would likely have the support of consumers. Moreover, the amount that consumers are willing to pay for such a scheme far exceed total levels of current consumer spending on digital content and total revenues lost by right holders due to online piracy. In other words, even the 'content industries' that would be most inclined to oppose the scheme would have a lot to gain.

Finally, in light of the ongoing proliferation of statutory remuneration schemes for private copying and reprography in the digital realm, the proposed universal right to remuneration would, in practice, be far less radical than it is sometimes portrayed – more of an evolution than a revolution.

Chapter 9

Borderlines of Copyright Protection: An Economic Analysis

Joost Poort*

9.1 INTRODUCTION[1]

Should copyright come into play when I want to bequeath my iTunes collection to my children? If I backup it up to the Cloud? If I forward an email? Or if I embed a link to a YouTube video on my webpage? In a 2007 article, John Tehranian described an ordinary day in the life of a hypothetical law professor John who, by the end of the day 'has committed at least eighty-three acts of infringement and faces liability in the amount of $12.45 million (to say nothing of potential criminal charges)' (Tehranian, 2007: p. 547). As digitization has rushed forward since 2007, including supplying us

* The author thanks the members of the project team (Bernt Hugenholtz, Stefan Bechtold, Séverine Dusollier, Martin Kretschmer, Ansgar Ohly and Alain Strowel), as well as Lionel Bently, Sari Depreeuw, Estelle Derclaye, Daniel Gervais, Jonathan Griffiths, Matthias Leistner, Bertin Martens, Giuseppe Mazziotti, João Pedro Quintais and Martin Senftleben, and the participants in the 'Reconstructing rights' symposium held on 26 September 2016 in Brussels for their valuable comments on earlier drafts of this chapter. All errors remain the author's.

1. The analysis in this chapter has served as a basis for the concretization of the 'Right to Reasonable Exploitation' chapter by Ole-Andreas Rognstad and Joost Poort in this volume. The legal foundations of that alternative model to redefine the economic rights in copyright from the starting point of a right to reasonable exploitation are presented in Rognstad (2015).

with smartphones and tablets, one can only expect these numbers to have increased.

This chapter explores the avenues for redefining the scope of copyright from a normative welfare economic perspective. The aim is to bring copyright more in line with today's world of ubiquitous connectivity, digitized works and the demise of physical information carriers such as CDs, DVDs and printed books, while preserving the incentives for the creation and active exploitation of works that copyright aims to provide.

Current copyright law grants the author of a work of literature, science or art moral rights and economic rights. The economic rights granted by copyright usually comprise the exclusive rights of *reproduction*, *communication to the public* and *distribution*. In European Union (EU) law, these core economic rights have been harmonized in Articles 2–4 of Directive 2001/29/EC (the 'Copyright Directive'). Another important economic right – not harmonized in EU law – is the right of adaptation, also referred to as the right to prepare *derivative works*. Such works include the translation of a song, the making of a movie from a book or the creation of a lunch box with a cartoon character. In principle, these economic rights are attributed to the creator or creators of a work, but much like any other property right, they can be subject to a licence, assignment or transfer. Irrespective of such transactions, the rights in question typically last for seventy years after the death of the last surviving author, in both the EU and the US.

Moral rights consist of the rights of attribution, integrity, disclosure and withdrawal and are not alienable or waivable. They are ignored in most of the economic literature on copyright (Rushton, 1998; Towse, 2006). In addition to these moral rights, which primarily aim to protect the reputation of the author, and the economic rights, which can be closely linked to the incentives to create and exploit works, copyright contains elements primarily aimed at promoting distributive justice. This is the case, for instance, for provisions designed to improve the position of authors towards publishers or other stakeholders through author's contract rights (e.g., *see* Hugenholtz & Guibault, 2004) or through provisions such as the *droit de suite* or resale right. Despite the fact that the distinction made here is not clear-cut since both moral rights and provisions aimed at improving distributive justice can affect the incentives to create and to exploit works (e.g., Towse, 2006; Poort & Theeuwes, 2010), the focus in the present chapter is on the economic rights as an incentive system. Accordingly, the *scope* of copyright is understood as the breadth of the economic rights: what is protected by copyright and what is not, and which acts (or even technologies) of third parties can be prohibited or can remuneration be claimed for with reference to copyright, and which cannot.[2]

2. Basically, the scope of the economic rights refers to anything other than the duration. Copyright duration, as well as exceptions and limitations to copyright (or fair use) are not

The economic rights in terms of *reproduction*, *communication to the public* and *distribution* no longer seem to match with the digital environment. Even though these acts are broad and general in the sense that they can be applied to music, books, films, etc., they appear to be more adequate and relevant in an analogue world of physical carriers, than in the digital environment. One can observe the Court of Justice of the EU (CJEU or 'Court') struggling with these concepts to take a position on relatively common issues such as linking and embedding, resale of digital content and making copies of digitally acquired content. In an analogue environment, it may have been logical to make reproduction an important element of the exclusive right of the creator, for instance, but in the current digital environment, this no longer seems the case. Accidental or transient copies of works, for instance, are constantly made in the process of consuming or distributing works; however, they do not seem to affect the exploitation opportunities for the right holder. In fact, reproducing a work without distributing these copies appears not to harm the incentives for the creator to create or to exploit a work.

This chapter starts with a brief overview of the basic economic analysis of copyright and a few trade-offs and insights concerning its scope, followed by an overview of how digitization has affected these trade-offs and insights (section 9.2). From thereon, five cases of 'borderline exploitation' are analysed, which the current copyright *acquis* can be argued to have problems making sense of. These cases are analysed through the lens of the welfare economic framework to determine how the scope of copyright could be reconstructed to be more in line with the twenty-first century. The first three cases, digital resale (section 9.3), private copying (section 9.4), and hyperlinking and embedding (section 9.5) will be dealt with more extensively; the last two, cable retransmission (section 9.6), and text and data mining (section 9.7) are discussed briefly. Section 9.8 offers a brief summary of findings and conclusions.

9.2 WELFARE ECONOMIC ANALYSIS OF COPYRIGHT

9.2.1 Copyright as a Solution to the Public Good Market Failure of Creative Works

In general, the economic literature on copyright links the rationale for copyright protection to the incentive to create and exploit works of literature, science and art, at the cost of creating a temporary monopoly over these

the main focus here, but will inevitably come up when considering suggestions for adjusting the scope of copyright.

works (e.g., Landes & Posner, 1989; Besen & Raskind, 1991; Posner, 2005; Miceli & Adelstein, 2006; Sag, 2006). Although this so-called utilitarian perspective is by no means undisputed, it is considered the most popular justification for copyright (Fisher, 2001) and it is certainly the most popular in the economic literature on copyright. Put simply, the exclusive right to certain acts of exploitation enables a right holder to generate revenues and to recoup the investment made to create and exploit the work. Like for many other economic activities, the costs of creating and exploiting works precede the benefits and this implies that future benefits need to be expected to provide proper incentives. This mechanism is highly relevant for creative works, since the initial (fixed) costs of creation are often very large in comparison to the (marginal) costs of reproduction, while copycats do not have to invest the fixed costs of creation.

Of course, this is a simplification as intrinsic motivation (or 'inner drive' or even 'inner necessity') is generally accepted to be very important to understand the professional activities of creators and performers. Nonetheless, extrinsic motivation (wages and other financial rewards) has been shown to play an important role, much like for any other profession (e.g., *see* Frey, 1997 & Towse, 2006). Moreover, economic considerations and incentives can be assumed to prevail over intrinsic motivations for publishers and intermediaries.

From this (utilitarian) welfare economic perspective, copyright aims to prevent a situation in which anyone could create and sell copies of a work without permission once the costs of its initial creation have been incurred. This would reduce the revenues for the initial creator though a loss of market share as well as a price drop towards the marginal costs of making a copy. In the short term this would be beneficial for consumers who gain access to works at low prices. But this would undermine the incentives for the creator to invest in the creation and exploitation of high-quality works, possibly leading to a loss of welfare in the long run. This mechanism, which represents the core dilemma of the economic analysis of copyright, is illustrated in Figures 9.1 and 9.2.

Figure 9.1 gives a highly stylized representation of the supply of and demand for a work with high fixed costs of creation and low marginal costs of reproduction. In such a case, the average costs per copy (the curved line) drop rapidly and converge to the marginal costs as the number of copies increases. If the right holder is the only supplier of the work (and can only charge a uniform price), he would choose price $p1$ to maximize his profits, which is the grey area in Figure 9.1 that equals the quantity $q1$ sold at price $p1$ times the difference between the price $p1$ and the average costs. At this price, consumers gain welfare as well, called consumer surplus. For each consumer, the individual welfare created is the difference between his or her maximum willingness to pay, depicted by the demand line, and the actual price paid. At the chosen fixed price *p*1, all consumers combined gain a consumer surplus represented by the dark triangle in Figure 9.1.

Figure 9.1 Stylized Supply and Demand Graph for a Copyright Work

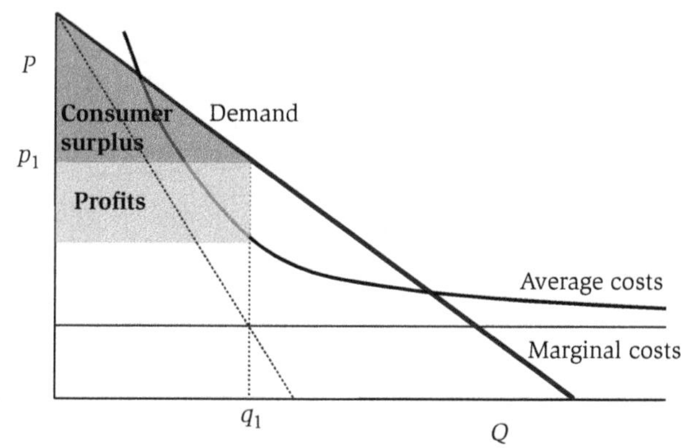

Now assume that the right holder faces competition from other suppliers of the same work – copycats – who have the same marginal costs of reproduction but no fixed costs. In that case, competition will bring the price down close to marginal costs, as is depicted in Figure 9.2. The total consumer surplus (the triangle) is much larger this time as a direct result of the lower price. However, no supplier is making a profit anymore in this extreme case, and the right holder has no way to recoup the initial investment.[3]

3. A few authors, most notably Boldrin & Levine (2002 2008) dispute this analysis, basically by emphasizing that in the initial sale to copycats, the creator can charge them for the profits they expect to make from subsequent reproductions. Although this type of argument will be accepted in certain special circumstances, it is rejected as a general argument against copyright. It requires rather theoretical assumptions, such as full appropriation of downstream rents upon sale, frictionless resale of copies by any copier at a uniform market price and no uncertainty about future demand. This is very remote from the current situation, in which a handful of copies of, for instance, a new film make their way to peer-to-peer exchange platforms. *See* McManis (2009) for a general critique of Boldrin & Levine (2008).

Figure 9.2 No Recoupment of Fixed Costs under Full Competition

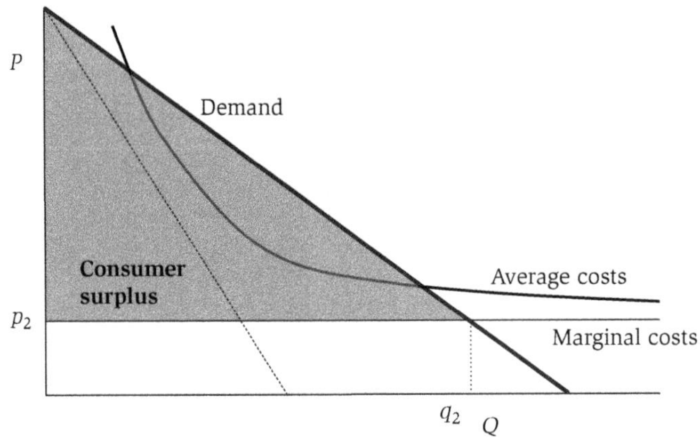

The optimum scope of copyright in the economic literature follows from the optimum long-term effect it has on total social welfare, taking account of the dynamic effects of copyright on the creation and quality of works, and the incentives it provides for their active exploitation. In such an analysis, consumer surplus and profits for producers are given equal weight and neither right holders nor consumers enjoy a privileged status. It should be stressed here that the concept of social welfare is much broader than the limited realm of monetary effects or wealth. In the welfare economic framework, non-monetary social norms such as privacy and freedom of speech also contribute to well-being and hence to social welfare. The utilitarian ambition would be for those norms, or more precisely the effect of certain acts or policy measures on those norms, to be expressed in monetary terms to allow for a comparison within the unified welfare economic framework. Only the distribution of welfare falls outside its theoretical scope.[4] Teulings et al. (2003), for instance, argue that ultimately there are only two goals for public policy making: efficiency and distributional issues. Ideally, these should be decided on independently. A few years earlier, the Dutch Scientific Council of Government Policy had identified five separate principles for good governance: democratic legitimation, equality before the law, legal certainty, effectiveness and efficiency (WRR 2000, 27–28). In response, Teulings et al. (2003) point out that effectiveness is not fundamentally distinct from efficiency, while they consider the first three principles to

4. *See* Stolwijk (2010) for a discussion of the broad economic concept of social welfare in policy analysis, contrasted with the narrower concept of GDP.

be procedural criteria, which are not goals in themselves but means to achieve the public interests of efficiency and an acceptable distribution of welfare.

In practice it seems almost impossible to realize this normative ambition to express any social norm or value other than equity in monetary terms and integrate it into a unified welfare economic framework. In fact, it will prove complicated enough to assess the static and dynamic effects of copyright issues for right holders and consumers, without integrating these other norms into the same framework. Focusing on these static and dynamic effects within the copyright industry and on consumers, and – if needed – later amending the outcomes of such a narrower economic analysis on the basis of these other norms therefore seems a more pragmatic solution than trying to incorporate these norms fully in the welfare economic framework. For instance, it could be decided that the economic position based solely on total welfare would lead to over- or under-protection since it insufficiently incorporates other social norms.

Thus, in economic terms, the main argument for copyright boils down to the observation that the rents from creation are not (or are insufficiently) *excludable* without some form of protection. This 'public good' market failure related to the creation of a work can justify copyright legislation and enforcement, but the extent to which this market failure occurs is not a given. It differs between types of works and has changed over time.

First, it depends on the *cost advantage* of the creator or publisher making copies of copyright-protected content: if the costs of making copies are much higher for third parties, the need for copyright protection is lower. In Figures 9.1 and 9.2, this point relates to the position of the marginal cost line for copycats compared to its position for the initial creator: the higher the marginal costs of copycats compared to those of the right holder, the more room there is for the right holder to recoup his investment.

Second, the need for protection will depend on the *substitutability* of 'originals' by copies. A painting by Marlene Dumas, for instance, is not only very hard to replicate adequately, but also derives much of its value from the fact that it is an original. Hence, creating a copy will be costly and will most likely yield no more than a poor substitute, which is why from an economic perspective, copyright protection would be less necessary here than for instance for an e-book.[5] Thus, the stronger the market preference for 'originals' over copies, the less need there is for copyright protection.[6]

Third, contractual arrangements – *private ordering* – are a potential substitute for copyright protection. In a world with perfect and enforceable private contracts, no copying without permission will occur and hence no copyright protection is required. The viability of private ordering as a substitute for copyright will depend on the enforceability and transaction costs of private contracts, as well as on the limits to contractual freedom and the enforcement of contracts on behalf of, for instance, competition policy, unfair business practices and privacy protection.

9.2.2 The Effects of Digitization on the Public Good Market Failure

Digitization has significantly affected all three of these factors relevant to the optimum scope of copyright protection. In the digital age, the costs of making good quality copies of many kinds of work have decreased sharply relative to the initial costs of creation, while the quality of third-party copies and hence the substitutability of originals by copies has increased. As a consequence, the 'natural protection' of the rents for the creator or follow-up right holder has diminished, making the situation depicted in Figure 9.2 a realistic scenario without adequate protection. Moreover, the Internet has dramatically decreased the cost of distributing digital copies.

Consider copying by private individuals, within small companies, within schools, etc. Photocopying a printed book in such an environment

---

5. That is setting aside the exclusive right to produce derivative works, which can also be part of the incentive system of an artist. In addition, the *droit de suite* for works of art should be mentioned in this context. This right entitles an artist or his heirs in some jurisdictions to a fee or share in the profits on resale of their work. This right is unrelated to the public good market failure at the foundation of copyright. Instead, it may be justified on other grounds. From a welfare economic perspective, it may be justified by information asymmetries, if buyers are believed to have better knowledge of the quality and market value of these works of art than the artists themselves. Also, it may be justified on distributional grounds, if the income or wealth position of artists or their heirs is believed to call for intervention or if buyers of works of art are generally believed to have market power vis-à-vis artists which need correcting for. As general rules, these justifications are contestable while the creation of a *droit de suite* can be expected to have a negative impact on the price in the first sale. For a critical welfare economic analysis of comparable legislative proposals to improve the position of authors, *see* Poort & Theeuwes (2010).
6. C.f. Landes & Posner (1989, p. 329): 'To generalize, when either the cost of making equivalent copies is higher for the copier than for the creator or the copier's product is a poor substitute for the original, the originator will be able to charge a price greater than his marginal cost, even without legal protection. And, obviously, the greater the difference in the costs of making copies and in the quality of copies between creator and copier … , the less need there is for copyright protection.'

used to be time-consuming and costly. Taking labour costs – or in the case of a private copy the opportunity costs of time – into account as well as the costs of copying paper and toner, the total costs of such a copy were probably higher than the production costs of an original by the publisher. At the same time, the quality of the photocopy compared poorly to the original. More or less the same held true for tape cassette copies of music records. In both cases, the cost of making copies and their inferior quality provided a natural protection for the original, even without copyright protection. Making copies from copies caused the quality to deteriorate even further, thus creating a natural barrier to the proliferation of copies.[7]

However, the costs for private individuals to make copies of digitized media such as CDs, DVDs and computer games are much lower, while the quality difference is much smaller. For works sold as digital files without any physical carrier, such as e-books, mp3 files, digital photos and video files, copying these files is easier still while there is no quality difference at all. As a result, the economic need and rationale for some form of copyright protection in the digital age may be stronger than before.

On the other hand, technical protection measures (TPMs) and digital rights management technology have been developed to prevent such copying or at least to increase the 'costs' of copying for individuals. Moreover, TPMs are increasingly used as tools for imposing end-user licence agreements, defining what buyers can and cannot do with the works they acquire. For instance, they allow consumers to only play content they have purchased on a limited number of devices or prevent them from reselling it or from giving it away by linking it to a user account. Thus, the more effective TPMs are, the more they enable private ordering. By doing so they serve not just to support or enforce copyright, but also to substitute it. As Elkin-Koren (2009) points out, 'TPMs could be designed to enforce copyright as defined by legislation, but also to expand the scope of protection by disabling uses which are explicitly exempted under copyright law.'

When perfectly effective, TPMs can resolve the previously described public good market failure, rendering copyright protection superfluous. But of course, TPMs are never infallible. They can be circumvented or removed, and if this is done well, the TPM-free version can no longer be traced back to the original buyer. This implies that the end-user licence agreement can no longer be effectively enforced. In addition, there is a natural tension between the aim of TPMs to restrict unlicensed uses, and the various interests of end users, for instance to access the content they acquired on different devices, as well as the public desire to safeguard the privacy and autonomy of users to some extent. In the early 2000s, TPMs on CDs caused computers to crash. Obviously, this conflicted with the bona fide expectation and wish of many consumers to use their computer for playing CDs. Eventually, the use of

7. Of course, this was different for 'industrial' copying e.g., by professional printers, but for these there was and is more room for copyright enforcement.

TPMs proved to be counterproductive for most of the music industry and was abandoned (Sinha, Machado & Sellman, 2010; Vernik, Purohit & Desai, 2011), while for audio-visual content, e-books and games it is still common. Also, the rapid emergence of access-based business models such as Spotify rekindled the use of TPMs for music. In light of the above, and despite their limitations, TPMs are regularly considered throughout this chapter, either as a means to support and enforce copyright, or as a potential substitute for it.

9.2.3 Societal Costs of Copyright Protection

Returning to the basic idea of copyright as a means to resolve the public good market failure associated with the creation and exploitation of works, it is important to stress that copyright protection comes with considerable costs to society. These costs need to be taken into account in any economic assessment of the optimum scope of copyright. Landes & Posner (1989) mention the costs of administering copyright, which are likely to increase with the number of works created and with the strength of protection. The administrative costs of licensing copyright or obtaining consent for certain acts which may be copyright-relevant are considered to fall within the same broad category of *transaction costs of copyright.* Posner (2005) adds that these costs increase over time, as identifying a copyright holder to license from usually becomes more difficult as time passes: the copyright holder may well be the heir of the initial creator, or a company obtaining the rights after the insolvency of a first company to which the initial creator transferred her economic rights, etc.

A second general type of cost of copyright protection stems from the fact that whenever it allows works to be priced above their marginal costs, this is likely to cause demand to decrease below the level that is optimum from a static perspective. This entails a static loss of welfare through so-called *dead-weight losses.* In Figure 9.1, these derive from all potential consumers who have a willingness to pay larger than the marginal costs but who are not serviced because the price *p*1 set by the right holder is larger than these marginal costs. Thus, every potential customer with a willingness to pay larger than the marginal costs who is not serviced entails a static loss of welfare. In a static economic framework, marginal cost pricing (as in Figure 9.2) would be preferable to a uniform price above marginal costs, but of course this raises the issue of how to recoup investment costs. Alternatively, refined price discrimination schemes may be used to minimize dead-weight losses but can have other economic and distributional drawbacks that are touched upon at the end of this section.

A third type of cost is related to the former but appears in a dynamic perspective. Works protected by copyright often serve as input for other works. Stronger economic rights will generally limit the possibilities for new creators to access works for inspiration or study, since they will cause works to be supplied at a profit-maximizing price. This will not be a strict monopoly price, since even under the strongest system of copyright protection there will be competition between works. Still, in many instances it will be higher than the price absent copyright protection, reducing demand from subsequent creators. Moreover, it will limit their ability to license works for transformative use and other forms of use, as this would likely be an infringement, or it will enhance uncertainty about whether the use of a work is allowed. These costs may cause dynamic welfare losses. Such dynamic effects imply that there is an inverted u-shaped relation between the strength of economic rights and creation: beyond some strength of copyright protection that yields the maximum level of creation, a further increase in strength leads to a *decrease* in the number of works created.

9.2.4 Economic Foundations for the Scope of Copyright

As a result of the three types of costs of copyright protection discussed in the previous section, the *welfare economic optimum* level of copyright protection lies *not* where creative output is highest in terms of volume and quality, but somewhere on the left-hand slope of this inverted u-shaped curve. The reasons for this are the increasing costs of administering copyright, and the dead-weight losses of stronger protection via the higher prices it entails, including its adverse effect on subsequent creation.

Where this optimum lies, for instance in terms of the duration of copyright, is essentially an empirical question, the answer to which may differ across types of work and forms of exploitation. For a more general economic assessment of the scope of copyright, however, one needs to go back to the general economic foundation of copyright protection, which is the resolution of the 'public good' market failure associated with the creation of works, so as to provide proper incentives for the creation and exploitation of works. As explained above, the costs of copying, the substitutability of originals by copies and the possibilities of private ordering as an alternative to copyright protection need to be borne in mind in such an assessment, as well as the various societal costs of copyright protection.

As a general principle, resolving the market failure requires giving a creator and follow-on right holders exclusive rights with respect to acts that, *as a consequence of this public good market failure, negatively and significantly affect his current or future exploitation opportunities* and hence negatively interfere with his incentives to create or exploit. Put differently, it requires entitling them to reasonably foreseeable or anticipated positive external effects from their creation. Acts that do not meet this criterion should – in an economic assessment of copyright – be considered 'copyright irrelevant'. In fact, they may even benefit the right holder. Hence the right holder requires no legal protection with respect to these acts.

Resolving the public good market failure must not generate new market failures by granting more or stronger rights than a creator would have in the absence of the initial market failure. Therefore, it should in itself be copyright irrelevant if a buyer of copyright-protected content manages to create surplus in a downstream market, as long as the public good market failure is not reintroduced by doing so. To illustrate this point, consider a company manufacturing cars. Once a car is sold, this company has no claim to the revenues created by this individual: whether he uses it for joyriding, for visiting clients or as a taxi. The car is an excludable private good and there is no economic reason for the manufacturer to have any claims on surplus created after its sale. The same argument holds for smartphones, shovels and sandwiches, as well as for a work of literature, science or art, once the public good market failure has been resolved, resulting in its sale or licensing. The differences in the value various buyers derive from a good give rise to the consumer surplus in Figure 9.1, which is larger for some buyers than for others. But the public good market failure associated with creative works gives no reason to entitle the creator to this surplus any more than in the case of other products and services.

Of course, an individual buyer may sell the car on the second-hand market and the manufacturer may argue that this second-hand market *negatively and significantly affects* the first-hand market. However, this argument can easily be reversed, since a strong second-hand market will affect the willingness to pay in the first-hand market.[8] Hence, the surplus in the secondary market can largely be appropriated in the first sale. In any case, in the car market, the argument that the second-hand market may negatively affect the market for new cars has not been accepted as a valid reason to prohibit the resale of used cars. Why should this be different for copyright-protected content? The arguments here imply that the exclusive rights of copyright should not extend beyond the first sale of a work any more than for other exhaustible goods. Once a physical or digital copy of a work has been sold, the market failure that justified copyright legislation has been resolved with respect to this specific copy. Like for any other product which does not suffer from this market failure, there is no economic justification for granting the initial creator automatic control over the secondary market or over the value created with the product downstream in the value chain, as this value is not an external effect that needs to be internalized to achieve a welfare optimum. Of course, altering the current copyright system to this end can affect the sales or licensing agreements upstream, and will impact the allocation of risks in the value chain.

The difference between copyright works and physical products such as smartphones or cars is of course that the initial buyer of a work could extend

8. A potentially appealing counter-argument that digital works are different as they do not degrade as physical products do will be discussed in the case study of digital exhaustion in section 9.3.

the market by selling *multiple* copies or by granting several new consumers access to the work. Thus, the initial buyer becomes a new seller (not just of what he bought), who can undercut the original creator and still make a profit because he has no investment in the initial creation to recoup. This is the scenario depicted in Figure 9.2 which reintroduces the initial 'public good' market failure and can justify intervention for the initial creator to regain control. This mechanism will be studied in more detail in sections 9.3 and 9.4, when discussing the issue of digital exhaustion and private copying.

To understand which acts ought to fall under copyright protection since they negatively and significantly affect the current or future exploitation opportunities of the right holder, it is essential to note that exploitation is a very wide and open concept here. The concept not only applies to the wide variety of business models that exist today, but also to future business models. Nowadays, exploitation can take many forms other than a simple exchange of a physical carrier or a content file – a copy of a work – for money. Exploitation can take the form of providing digital access to works on a temporary or permanent basis – for instance by licensing digital streaming platforms such as Spotify and Netflix. And a monetary payment by the end user in exchange for a work or access to a work is just one of several possible business models. Others may rely on advertising revenues (e.g., YouTube, Spotify Free, Readfy), collecting data about consumers, creating an environment of cross-selling other works or products, building a fan base or reputation which can be monetized in the future, and whatnot. For the right holders of works on free platforms such as YouTube or even SSRN, the number of views or downloads can be an important incentive for creating and posting works, as views or downloads may be monetized directly through a share in advertising revenues, or indirectly as a proof of reputation or fame which contributes to the career opportunities of the creator. When the challenges of copyright in the digital age became apparent, in particular in the context of unauthorized file sharing, an often-heard recommendation was for the content industry to develop new business models (e.g., Van Eijk, Poort & Rutten, 2010). Now that various such business models have emerged, it is important to take into account their existence when considering how acts by third parties may affect current or future exploitation opportunities. This does not imply that any current exploitation model must be respected and protected by copyright. But it does mean that the scope of copyright should be broad enough to allow for many of the current exploitation models, and general enough to account for new models yet to be developed.

The central notion for all of the models mentioned above is that of *control*. This control – deriving from the exclusive nature of the economic right – enables the right holder to exchange access to a work for something which generates value for him, be it money, website traffic, attention or personal data. A right holder exploiting a work can control who can consume a work and under what circumstances, and choose an exploitation model which seems fit. This control to exclude consumers is what is lacking without copyright protection, due to the 'public good' nature of a work. However, from an economic incentive perspective, control is only justified to the extent that a lack of control would, as a consequence of the public good market failure that is described, negatively and significantly affect the current or future exploitation opportunities for the right holder.

But even if a negative and significant effect may occur, the extent of the market failure – in light of the cost for third parties to make copies, the substitutability of originals by copies and the opportunities for private ordering – as well as the various 'costs' of copyright protection need to be considered in order to define the optimum scope of copyright. As said, this is an empirical question, the answer to which may differ between types of work and forms of exploitation.

First, *transaction costs* may justify curtailing copyright and placing certain acts that negatively and significantly affect the current or future exploitation opportunities for the right holder nonetheless outside the scope of copyright protection.

Second, there is the issue of *dead-weight losses* that result from above marginal cost pricing. In theory, the interests of society at large and the right holders in minimizing these costs are aligned. To minimize dead-weight losses and to maximize profits, right holders can be expected to develop price discrimination schemes, just as entrepreneurs in many other industries do, as soon as the conditions for price discrimination are met. That is, the seller needs to have at least some market power to be able to set prices above marginal costs; he needs to be able to distinguish between consumers to know which price to charge to whom; and resale needs to be impractical, costly or outright forbidden in order to prevent arbitrage between customers. Note that the last condition has a direct link with private ordering and end-user licence agreements, which implies the opportunities for price discrimination when using TPMs are abundant.[9]

In practice, given the fact that perfect (first degree) price discrimination is not achievable, a right holder will be inclined to accept dead-weight losses if it helps to maximize revenues. There is a vast literature on the outcomes and welfare effects of price discrimination in various different competitive settings and under various assumptions about consumer demand, the information consumers and producers have, producers' ability to commit to prices, etc. These effects turn out to be ambiguous. As Miller (2013) observes: 'economic models of price discrimination tend to predict a positive increase in overall social welfare compared with flat rate pricing'. A general rule of thumb is that for price discrimination to be welfare enhancing, it must lead to a substantial increase in total output by serving markets that were previously unserved.

---

9. For example Varian, 1989. *See* in the context of price discrimination for copyright works also Fisher (2001: pp. 196–198).

An extreme, but not unrealistic, illustration of this is provided in Figure 9.3. This figure is largely identical to Figure 9.1, with the notable difference that the average cost curve lies to the right of the demand line. For any quantity sold, the average costs are larger than the corresponding uniform price. This implies that the right holder will need to price discriminate in order to recoup the initial investment. Nevertheless, the creation and exploitation of the product generates welfare: it is readily seen that the total losses the right holder incurs at a price *p*3 are much smaller than the total consumer surplus that is generated. Price discrimination can be a way for the right holder in Figure 9.3 to extract some of the consumer surplus and to recoup the investment after all.

Figure 9.3 Product for Which no Uniform Price Recovers the Fixed Costs

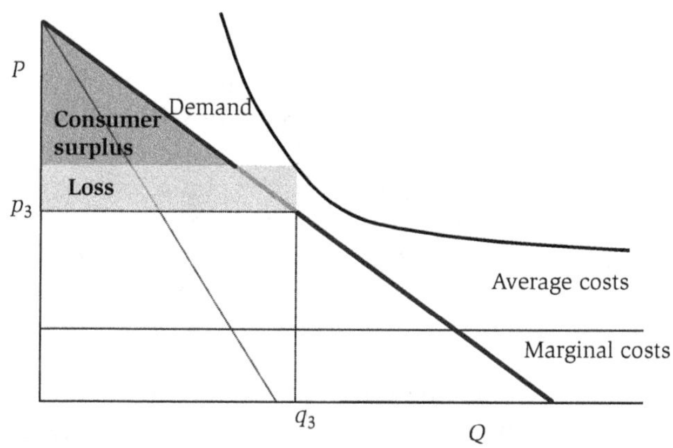

In situations such as that depicted in Figure 9.3, and also in less extreme cases, price discrimination can be welfare enhancing. But even then, total consumer surplus will be reduced at the expense of producer surplus, raising distributional concerns. In other cases even producers can suffer a welfare loss, due to intensified competition. These considerations are general and not specific for copyright works. Therefore, a welfare economic assessment of the scope of copyright may involve limits to the ability of right holders to price discriminate, but in principle these limits should be no more or less stringent than for other products and services.[10]

Lastly, as stated at the start of this section, it may be necessary to amend the normative economic stance on the optimum scope of copyright on the

10. Note a strong analogy with antitrust policy here: if a right holder is given monopolistic control over the exploitation of a work, there may be cause for antitrust intervention like in other industries where dominant players exist.

basis of other societal norms such as freedom of speech and privacy, as long as such norms have not been incorporated in the normative economic framework itself.

9.3 DIGITAL RESALE

The issue of the resale of digital content has already been mentioned in the previous section. Here, this case is studied in more detail. The question is whether an end user should be allowed to resell digitally acquired copyright works such as e-books, music files, video files and games, or to give them away, barter them or lend them to friends, just like works obtained on physical carriers.

9.3.1 Legal Treatment

The 'exhaustion' or 'first sale' doctrines refer to the general principle that once an original or copy of a work, such as a book or CD, has been sold by or under the authorization of the copyright holder, the exclusive right to authorize or prohibit any further distribution to the public of that original or copy, by sale or otherwise, is 'exhausted' (Article 4(2) of the Copyright Directive). In other words, the buyer can resell or give it to other parties as he sees fit and, in this respect, a physical carrier containing a copy of a work is treated identically to other products (although in EU copyright, the exhaustion rule does not encompass rental and lending). For digitally acquired works, however, this may be different as exhaustion does not apply to communication to the public (Article 3(3) of the Copyright Directive).

In a case relating to software, some room for digital resale was created by the CJEU. In Case C-128/11 – *UsedSoft*, the CJEU ruled that under certain conditions the exhaustion doctrine also applies to software bought by way of downloading it from the Internet, which means software can be resold 'second-hand' provided it is deleted by the initial buyer. Volume (multi-user) licences can only be resold as a whole and not partially, however. An important element in the reasoning of the Court was the fact that the Oracle software in this case could be used 'for an unlimited period' (CJEU, *UsedSoft*, paragraph 45), which lead the Court to conclude it involves 'the transfer of the right of ownership of the copy of the computer program in question' (CJEU, *UsedSoft*, paragraph 46). Further on, the Court argues that:

> from an economic point of view, the sale of a computer program on CD–ROM or DVD and the sale of a program by downloading from the internet are similar. The on-line transmission method is the functional equivalent of the supply of a material medium. Interpreting Article 4(2) of Directive 2009/24 in the light of the principle of equal treatment

> confirms that the exhaustion of the distribution right under that provision takes effect after the first sale in the European Union of a copy of a computer program by the copyright holder or with his consent, regardless of whether the sale relates to a tangible or an intangible copy of the program. (CJEU, UsedSoft, para. 61)

Hence, with respect to exhaustion, the CJEU makes no fundamental distinction between software bought on a physical carrier and software downloaded from the Internet without such a carrier. Commentators have stressed that in practice it will be hard to distinguish between authorized and unauthorized copies, as a result of which this ruling opens the door for uncontrollable piracy. On the other hand, the applicability of the ruling seems limited: first, it applies to software and not to other types of work. Second, it appears easy to circumvent this ruling by either offering a software licence for a limited time or offering it as a service instead of a product.[11]

However, in the case *Tom Kabinet v. Nederlands Uitgeversverbond* concerning the second-hand sale of e-books, the Amsterdam Court of Appeal held in 2015 that, in principle, the *UsedSoft* ruling can also be said to apply to e-books and therefore that the second-hand resale of e-books should in principle be allowed, as long as the reseller can guarantee the legitimacy of the e-books on sale. This case has now led to a preliminary reference to the CJEU.[12] Moreover, in Case C-174/15 – *Vereniging Openbare Bibliotheken v. Stichting Leenrecht*, the CJEU ruled that public libraries can lend digital copies of e-books, provided that 'only one copy may be downloaded during the lending period and that, after that period has expired, the downloaded copy can no longer be used by that user'. (CJEU, *Vereniging Openbare Bibliotheken v. Stichting Leenrecht*, paragraph 74). Both rulings suggest at least some room for applying the exhaustion doctrine to digital content.

9.3.2 Economic Analysis

One may question the economic significance of resale of digital content. Before embarking on a normative economic analysis of digital exhaustion, the following subsection aims to scratch the surface of the potential market for second-hand digital content.

9.3.2.1 The Potential Market for Second-Hand Digital Content

It is uncontroversial that the exhaustion doctrine applies to physical carriers such as CDs, DVDs and printed books and is simply irrelevant for

11. *See* Hugenholtz (2013b). For an extensive legal analysis of the *UsedSoft* case and digital exhaustion in EU and US law, *see* for instance Linklater (2014) and Mezei (2015).
12. ECLI:NL:RBDHA:2017:7543.

subscription services which, once cancelled, leave the consumer with no collection that could be resold. The issue to be discussed here is whether – from a welfare economic perspective – it ought to apply to *digital downloads* of copies of works. To estimate the potential market for second-hand digital content, this subsection first assesses the share of digital downloads in the various content markets.

In the music industry, digital downloads and physical formats are rapidly losing ground while subscription services are booming. In 2016, global revenues from recorded music totalled USD 15.7 billion, a growth of 5.9% compared to 2015 and the second consecutive year of global growth after two decades of decline (IFPI, 2017: p. 11). Digital sales (downloads plus subscription services) accounted for 50% of total revenues (USD 7.8 billion), while physical formats were down to a 34% share. Performance rights and synchronization rights were responsible for the remaining 16% of global revenues. Within the digital revenues share, the market is rapidly tilting towards streaming services. In 2016, streaming grew by 60% to account for 59% of digital revenues, while revenues from downloads declined by 21% (IFPI, 2017: p. 12). Considering the growth and decline of these digital formats over the past few years, streaming can be expected to grow further at the expense of both physical formats and digital downloads in the years to come. This implies that the potential market for second-hand digital music will shrink as the consumption on the first-hand market declines. On the other hand, the revenue share of digital music downloads could stabilize at some still-significant level. Moreover, there could be a surge in consumers who have switched to streaming services and therefore want to resell their digital collections.

Compared with music, the market for audio-visual content is more fragmented between genres and windows with very different backgrounds and business models, such as linear television (free-to-air or subscription-based), on-demand services and over the top (OTT) services such as Netflix. Films can be made available through all of these channels, but also have the theatrical window which series and other audio-visual content do not. Like for digital music, revenues for digital audio-visual content are growing rapidly, but for audio-visual, physical carriers are still the dominant format.

In 2016, total spending in Europe on buying and renting physical and digital video was EUR 9.7 billion (International Video Federation 2017). Physical DVDs and Blu-ray discs accounted for EUR 4.2 billion of that, down by 18% in 2016, while digital video and video on demand grew by 27% in that period to EUR 5.4 billion. Of that, digital retail is only a small portion and it remains uncertain whether digital retail will ever gain a substantial share in this market, given the rapid growth of subscription services. The fact that most adults do not consume audio-visual content repeatedly, as they do music, makes this market even more fit for digital rental or subscription services than music, but also implies that people might want to resell digital downloads if they can.

The market for video games is also very fragmented by platform (PC games, console games, smartphone and tablet games) and acquisition channel (physical formats, rentals, subscription services, web downloads and downloads from app stores). SuperData Research estimated the global market for *digital* games at USD 61 billion in 2015, 8% growth from 2014.[13] Of that USD 61 billion, tablet and smartphone games accounted for USD 25.1 billion and digital PC games for USD 32 billion. Digital console games accounted for only about USD 4 billion. In theory, a substantial percentage of this market for digital games could be relevant for digital resale.

Systematic, internationally comparable data for the e-book market are not available and different sources differ even when reporting for the same country (Poort & van Eijk, 2015). In 2013, e-book adoption was by far the highest in the US, where turnover from e-books amounted to about 19% of industry revenues. The UK came in second, with a 2013 market share for e-books of 15%, followed at some distance by countries such as Denmark (5%), the Netherlands (4.7%), Germany (3.9%), Spain (3%–5%), France (1.5%–2.3%) and Sweden (1%). Overall, e-books accounted for only 3% of book sales in Europe in 2013 (Wischenbart et al. 2014). More recent figures for the US e-book market suggest its share of total revenues has levelled off, at around 20% since 2012.[14] There are some subscription services for e-books, such as Kindle Unlimited, but these have not yet picked up a large market share. This suggests that there could be a substantial potential market for second-hand e-books.

To summarize: despite the fact that physical formats are still dominant for books and that access-based models (subscription and rental) dominate digital sales in music and audio-visual, there is still a large market for the sale of digital content. This raises the question of whether or not to allow digital resale. Apart from the potential size of this second-hand digital content market, there are other reasons (both economic and non-economic) for advocating the existence of such a market. Reis (2015: pp. 189–194) lists improved access to content, preservation, privacy, transactional clarity, innovation, platform competition and reducing piracy.[15]

---

13. http://www.cnbc.com/2016/01/26/digital-gaming-sales-hit-record-61-billion-in-2015-report.html (accessed 24 August 2017).
14. Association of American Publishers (AAP) (27 January 2016). *AAP StatShot: Publisher Net Revenue from Book Sales Declines 2.0% Through Third Quarter of 2015*, Press release.
15. Similar arguments are provided by Rubí Puig (2013), who proposes a set of 'factors that can be considered by courts and policymakers in applying rules on exhaustion more flexibly in some settings'. Taking such factors into account, right holders could formulate an efficiency defence for enforcing a contract limiting exhaustion.

9.3.2.2 No Economically Relevant Difference Between Physical and Digital Formats?

Section 9.2.4 stated that, as a default, control over a copy should not extend beyond its first sale any more than for any exhaustible good: once a digital or physical copy of a work has been sold, the market failure that justified copyright legislation has been resolved with respect to this specific copy. As for any other product which does not suffer from this market failure, there is sound economic justification for granting the initial creator automatic control over the secondary market or over the value created with the product downstream in the value chain.

As argued, this does not imply that a right holder would not *want* to control or extract rents from the secondary market or from value creation downstream. As Boldrin & Levine (2002: p. 3) write: ‘All producers would impose downstream licensing agreements if they could: producers prefer not to compete against their customers. But the absence of competition leads to monopoly, and economists as a rule frown upon monopoly’. A car manufacturer, for instance, might want to forbid or otherwise control the secondary market for cars in order to prevent competition from the market for used cars in the market for new ones. The closer substitute used cars are to new ones for consumers, the more new and used cars become part of the same relevant market, which implies that the price of new cars will be depressed by the price of used ones. At the same time, however, the option to sell a car on the secondary market increases the value of a new car for a consumer and part of this value can be extracted by the manufacturer in the initial sale.

For the car manufacturer, it might seem a good idea to receive royalties for the profits made by a company using its cars or for any resale in the second-hand market. In fact, such a royalty on the digital resale of copyright works is proposed by Reis (2015) and has been agreed upon between the Dutch reseller of second-hand e-books Tom Kabinet, and right holders: authors receive EUR 0.50 for each e-book sold second-hand on this website.[16] The idea of such a royalty for digital resale resembles the *droit de suite* or resale right which was discussed briefly in the introduction (section 9.1). The difference is that the *droit de suite* serves the purpose of improving distributive justice for artists whose work increases substantially in value after the first sale, or of protecting them against information asymmetries or possibly myopia; not of giving publishers or e-tailers control over downstream markets.

From an economic perspective, such a royalty should be rejected, since profits in downstream markets are not external effects and do not stem from the public good market failure of copyright works. A royalty on resale could hence be called a *jealousy tax* with no sound economic justification. In specific cases, such a royalty may improve the incentives for the production

16. http://www.tomkabinet.nl/en/faq/ (accessed 24 August 2017).

of cars. But as a general rule, this is more likely to introduce or worsen market failures downstream and lead to an overall welfare loss. From general economic theory it follows that the welfare effects on downstream markets, caused by investments in a market, may only be significant if significant market failures exist in these downstream markets. Only in such cases might the investment increase or reduce market failure (e.g., market power) in downstream markets and generate additional welfare effects there.[17]

A point which is often raised to argue that resale of digital content is different and that exhaustion should therefore not apply, is that digital content does not degrade or depreciate (e.g., Reis, 2015). A second-hand version of an e-book has no coffee stains or dog ears and is just as good as a new one. This could imply that first and second-hand versions are perfect substitutes, meaning the right holder may face stiff competition from the second-hand market. Three points can be made to counter this argument.

First, it was already pointed out that part of the value consumers anticipate from resale can be extracted in the initial sale.[18]

Second, depreciation of copyright works is not just physical but primarily commercial. Although there are certainly differences between types of works, genres and specific titles in this respect, books, music albums, films, series and games are generally 'fast-selling products' and generate most of their revenues during a short period of time. For games, this may be less than a week, but for popular music, books and audio-visual content too, sales fall off very rapidly over time.

To illustrate this: Adele's album '25' sold 2.3 million copies in the US during the first three days, making it one of twenty albums to have ever sold over a million copies within a week. Interestingly, the list of albums to *ever* sell over a million copies is identical to the list of albums selling over a million copies within a week, which implies that *no album to ever sell over a million copies did not do so within a week.*[19] Most books also have a short commercial life cycle. For the Netherlands it was ascertained that, around 2010, an average book generated more than half of its turnover in the first year after publication and about three quarters in the first two years (Poort et al. 2012: p. 33). The content industries deploy windowing strategies to encourage and to exploit this phenomenon: books are often first published in a more expensive hardcover edition and gradually become cheaper. For films, windowing has evolved into a complex timeline, starting with the theatrical window and ending with free-to-air television, with windows in between for video on demand, digital sales, rental and pay television (Weda

17. For example *see*: Romijn & Renes, 2013: p. 63.
18. Under the assumptions in the models of Boldrin & Levine (2002–2008), full extraction occurs even if buyers start producing and selling multiple copies, which is not advocated here.
19. http://www.billboard.com/articles/columns/chart-beat/6770482/adele-25-other-million-selling-albums (accessed 24 August 2017).

et al. 2012: p. 37). For video games, frequent updates boost people's preference for originals over second-hand products. Hence, the commercial depreciation of copyright works is well-established and limits the threat the second-hand market may be for the first-hand market. By the time second-hand works enter the market, most of the money has already been made.

Third, like in any second-hand market, there are information asymmetries and transaction costs associated with digital resale. These derive from questions such as: will the file format of this e-book or film be supported by my hardware and, if not, will I be able to get my money back? Will this video game be virus-free? Is it a corrupted version or illegal copy which does not give me updates and support? Jewellery is an interesting analogy, fitting the first and this third points: like digital works, jewels barely degrade physically, but the option to resell or pawn them is part of the reason people are willing to pay large sums for them. Moreover, information asymmetries and transactions costs make many people think twice before buying expensive jewellery from street vendors or on eBay.

Yet another line of argument *against* digital resale starts from the perspective of private ordering. The point would be that contractual freedom should prevail and override digital exhaustion, implying that if buyer and seller agree on a contract which precludes resale, they should have a right to do so. If both parties agree on such a contract, it is likely to be in the interest of both parties and forbidding such a contract is likely to decrease welfare. Such a position is taken by Epstein (2010: pp. 503–511) who argues that there is no good reason to forbid contractual arrangements that restrict or put conditions on resale, unless a monopoly position is bolstered by them.

The arguments for and against such a position are very similar to other debates on vertical restraints, such as retail price maintenance or agency pricing, as introduced and abandoned for e-books. Under certain conditions, some such restrains can be welfare enhancing,[20] but a general observation is that in a perfectly competitive market, a manufacturer will have neither the power nor the desire to push such contracts. Only in the presence of market power or other market failures such as information asymmetry, may a manufacturer be likely to want to restrict resale in downstream markets, which can in some cases be pro-competitive and in others anti-competitive. For instance, a publisher may exploit information asymmetries or myopia at the expense of consumers who are not aware the music file or e-book they buy cannot be resold or even be inherited or given away.[21] Or publishers may all collude by orchestrating a contractual restriction on resale. In such cases,

20. For a discussion of the arguments concerning retail price maintenance for books and e-books, *see* Poort & van Eijk (2015).

21. For example *The Guardian* 3 September 2012, 'Bruce Willis to fight Apple over right to leave iTunes library in will' (http://www.theguardian.com/film/2012/sep/03/bruce-willis-apple-itunes-library, accessed 24 August 2017). For e-books, this lack of transparency and awareness for consumers is discussed in Reis (2015: pp. 197–200).

restrictions on resale are likely to be profitable for publishers but welfare decreasing for society at large. Downes (2013) suggests consumers might need time to lose the mindset of ownership of products bought, encouraged since the Industrial Revolution. It may take 're-education' for consumers to get used to buying content as a service, subject to certain conditions. However, the immense popularity of streaming services such as Spotify and Netflix shows that consumers are quick learners and easily accept temporary access-based models as long as it is clear what they can expect.

9.3.3 Conclusions

As a general response to the argument of contractual freedom, one can take the stance that – as in section 9.2.4 – control over a copy should not extend beyond its first sale as a default rule, while any contractual arrangements that aim to override this should be subject to general rules concerning fair business practices and competition law. For one thing, this implies that any market-wide contractual restriction on resale should be looked upon with much suspicion as it may very well be a sign of collusion – tacit or not. Also, a prohibition on resale should not exploit information asymmetries by hiding behind terms and conditions which no one reads or understands. There are no economic justifications for granting copyright-protected works a special status in these respects. Once a digital or physical copy of a work has been sold, the market failure that justified copyright protection has been resolved with respect to this specific copy and any profits on resale do not derive from non-excludability or external effects. To the extent that copyright grants monopoly power over a specific work, the risk that contractual arrangements and vertical restraints are used to exploit this further are likely to be larger than in many other industries.

The logic behind the CJEU ruling in *UsedSoft* – accepting a form of exhaustion and allowing resale for software clients could use for an unlimited period – as well as the ruling in *Vereniging Openbare Bibliotheken v Stichting Leenrecht* – allowing a public library to lend e-books under certain conditions without any additional contract – is in line with this economic reasoning for allowing resale as a general rule. Yet there is a need for refining the approach with regard to the possibilities for product and price discrimination, for which resale was required to be impractical, costly or outright forbidden (*see* section 9.2.4 above): it can be welfare enhancing for a company to aim to prevent discounted student licences for software being resold to companies. Similarly, preventing resale of promotional copies of CDs or student copies of books may well be welfare enhancing as a way to segment the market. Also, partial reselling of multi-user licences would constitute a serious threat to price discrimination, as it would undermine volume-based price discrimination.

However, in digital markets a publisher can try to uphold price discrimination without contractual arrangements, for instance by versioning or offering additional services or by offering subscriptions and streaming services instead of one-off fees for an unlimited time. In fact, this happens all the time. Versioning may seem wasteful at first glance, but often it is a welfare enhancing way to service both high- and low-end customers. Also, a publisher can offer a discount on a newer version if you hand back your earlier version. Under such business strategies, there is less need for contractual arrangements that prevent resale, let alone legislation which supports right holders in their efforts to price discriminate.

So far, it has been implicitly assumed in this section that digital resale really involves the transfer of a digital content file. That is, the initial buyer actually deletes the music file, e-book, game or video file from his computer. In practice, this may be problematic to ensure or to monitor. In section 9.2.4, it was observed that the public good market failure re-emerges if the secondary market can lead to market extension, where buyers can resell multiple copies or grant several new consumers access to the work, undercutting the original creator because they have no investment in the initial creation to recoup. Without TPMs that help guarantee that such market extension does not occur, a right holder has next to no opportunity to monitor whether the initial version is really deleted or uninstalled after resale.

There are two options to address this issue. The first is to accept this and still allow digital resale as a general rule. In this approach, right holders can regain control by implementing strong copy protection through TPMs or by contractually limiting or forbidding such resale, in which case such a contract is subject to general rules concerning fair business practices and competition law. A disadvantage of this approach is that it encourages right holders to use TPMs, despite the transaction costs and dead-weight losses this entails, because copy protected works are in many cases less user-friendly. A second option is to only allow digital resale for works protected by TPMs. As long as this condition is transparent on sale, it is not an obstacle for consumers, and market places can easily monitor to ensure that only TPM-protected works can be resold. For TPM-free material, monitoring the legitimacy of the secondary market is not possible and therefore control is exercised by having exclusive rights to the secondary market.

9.4 PRIVATE COPYING

Like in the case of digital resale, the key issue in the economic analysis of private copying is whether it is welfare enhancing for right holders to be able to control or be remunerated for certain uses of content after its sale.

9.4.1 Legal Treatment

Article 5(2)(b) of the Copyright Directive provides Member States with the option to implement a private copying exception to the exclusive right of authors, subject to payment of fair compensation:

> [M]ember States may provide for exceptions or limitations to the reproduction right … in respect of reproductions on any medium made by a natural person for private use and for ends that are neither directly nor indirectly commercial, on condition that the rightholders receive fair compensation which takes account of the application or non-application of technological measures referred to in Article 6 to the work or subject-matter concerned.

> [M]ember States may provide for exceptions or limitations to the reproduction right … in respect of reproductions on any medium made by a natural person for private use and for ends that are neither directly nor indirectly commercial, on condition that the rightholders receive fair compensation which takes account of the application or non-application of technological measures referred to in Article 6 to the work or subject-matter concerned.

In most Member States, such fair compensation is provided through a system of levies on blank media and equipment used for making private copies. Despite the shared legislative background – the Copyright Directive – there is much variation between Member States in the choices made concerning the equipment and blank media on which levies are imposed, the levy tariffs applied and the per capita revenues collected annually (WIPO/ Wijminga et al., 2017: 3–27).

Since 2010, the CJEU has dealt with a series of cases in relation to private copying and private copying levies. For the purposes of this chapter, the most relevant judgments of the CJEU are: Case C-467/08 –*Padawan*; Joined Cases C-457/11 to C-460/11 – *VG Wort*; Case C-435/12 – *ACI Adam*; and Case C-463/12 – *Copydan*.

In *Padawan* the Court ruled that private copying levies should not compensate for copies made for professional use. The latter do not fall under the exception of Article 5(2)(b), and hence there can be no compensation for such copies, nor is a system allowed that accounts for this by reducing levies for both private and professional users (so-called mutualization).

In *VG Wort* and *Copydan* the CJEU dealt with the issue of licensed copies. The Court held that if the private copying exception is introduced into national law, a licence allowing consumers to make multiple copies for personal use is null and void. Therefore, it can have no impact on the levy that is due.

Finally, in *ACI Adam* the CJEU held that copies made through downloading from illegal sources are outside the scope of the private copying exception. Hence, private copying levies cannot be due to compensate for such downloading.

9.4.2 Economic Analysis

Like the previous section on digital resale (section 9.3), the economic analysis in this section starts off with a brief assessment of the economic footprint of the phenomenon. Making private copies is something which an average person does almost every day, even without noticing: private copies in the legal sense are not only made when copying a CD or DVD or ripping it for playback on a smartphone, but also when making a backup of legally obtained e-books, transferring one's digital music collection to a new smartphone, recording a film on TV to watch it the next day, etc.

In the Netherlands for instance, annual surveys are held to assess the number of private copies made in order to provide information for setting and redistributing levies. In the 2017 edition of the survey, the total number of works copied per person was estimated at more than six hundred per year, 80% of which were considered to require fair compensation through a levy. Of the latter, about 60% consisted of audio files such as music and radio programmes; about 20% were audio-visual material such as movies, TV series, documentaries and music videos; and the rest were images, e-books and material from publications (Verhue & De Gier, 2017: Tables 7–9). The value of all such copies for users and the potential damage to right holders are key issues in discussions on levy setting in any country.

Annual revenues from levies within a country tend to fluctuate much more than the number of copies made. This is partly due to the rapid changes in the markets for consumer electronics, as a result of which the equipment and media used for making copies change rapidly so that levy systems need constant maintenance to keep pace. A second driver of volatility is litigation concerning which levy systems are congruent with EU law and which are not. As a result, even total revenues collected in all EU Member States together fluctuate substantially: between 2007 and 2015, revenues grew from EUR 549 million to EUR 582 million, but amounted to only EUR 406 million in 2012, while reaching EUR 722 million in 2014. Per person per year, average revenues in the EU increased from EUR 1.37 to EUR 1.42 between 2007 and 2015. Between EU Member States, the differences are more than two orders of magnitude: in 2015 the average revenues per person were EUR 3.38 in France but less than EUR 0.01 in Estonia (WIPO/Wijminga, et al., 2017: pp. 16–22).

For an economic analysis of private copying levies along the lines of this chapter, one needs to establish whether private copying affects the ability of a creator to *control* access to a work and to exchange it for something which is valuable to him and, if so, whether it negatively and significantly affects the current or future exploitation opportunities for the right holder. To answer these questions, it is useful to distinguish different kinds of private copies:[22]

(1) Making '*clone copies*' of or '*format shifting*' CDs, DVDs and media files, or storing streaming audio and video for offline playback (also known as stream 'ripping' or 'capture').
(2) Making *backup copies* of works.
(3) Making copies of broadcast works for *time shifting,* such as storing radio or TV content on a recording device to watch it another time, and repeatedly if desired.
(4) Making clone copies or format shifting to *share* works with members of your *household, family and friends.*
(5) Making clone copies or format shifting of works from media *rented* or *borrowed* from libraries or commercial renters.
(6) *Downloading* and storing works from *unauthorized sources* on the Internet (and making subsequent copies thereof).

Typically, private copies of types (1) to (5) are allowed under the private copying exception. However, types (1), (2), (4) and (5) may in practice be prohibited or restricted by TPMs and licence or rental agreements. Downloading from unauthorized sources on the Internet (type (6)) is explicitly prohibited following the *ACI Adam* ruling of the CJEU.

With regard to the question of whether private copies negatively and significantly affect the exploitation opportunities for the right holder, there are relevant economic differences between these types of copy.

Copies of type (1) enhance the utility that consumers derive from their legitimate purchase or subscription. Such copies enable them to consume this content on a more practical device or without carrying discs and devices around. For instance, they can keep a copy of their favourite CDs in their car or vacation home or play them on their computer, smartphone or mp3 player. In all these ways, such copies may generate additional consumer surplus, but one can dispute whether it affects the control of a creator to exchange access to a work for something which is valuable to him. Right holders could argue that such copies affect their ability to charge for access to copies *offline* or in a more convenient format (e.g., mp3 instead of a CD), but unlimited access to the works themselves had already been obtained by the users, for instance by buying the CD. The mere effect of copies of type (1) is that they make accessing these works more convenient for consumers or allow them to access the works under new circumstances, for instance when they do not have an Internet connection. The same goes for backup copies (2), which do not provide utility directly, but act as an insurance against mishaps.

This insight suggests that from an economic perspective, private copies of types (1) and (2) are largely copyright irrelevant and need not fall under an exclusive right or be compensated for by way of a copyright levy. The

22. The typology here and part of this section are taken from Poort & Quintais (2013).

economic reason for this is that the value an average consumer derives from these copies is largely foreseeable and can be anticipated by both the buyer and the seller and therefore appropriated in the initial sale, much as it was argued in the case of digital resale in the previous section. Of course, some consumers would appreciate the option to make such copies more than others, but such differences in the utility consumers derive from a good are a fact of ordinary economic life. Such differences underlie the sloping demand line and as a result of that the consumer surplus in Figure 9.1. The argument can be made that, to the extent any harm from such copies cannot be appropriated in the initial sale, it is minimal (*de minimis*).

Some additional sales could be foregone as a result of such copying, for instance when a person would have bought his favourite CD twice to play it at home and in his car. But, to the extent that consumers can broadly anticipate their copying behaviour, the option to copy will be reflected by the demand for originals and priced into the initial purchase by right holders. This implies that in such a case a copyright levy that charges consumers for the value they attach to the additional copies would lead to double payment and could in fact reduce the willingness to pay for originals.

Having said that, the demand curve will not reflect the utility of *unforeseen* copying possibilities: in the first decade after the introduction of the CD, consumers would not have anticipated that twenty years later they would be able to make perfect home copies of their CDs, let alone rip five hundred CDs onto a portable device the size of a matchbox. Hence, the utility they derive from copying and ripping these CDs will not have been reflected in their initial purchase at the time. However, nor was such unforeseen utility as a result of technological change a consideration for creating the work in the first place. Hence, there is no welfare economic reason to entitle right holders to a part of these unforeseen benefits.

The same argument largely holds for time shifting copies (type (3)), but not entirely. Where time shifting also involves systematically skipping advertisements in an ad-based exploitation model (or time shifting to a moment in time where the ads surrounding a radio or television broadcast no longer have their initial commercial value), it may undermine the exploitation opportunities for the right holder to some extent.[23] Advertisers will be aware that some of their ads will be skipped when consumers watch programmes they have recorded, which will lower advertising revenues for channels. Therefore, copies of type (3) may be looked upon differently than types (1) and (2) and may justify an alternative way of remuneration for right holders, such as a levy on welfare economic grounds, provided the transaction costs and dead-weight losses of these levies do not outweigh the positive incentive effects.

23. There is an analogy with embedding (section 9.5 below) here, where content may also be stripped from its exploitation model.

Copies of types (4) and (5) differ from the former in that they extend the circle of consumers who derive utility from an original unit of content.[24] Unauthorized downloading (6) resembles these types, with the notable difference that the extended circle of consumers is anonymous and potentially unlimited. These types of private copy do affect a creator's control – new consumers gain access to the content – but there is a substantial difference between unauthorized downloading (6) and the other types of copy in respect of the extent to which it is likely to affect the current or future exploitation opportunities for the right holder.

This difference can be translated into the *harm* that private copying may cause to copyright holders. The crucial economic concept here is *indirect appropriability*. This term refers to the economic mechanism according to which, under certain conditions, the demand for originals will reflect the value that consumers place on both the originals and subsequent copies they may make.[25] As will be discussed below, the value of private copies of types (4) and (5) can – just like (1) and (2) – largely be priced into the initial purchase and, by doing so, this value is *indirectly appropriated.*

A seminal contribution to this issue is provided by Stan Liebowitz (1985), who studied the effect of photocopying on the demand for journals and writes: 'The evidence indicates that publishers can indirectly appropriate revenues from users who do not directly purchase journals and that photocopying has not harmed journal publishers.' The value consumers (or scholars) derive from copies contributes to libraries' willingness to pay. Hence, publishers end up selling fewer originals at a higher price, which may even raise profits. If the number of copies per original varies substantially, such *indirect appropriability* depends on the ability to price discriminate: charging a higher price for users who are likely to enable extensive copying while preventing arbitrage through a secondary market or other ways of circumventing price discrimination. In practice, this is done by setting a higher price for libraries and a lower price for individuals.

In general, selling fewer originals at a higher price introduces two opposing effects which may lead to both higher and lower profits. This issue was further studied by Besen and Kirby (1989), who model private copying while distinguishing: (1) the extent to which originals and copies are perfect substitutes, and (2) whether private copying has constant or increasing marginal costs.[26] Increasing marginal costs may stem not only from the

24. Alternatively, one could argue that making copies of legally borrowed or rented content – type (5) – is a form of time shifting (beyond the rental period) rather than an extension of the circle of consumers.
25. This is very like the argument in section 9.3 that the value consumers may derive from the resale of digital content can also be priced into the purchase as well as the central argument in Boldin & Levine (2002–2008).
26. Besen and Kirby's models ignore possible positive dynamic effects of the consumption of copies on future sales (the so-called sampling effect) and negative effects of lost sales on the future production of content.

technology itself, but also from the 'costs' of organizing the copying process within sharing groups. Besen and Kirby conclude that the effect of private copying on consumer and producer surplus and total welfare depends strongly on the assumptions about substitutability and the costs of copying. When the marginal costs of copying are *constant*, copies will be distributed at marginal cost and the value of copies cannot be appropriated. The introduction of (relatively cheap) copying technology will then lower the price of originals and profits will subsequently decline. Consumer surplus will increase, while the effect on total welfare is ambiguous. If the marginal costs of copies are *increasing*, copying leads to fewer originals sold at a higher price. Besen and Kirby conclude that the effect on welfare will depend on whether or not copying is cheaper than producing originals:

> in the case where the size of the sharing group is fixed, consumer and producer welfare generally increase when copying is efficient and decline when it is not. When the costs of both originals and copies are low, however, producers will generally lose and consumers will gain from the introduction of copying. (Besen & Kirby, 1989: p. 280).

The scenario of constant (near-zero) marginal costs of copying resembles the situation of unauthorized file sharing over the Internet, even though such file sharing did not exist when Besen and Kirby wrote their paper. Their analysis implies that indirect appropriability is not feasible in the face of online file sharing (type (6) above). This also follows from the fact that through online file sharing the number of copies generated per original sold will differ immensely: some content will not be copied at all, while other content will be uploaded to torrent sites to be downloaded by millions of users. This makes adequate price discrimination – and by extension indirect appropriation – practically impossible: one cannot charge a buyer of a CD or e-book for the surplus all downloaders derive from it if he chooses to distribute it illegally over the Internet.

The scenario of *increasing* marginal costs will apply to copies of types (4) and (5): such activities have a natural limit to their scope. Copies of these types may or may not cause harm, depending on the costs and value of copies in comparison to originals and the size of sharing groups. Depending on the assumptions about these, copying may cause no harm at all to copyright holders, or it may constrain the price the copyright holder can charge for originals and reduce profits substantially (Varian, 2005).

Empirical testing of the net effect on profits of private copying of types (1) to (5) is lacking.[27] Surveys carried out in the context of the levy-setting process in various countries (such as Verhue & De Gier, 2017) typically focus on the number of private copies and sometimes the self-reported substitution rate, but ignore the effect of private copying on the demand for

27. Empirical evidence on the effect of copying from illegal sources (type (6)) will be discussed briefly in section 9.5 below.

the first original and the complex dynamics of indirect appropriability. The net effect can be expected to differ for the various types of private copies discussed above. As mentioned there, private copies of types (1) and (2) do not extend the circle of consumers that derive utility from an original unit of content and are largely copyright irrelevant. No 'copying groups' are formed in which copies become competitors to the original.

Turning to copies shared within one's household, and with family and friends (type (4)), the models of Besen and Kirby and Varian are more likely to apply, and private copying might be harmful to copyright holders even though some of the additional utility can be appropriated indirectly. This is partly due to the fact that the size of such copying groups is variable and price discrimination according to group size is not possible. The utility of copies of type (5) could in theory be appropriated indirectly through rental prices, unless restrictions put on the rental price prohibit doing so. For the right holder, this implies that price discrimination will be required between libraries and commercial renters – who, as in Stan Liebowitz's example, would pay a higher price to account for the utility of subsequent copies – and end consumers.[28] If these markets cannot be separated, copying groups will be too variable in size to adequately price copying into the purchase and a private copying levy or lending right will still be justified on welfare economic grounds.

9.4.3 Conclusions

Economic analysis has shown that the utility consumers derive from offline private copies can to a large extent be appropriated indirectly. Hence, the harm caused by these acts will be substantially smaller than the utility consumers derive from private copies or even the sales forgone by such copying. For *format shifting* and *clone copying* for personal use – copies that do not lead to a proliferation of content – this is likely to be the case almost entirely, after an initial shock wave caused by the introduction of cheap digital copying and ripping technology for consumers. Now that both consumers and producers are aware of this technology, indirect appropriability will apply and harm will be minimal. In such cases, levies aimed at compensating for this minimal harm are ill-advised, given the administrative and transaction costs they incur and their potential to take away incentives for smart pricing.

For *(large scale) time shifting* which significantly affects a consumer's exposure to advertisements in ad-based exploitation models, and for copies *made within the accepted circle of family and friends*, on the other hand, indirect appropriation may not be sufficiently possible (e.g., due to varying sharing group size) and harm from such private copies may indeed occur.

28. Alternatively, lending rights can serve this purpose.

The argument of indirect appropriability does not apply to unauthorized online file sharing, as there is no relation between the uploader (including any unlawful content provider) and the downloader. Also, the number of copies made from an original will vary dramatically, which makes it impossible to price such copies into the purchase. Hence, there are sound economic arguments for such copies falling under the exclusive right of the creator, or for introducing some form of compensation system to the extent that such copying cannot be controlled. [29]

9.5 HYPERLINKING AND EMBEDDING

The third case to be discussed concerns what is arguably the essence of the World Wide Web: hyperlinking to web pages and embedding content from other web pages on one's own.

9.5.1 Legal Treatment

The legal nature of hyperlinking and embedding, and subsequently the question of whether or not such linking without prior authorization constitutes a copyright infringement, has been debated in four CJEU cases: Case C-466/12 – *Svensson*, Case C-348/13 – *Bestwater*, Case C-279/13 – *C More Entertainment*, and Case C-160/15 – *GS Media*. It is generally acknowledged that linking or embedding does not concern acts of reproduction, rather disputes focus on the question of whether or not it involves a communication to the public under Article 3 of the Copyright Directive and, if so, whether it requires the prior authorization of the right holder.

In *Svensson*, the CJEU ruled that hyperlinking can be considered a communication to the public and thus fall within the scope of copyright. However, unless hyperlinking results in the circumvention of access restrictions, it does not lead to works being communicated to a *new* public, i.e., a public which the right holder did not consider when making the work available online. Given these considerations, hyperlinking is not considered an infringement and in this respect no difference is made between hyperlinking, framing or embedding.[30]

In a later decision, *Bestwater*, the CJEU confirmed that hyperlinking and embedding were to be considered equivalent as regards their copyright relevancy. In the case at hand, sales representatives had embedded a

29. *See* the chapter by Quintais and Hugenholtz in this volume.
30. ALAI (2013) suggests no difference between framing and linking, but a difference between referring links and links that provide access. It suggests that site owners can program so as to decide if deep linking/embedding is possible.

promotion video made by Bestwater on their website. The video had been posted on YouTube, allegedly without the consent of Bestwater.

Another five months later, the CJEU delivered its ruling in *C More Entertainment*. Of the five initial questions, four had been withdrawn by the referring court after the *Svensson* judgment, leaving only a question on the issue of linking to or embedding of live broadcasts. The CJEU ruled that national legislators can implement the protection of these rights in such a way that such linking or embedding without authorization is an infringement. As a consequence, linking to live broadcasts may be allowed in some Member States and an infringement in others, regardless of whether technical protection measures are circumvented in doing so.

In September 2016, the Court delivered its judgment in *GS Media*, a case that dealt with linking to *unauthorized* content. It concerned a Dutch website operated by GS Media BV that posted links to an Australian site hosting nude pictures of a Dutch woman without authorization, and even prior to their official publication in Playboy magazine. The Dutch Supreme Court asked the CJEU whether linking to unauthorized content constitutes a communication to the public; whether it makes a difference if the linked to content has been previously communicated with the right holder's consent; whether it makes a difference if the hyperlinker is aware of these things; whether it makes a difference if the site communicating the unauthorized content is not easily locatable without the link; and whether any other circumstances are relevant regarding linking to content communicated without consent (CJEU, *GS Media*, paragraph 24).

In its decision, the CJEU reiterated that linking to *authorized* content is not a communication to a new public. Regarding *unauthorized* content, the Court makes a distinction based on the nature and knowledge of the linking party, due to the complexity involved in ascertaining whether content is posted with authorization. If the party linking to unauthorized content is a person who does not act for profit, he or she is not assumed to have knowledge of the authorized or unauthorized nature of the content linked to. Therefore, the link is not considered a communication to the public.

However, if a person knew the content was unauthorized, or ought to have known this, the link *is* considered a communication to the public (CJEU, *GS Media*, paragraphs 44–49). Also, if the posting of links is carried out for profit, 'it must be presumed that that posting has occurred with the full knowledge of the protected nature of that work and the possible lack of consent to publication on the internet by the copyright holder' (CJEU, *GS Media*, paragraph 50). Hence, linking to unauthorized content by a for-profit website or entity is a communication to the public and requires authorization from the right holder.[31]

---

31. Relatedly, in April 2017, the CJEU delivered its ruling in Case C-527/15 – *Filmspeler*. In the case, Brein opposed a provider of a media player with add-ons containing pre-installed links to unauthorized content (Filmspeler). The questions referred to the

9.5.2 Economic Analysis

To start an economic analysis, it is important to realize that hyperlinking and embedding are key features of the web. The number of unique websites is estimated at more than 1.2 billion,[32] while the number of individual *pages* indexed by Google in 2014 was reported to be 30 trillion.[33] Another source mentions an average of 60 links per page,[34] which would imply a total of around 2 quadrillion (2×10^{15}) links on the Internet. In addition, hyperlinks can be included in word files, pdfs, etc., which can also be made available on the Internet. This implies that any legal decision which curtails the practice of linking – as the *GS Media* ruling (C-160/15) does – may not just affect the nature of the web, but may also have massive economic effects in terms of transaction costs and dead-weight losses.

To assess the optimum scope of copyright with respect to linking and embedding from a welfare economic perspective, the first question is to determine whether and to what extent linking and embedding affect the ability of a creator to *control* access to a work and exchange this for something which is valuable to him, against the background of the public good market failure of works. If control is affected, the next question is whether it negatively and significantly affects the current or future exploitation opportunities for the right holder.

9.5.2.1 Linking to or Embedding of Authorized Sources

Focusing first on the issue of linking to or embedding of *authorized* sources (as dealt with in *Svensson*), it is relevant to distinguish different types of hyperlinking and embedding on the Internet, which can have different effects on the control, and hence the exploitation opportunities of the right holder:[35]

(1) Linking:

- *Link to homepage*, the primary domain where content can be found (e.g., www.abc.com). People following this link will generally need to navigate further on this homepage to the actual information referred to.

CJEU focused on the status of streaming from an unauthorized source rather than on the issue of linking or embedding. The CJEU ruled that the sale of a multimedia player such as that of Filmspeler is a communication to the public. On the issue of streaming from unauthorized sources, it ruled that this is an infringement.

32. http://www.internetlivestats.com/total-number-of-websites/ (accessed 24 August 2017).
33. http://www.statisticbrain.com/total-number-of-pages-indexed-by-google/ (accessed 24 August 2017).
34. http://edition.cnn.com/2011/TECH/web/09/12/web.index/ (accessed 24 August 2017).
35. A similar typology is presented in Tsoutsanis (2014).

- *Deep link* to a subpage, which contains the information referred to (e.g., http://abc.go.com/shows/the-muppets).
- *Deep link to image*, which does not contain any of the context in which the image is shown or for instance advertisements surrounding it (e.g., http://cdn1.edgedatg.com/aws/v2/abc/TheMuppets/person/857714/535c2ae0b818dc2da74266fca8e73046/512x535c2ae0b818dc2da74266fca8e73046/512x288-Q90_535c2ae0b818dc2da74266fca8e73046.jpg).
- Note that all these links can be presented as a URL or as text or even a symbol which does not immediately reveal the address or nature of the referred content (e.g., kermit or even 🎭).

(2) Embedding or framing: this is a quite different technique, which can be used to present content on a site while it is hosted somewhere else. This technique was utilized for instance in the *Bestwater* case.

Note that the typology presented here is time and technology specific. A robust proposal for copyright legislation should stay away from being technology specific but set out general principles. Having said that, the main demarcation here lies between the various types of linking on the one hand, which push the visitor to a different location, and embedding or framing on the other, which pull information from another location (*see also* Tsoutsanis, 2014: 497).

The relevance of the distinction between linking and embedding or framing can be illustrated by an offline analogy, referring to content in a book. Linking to a homepage would correspond to mentioning a book where certain information can be found. Deep linking would correspond to citing the book and the page number where the information can be found. An analogy to deep linking to an image is harder to find: it would involve referring to a clipping from a book on an otherwise blank page. This analogy leads some commentators to conclude that hyperlinks are 'nothing more than a reference or a footnote' (e.g., Tim Berners-Lee and Jessica Litman cited in Bently et al., 2013).

In all of these cases, a relevant difference between referencing or footnoting on the one hand, and linking on the other, is that through linking, clear and highly convenient directions are given to where the referenced information can be found: *as long as the link is working*, a website visitor is no more than one click away from the information referred to, which implies that the transaction costs of following up on the reference are dramatically lower than in the offline world. Obviously, such a dramatic decrease in transaction costs compared to footnoting will have significant consequences. A website visitor will be much more likely to follow up on a link and visit the website with the work which is referred to, than he would be to go to a library or bookstore to follow up on a footnote. Hence a 'simple' decrease in transaction costs will have significant and positive effects on the consumption of a work.

Embedding or framing is quite different again. The analogy might be to show a picture from a book page, without making clear which book it is or where it can be found. The picture may even *appear* to be part of the source referring to it instead of a separate source. Like linking, this can have significant and positive effects on the number of people viewing the embedded picture (or watching the video or listening to the stream), but consumers of the work may be much less aware which work they consume, who the author is and in what context it is presented.

For both linking and embedding, the *right holder remains in control* of the availability and integrity of the relevant content. This is the catch of the condition 'as long as the link is working' above: if the right holder removes the content from his site or introduces some form of access restriction, the content will no longer be available through linking and embedding. If the right holder decides to make changes to the content, the changes will immediately extend to the linking or embedding sites. This is a fundamental difference between linking or embedding, and downloading content to send it to someone else by email or post it on a different site. In the latter case, the right holder's control over the availability and integrity of the content is lost. This is why it can be disputed whether the work is communicated/made available to the public by linking or embedding as the CJEU argues. Control over the availability and integrity of the information continues to lie exclusively with the referred site.

In section 9.2, the general principle was laid out that resolving the public good market failure of creative works could require giving a creator certain exclusive rights with respect to acts that *negatively and significantly affect his current or future exploitation opportunities* and hence negatively interfere with his incentives to create or to exploit. In light of this principle, there is a substantial difference between linking and embedding. In the case of linking, the right holder cannot only control the availability and integrity of the work, but also the environment in which the work can be accessed.

It was also stressed in section 9.2 that exploitation of a work in the digital environment can take many forms, and linking does not seem to affect any of these negatively. Linking can have significant and *positive* effects on the consumption of a work, if the linking page has a large number of visitors. Thus, it is hard to see how linking to a homepage or deep linking may negatively and significantly affect the current or future exploitation opportunities for the right holder. The contextual information and advertisements surrounding a link will still be seen. The right holder remains in control of the information that is made public and the conditions under which it is made public (e.g., payment, registration, advertisements). Hence, it seems that linking to a homepage or deep linking can only *positively* affect the current or future exploitation opportunities for the right holder, if it affects them at all. Therefore, there seems very little room for making the case that linking to authorized content should amount to copyright infringement.

From an economic perspective, embedding and framing are fundamentally different. Embedding is much closer to the exploitation of a work than linking; also, contrary to linking, embedding can be a substitute to licensing. In such cases, the right holder still has control over the availability and integrity of the work, but loses most of his control over the environment in which the work is accessed. This can negatively and significantly affect the exploitation opportunities for the right holder, as they entail that the right holder's site does not need to be visited, and so advertisements or other information on this site are not seen and even the page visit may not be counted properly. Depriving right holders from a certain exclusivity by doing this could negatively affect their exploitation opportunities.

However, before jumping to the conclusion that embedding might therefore be an act that should fall within the scope of copyright and hence require a licence, the transaction costs and dead-weight losses of doing so need to be taken into consideration. It goes without saying that the majority of right holders do not mind if their content is embedded, or even encourage it. Hence, it would entail enormous transaction costs to require a licence for any such embedding. As a result, many sites would refrain from embedding certain content, leading to dead-weight losses. The total number of links on the world wide web was estimated above at around 2 quadrillion (2×10^{15}). Assume that this estimate – which is very rough – overestimates the number of links by a factor of 100, and that for every 10,000 links there is one instance of embedding. This would still yield a staggering 2 billion embedded links (2×10^{15}/ 100 / 10,000 = 2×10^{9}).[36] The point here is not to claim that this number is accurate, but rather to give a ballpark figure for how large the number is likely to be. As a consequence, the transaction costs and dead-weight losses of licensing or otherwise actively acquiring authorization for linking, or even embedding, will be enormous. Likewise, the transaction costs and dead-weight losses of the CJEU ruling in *GS Media* – if acted upon – could be overwhelming.

A way to minimize transaction costs would be to implement a technical solution which precludes embedding a website that does not want to be embedded. In fact, such a technical solution already seems to exist,[37] even though in the context of this study it is not possible to judge how robust such a solution is against new ways of embedding or wilful circumvention. Alternatively, some standardized information in the meta-text of a web page could state whether the information can be embedded without consent. This

36. As a rough sanity check, compare this to an estimated 1.2 billion videos uploaded to YouTube between 2005 and 2015 (*see*: http://www.reelseo.com/youtube-changes-33-percent-a-year/, accessed 24 August 2017).

37. *See*: https://developer.mozilla.org/en-US/docs/Web/HTTP/Headers/X-Frame-Options (accessed 24 August 2017).

could be either a 'do not embed' line (opt-out), or an 'okay to embed' line (opt-in). The preferable choice from an economic perspective is the one which involves the lowest transaction costs. Taking into account the vast number of instances of embedding that currently exist, and assuming that a large majority of the website owners do not mind being embedded, an opt-out or the application of a technical measure that prevents embedding would be preferable.

Note that this proposal involves a (light) form of private ordering and therefore could be considered outside the scope of copyright, as long as the 'do not embed' line is legally enforceable. Either way, if a website were to ignore such an opt-out, or wilfully circumvent a technical measure, it could be held liable for copyright infringement and therefore subject to enforcement measures, such as a notice and takedown, blocking or fines. In an opt-out scheme that does not involve a technical solution precluding embedding, a subsequent issue would be how to deal with a source that changed its mind and no longer wants to be embedded. It may take time and notifications for linking sites to become aware of that. Of course, an immediate way for the source to invalidate existing instances of embedding would be to change the exact location of the embedded content. In principle, the solution described here could also be applied to linking, but as discussed, in the case of linking it is much less likely that a right holder has legitimate reasons to prevent linking on the ground of reasonable exploitation.

In *C More Entertainment*, the CJEU considered circumvention of an access restriction in the act of linking or embedding to be a relevant criterion. From the perspective of control and the effect on the exploitation opportunities for the right holder, circumventing an access restriction such as a login or registration can indeed be relevant. The application of an access restriction suggests that the right holder intends to rely on access restriction (e.g., a subscription or pay-per-view model) as an exploitation model and circumventing it could deprive a right holder of the necessary control.

However, taking transaction costs into account suggests otherwise. The *C More Entertainment* case shows that it is rather simple to implement an access restriction to prevent deep linking or embedding by unauthorized users. Between the first and second sports matches at stake, C More installed such restrictions (CJEU, *C More Entertainment*, paragraph 14). Rather than having a linking party check whether an access restriction may be circumvented by deep linking or embedding, it does not seem unreasonably onerous to hold a right holder responsible for implementing the access restriction in such a way that it cannot be circumvented by deep linking.

One could consider stretching this point further and requiring a website owner to install an effective access restriction whenever he does not appreciate linking to or embedding of his content. This would probably be more effective than a 'do not embed' line in the meta-text of a webpage, but the transaction costs and dead-weight losses of this suggestion will be very large, making it a less efficient solution: It would deprive the website holder of the possibility of offering users hassle-free access without having to set up an account and log in, which will have a dramatically negative effect on website traffic.

9.5.2.2 Linking to or Embedding of Unauthorized Sources

Having dealt with the cases of linking to and embedding of lawful sources and of linking to sources behind some faulty form of access restriction, it is time to consider linking to unauthorized sources. This is the central matter at stake in *GS Media.*

Starting with the unauthorized source which is embedded or linked to, this clearly affects the control a creator has over exchanging access to a work for something which is valuable to him. This is the essence of the public good market failure, that without protection, works of literature, science and art are non-excludable if the costs of copying are low. *GS Media* illustrates an even more striking loss of control, since the pictures relevant to this case were uploaded and subsequently linked to without permission, prior to their publication in Playboy magazine.

The empirical question of whether unauthorized publication negatively and significantly affects the current or future exploitation opportunities for the right holder, has proven to be more cumbersome. Over the past ten years, a large body of literature emerged on the effect of unauthorized file sharing on the legal sales of music, and to a lesser extent video content and games, albeit to no general consensus. In theory, file sharing can have several opposing effects on legal sales and the sales of related products and services. Van Eijk, Poort and Rutten (2010) distinguish nine different interactions. Perhaps the most obvious, and certainly the one that is stressed most by copyright holders, is *substitution*: file sharing may substitute for the online or offline purchase of recorded music, films or series, books, games or for cinema visits. Opposing this is the so-called *sampling effect*: file sharing may introduce consumers to works, artists and genres which increases their demand for these works or other works by the same artists or in the same genre. Another positive effect may be an increased demand for related products or services, such as concerts or merchandise (e.g., Dewenter, Haucap & Wenzel, 2012; Mortimer, Nosko & Sorensen, 2012). Neutral effects with respect to sales occur when file sharing meets the demand of consumers with insufficient willingness to pay, or who have demand for a work (or a work in a specific technical quality or file type) that is not on offer.

This variety of different and opposing interactions is one of the reasons why the effect of file sharing on sales is hard to determine empirically. Early contributions focus on the music industry – e.g., Peitz & Waelbroeck (2004), Rob & Waldfogel (2006), Zentner (2006), Liebowitz (2006) and Oberholzer-Gee & Strumpf (2007). A smaller number of studies deal with the effect for movies – e.g., Bounie, Bourreau & Waelbroeck (2006), Hennig-Thurau,

Henning & Sattler (2007) and Rob & Waldfogel (2007). In literature reviews (e.g., Handke, 2012; Smith & Telang, 2012; and Watson, Zizzo & Fleming, 2014), it is observed that there are hardly any studies concerning other markets such as games, books and software. Smith & Telang (2012) conclude that 'the vast majority of the literature … finds evidence that piracy harms media sales'. However, this evidence generally suggests a much smaller effect than a one-to-one displacement of sales by illegal copies. The effect most studies report is also substantially smaller than the loss of revenues from recorded music that the industry has experienced since the late 1990s.

From the analysis above, it follows that in general there is justification for the claim that unauthorized publication of works negatively and significantly affects the current or future exploitation opportunities for the right holder. As a consequence, linking to content that has been made public without authorization can have the same effect, irrespective of the fact that the linking (or embedding) party may not himself be hosting this content without authorization. Quantitative estimates of this vary largely and are likely to differ between types of works (music, films, games, books), between genres and between right holders within genres.[38] In *GS Media*, it is safe to say that without the links on the Dutch website, the mere posting of the pictures on an Australian site (which was not even indexed by search engines) would not have generated any interest anywhere and would have had no effect whatsoever on the exploitation opportunities for the copyright holder in the Netherlands.

This suggests that linking to or embedding of *unauthorized* content should be deemed infringing. Yet before arriving at such a conclusion, the societal costs it involves need to be considered: holding any linking party liable for infringement without prior warning would entail enormous transaction costs and potential dead-weight losses. The linker would have to make sure that the linked content is made available with authorization. Recall the enormous number of links on the Internet; requiring linking websites to assess whether or not the content they link to is lawful would generate equally enormous welfare losses. Assuming again that the number of hyperlinks is overestimated by a factor of one hundred and assuming transaction costs or dead-weight losses of EUR 0.01 cent per link, the welfare costs of 'clearing the rights' for all current hyperlinks would be EUR 200 billion. This dwarfs even the highest estimates of the global losses resulting from the unauthorized consumption of copyright material.

Limiting the obligation to ascertain the legality of the linked content to parties that pursue financial gain, as the CJEU does, hardly makes things any

38. Some studies find indications that more popular musicians and albums (Blackburn, 2004; Mortimer et al., 2012) and blockbuster movies (Peukert, Claussen & Kretschmer, 2013) suffer more from the substitution effect, while less well-known productions may even benefit as the opposing sampling effect prevails. However, other studies find an opposite effect (Bhattacharjee, Gopal, Lertwachara, Marsden & Telang, 2007; Hammond, 2013).

better. For one thing, the concept of financial gain is very wide and open and can be argued to include all news media, politicians, academics and any blogger with the slightest professional ambition. Thus, linking to unauthorized content may have a significant negative effect on the exploitation opportunities for creators and hence on creation itself, but making such links ex ante infringements would involve even more significant welfare costs through transaction costs and dead-weight losses.

A way to partially resolve this would be a procedure of notice and take down for links to illegal content (in line with the legal doctrine of contributory or secondary liability). The idea would be that in general linking and embedding are acceptable and do not require consent or a licence, nor do they require any ex ante knowledge of whether the linked content has been made available with authorization. Only if the copyright holder alerts the linking site that the content on the linked site is made available without authorization, would there be an obligation to remove the link. For a careful procedure and to make sure links are not removed unjustly, one could require a court order for this. However, this would increase the transaction costs and the response time of such a procedure substantially, and by doing so thwart its effectiveness and efficiency. In practice, a simple procedure without any court intervention necessary, but with a procedure to reinstall links that have been removed unjustly could work, much like the procedure YouTube has in place for removing unauthorized content.[39]

9.5.3 Conclusions

From a welfare economic perspective, it is useful to distinguish between hyperlinking, embedding and linking to unauthorized sources. An 'outward' or 'push' link to an authorized source, whether a link to a homepage or a deep link, can hardly be argued to have a negative effect on the exploitation opportunities of the right holder of the linked content. Therefore, from the framework established in this chapter, there is no economic justification for such links to fall within the scope of copyright.

Embedded or 'pull' links can be different in that respect, as through the use of such links right holders lose most of their control over the environment in which the work is accessed. Indeed, this can negatively and significantly affect the exploitation opportunities for the right holder, e.g., by depriving them of advertising revenues. However, the transaction costs and dead-weight losses of requiring a licence or explicit authorization for every embedded link are expected to be enormous. That suggests alternative 'opt-out' solutions, such as technical measures to be taken by websites that

39. *See*: https://support.google.com/youtube/answer/2807622?hl=en (accessed 24 August 2017).

do not want to be embedded, or a 'do not embed' line in the meta-text of web pages, which linking sites need to respect.

Linking to unauthorized sources is different: there is substantial empirical evidence that linking to such sources can have a significant and negative effect on the exploitation opportunities and indeed on the revenues of right holders. This would suggest making linking to unauthorized content a protected act within the scope of copyright. However, the transaction costs and dead-weight losses of a general ex ante prohibition of linking to unauthorized content are expected to be overwhelmingly large and the same holds for presuming knowledge for any for-profit linker. From a welfare economic perspective, a procedure of notice and take down for links to unauthorized content is preferable.

As *GS Media* illustrates, this will not resolve the issue of linking to unauthorized content entirely, as a stubborn or malicious site owner may link to a new unauthorized source each time a link is removed. In such cases, it would be for courts to decide whether in practice such behaviour of persistent linking to 'obviously unlawful sources' is equivalent to a refusal to remove a link, and therefore should be considered an infringement ex ante.

A final issue remains what can be done about linking sites and linked sites that are outside the jurisdiction of copyright legislation. Taking down such sites has proven to be legally difficult as well as rather ineffective: mirror sites are easily created once a site is taken down. Ordering Internet service providers (ISPs) to block access to such sites is often proposed and even implemented as a remedy, but – apart from any legal objections one may have related to e.g., freedom of speech and censorship – is rather ineffective as well (Poort et al., 2014). It can easily be circumvented by using mirror sites and by using Virtual Private Networks for instance.

Hence, it is illusory to think that linking to and (more importantly) downloading and streaming from unauthorized sources can be eradicated entirely. Acknowledging this, several academic authors have proposed introducing some form of 'statutory licensing scheme' with a levy system to compensate for this practice (e.g., Ku, 2002; Netanel, 2003; Fisher, 2004; Litman, 2004; Gratz, 2004; and Oksanen & Valimaki, 2005). For an extensive analysis of this literature, *see also* Quintais (2017: Chapter 3). Such proposals are also known as for instance 'content flat rate' or 'alternative compensation schemes'.[40]

9.6 RETRANSMISSION

The next case study is considerably more concise. It outlines how the economic framework developed in this chapter applies to instances of

40. *See also* the chapter by Quintais and Hugenholtz in this volume.

retransmission of radio or television broadcasts. The argument will be made that, in hindsight, the analysis is rather similar to that of hyperlinking.

9.6.1 Legal Treatment

Several CJEU cases concern such retransmission of television or radio broadcasts. Only some of these cases are relevant for the purposes of this section. In Case C-306/05 – *SGAE*, the owner of the Rafael hotels was sued for 'retransmitting' television broadcasts picked up with one central hotel aerial to the individual hotel rooms. Joint cases C-403/08 and C-429/08 – *Premier League* concerned a pub owner who had acquired a Greek smart card for decoding satellite broadcasts of Premier League football matches and used it to display those matches in a pub in the UK. Case C-135/10 – *Del Corso* concerned a dentist who played radio in his waiting room to ease the sound of drilling. Case C-607/11 – *ITV Broadcasting* involved a company (TVCatchup) live streaming a number of British television channels over the Internet. Finally, Case C-325/14 – *SBS* concerned the question of whether a broadcasting organization is communicating to the public if it broadcasts its programmes by 'direct injection', meaning signals are transmitted exclusively to distributors such as cable networks, without being accessible to the general public at this stage.

In a nutshell, the central legal question in all of these cases is whether these acts qualify under the exclusive economic right of communication to the public. To make that assessment, the CJEU typically identifies two cumulative criteria. First, that there is an active intervention that qualifies as an 'act of communication'. Second, that the act of communication is made to a public, in which case the communication can either be made through a specific technical means (e.g., in *ITV Broadcasting*), or to a new public, i.e., a public which the right holder did not consider in its initial communication (like in *SGAE*). If the answer to these questions is affirmative, then the acts in question require the authorization of the copyright holder. In *Del Corso* and *SBS*, the Court ruled that the acts under analysis did *not* meet these requirements, and therefore did not constitute restricted communications to the public. In all other cases, the CJEU's answer to both questions was 'yes'.

In *ITV Broadcasting*, the CJEU noted that the act involved a communication to the public, even though subscribers of TVCatchup 'are within the area of reception of that terrestrial television broadcast and may lawfully receive the broadcast on a television receiver'. Moreover, the Court noted that this decision 'is not influenced by the fact that a retransmission, such as that at issue in the main proceedings, is funded by advertising and is therefore of a profit-making nature'. (CJEU, *ITV Broadcasting*, paragraph 48).

It is noteworthy that this case strongly resembles the *Aereo* case in the US, which also involved centralized reception and subsequent online transmission of free-to-air television signals which the subscribers of Aereo, Inc. could have received for free with a rooftop antenna.[41] A notable technical difference is that Aereo used a large number of tiny antennae – one dedicated antenna per user at the time – to avoid having to pay transmission fees. Both Aereo and TVCatchup lost their cases.

As regards the concept of a 'public', Hugenholtz (2013a) stresses that this seems to be rather blurry in these rulings: in *SGAE*, the individual hotel guests were considered to be a public, while in *Del Corso* the dentist's patients were not. In *ITV Broadcasting*, individual streams were considered by the Court to add up to a public, while not deeming it relevant whether or not this was also to be considered a 'new public'. However, Hugenholtz (2013a) criticizes this argument for being unclear and argues that the whole concept of 'new public' is flawed and circular. Instead, he suggests considering the question whether a communication is to a 'separate public', i.e., reaching a separate market (segment).

9.6.2 Economic Analysis

Without a doubt, the economic significance of retransmission of television broadcasts (and to a lesser extent radio broadcasts) is large, in particular when including retransmission by cable companies and other telecommunications networks. Television sets are a standard item in most hotel rooms and can be expected on average to add value to the offer. Also, the market for live-streaming television broadcasts over the Internet is presumably substantial and will grow as more households cancel their TV subscription ('cut the cord'). Likewise, there is substantial commercial value in displaying football matches or other sports in pubs.

However, the economic value that may be created by retransmission does not automatically imply that it should fall within the scope of copyright from an economic point of view. In the legal treatment discussed above, as well as in an economic analysis, there are strong resemblances between retransmission and hyperlinking. The legal analysis by the CJEU focused on the question of whether or not the acts discussed here involve a communication to a (new) public. In general terms this 'new public' criterion is congruent with the economic observation that both hyperlinking and live retransmission do not in themselves affect a right holder's control over the broadcast, provided access restrictions are not circumvented implying subscription fees are forfeited and that retransmission occurs within the reception area of the broadcast.

First, consider *free-to-air* radio or television, which anyone with the proper hardware in the reception area can receive *without a smart card or*

41. For discussions of the Aereo case from a legal or law and economics perspective, *see* Giblin & Ginsburg (2014a, b) and Lunney (2014).

subscription. Such broadcasts either receive their revenues from commercial sources such as advertisements, product placement, sponsored content, texting, etc. or from public funding, or from a combination of these. In either case, having a larger audience will be in the commercial or societal interest of the broadcaster, which implies that linear live or near-live retransmission within the reception area will not negatively affect the exploitation opportunities for the broadcaster.

On the contrary: the more viewers or listeners, the better, and there is no market failure to justify control over a downstream market, regardless of whether this is a single household with a rooftop antenna, a hotel with twenty rooms or a cable company with one million connected households. Such broadcasts are free to all by choice, not because of a market failure. This is analogous to linking to a website without access restrictions, which in general will only benefit from more visitors. Of course, surplus may be created by the party involved in the retransmission, just as a website providing links to other sites may create surplus and a car owner may create surplus with a car. But in this free-to-air scenario, this does not entitle the initial broadcaster to a share of this surplus, any more than it does the linked website or the car manufacturer. It is not an external effect that warrants 'internalization' through transmission fees. Like in the case of digital resale, claiming a share in these downstream profits would be akin to a jealousy tax.

It goes without saying that abolishing retransmission fees will affect the financial agreements upstream: if creators, performers and other right holders of audio-visual content no longer receive retransmission fees, this will change the deals they make with broadcasters. Broadcasters in turn may reconsider the viability of free-to-air television, which is currently partly financed by cable companies through retransmission fees. They may renegotiate their deals for injecting their signal directly into cable networks. The argument here abstracts from such effects in the value chain by making the point that free-to-air television is free-to-air by choice and hence ought to be self-sufficient as a business model. Put differently, it is hard to see the economic logic of why a cable subscriber should pay for retransmission of a free-to-air channel via his cable fee, while someone who uses a rooftop antenna to pick up the same channel at the same location should not.

The argument above applies to the *SGAE*, *Del Corso* and *ITV Broadcasting* cases. It is different in *SBS*, since in that case the signals had not been made publicly and freely accessible before distribution to the networks, which implies that the argument above that the broadcasts are a public good by choice does not apply. Also, it does not hold for broadcasts that are not free-to-air. Such broadcasters can negotiate a fee themselves for transmission to the subscribers of cable networks or any other platform such as satellite or digital terrestrial television. These contracts make additional retransmission fees obsolete. In their contract with end users, they can opt for a subscription or pay-per-view model. In such cases, the exploitation model exchanges access for subscription fees or direct payment and retransmitting the unscrambled programme would undermine this.

This situation is much like the initial market failure discussed in section 9.2 above; that without protection, the rents of copying are not excludable by the creator. Contrary to free-to-air broadcasts, a subscription will involve contracts between the broadcaster, the network and the recipient, which can contain clauses forbidding retransmission of the unscrambled signal by the network or a hotel owner.[42] From an economic perspective, such a clause can be justified as second degree (volume-based) price discrimination, which is common in many industries and may very well pass the test of being beneficial for aggregate welfare. Hence, if a hotel were to unscramble the signal using one smart card and to retransmit the unscrambled signal to all rooms, this would not be a copyright issue but a breach of contract. It could be left to general competition law and unfair business practices to decide if such a clause is acceptable and the hotel owner liable.

Premier League also boils down to the issue of what is permissible to circumvent price discrimination, and what to enforce it. In these cases, price discrimination is not volume-based but geographic. Starting from the observation that the willingness to pay for TV subscriptions for British football matches is much lower in Greece than in the UK, licence fees had been set accordingly. The issue at stake was whether arbitrage of the ensuing user fees – by using Greek smart cards in the UK – can be prohibited. The CJEU ruled that competition policy and free trade in the internal EU market should prevail, in the sense that legislation which prohibits arbitrage is denounced. Note that this case does not concern unauthorized retransmission of a signal outside the original reception area, but circumvention of price discrimination by consumers. Against that background, the CJEU ruling makes much sense from a welfare economics perspective: as the welfare effects of price discrimination are highly ambiguous (*see* section 9.2), categorical legislative support for it is ill-advised. Rather, it is left to suppliers to try to use smart pricing, and to consumers to outsmart suppliers by finding the best deal.

Note that the arguments here do not hold for catch-up services. Similarly, recording live television and offering a (large scale) catch-up service that might even skip or replace advertisements undermines the exploitation model of the initial broadcaster and takes away control or opportunities to make money on reruns. This is analogous to the distinction between linking to a document on a website on the one hand, and downloading and sending it out on the other. In the latter case, the right holder no longer has any control over the exploitation environment and hence his exploitation opportunities are negatively affected.

42. Compare how Netflix or Spotify subscriptions differentiate in the number of streams that are allowed simultaneously.

9.7 TEXT AND DATA MINING

A final brief case study in this chapter deals with the issue of text and data mining. Text and data mining, often referred to as 'TDM' (or 'DM' for data mining), is a rapidly up-and-coming technology. Hand et al. (2001) define it as 'the discovery of interesting, unexpected or valuable structures in large datasets'. Over the past few years it has become a promising branch of research, as can be illustrated by an article in Nature Genetics: 'Big data mining yields novel insights on cancer' (Jiang & Liu, 2015).

9.7.1 Legal Treatment

There are no CJEU references that deal specifically with TDM, although the *Infopaq* cases could be considered relevant. In Case C-5/08 – *Infopaq I*, the CJEU ruled that the use and printing of extracts of only eleven words, resulting from data capture by the media analysis company Infopaq International A/S does not qualify as a transient copy under Article 5(1) Copyright Directive, and might amount to copyright infringement unless prior consent from right holders has been obtained. Two and a half years later, in Case C-302/10 – *Infopaq II*, the CJEU ruled that, provided certain conditions are met, data capture 'may not conflict with a normal exploitation of the work or unreasonably prejudice the legitimate interests of the rightholder' and therefore could be allowed without prior authorization. On the other hand, one of the conditions mentioned, in line with Article 5(1) Copyright Directive, is that it 'must not have an independent economic significance'. A second condition is that it 'does not enable the generation of an additional profit going beyond that derived from the lawful use of the protected work'.

Be that as it may, whereas TDM does not seem to require authorization in fair use countries such as the US, it is often believed to fall within the scope of the exclusive economic rights in the EU and for that reason licensing solutions have been sought.[43] In Article 3 of the proposal for a Directive on *copyright in the Digital Single Market* (COM (2016) 593), a mandatory exception is proposed for research organizations to perform 'text and data mining of works and other subject-matter to which they have lawful access for the purpose of scientific research'. Contractual provisions contrary to this shall be unenforceable.

9.7.2 Economic Analysis

As already mentioned, TDM is an up-and-coming and promising field of research. McDonald (2012: p. 4) stresses the benefits, which include

43. Boulanger et. al., 2014: p. 3, Van der Noll *et al.*, 2012: pp. 20–21.

increased researcher efficiency and unlocking hidden information and developing new knowledge, which lead to 'cost savings and productivity gains, innovative new service development, new business models and new medical treatments'. Hence, the dynamic dead-weight losses due to licensing requirements or uncertainty about such requirements could be substantial. In fact, Handke, Guibault & Vallbé (2015) have found that academic researchers in the EU/EEA have a weaker performance in this kind of research, which suggests such losses are currently incurred. In their economic assessment of TDM for the European Commission, Boulanger et al. (2014: p. 67) also mention the transaction costs that may be involved in licensing, but suggest these transaction costs have diminished as a result of standardized contracts, while licences may also give incentives to right holders to facilitate effective access.

The economic arguments for retrospectively placing TDM within the scope of the economic rights are weak. In *Infopaq II*, the CJEU seems to reason that any unlicensed use which has economic significance and generates additional profits as a consequence unreasonably prejudices the legitimate interests of the right holder and therefore should be licensed. Such reasoning resembles the argument criticized in previous sections, for instance in the case of digital resale, that authors should somehow be entitled to a share of any surpluses created by or with works in downstream markets.

However, while in the case of digital resale the market failure can be considered resolved for any physical or digital copy that is sold (as long as it is not subsequently copied and redistributed, *see* section 9.3), in the case of text and data mining, it can be observed that there never was a market failure in relation to TDM that needs to be resolved, provided *access* to articles or data to engage in TDM is lawfully obtained. The additional profits generated by it have never been part of the incentive system of the authors. Now that TDM is an emerging field of research, it may have become part of the incentive system for publishers aggregating large databases of articles. But to the extent that TDM was unforeseen in existing contracts for accessing such databases, this can be assumed not to have been the case.

Retrospectively providing rights that require licensing would create windfall profits for publishers without any incentive effect, while imposing dead-weight losses on text and data mining, as well as transaction costs of licensing. For future contracts, the value users derive from TDM can largely be priced into ordinary access contracts without specific contractual clauses. Thus, a mandatory exception, as proposed by the European Commission, is in line with the economic framework of this chapter. The unenforceability of contractual provisions that forbid TDM could serve as a safeguard against windfall profits for publishers. Having said that, one can dispute whether a right to engage in TDM should be phrased as an exception or a rule. Moreover, limiting this right to non-profit or public interest research organizations, as the proposal does, seems to be hard to defend from a welfare economic point of view.

9.8 CONCLUSIONS

This chapter has explored the avenues for redefining the scope of copyright from a normative, welfare economic perspective, to bring copyright more in line with today's digital world. A welfare economic analysis of copyright sees it as a tool that aims to provide incentives for the creation and exploitation of works, by resolving the public good market failure associated with creative works. In this framework, the optimum scope of copyright follows from the optimum long-term effect it has on total social welfare, taking account of the dynamic effects of copyright on the creation and quality of works, and on the incentives it provides for their active exploitation. Transaction costs and dead-weight losses generated by copyright protection need to be taken into account to determine that optimum.

On the one hand, digitization has strengthened the need for copyright protection through the reduced cost of copying – not just for right holders but also for infringers – and the increased substitutability of originals by copies. On the other, contractual arrangements supported by technical protection measures that determine what can and cannot be done with the content acquired are a powerful counterforce to protect the interests of right holders.

To redefine the scope of copyright from an economic perspective in this digital world, the technology-neutral principle is formulated such that the public good market failure requires giving a creator and follow-on right holders exclusive rights with respect to acts that, as a consequence of this public good market failure, negatively and significantly affect his current or future exploitation opportunities and hence negatively interfere with his incentives to create or exploit, while taking account of the transaction costs and dead-weight losses generated by protection. On top of that, resolving the public good market failure must not generate new market failures by granting more or stronger rights than a creator would have in the absence of the initial market failure.

From the case studies in this chapter, it can be observed that digitization has caused 'mission creep' for copyright, extending to acts that lack the underlying market failure to justify protection and that would not be accepted in 'ordinary markets', such as controlling or extraction rents generated in downstream markets – criticized here as a 'jealousy tax' – or legislative backup for price discrimination. This is the case for digital resale, most copying for private use, linking to authorized content, text and data mining in databases a user has legitimate access to, and even retransmission of free-to-air television and radio stations within the reception area of the signal. In general, the analysis in this chapter suggests treating content markets no differently from other markets, once the public good market failure has been resolved, and to apply competition law and regulations concerning unfair business practices accordingly.

All this should not be mistaken for a plea against copyright in the digital domain. For instance, economic arguments remain valid to somehow prevent linking to unauthorized content. Also, the potentially negative effect of embedding on the exploitation opportunities for a right holder is acknowledged. However, a solution to counter this negative effect should take account of transaction costs and dead-weight losses, which dictates opt-out solutions for right holders that do not want to be embedded.

LITERATURE

ALAI (2013), REPORT and OPINION on the making available and communication to the public in the internet environment – focus on linking techniques on the Internet.

Association of American Publishers (AAP) (27 January 2016). *AAP StatShot: Publisher Net Revenue from Book Sales Declines 2.0% Through Third Quarter of 2015*, Press release.

Bently, L.A.F., et al. (2013), *European Copyright Society Opinion on The Reference to the CJEU in Case C-466/12 Svensson*, 15 February 2013. Retrieved from: http://ssrn.com/abstract=2220326 (accessed 24 August 2017).

Besen, S.M. & Kirby, S.N. (1989), *Private Copying, Appropriability, and Optimal Copying Royalties*, *Journal of Law and Economics* 32(2), 255–280.

Besen, S.M. and Raskind, L.J. (1991). An Introduction to the Law and Economics of Intellectual Property. *The Journal of Economic Perspectives*, 5(1) Winter 1991, 3–27.

Bhattacharjee, S., Gopal, R.D., Lertwachara, K., Marsden, J.D. & Telang, R. (2007). The Effect of Digital Sharing Technologies on Music Markets: A Survival Analysis of Albums on Ranking Charts. *Management Science*, 53(9), 1359–1374.

Blackburn, D. (2004). *Does File Sharing Affect Record Sales?* Cambridge, Mass.: Harvard University, Department of Economics.

Boldrin, M. & Levine, D.K. (2002). The Case Against Intellectual Property. *CEPR Discussion Paper No. 3273.* Retrieved from: http://ssrn.com/abstract=307859 (accessed 24 August 2017).

Boldrin, M. & Levine, D.K. (2004). 2003 Lawrence R. Klein Lecture. The Case Against Intellectual Monopoly. *International Economic Review*, 45(2), 327–350.

Boldrin, M. & Levine, D.K. (2005). The Economics of Ideas and Intellectual Property. *Proceedings of the National Academy of Sciences of the United States of America (PNAS)*, 102(4), 1252–1256.

Boldrin, M. & Levine, D.K. (2008). *Against Intellectual Monopoly.* Cambridge University Press.

Bounie, D., Bourreau, M. & Waelbroeck, P. (2006). Piracy and the Demand for Films: Analysis of Piracy Behavior in French Universities. *Review of Economic Research on Copyright Issues*, 3(2), 15–27.

Boulanger, J., Carbonnel, A., De Coninck, R. & Langus, G. (2014). *Assessing the Economic Impacts of Adapting Certain Limitations and Exceptions to Copyright and Related Rights in the EU. Analysis of Specific Policy Options.* Charles River Associates.

Dewenter, R., Haucap, J. & Wenzel, T. (2012). On File Sharing with Indirect Network Effects Between Concert Ticket Sales and Music Recordings. *Journal of Media Economics*, 25(3), 168–178.

Directive 2001/29/EC of the European Parliament and of the Council of 22 May 2001 on the harmonisation of certain aspects of copyright and related rights in the information society. *Official Journal of the European Communities L167/16.*

Downes, L. (2013). Will We Get a Second-Hand Market for Digital Goods? *Harvard Business Review*, 27 March 2013.

Eijk, N. van, Poort, J. & Rutten, P. (2010). Legal, Economic and Cultural Aspects of File Sharing. *Communications & Strategies*, 77, (1st Q. 2010), 35–54.

Elkin-Koren, N. (2009). Governing Access to Users-Generated-Content: The Changing Nature of Private Ordering in Digital Networks, in: Brousseau, E, Marzouki, M. & Meadel C. eds., *Governance, Regulations and Powers on the Internet,* Cambridge University Press.

Epstein, R.A. (2010). The Disintegration of Intellectual Property? A Classical Liberal Response to a Premature Obituary, *Stanford Law Review* 62(2), 455–524.

Fisher, W. (2001). 'Theories of Intellectual Property', Chapter 6 in: Munzer, S.R. (ed.) *New Essays in the Legal and Political Theory of Property*, Cambridge University Press, pp. 168–199.

Fisher, W. (2004). 'An Alternative Compensation System', Chapter 6 in: *Promises to Keep: Technology, Law, and the Future of Entertainment*, Stanfort, CA: Stanford University Press, pp. 199–258.

Frey, B. (1997). *Not Just for the Money*, Cheltenham: Edward Elgar Publishing.

Giblin, R. & Ginsburg, J.C. (2014a). We (still) Need to Talk About *Aereo*: New Controversies and Unresolved Questions After the Supreme Court's Decision. *Columbia Journal of Law & the Arts*, 38(2), 109–156.

Giblin, R. & Ginsburg, J.C. (2014b). Asking the Right Questions in Copyright Cases: Lessons from *Aereo* and its International Brethren. *Columbia Law School Working Paper No. 504.*

Gratz, J. (2004). 'Reform In The "Brave Kingdom": Alternative Compensation Systems for Peer-To-Peer File Sharing', *Minnesota Journal of Law, Science & Technology*, 6, 399–430.

Hammond, R.G. (2013). Profit Leak? Pre-Release File Sharing and the Music Industry. *Southern Economic Journal* 81(2), 387–408.

Hand, D.J., Mannilla, H., Smyth, P. (2001). *Principles of Data Mining*. MIT Press, Cambridge.

Handke, C., Guibault, L. & Vallbé, J. (2015). *Is Europe Falling Behind in Data Mining? Copyright's Impact on Data Mining in Academic Research.* Retrieved from: http://ssrn.com/abstract=2608513 (accessed 24 August 2017).

Handke, C. (2012). A Taxonomy of Empirical Research on Copyright: How Do We Inform Policy? *Review of Economic Research on Copyright Issues*, 9(1), 47–92.

Hennig-Thurau, T., Henning, V. & Sattler, H. (2007). Consumer File Sharing of Motion Pictures. *Journal of Marketing*, 71 (October), 1–18.

Hugenholtz, P.B. (2013a), Noot onder Hof van Justitie EU 7 maart 2013, zaak C-607/11 (ITV Broadcasting Ltd e.a./TVCatchup Ltd), *Nederlandse Jurisprudentie* 2013, 42, nr 444.

Hugenholtz, P.B. (2013b), Noot onder HvJEU 3 juli 2012, zaak C-128/11 (UsedSoft/Oracle International), *Nederlandse Jurisprudentie* 2013-11, nr. 118, pp. 1337–1349.

Hugenholtz, P.B., Guibault, L. (2004). *Auteurscontractenrecht: naar een wettelijke regeling?*, IViR, Amsterdam. Retrieved from: http://www.ivir.nl/publicaties/download/328 (accessed 24 August 2017).

IFPI (2017). *Global Music Report 2017. Annual state of the industry 2016.* Retrieved from: www.ifpi.org/downloads/GMR2017.pdf (accessed 24 August 2017).

International Video Federation (2017). *European Video Market 2017.*

International Video Federation (2014). *European Video Yearbook 2014.*

Jiang, P. & Liu, X.S. (2015) Big Data Mining Yields Novel Insights on Cancer. *Nature Genetics*, 47-2, 103–104.

Ku, R. (2002), 'The Creative Destruction of Copyright: Napster and the New Economics of Digital Technology', *University of Chicago Law Review*, 69(1), 263–324.

Landes, W.M. and Posner, R.A. (1989). An Economic Analysis of Copyright Law. *The Journal of Legal* Studies, 18(2) June 1989, 325–363.

Liebowitz, S.J. (1985). *Copying and Indirect Appropriability: Photocopying of Journals*, Journal of Political Economy, 93(5), 945–957.

Liebowitz, S.J. (2006). File-Sharing: Creative Destruction or Just Plain Destruction? *Journal of Law and Economics*, XLIX (April 2006), 1–27.

Linklater, E. (2014). UsedSoft and the Big Bang Theory: Is the e-Exhaustion Meteor about to Strike? *Journal of Intellectual Property, Information Technology and Electronic Commerce Law* (*JIPITEC*) 5(1), pp. 12–22.

Litman, J. (2004), 'Sharing and Stealing', *Hastings Communications and Entertainment Law Journal,* 17(1).

Lunney, G.S. Jr. (2014). Aereo and Copyright's Private-Public Performance Line. 162 *University of Pennsylvania Law Review Online* 205. Retrieved from: http://scholarship.law.tamu.edu/facscholar/358 (accessed 24 August 2017).

McDonald, D. (2012). *Value and Benefits of Text Mining*, London, JISC.

McManis, C. (2009). A Rhetorical Response to Boldrin & Levine: Against Intellectual Monopoly. *Review of Law and Economics*, 5(3), 1081–1100.

Mezei, P. (2015). Digital First Sale Doctrine Ante Portas: Exhaustion in the Online Environment. *Journal of Intellectual Property, Information Technology and Electronic Commerce Law (JIPITEC)* 6(1), 23–71.

Miceli, T.J. & Adelstein, R.P. (2006). An Economic Model of Fair Use. *Information Economics and Policy*, 2006(18), 359–373.

Miller, A.A. (2013). What Do We Worry About When We Worry About Price Discrimination? The Law and Ethics of Using Personal Information for Pricing. *Journal of Technology Law & Policy*, 19, 41–104.

Mortimer, J.H., Nosko, C. & Sorensen, A. (2012). Supply Responses to Digital Distribution: Recorded Music and Live Performances. *Information Economics and Policy*, 24(1), 3–14.

Netanel, N.W. (2003), 'Impose a Noncommercial Use Levy to Allow Free Peer-to-Peer File Sharing', *Harvard Journal of Law & Technology*, 17(1), 1-1-84.

Noll, R. van der, Gompel, S. van, Guibault, L., Weda, J. Poort, J., Akker, I. & Breemen, K. (2012). *Flexible Copyright. The Law and Economics of Introducing an Open Norm in the Netherlands*, SEO/IViR, Amsterdam, SEO-rapport nr. 2012-60.

Oberholzer-Gee, F. & Strumpf, K. (2007). The Effect of File Sharing on Record Sales: An Empirical Analysis. *Journal of Political Economy*, 115(1), 1–42.

Oksanen, V. & Valimaki, M. (2005), Copyright Levies as an Alternative Compensation Method for Recording Artists and Technological Development, *Review of Economic Research on Copyright Issues*, 2(2), 25–39.

Peitz, M. & Waelbroeck, P. (2004). The Effect of Internet Piracy on Music Sales: Cross-Section Evidence. *Review of Economic Research on Copyright Issues*, 1(2), 71–79.

Peukert, C., Claussen, J. & Kretschmer, T. (2013). Piracy and Movie Revenues: Evidence from Megaupload: A Tale of the Long Tail?: Retrieved from: http://ssrn.com/abstract=2176246 (accessed 24 August 2017).

Poort, J. Akker, I, Eijk, N. van, Sloot, B. van der, Rutten, P., (2012). *Digitally Binding. Examining the Feasibility of Charging a Fixed Price for e-books.* SEO-report 2012-18.

Poort, J., van Eijk, N. (2015). Digital Fixation: The Law and Economics of a Fixed e-book Price. *International Journal of Cultural Policy,* DOI: 10.1080/10286632.2015.1061516.

Poort, J., Leenheer, J., Van der Ham, J. Dumitru, C. (2014). Baywatch: Two Approaches to Measure the Effects of Blocking Access to the Pirate Bay. *Telecommunications Policy* 38 (2014), pp. 383–392.

Poort, J., Quintais, J.P. (2013). The Levy Runs Dry: A Legal and Economic Analysis of EU Private Copying Levies. *Journal of Intellectual Property,*

Information Technology and Electronic Commerce Law (*JIPITEC*) 4(3), pp. 205–224.

Poort, J.P. & Theeuwes, J.J.M. (2010). Prova d'Orchestra: een economische analyse van het voorontwerp auteurscontractenrecht. *Tijdschrift voor Auteurs-, Media- en Informatierecht (AMI)*, 34, (5), 137–145.

Posner, R.A. (2005). Intellectual Property: The Law and Economics Approach. *Journal of Economic Perspectives,* 19(2), 57–73.

Proposal for a Directive of the European Parliament and of the Council on copyright in the Digital Single Market, COM(2016) 593 final, Brussels 14-9-2016.

Quintais, J. P. (2017). *Copyright in the Age of Online Access: Alternative Compensation Systems in EU Law.* Kluwer Law International (Information Law Series Volume 40).

Reis, S. (2015). Toward a 'Digital Transfer Doctrine'? The First Sale Doctrine in the Digital Era. Notes and Comments. *Northwestern University Law Review*, 109(1), 173–208.

Rob, R. & Waldfogel, J. (2006). Piracy on the High C's: Music Downloading, Sales Displacement, and Social Welfare in a Sample of College Students. *Journal of Law and Economics*, XLIX (April 2006), 29–62.

Rob, R. & Waldfogel, J. (2007). Piracy on the Silver Screen. *The Journal of Industrial Economics*, 55(3), 379–395.

Rognstad, O-A. (2015). Restructuring the Economic Rights in Copyright – Some Reflections on an 'Alternative Model'. *Journal of the Copyright Society of the USA*, 62, 503–544.

Romijn, G. and Renes, G. (2013). *Algemene leidraad voor maatschappelijke kosten-batenanalyse.* CPB/PBL, Den Haag.

Rubí Puig, A. (2013). Copyright Exhaustion Rationales and Used Software: A Law and Economics Approach to Oracle v. UsedSoft. *Journal of Intellectual Property, Information Technology and Electronic Commerce Law* (*JIPITEC*) 4(3), pp. 159–178.

Rushton, M. (1998). The Moral Rights of Artists: Droit Moral ou Droit Pécuniaire? *Journal of Cultural Economics*, 22, 15–32.

Sag, M.J. (2006). Beyond Abstraction: The Law and Economics of Copyright Scope and Doctrinal Efficiency. *Tulane Law Review*, 81; Northwestern Law & Econ Research Paper No. 916603. Retrieved from: http://ssrn.com/abstract=916603 (accessed 24 August 2017).

Sinha, R.K., Machado, F.S. & Sellman, C. (2010). Don't Think Twice, It's All Right: Music Piracy and Pricing in a DRM-Free Environment. *Journal of Marketing*, 74(2), 40–54.

Smith, M.D. & Telang, R. (2012). Assessing the Academic Literature Regarding the Impact of Media Piracy on Sales: Retrieved from: http://ssrn.com/abstract=2132153 (accessed 24 August 2017).

Stolwijk, H.J.J. (2010). *Economische beleidsevaluaties en welvaart.* CPB Memorandum 245. CPB, Den Haag, The Netherlands.

Teulings, C.N., Bovenberg, A.L. & van Dalen, H.P. (2003). *De Calculus van het publieke belang.* Kenniscentrum voor Ordeningsvraagstukken, Den Haag, The Netherlands.

Tehranian, J. (2007). Infringement Nation: Copyright Reform and the Law/Norm Gap, *Utah Law Review*, 2007-3, 537–550.

Towse, R. (2006). Copyright and Artists: A View From Cultural Economics, *Journal of Economic Studies*. 20-4, 567.

Tsoutsanis, A. (2014). Why Copyright and Linking can Tango. *Journal of Intellectual Property Law & Practice*, 9(6), 495–509.

Varian H.R. (1989). 'Price Discrimination' in Schmalensee, R. & Willig, R. (eds), *Handbook of industrial organisation* (Elsevier 1989), p. 599.

Varian, H.R. (2005). Copying and Copyright, *Journal of Economic Perspectives*, 19(2), 121–138.

Verhue, D. & De Gier, M. (2017). *Privékopiëren – editie 2017.* Bureau Veldkamp, Amsterdam.

Vernik, D.A., Purohit, D. & Desai, P.S. (2011). Music Downloads and the Flip Side of Digital Rights Management. *Marketing Science*, 30(6), 1011–1027.

Watson, S.J., Zizzo, D.J. & Fleming, P. (2014). *Determinants and Welfare Implications of Unlawful File Sharing: A Scoping Review.* Glasgow: CREATe.

Weda, J., Van der Noll, R., Akker, I., Poort, J., Van Gompel, S., Leenheer, J. (2012). *Digitale drempels. Knelpunten voor legaal digitaal aanbod in de creatieve industrie.* SEO/IViR/CentERdata, Amsterdam, SEO-rapport nr. 2012-41.

WIPO/Wijminga, H., Klomp, W., Jagt, M. van der, Poort, J. (2017). *International Survey on Private Copying. Law & practice 2016*, WIPO Publication No. 1037E/17. WIPO, Geneva.

Wischenbart, R., et al. (2014). *Global eBook: A Report on Market Trends and Developments: Update Fall 2014*, Rüdiger Wischenbart Content & Consulting.

WRR. (2000). *Het borgen van publiek belang.* Wetenschappelijke Raad voor het Regeringsbeleid, Rapporten aan de Regering 56. Den Haag, The Netherlands.

Zentner, A. (2006). Measuring the Effect of File Sharing on Music Purchases. *Journal of Law and Economics*, XLIX (April 2006), 63–90.

CASE LAW

C-306/05, Judgment of the Court (Third Chamber), 7 December 2006 ('*SGAE*').

C-5/08, Judgment of the Court (Fourth Chamber), 16 July 2009 ('*Infopaq I*').

C-403/08, Judgment of the Court, (Grand Chamber) of 4 October 2011 ('*Premier League*').

C-429/08, Judgment of the Court, (Grand Chamber) of 4 October 2011 ('*Murphy*').
C-467/08, Judgment of the Court, (Third Chamber), 21 October 2010 ('*Padawan*').
C-135/10, Judgment of the Court (Third Chamber), 15 March 2012 ('*Del Corso*').
C-302/10, Judgment of the Court (Third Chamber), 17 January 2012 ('*Infopaq II*').
C-607/11, Judgment of the Court (Fourth Chamber), 7 March 2013 ('*ITV Broadcasting*').
C-128/11, Judgment of the Court, (Second Chamber), 12 July 2012 ('*Used-Soft*').
C-457/11 – C-460/11, Judgment of the Court, (Fourth Chamber), 27 June 2013 ('*VG Wort*')
C-435/12, Judgment of the Court, (Fourth Chamber), 10 April 2014 ('*ACI Adam*')
C-463/12, Judgment of the Court, (Fourth Chamber), 5 March 2015 ('*Copydan*')
C-466/12, Judgment of the Court, (Fourth Chamber), 13 February 2014 ('*Svensson*').
C-279/13, Judgment of the Court, (Ninth Chamber), 26 March 2015 ('*C More Entertainment*').
C-348/13, Judgment of the Court, (Ninth Chamber), 21 October 2014 ('*Bestwater*').
C-325/14, Judgment of the Court (Ninth Chamber), 19 November 2015 ('*SBS*').
C-160/15, Judgment of the Court (Second Chamber), 8 September 2016 ('*GS Media*').
C-174/15, Judgment of the Court (Third Chamber), 10 November 2016 ('*Vereniging Openbare Bibliotheken v Stichting Leenrecht*').
C-527/15, Judgment of the Court (Second Chamber), 26 April 2017 ('*Filmspeler*').
Amsterdam Court of Appeal, 20-01-2015, *Tom Kabinet v. Nederlands Uitgeversverbond* (ECLI:NL:GHAMS:2015:66).
Court of The Hague, 12-07-2017, *Nederlands Uitgeversverbond, Groep Algemene Uitgevers v. Tom Kabinet* (ECLI:NL:RBDHA:2017:7543).

INFORMATION LAW SERIES

1. Egbert J. Dommering & P. Bernt Hugenholtz, *Protecting Works of Fact: Copyright, Freedom of Expression and Information Law,* 1991 (ISBN 90-654-4567-6).
2. Willem F. Korthals Altes, Egbert J. Dommering, P. Bernt Hugenholtz & Jan J.C. Kabel, *Information Law Towards the 21st Century,* 1992 (ISBN 90-654-4627-3).
3. Jacqueline M.B. Seignette, *Challenges to the Creator Doctrine: Authorship, Copyright Ownership and the Exploitation of Creative Works in the Netherlands, Germany and The United States,* 1994 (ISBN 90-654-4876-4).
4. P. Bernt Hugenholtz, *The Future of Copyright in a Digital Environment, Proceedings of the Royal Academy Colloquium,* 1996 (ISBN 90-411-0267-1).
5. Julius C.S. Pinckaers, *From Privacy Toward a New Intellectual Property Right in Persona,* 1996 (ISBN 90-411-0355-4).
6. Jan J.C. Kabel & Gerard J.H.M. Mom, *Intellectual Property and Information Law: Essays in Honour of Herman Cohen Jehoram,* 1998 (ISBN 90-411-9702-8).
7. Ysolde Gendreau, Axel Nordemann & Rainer Oesch, *Copyright and Photographs: An International Survey,* 1999 (ISBN 90-411-9722-2).
8. P. Bernt Hugenholtz, *Copyright and Electronic Commerce: Legal Aspects of Electronic Copyright Management,* 2000 (ISBN 90-411-9785-0).
9. Lucie M.C.R. Guibault, *Copyright Limitations and Contracts: An Analysis of the Contractual Overridability of Limitations on Copyright,* 2002 (ISBN 90-411-9867-9).
10. Lee A. Bygrave, *Data Protection Law: Approaching its Rationale, Logic and Limits,* 2002 (ISBN 90-411-9870-9).
11. Niva Elkin-Koren & Neil Weinstock Netanel, *The Commodification of Information,* 2002 (ISBN 90-411-9876-8).
12. Mireille M.M. van Eechoud, *Choice of Law in Copyright and Related Rights: Alternatives to the Lex Protectionis,* 2003 (ISBN 90-411-2071-8).
13. Martin Senftleben, *Copyright, Limitations and the Three-Step Test: An Analysis of the Three-Step Test in International and EC Copyright Law,* 2004 (ISBN 90-411-2267-2).
14. Paul L.C. Torremans, *Copyright and Human Rights: Freedom of Expression – Intellectual Property – Privacy,* 2004 (ISBN 90-411-2278-8).
15. Natali Helberger, *Controlling Access to Content: Regulating Conditional Access in Digital Broadcasting,* 2005 (ISBN 90-411-2345-8).
16. Lucie M.C.R. Guibault & P. Bernt Hugenholtz, *The Future of the Public Domain: Identifying the Commons in Information Law,* 2006 (ISBN 978-90-411-2435-7).

17. Irini Katsirea, *Public Broadcasting and European Law: A Comparative Examination of Public Service Obligations in Six Member States,* 2008 (ISBN 978-90-411-2500-2).
18. Paul L.C. Torremans, *Intellectual Property and Human Rights: Enhanced Edition of Copyright and Human Rights,* 2008 (ISBN 978-90-411-2653-5).
19. Mireille van Eechoud, P. Bernt Hugenholtz, Stef van Gompel, Lucie Guibault & Natali Helberger, *Harmonizing European Copyright Law: The Challenges of Better Lawmaking,* 2009 (ISBN 978-90-411-3130-0).
20. Ashwin van Rooijen, *The Software Interface between Copyright and Competition Law: A Legal Analysis of Interoperability in Computer Programs,* 2010 (ISBN 978-90-411-3193-5).
21. Irini A. Stamatoudi, *Copyright Enforcement and the Internet,* 2010 (ISBN 978-90-411-3346-5).
22. Wolfgang Sakulin, *Trademark Protection and Freedom of Expression: An Inquiry into the Conflict between Trademark Rights and Freedom of Expression under European Law,* 2011 (ISBN 978-90-411-3415-8).
23. Stef van Gompel, *Formalities in Copyright Law: An Analysis of their History, Rationales and Possible Future,* 2011 (ISBN 978-90-411-3418-9).
24. Nadezhda Purtova, *Property Rights in Personal Data: A European Perspective,* 2012 (ISBN 978-90-411-3802-6).
25. Brad Sherman & Leanne Wiseman, *Copyright and the Challenge of the New,* 2012 (ISBN 978-90-411-3669-5).
26. Ewa Komorek, *Media Pluralism and European Law*, 2012 (ISBN 978-90-411-3894-1).
27. Joris van Hoboken, *Search Engine Freedom: On the Implications of the Right to Freedom of Expression for the Legal Governance of Web Search Engines,* 2012 (ISBN 978-90-411-4128-6).
28. Natali Helberger, Lucie Guibault, Marco Loos, Chantal Mak, Lodewijk Pessers & Bart van der Sloot, *Digital Consumers and the Law: Towards a Cohesive European Framework*, 2012 (ISBN 978-90-411-4049-4).
29. Tatiana-Eleni Synodinou, *Codification of European Copyright Law: Challenges and Perspectives,* 2012 (ISBN 978-90-411-4145-3).
30. Heather Ann Forrest, *Protection of Geographic Names in International Law and Domain Name System Policy*, Second Edition, 2017 (ISBN 978-90-411-8839-7).
31. Sari Depreeuw, *The Variable Scope of the Exclusive Economic Rights in Copyright*, 2014 (ISBN 978-90-411-4915-2).
32. Vikrant Narayan Vasudeva, *Open Source Software and Intellectual Property Rights*, 2014 (ISBN 978-90-411-5228-2).

33. Frederik J. Zuiderveen Borgesius, *Improving Privacy Protection in the Area of Behavioural Targeting*, 2015 (ISBN 978-90-411-5990-8).
34. Paul L.C. Torremans, *Intellectual Property Law and Human Rights*, Third Edition, 2015 (ISBN 978-90-411-5836-9).
35. Irini A. Stamatoudi, *New Developments in EU and International Copyright Law*, 2016 (ISBN 978-90-411-5991-5).
36. Lodewijk W.P. Pessers, *The Inventiveness Requirement in Patent Law: An Exploration of Its Foundations and Functioning*, 2016 (ISBN 978-90-411-6731-6).
37. Susy Frankel & Daniel Gervais, *The Internet and the Emerging Importance of New Forms of Intellectual Property*, 2016 (ISBN 978-90-411-6789-7).
38. Axel M. Arnbak, *Securing Private Communications: Protecting Private Communications Security in EU Law – Fundamental Rights, Functional Value Chains, and Market Incentives*, 2016 (ISBN 978-90-411-6737-8).
39. Christina Angelopoulos, *European Intermediary Liability in Copyright: A Tort-Based Analysis*, 2017 (ISBN 978-90-411-6835-1).
40. João Pedro Quintais, *Copyright in the Age of Online Access: Alternative Compensation Systems in EU Law*, 2017 (ISBN 978-90-411-8667-6).
41. P. Bernt Hugenholtz, *Copyright Reconstructed: Rethinking Copyright's Economic Rights in a Time of Highly Dynamic Technological and Economic Change,* 2018 (ISBN 978-90-411-9103-8).

www.ingramcontent.com/pod-product-compliance
Lightning Source LLC
Chambersburg PA
CBHW071238230926
51849CB00001B/149
* 9 7 8 9 0 4 1 1 9 1 0 3 8 *